CompTIA Security+: SY0-601 Certification Guide

Second Edition

Complete coverage of the new CompTIA Security+ (SY0-601) exam to help you pass on the first attempt

Ian Neil

BIRMINGHAM—MUMBAI

CompTIA Security+: SY0-601 Certification Guide
Second Edition

Commissioning Editor: Vijin Boricha

Acquisition Editor: Rahul Nair

Senior Editor: Arun Nadar

Content Development Editor: Pratik Andrade

Technical Editor: Yoginee Marathe

Copy Editor: Safis Editing

Project Coordinator: Neil Dmello

Proofreader: Safis Editing

Indexer: Rekha Nair

Production Designer: Vijay Kamble

First published: September 2018
Second published: December 2020

Production reference: 1221220

Published by Packt Publishing Ltd.
Livery Place
35 Livery Street
Birmingham
B3 2PB, UK.

ISBN 978-1-80056-424-4

www.packt.com

Packt>

Packt.com

Subscribe to our online digital library for full access to over 7,000 books and videos, as well as industry leading tools to help you plan your personal development and advance your career. For more information, please visit our website.

Why subscribe?

- Spend less time learning and more time coding with practical eBooks and Videos from over 4,000 industry professionals

- Improve your learning with Skill Plans built especially for you

- Get a free eBook or video every month

- Fully searchable for easy access to vital information

- Copy and paste, print, and bookmark content

Did you know that Packt offers eBook versions of every book published, with PDF and ePub files available? You can upgrade to the eBook version at packt.com and as a print book customer, you are entitled to a discount on the eBook copy. Get in touch with us at customercare@packtpub.com for more details.

At www.packt.com, you can also read a collection of free technical articles, sign up for a range of free newsletters, and receive exclusive discounts and offers on Packt books and eBooks.

Contributors

About the author

Ian Neil is one of the world's top trainers of Security+ he has the ability to break down the information into manageable chunks so that people with no background knowledge can gain the skills required to become certified. He has recently worked for the US Army in Europe and designed a Security+ course that catered for people from all backgrounds (not just the IT professional), with an extremely successful pass rate. He is an MCT, MCSE, A+, Network+, Security+, CASP, and RESILIA practitioner, who over the past 23 years, has worked with high-end training providers and was one of the first technical trainers to train Microsoft internal staff when they opened their Bucharest Office in 2006.

About the reviewers

Crystal Voiles is an IT specialist with more than 30 years of IT experience ranging from help desk support, desktop support, system administration, and cyber security support.

For the last 10 years, she has served as a cyber security specialist, managing several cyber security tools, including **Assured Compliance Assessment Solution (ACAS)**, **Host-Based Security System (HBSS)**, Tanium, **System Center Configuration Manager (SCCM)**, and **Enterprise Mission Assurance Support Service (eMASS)**.

Currently serving as the **Information Systems Security Manager (ISSM)** for a small medical organization responsible for coordination and execution of security policies and controls, as well as assessing vulnerabilities within a medical company. She is responsible for data and network security processing, security systems management, and security violation investigations. She manages backup and security systems, employee training for approximately 900 end user accounts, security planning measures, and recovery of data in disaster testing situations.

Her certifications include **Certified Information Systems Security Professional (CISSP)**, **CompTIA Advanced Security Practitioner (CASP+)**, Security +, **Microsoft Certified Professional (MCP)**, SCCM, and ITIL Foundations.

Rebecca Moffitt is an experienced information security and risk consultant with 8 years of experience in the industry.

Rebecca joined QA in October of 2018, and since then has been working as a cyber security technical specialist. Her areas of training have been primarily related to cyber security, information security, information assurance, and risk management. She most recently obtained her CISM via ISACA, and her CSRM via PECB. She is a certified Information Security Management Systems Lead Implementer and is proficient in ISO 27001, 27002, 27005, and has knowledge of ISO 31000, 27035, and 19011, as well as various cyber, information, and risk frameworks.

Rebecca is passionate about her profession and has spent time working with the younger generations, raising their awareness of the field of cyber/information security and sparking enthusiasm in them about a potential career in cyber security.

On a personal level, Rebecca is Canadian. The country lifestyle is rooted within her. She loves all things related to the East Coast lifestyle: kitchen parties, country music, and fiddleheads.

I would like to thank my family always, for their continual love and support.

- Rebecca Moffitt

Packt is searching for authors like you

If you're interested in becoming an author for Packt, please visit `authors.packtpub.com` and apply today. We have worked with thousands of developers and tech professionals, just like you, to help them share their insight with the global tech community. You can make a general application, apply for a specific hot topic that we are recruiting an author for, or submit your own idea.

Table of Contents

2

Implementing Public Key Infrastructure

3
Investigating Identity and Access Management

4
Exploring Virtualization and Cloud Concepts

Section 2: Monitoring the Security Infrastructure

5

Monitoring, Scanning, and Penetration Testing

6

Understanding Secure and Insecure Protocols

7

Delving into Network and Security Concepts

8

Securing Wireless and Mobile Solutions

Section 3: Protecting the Security Environment

9

Identifying Threats, Attacks, and Vulnerabilities

10

Governance, Risk, and Compliance

11
Managing Application Security

12

Dealing with Incident Response Procedures

Section 4: Mock Tests

13

Mock Exam 1

Mock Exam 1 Assessment

14

Preface

This book will help you to understand security fundamentals, ranging from the CIA triad right through to identity and access management. This book describes network infrastructure and how it is evolving with the implementation of virtualization and different cloud models and their storage. You will learn how to secure devices and applications that are used by a company.

Who this book is for

This book is designed for anyone who is seeking to pass the CompTIA Security+ SY0-601 exam. It is a stepping-stone for anyone who wants to become a security professional or move into cybersecurity.

What this book covers

Chapter 1, Understanding Security Fundamentals, covers some security fundamentals that will be expanded upon in later chapters.

Chapter 2, Implementing Public Key Infrastructure, goes into the different encryption types and teaches how certificates are issued and used.

Chapter 3, Investigating Identity and Access Management, looks at different types of authentication. We will look at the concepts of identity and access management.

Chapter 4, Exploring Virtualization and Cloud Concepts, gets you acquainted with various cloud models and cloud security, looking at their deployment and storage environments.

Chapter 5, Monitoring, Scanning, and Penetration Testing, looks at penetration testing, exercise types, scanning, threat hunting, and SIEM systems.

Chapter 6, Understanding Secure and Insecure Protocols, looks at when to use certain secure protocols.

Chapter 7, Delving into Network and Security Concepts, looks at network components, remote access, and network reconnaissance tools.

Chapter 8, Securing Wireless and Mobile Solutions, looks at wireless solutions and secure mobile solutions.

Chapter 9, Identifying Threats, Attacks, and Vulnerabilities, explores attacks and vulnerabilities, taking each type of attack in turn and its unique characteristics. This chapter is probably the most heavily tested module in the Security+ exam.

Chapter 10, Governance, Risk, and Compliance, looks at risk management and regulations and frameworks.

Chapter11, Managing Application Security, looks at application development and security.

Chapter 12, Dealing with Incident Response Procedures, looks at preparing for disaster recovery incidents and how to recover.

Chapter 13, Mock Exam 1, includes mock questions, along with explanations, which will help assess whether you're ready for the test.

Chapter 14, Mock Exam 2, includes more mock questions, along with explanations, which will help assess whether you're ready for the test.

To get the most out of this book

This certification guide assumes no prior knowledge of the product. You need to understand the information fully to become certified.

Download the color images

We also provide a PDF file that has color images of the screenshots/diagrams used in this book. You can download it here: `http://www.packtpub.com/sites/default/files/downloads/9781800564244_ColorImages.pdf`.

Conventions used

There are a number of text conventions used throughout this book.

`Code in text`: Indicates code words in text, database table names, folder names, filenames, file extensions, pathnames, dummy URLs, user input, and Twitter handles. Here is an example: "The problem that arises is that `strcpy` cannot limit the size of characters being copied."

A block of code is set as follows:

```
int fun (char data [256]) {
int I
char tmp [64]; strcpy (tmp, data);
}
```

Any command-line input or output is written as follows:

```
Set-ExecutionPolicy Restricted
```

Bold: Indicates a new term, an important word, or words that you see onscreen. For example, words in menus or dialog boxes appear in the text like this. Here is an example: "The SSID is still enabled. The administrator should check the box next to **Disable Broadcast SSID**."

> **Tips or important notes**
> Appear like this.

Get in touch

Feedback from our readers is always welcome.

General feedback: If you have questions about any aspect of this book, mention the book title in the subject of your message and email us at customercare@packtpub.com.

Errata: Although we have taken every care to ensure the accuracy of our content, mistakes do happen. If you have found a mistake in this book, we would be grateful if you would report this to us. Please visit www.packtpub.com/support/errata, selecting your book, clicking on the Errata Submission Form link, and entering the details.

Piracy: If you come across any illegal copies of our works in any form on the Internet, we would be grateful if you would provide us with the location address or website name. Please contact us at copyright@packt.com with a link to the material.

If you are interested in becoming an author: If there is a topic that you have expertise in and you are interested in either writing or contributing to a book, please visit authors. packtpub.com.

Reviews

Please leave a review. Once you have read and used this book, why not leave a review on the site that you purchased it from? Potential readers can then see and use your unbiased opinion to make purchase decisions, we at Packt can understand what you think about our products, and our authors can see your feedback on their book. Thank you!

For more information about Packt, please visit `packt.com`.

Section 1: Security Aims and Objectives

In this section, you will learn about security fundamentals, from the CIA triad through to identify and access management.

This section comprises the following chapters:

- *Chapter 1, Understanding Security Fundamentals*
- *Chapter 2, Implementing Public Key Infrastructure*
- *Chapter 3, Investigating Identity and Access Management*
- *Chapter 4, Exploring Virtualization and Cloud Concepts*

1
Understanding Security Fundamentals

In this chapter, we are going to look at some security fundamentals that will help you identify security threats in the system and mitigate them. With cybercrime increasing day by day, as an **Information Technology (IT)** professional, it is essential to first understand these fundamental concepts.

In this chapter, we will be covering the following topics:

- Security Fundamentals
- Comparing Control Types
- Physical Security Controls
- Understanding Digital Forensics

Let's start off by looking at security fundamentals.

Security Fundamentals

The fundamentals of security are the foundation of protecting our assets, and there must be a strategy or methodology that we adapt for security. This is the CIA triad; let's look at its breakdown.

CIA Triad Concept

Most security books start with the basics of security by featuring the CIA triad—this is a conceptual model designed to help those writing information security policies within an organization. It is a widely used security model and it stands for confidentiality, integrity, and availability, the three key principles that should be used to guarantee you have a secure system:

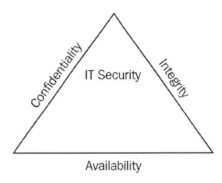

Figure 1.1 – CIA triad

We'll discuss these principles in more depth here:

- **Confidentiality**: Prevents the disclosure of data to unauthorized people so that only authorized people have access to data. This is known as the need-to-know basis. Only those who should know the contents should be given access. An example would be that your medical history is only available to your doctor and nobody else.

   We also tend to encrypt data to keep it confidential. There are two types of encryption, known as symmetric and asymmetric. Symmetric encryption uses one key, known as the private key or shared key. Asymmetric encryption uses two keys, known as the private key and the public key.

- **Integrity**: This means that you know that data has not been altered or tampered with. We use a technique called hashing that takes the data and converts it into a numerical value called a hash or message digest. When you suspect changes have taken place, you would check the hash value against the original. If the hash value has changed, then the data has been tampered with. Common hashing algorithms covered in the exam are **Secure Hash Algorithm Version 1 (SHA1)** 160-bit, SHA2 256-bit, SHA3 512-bit, and **Message Digest Version 5 (MD5)** 128-bit. SHA1 is more secure than MD5; however, MD5 is faster. The higher the number of bits, the more secure, and the lower the number, the faster it is.

- **Availability**: Availability ensures that data is always available; an example would be if you wanted to purchase an airplane ticket and the system came back with an error saying that you could not purchase it. This could be frustrating and hence, availability is important. Examples of availability could be using **Redundant Array of Independent Disks (RAID)**, maybe a fail-over cluster, a data backup, or **Heating Ventilation Air Conditioning (HVAC)** to regulate the system for critical servers.

Least Privilege

Least Privilege is where you give someone only the most limited access required so that they can perform their job role; this is known as a *need-to-know* basis. The company will write a least privilege policy so that the administrators know how to manage it.

Defense in Depth Model

Defense in Depth is the concept of protecting a company's data with a series of protective layers so that if one layer fails, another layer will already be in place to thwart an attack. We start with our data, then we encrypt it to protect it:

- The data is stored on a server.
- The data has file permissions.
- The data is encrypted.
- The data is in a secure area of the building.
- There is a security guard at the building entrance checking identification.
- There is CCTV around the perimeter.
- There is a high fence around the perimeter.

Let's look at this from the intruder's perspective, trying to jump the fence, and see how many layers they have to circumvent:

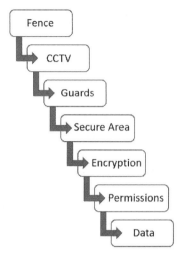

Figure 1.2 – Defense in Depth model

Let's now compare the different control types.

Comparing Control Types

There is a wide variety of different security controls that are used to mitigate the risk of being attacked; the three main categories are managerial, operational, and technical. We are going to look at these in more detail; you need to be familiar with each of these controls and when each of them should be applied. Let's start by looking at the three main controls.

Managerial Controls

Managerial Controls are written by managers to create organizational policies and procedures to reduce risk within companies. They incorporate regulatory frameworks so that the companies are legally compliant. The following are examples of management controls:

- **Annual Risk Assessment**: A company will have a risk register where the financial director will look at all of the risks associated with money and the IT manager will look at all of the risks posed by the IT infrastructure. As technology changes and hackers get more sophisticated, the risks can become greater. Each department will identify their risks and the risk treatments, and place them in the risk register. These should be reviewed annually.

- **Penetration Testing/Vulnerability Scanning**: A vulnerability scan is not intrusive as it merely checks for vulnerabilities, whereas a penetration test is more intrusive and can exploit vulnerabilities. These will be explained further later in this book.

Operational Controls

Operational controls are executed by company personnel during their day-to-day operations. Examples of these are the following:

- **Annual Security Awareness Training**: This is an annual event where you are reminded about what you should be doing on a daily basis to keep the company safe:

    a. **Example 1** – When you are finished for the day, you clear your desk and lock all documents away; another employee would remind you that your identity badge should be worn at all times and you should challenge anyone not wearing a badge.

    b. **Example 2** – Companies need their employees to complete annual cybersecurity training as the risk is getting greater each day.

- **Change Management**: This is a process that a company adopts so that changes made don't cause any security risks to the company. A change to one department could impact another department. The **Change Advisory Board (CAB)** assists with the prioritization of changes; they also look at the financial benefits of the change and they may accept or reject the changes proposed for the benefit of the company. IT evolves rapidly and our processes will need to change to cope with the potential security risks associated with newer technology.

- **Business Continuity Plan**: This is contingency planning to keep the business up and running when a disaster occurs by identifying any single point of failure that would prevent the company from remaining operational.

Technical Controls

Technical Controls are those implemented by the IT team to reduce the risk to the business.

These could include the following:

- **Firewall Rules**: Firewalls prevent unauthorized access to the network by IP address, application, or protocol. These are covered in depth later in this book.

- **Antivirus/Antimalware**: This is the most common threat to a business, and we must ensure that all servers and desktops are protected and up to date.

- **Screen Savers**: These log computers off when they are idle, preventing access.

- **Screen Filters**: These prevent people that are walking past from reading the data on your screen.

- **Intrusion Prevention Systems (IPS)/Intrusion Detection Systems (IDS)**: An IDS monitors the network for any changes and an IPS stops the attacks. If you do not have an IDS, the IPS has the ability to fulfill the role of the IDS.

Let's now look at other control types, from deterrents to physical controls, when we try and stop attacks at the source.

Deterrent Controls

Deterrent Controls could be CCTV and motion sensors. When someone is walking past a building and the motion sensors detect them, it turns the lights on to deter them. A building with a sign saying that it is being filmed with CCTV prevents someone from breaking into your premises, even though there may not be film inside the camera—but they don't know that!

Detective Controls

Detective Controls are used to investigate an incident that has happened and needs to be investigated; these could include the following:

- **CCTV** records events as they happen and from that, you can see who has entered a particular room or has climbed through a window at the rear of a building. CCTV can capture motion and provide non-repudiation.

- **Log Files** are text files that record events and the times that they occurred; they can log trends and patterns over a period of time. For example, servers, desktops, and firewalls all have event logs that detail actions that happen. Once you know the time and date of an event, you can gather information from various log files. These can be stored in **Write-Once Read-Many** (**WORM**) drives so that they can be read but not tampered with.

Corrective Controls

Corrective Controls are the actions you take to recover from an incident. You may lose a hard drive that contained data; in that case, you would replace the data from a backup you had previously taken.

Fire Suppression Systems are another form of corrective control. There may have been a fire in your data center that destroyed many servers, therefore when you purchase a replacement, you may install an oxygen suppressant system that will starve a fire of the oxygen needed. This method uses argon/nitrogen and carbon dioxide to displace the oxygen in the server room.

Compensating Controls

Compensating Controls can also be called **Alternative** or **Secondary Controls** and can be used instead of a primary control that has failed or is not available. Once a primary control has failed, we need a secondary control. This is similar to when you go shopping and you have $100 in cash—once you have spent your cash, you will have to use a credit card as a compensating control.

Example: When a new employee arrives, they should log in using a smart card and PIN. It may take 3–5 days to get a new smart card, so during the waiting period, they may log in using a username and password.

Preventative Controls

Preventative Controls are in place to deter any attack; this could be having a security guard with a large dog walking around the perimeter of your building. This would make someone trying to break in think twice about doing so. Some of the preventive measures that can be taken are as follows:

- **Disable User Accounts**: When someone leaves a company, the first thing that happens is that their account is disabled, as we don't want to lose information that they have access to, and then we change the password so that they cannot access it. We may also disable an account while people are on secondment or maternity leave.

- **Operating System Hardening**: This makes a computer more secure, where we ensure that the operating system is fully patched and turn off unused features and services. This will ensure that there will be no vulnerabilities.

Access Controls

The three main parts of access controls are identifying an individual, authenticating them when they insert a password or PIN, and then authorization, where an individual is granted permission to the different forms of data. For example, someone working in finance will need a higher level of security clearance and have to access different data than a person who dispatches an order in finished goods:

- **Identification**: This is similar to everyone having their own bank account; the account is identified by the account details on the bank card. Identification in a security environment may involve having a user account, a smart card, or maybe a fingerprint reader—this is unique to each individual. Each person has their own **Security Identifier** (**SID**) for their account, which is like an account serial number.

- **Authentication**: Once the individual inserts their method of identification, they next have to be authenticated, for example, by inserting a password or a PIN.

- **Authorization**: This is the level of access or permissions that you have to apply to selected data. You are normally a member of certain groups, for example, a sales manager could access data from the sales group and then access data from the managers group. You will only be given the minimum amount of access required to perform your job; this is known as least privilege.

Discretionary Access Control

Discretionary Access Control involves **New Technology File System** (**NTFS**) file permissions, which are used in Microsoft operating systems. The user is only given the access that they need to perform their job. They are sometimes referred to as user-based or user-centric. The permissions are as follows:

- **Full Control**: Full access.
- **Modify**: Change data, read, and read and execute.
- **Read and Execute**: Read the file and run a program if one is inside it.
- **List Folder Contents**: Expand a folder to see the subfolders inside it.
- **Read**: Read the contents.
- **Write**: Allows you to write to the file.
- **Special Permissions**: Allows granular access; for example, it breaks each of the previous permissions down to a more granular level.
- **Data Creator/Owner**: The person that creates the unclassified data is called the owner and they are responsible for authorizing who has access to that data.

The following diagram shows a user called *Ian* who had **Read** and **Read & execute** permissions:

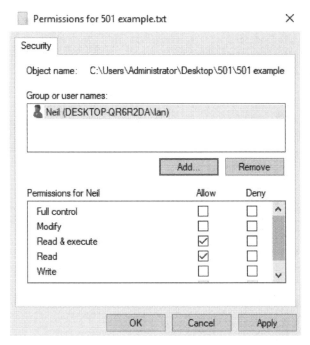

Figure 1.3 – DAC file permissions

Mandatory Access Control

Mandatory Access Control (**MAC**) is based on the classification level of the data. MAC looks at how much damage could be inflicted to the interests of the nation. These are as follows:

- **Top secret**: Highest level, exceptionally grave damage
- **Secret**: Causes serious damage
- **Confidential**: Causes damage
- **Restricted**: Undesirable effects

Examples of MAC based on the classification level of data are as follows:

- **Top secret**: Nuclear energy project
- **Secret**: Research and development
- **Confidential**: Ongoing legal issues

MAC Roles

Once classified data has been written, it is owned by the company. For example, if a Colonel writes a classified document, it belongs to the Army. Let's look at three roles:

- **Owner**: This is the person who writes data, and they are the only person that can determine the classification. For example, if they are writing a secret document, they will pitch it at that level, no higher.

- **Steward**: This is the person responsible for labeling the data.

- **Custodian**: The custodian is the person who stores and manages classified data.

- **Security Administrator**: The security administrator is the person who gives access to classified data once clearance has been approved.

Role-Based Access Control

Role-based access control is a subset of the department carrying out a subset of duties within a department. An example would be two people within the finance department who only handle petty cash. In IT terms, it could be that only two people of the IT team administer the email server.

Rule-Based Access Control

In **Rule-Based Access Control (RBAC)**, a rule is applied to all of the people within a department, for example, contractors will only have access between 8 a.m. and 5 p.m., and the help desk people will only be able to access building 1, where their place of work is. It can be time-based or have some sort of restriction, but it applies to the whole department.

Attribute-Based Access Control

In **Attribute-Based Access Control (ABAC)**, access is restricted based on an attribute in the account. John could be an executive and some data could be restricted to only those with the executive attribute. This is a user attribute from the directory services, such as a department or a location. You may wish to give different levels of control to different departments.

Group-Based Access Control

To control access to data, people may be put into groups to simplify access. An example would be if there were two people who worked in IT who needed access to IT data. For example, let's call them *Bill* and *Ben*. We first of all place them into the IT group, and then that group is given access to the data:

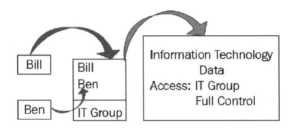

Figure 1.4 – Group-based access

Another example is where members of a sales team may have full control of the sales data by using group-based access, but you may need two new starters to have only read access. In this case, you would create a group called new starters and give those people inside that group only read permission to the data.

Linux-Based Access Control

In this section, we are going to look at Linux file permissions. These appear frequently in the Security+ exam even though they are not covered in the exam objectives.

Linux File Permissions (not SELinux)

Linux file permissions come in a numerical format; the first number represents the owner, the second number represents the group, and the third number represents all other users:

a. Permissions:

- **Owner**: First number
- **Group**: Second number
- **All other users**: Third number

b. Numerical values:

- **4**: Read
- **2**: Write
- **1**: Execute

Unlike a Windows permission that will execute an application, the execute function in Linux allows you to view or search. A permission of 6 would be read and write. A value of 2 would be write, and a value of 7 would be read, write, and execute. Some examples are as follows:

- **Example 1**: If I have *764* access to *File A*, this could be broken down as follows:

  a. **Owner**: Read, write, and execute

  b. **Group**: Read and write

  c. **All other users**: Read

  Another way the permissions can be set is by alphabetical values, as shown:

  a. **R**: Read

  b. **W**: Write

  c. **X**: Execute

  When using alphabetical values, each set of permission is shown as three dashes. Full control for the three entities are as follows:

  a. **Owner Full Control**: `rwx --- ---`

  b. **Group Full Control**: `--- rwx ---`

  c. **User Full Control**: `--- --- rwx`

- **Example 2**: If a file has an access level of `rwx rwx rw-`, what does this mean?

  a. Owner has read, write, and execute (full control).

  b. Group has read, write, and execute (full control).

  c. Others have only read and write permissions.

Physical Security Controls

Physical security controls are put in place to stop unauthorized access to the company or accessing the data. Physical security controls are easily identifiable as you can touch them. Let's look at each of them in turn.

Perimeter Security

In this section, we will look at different types of perimeter security systems:

- **Signage**: Before anyone reaches your main entrance, there should be highly visible signs warning them that they are entering a secure area with armed guards and dogs. This is used as a deterrent to prevent possible intruders.

- **Fences/Gates**: The first line of defense should be a perimeter fence as the openness of many sites renders them highly vulnerable to intruders. Access to the site can be controlled by using a gate either manned by a security guard or with a proximity reader. You could place bollards in front of a building to stop a car driving through the entrance. You may even have different zones, such as a research and development department, with their own perimeter security.

- **Access Control**: Armed guards at the gates should be checking the identity of those entering. There should be an access control list for visitors who are sponsored by an internal department. The guards checking identities should be behind one-way toughened glass so that visitors cannot see inside the gatehouse.

- **Lighting**: Lighting is installed for two main reasons: the first reason is so that anyone trying to enter your site at night can be seen and the second reason is for safety.

- **Cameras**: Cameras can be set up at areas around the perimeter and on doorways to detect motion. They can be set up to detect objects in both day and night to alert the security team by raising an alarm.

- **Robot Sentries**: These can be set up to patrol the perimeter and can shout out warnings to deter any intruders. These sentries patrol the DMZ between North and South Korea and they can be armed:

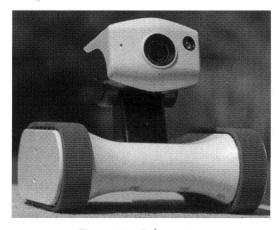

Figure 1.5 – Robot sentry

> **Tip**
> Robot sentries can shout out warnings to deter intruders. They could also be armed.

- **Industrial Camouflage**: When you are trying to protect a highly secure area, you would design the building so that it is obscured from aerial photographs by making some of the building look like residential housing. You would disguise the entrances as well. This would make it difficult for surveillance operatives to spot it.

Building Security

In this section, we will look at different types of building security systems:

- **Security Guards**: They work at the entrance reception desk to check the identity cards of people entering the building to stop unauthorized access. These guards should be armed and one of the guards should be a dog handler. An access control list is provided to them to ensure that unauthorized personnel is denied access.

- **Two-Person Integrity/Control**: This increases the security level at the entrance to a building, ensuring that someone is available to deal with visitors even when the other person is on the phone. This would also reduce the risk of a malicious insider attack.

- **Badges**: Visitors sign the visitor book and are allocated a badge that is a different color to that of employees. These badges should have a photograph, name, and signature of the holder. These badges should be visible at all times and anyone that isn't displaying a badge should be challenged.

- **Key Management**: This is where departmental keys are signed out and signed back in daily to prevent someone from taking the keys away and cutting copies of them.

- **Mantraps**: These are turnstile devices that only allow one person in at a time. They maintain a safe and secure environment, mainly for a data center. A data center hosts many servers for different companies.

- **Proximity Cards**: These are contactless devices where a smart card is put near the proximity card device to gain access to a door or building.

- **Tokens**: Tokens are small physical devices where you touch the proximity card to enter a restricted area of a building. Some tokens allow you to open and lock doors by pressing the middle of the token itself; others display a code for a number of seconds before it expires.

- **Biometric Locks**: Biometrics are unique to each person; examples would be using their fingerprint, retina, palm, voice, an iris scanner, or facial recognition.

- **Electronic Locks**: With electronic locks, you no longer need a key to access a building; you only need a PIN. They can be set to fail open, where the door opens when a power cut is detected, or fail safe, where the door remains locked.

- **Burglar Alarms**: These are set when the premises are not occupied, so when someone tries to break into your premises, it will trigger the alarm and notify the monitoring company or local police.

- **Fire Alarms/Smoke Detectors**: In a company building, there will be fire alarms or smoke detectors in every room so that when a fire breaks out and the alarms go off, the people inside the premises are given the opportunity to escape.

- **Internal Protection**: You could have safe areas and secure enclosures; the first example would be a toughened glass container or a sturdy mesh, both with locks to reduce access. You could also have protected distribution for cabling; this looks like metal poles that would have network cables inside. Screen filters used on a desktop could prevent someone from reading the screen.

- **Conduits**: Conduits or cable distribution have cables placed inside. This protects the cables from tampering or being chewed by rodents.

> Tip
> Conduits and cable distribution protect the Ethernet cable between the wall jack and the patch panel.

- **Environmental Controls**: HVAC and fire suppression systems are also security controls. In a data center or a server room, the temperature needs to be kept cool or the servers inside will overheat and fail. They use a technique called hot and cold aisles to regulate the temperature.

Device Protection

In this section, we will look at different device protection systems:

- **Cable Locks**: These are attached to laptops or tablets to secure them so that nobody can steal them.

- **Air Gap**: A computer is taken off the network and has no cable or wireless connection to ensure that the data is not stolen. An example of this would be a computer in the research and development department, as we want to prevent access to it via a network cable.

> **Tip**
> An air gap is an isolated computer; the only way to extract data is by using a USB or CD ROM.

- **Laptop Safe**: Laptops and tablets are expensive, but the data they hold could be priceless, therefore there are safes for the storage of laptops and tablets.

- **USB Data Blocker**: This device blocks the data pins on the USB device, which prevents a hacker from juice jacking, where data is stolen when you are charging your USB device.

- **Vault**: This is where data can be encrypted and stored in the cloud, giving you an extra-secure storage area.

- **Faraday Cage**: This is a metal structure, like a metal mesh used to house chickens. The cage prevents wireless or cellular phones from working inside the company. This could be built into the structure of a room used as a secure area. They would also prevent any kind of emissions from escaping from your company.

Understanding Digital Forensics

Digital forensics is used by the police when they are investigating crimes and need to find digital evidence so that they can secure a conviction. We will be looking at computer- and web-based attacks.

In 2006, Forensic Process 19, proposed by NIST, consisted of four different phases: collection, examination, analysis, and reporting. Here's a diagram showing these phases:

Figure 1.6 – Forensics cycle

Let's look at each of these phases:

- **Collection**: Here, the data is examined, then extracted from the media that it is on, and then converted into a format that can be examined by forensic tools.

- **Examination**: Prior to examination, the data will be hashed, and then an investigation will be carried out with the relevant forensic tool. When the examination has concluded, the data is once again hashed to ensure that the examiner or the tools have not tampered with it. We could use a USB write blocker that allows only read access to storage media.

- **Analysis**: When all of the forensic data has been collected, it is analyzed and then transformed into information that can be used as evidence.

- **Reporting**: A report is compiled that can be used as evidence for conviction.

There are many different components to a forensic investigation; we will look at each of them in turn:

- **Admissibility**: All evidence relevant to the case is deemed admissible only if it is relevant to the disputed facts of the case and does not violate any laws or legal statutes.

- **Order of Volatility**: Say you are a firefighter and you arrive at a house on fire; you can only save items one at a time and there are two items inside. The first is a snowman, and the second is a rib of beef. You now have a dilemma: which one should you choose? Easy! You save the snowman first as it is melting, and you let the rib of beef cook some more so that the other firefighters can have a nice supper! So, when we want to ascertain the order of volatility, we are looking to secure the most perishable evidence first. We do not try and stop the attack until we have secured the volatile evidence so that the source can be identified. This is known as the order of volatility. Let's look at a few examples.

  Example 1 – Web-Based Attack: An attacker is attacking the company website and the security team is trying to capture the network traffic to find the source of the attack. This is the most volatile evidence.

  Example 2 – Attack inside a Computer: When someone has attacked your computer, you need to capture the evidence in accordance with the order of volatility:

  a. **CPU Cache**: Fast block of volatile memory used by the CPU

  b. **Random Access Memory (RAM)**: Volatile memory used to run applications

c. **Swap/Page File/Virtual Memory**: Used for running applications when RAM is totally exhausted.

d. **Hard Drive**: Data at rest for storing data

Example 3 – Removable Storage Drive Attached to a Computer/Server: Someone has left a USB flash drive plugged into your fileserver. When it is in use, programs such as Word are launched in RAM, so we would capture the volatile memory first.

Example 4 – Command-Line Tools: You need to know which command-line tool provides information that could disappear if you reboot the computer, and that would be `netstat`. With `netstat -an`, the listening and established ports are shown. If you reboot the computer, all of the established connections will be lost.

> Tip
> Order of volatility is collecting the most perishable evidence first. In a web-based attack, we should collect the network traffic with a packet sniffer.

Five-Minute Practical

Open up Command Prompt on your computer and type `netstat -an`. You should now see the listening and established ports; count them, and write the numbers down. Run the `shutdown /r /t 0` command to immediately reboot the machine. Log back in, go to Command Prompt, and run `netstat -an`; what is the difference? You will see that you have lost information that could have been used as evidence.

Collection of Evidence

In this section, we will look at different types of evidence collection:

- **E-Discovery**: During e-discovery, companies may be subpoenaed so that we can collect, review, and interpret electronic documents located on hard disks, USB drives, and other forms of storage.

- **Chain of Custody**: The chain of custody is one of the most crucial aspects of digital forensics, ensuring the evidence has been collected and there is not a break in the chain. It starts when the evidence has been collected, bagged, tied, and tagged, ensuring the evidence has not been tampered with. It lists the evidence and who has handled it along the way. For example, Sergeant Smith handed 15 kg of illegal substance to Sergeant Jones following a drugs raid. However, when it is handed in to the property room, 1 kg is missing. In this event, we would need to investigate the chain of custody. In this scenario, Sergeant Jones would be liable for the loss. Chain of custody examples are as follows:

Example 1 – Missing Entry on the Chain of Custody Document: On Monday, 15 laptops were collected by the system administrator. The next day, the system administrator passed them on to the IT manager. On Wednesday, the IT director presents the 15 laptops as evidence to the court. The judge looks at the chain of custody document and notices that there was no formal handover between the IT manager and the IT director. With the handover missing, the judge wants to investigate the chain of custody.

Example 2 – Evidence Leaves the Detective's Possession: The FBI arrests a known criminal and collects 43 hard drives that they bag and tag, before placing them in two bags. They arrest the criminal and take him from Arizona to New York by airplane. One detective is handcuffed to the criminal while the other carries the two bags.

When they arrived at check-in, the airline clerk tells them that the carry-on bags are more than the 8 kg allowance, and therefore they are too heavy and need to go in the hold. The detective complies, but locks the suitcases to prevent theft. Because the evidence is not physically in their possession at all times, the chain of custody is broken as there is a chance that someone working for the airline could tamper with the evidence. Therefore, they cannot prove to the court that the integrity of the evidence has been kept intact at all times.

- **Provenance**: When the chain of custody has been carried out properly and the original data presented to the court has not been tampered with, it is known as data provenance.

- **Legal Hold**: Legal hold is the process of protecting any documents that can be used in evidence from being altered or destroyed. Sometimes, this is also known as litigation hold.

  Example: Dr. Death has been prescribing new drugs to patients in a large hospital who have been dying. An auditor has been sent to investigate the possibility of foul play, and then following the audit, the FBI is notified. The doctor has been emailing a pharmaceutical company that has been supplying the drugs for a trial. The FBI does not want the doctor to be alerted, so they have the hospital's IT team put his mailbox on legal hold. When the mailbox is on legal hold, the mailbox limit is lifted; the doctor can still send and receive emails, but cannot delete anything. This way, they are not alerted to the fact that they are under investigation.

- **Data Acquisition**: This is the process of collecting all of the evidence from devices, such as USB flash drives, cameras, and computers; as well as data in paper format, such as letters and bank statements. The first step in data acquisition is to collect the volatile evidence so that it is secured. The data must be bagged and tagged and included in the evidence log.

- **Artifacts**: This can be log files, registry hives, DNA, fingerprints, or fibers of clothing normally invisible to the naked eye.

- **Time Offset**: When we collect evidence from computers, we should record the time offset. This is the regional time so that in a multinational investigation, we can put them into a time sequence—this is known as time normalization.

- **Time Normalization**: This is where evidence is collected across multiple time zones, then a common time zone, such as GMT, is used so that it can be put into a meaningful sequence.

  Example: The police in three separate countries are trying to identify where the data started from in a chain, then who handled the data along the line. They have the following information about when it was first created:

  a. **New York**: Created 3 a.m.

  b. **London**: Created 4 a.m.

  c. **Berlin**: Created 4.30 a.m.

  By recording the time offset, it looks as if it started off in New York, but if we apply time normalization, when it is 4 a.m. in London, the time in New York is 11 p.m. the day before, so it cannot be New York. When it is 4.30 a.m. in Berlin, it is only 3.30 a.m. in London; therefore, it originated in Berlin. This looked the least unlikely before the time offset of the data collection had time normalization applied.

- **Time Stamps**: Each file has time stamps showing when files were created, last modified, and last accessed:

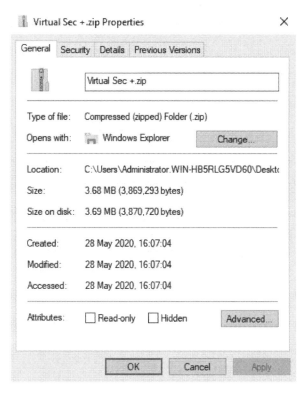

Figure 1.7 – Time stamps

- **Forensic Copies**: If we are going to analyze removable data that we have acquired, we would first of all take a forensic copy and keep the original data intact. We would then use the copy to analyze the data so that we keep the original data unaltered, as it needs to be used in its original state and presented as evidence to the courts. It would be hashed at the beginning and the end to confirm that the evidence has not been tampered with.

- **Capturing System Images**: When the police are taking evidence from laptops and desktops, they take a complete system image. The original image is kept intact and the system is analyzed to find evidence of any criminal activity. It would be hashed at the beginning and the end to confirm that the evidence has not been tampered with.

- **Firmware**: Firmware, sometimes called embedded systems, could be reversed engineered by an attacker, therefore it is important that we compare the source code that the developer wrote against the current source code in use. We would employ a coding expert to compare both lots of source code in a technique called regression testing. Types of attacks that affect embedded systems could be rootkit and backdoor.

- **Snapshots**: If the evidence is from a virtual machine, a snapshot of the virtual machine can be exported for investigation.

- **Screenshots**: You may also take screenshots of applications or viruses on the desktops and keep them as evidence. A better way of doing this would be to use a modern smartphone that would geotag the evidence.

> **Tip**
> You should capture a system image from a laptop and take a forensic copy from a removable drive

- **Taking Hashes**: When either the forensic copy or the system image is being analyzed, the data and applications are hashed at the beginning of the investigation. It can be used as a checksum to ensure integrity. At the end, it is re-hashed and should match the original hash value to prove data integrity.

- **Network Traffic and Logs**: When investigating a web-based or remote attack, we should first capture the volatile network traffic before stopping the attack. This will help us identify the source of the attack. In addition to this, we should look at different log files from the firewall, NIPS, NIDS, and any server involved. If we use a **Security Information Event Management** (**SIEM**) system, this can help collate these entries and give a good picture of any attack. However, if it is a rapidly expanding virus, we would quarantine it.

  Example: Your company uses an account lockout of three attempts. If an attacker tries to log in once to three separate computers, each computer would not identify it as an attack, as it is a single attempt on each computer, but a SIEM system would pick up these attempts as three failed logins attempts and alert the administrators in real time.

> **Tip**
> You should remove a computer with a dynamically expanding virus immediately rather than collect the network traffic.

- **Capturing Video**: CCTV can be a good source of evidence for helping to identify attackers and the time the attack was launched. This can be vital in apprehending suspects.

- **Interviews**: The police may also take witness statements to try and get a picture of who was involved and maybe then use photo-fits so that they can be apprehended.

- **Preservation**: Data needs to be preserved in its original state so that it can be produced as evidence in court. This is why we take copies and analyze the copies so that the original data is not altered and is pristine. Putting a copy of the most vital evidence in a WORM drive will prevent any tampering with the evidence, as you cannot delete data from a WORM drive. You could also write-protect the storage drives.

- **Recovery**: When the incident has been eradicated, we may have to recover the data from a backup; a faster method would be a hot site that is already up and running with data less than 1 hour old. We may also have to purchase additional hardware if the original hardware was damaged during the incident.

- **Strategic Intelligence/Counterintelligence Gathering**: This is where different governments exchange data about cyber criminals so that they can work together to reduce threats. It is also possible for companies who have suffered an attack to log as much information as they can and have a third party who specializes in incident response to help them find a way to prevent re-occurrence.

- **Active Logging**: To track incidents, we need to be actively monitoring and actively logging changes to patterns in our log files or traffic patterns in our network. Installing a SIEM system that provides real-time monitoring can help collate all entries in the log files, ensuring that duplicate data is not used so that a true picture can be taken. Alerts based on certain triggers can be set up on our SIEM system so that we are notified as soon as the event happens.

Cloud Forensics

In the last few years, the growth of cloud computing and resources has been increasing year on year. Cloud forensics has different needs than that of traditional forensics. One of the primary aspects that a cloud provider must provide is security of the data stored in the cloud.

In 2012, Cloud Forensic Process 26 was created to focus on the competence and admissibility of evidence. The stages are as follows:

- **Stage A** – Verify the purpose of cloud forensics.

- **Stage B** – Verify the type of cloud service.

- **Stage C** – Verify the type of technology behind the cloud.

- **Stage D** – Verify the role of the user and negotiate with the **Cloud Service Provider (CSP)** to collect the evidence required.

Cloud services, because of the nature of their business, create virtual machines and then destroy them on a regular basis. This prevents the collection of forensic evidence. The forensic team needs to prove to the cloud provider their reasons for the collection of the evidence and they have to rely on the cloud provider sending them the correct evidence that they require.

Right-to-Audit Clauses

By inserting right-to-audit clauses into supply chain contracts, an auditor can visit the premises without notice and inspect the contractor's books and records to ensure that the contractor is complying with its obligation under the contract. This would help them identify the following:

- Faulty or inferior quality of goods

- Short shipments

- Goods not delivered

- Kickbacks

- Gifts and gratuities to company employees

- Commissions to brokers and others

- Services allegedly performed that weren't needed in the first place, such as equipment repairs

Regulatory and Jurisdiction

Cloud data should be stored and have data sovereignty in regions. The US introduced the CLOUD Act in 2018 due to the problems that the FBI faced in forcing Microsoft to hand over data stored in Ireland. In 2019, the UK received royal assent for the Overseas Production Act (COPOA), which allows the UK to seek data stored overseas as part of a criminal investigation. In 2019, the US and the UK signed a data-sharing agreement to give law enforcement agencies in each country faster access to evidence held by providers, such as social media or web hosting. In 2016, a similar agreement was set between the US and the EU; however, with the introduction of **General Data Protection Regulation (GDPR)**, all websites in the US that have consumers from the EU have to abide by GDPR.

Data Breach Notifications/Laws

If a data breach occurs, a company can be fined more than £10 million for failing to report a breach. The EU uses GDPR, and notifications of data breaches must be reported within 72 hours. Other countries have their own reporting timescale.

Review Questions

Now it's time to check your knowledge. Answer these questions and check your answers, found in the *Assessment* section at the end of the book:

1. What are the three components of the CIA triad?

2. Why might a CCTV camera be situated outside a building without any film inside?

3. What does confidentiality mean?

4. How can we control access of personnel to a data center?

5. What is the purpose of an air gap?

6. Name three main control categories.

7. Name three physical controls.

8. Following an incident, what type of control will be used when researching how the incident happened?

9. How do I know whether the integrity of my data is intact?

10. What is a corrective control?

11. What type of control is it when you change the firewall rules?

12. What is used to log in to a system that works in conjunction with a PIN?

13. What is the name of the person who looks after classified data and who is the person that gives people access to the classified data?

14. When you use a DAC model for access, who determines who gains access to the data?

15. What is least privilege?

16. What is the Linux permission of 764? What access does it give you?

17. The sales team are allowed to log in to the company system between 9 a.m. and 10 p.m. What type of access control is being used?

18. Two people from the finance team are only allowed to authorize the payment of checks; what type of access control are they using?

19. What is the purpose of the defense in depth model?

20. When someone leaves the company, what is the first thing we should do with their user account?

21. What do US companies that host websites in the US have to comply with if customers are based in Poland?

22. How can a company discover that their suppliers are using inferior products?

23. What is one of the most important factors between someone being arrested and their appearance before the judge in court?

24. Can you explain what the purpose of the CLOUD Act and COPOA is?

25. What is Stage C of Cloud Forensic Process 26?

2

Implementing Public Key Infrastructure

Public Key Infrastructure (**PKI**) is asymmetric encryption that has a Certificate Authority and the associated infrastructure to support issuing and managing certificates. Certificates are used for both encryption and authentication, and in this chapter, we are going to look at different encryption types and how certificates are issued and used. This is the most difficult module for students to understand, so we have focused on making the most difficult aspects seem easy. If you are going to be successful in the Security+ exam, you must know this module thoroughly.

In this chapter, we are going to cover the following topics:

- Public Key Infrastructure Concepts
- Asymmetric and Symmetric Encryption
- Cryptography Algorithms and Their Characteristics
- Comparing and Contrasting the Basic Concepts of Cryptography

PKI Concepts

The PKI provides asymmetric techniques using two keys: a public key and a private key. There is a certificate hierarchy, which is called the Certificate Authority, that manages, signs, issues, validates, and revokes certificates. Let's first look at the components of the certificate hierarchy. A certificate is known as an X509 certificate.

Certificate Hierarchy

The **Certificate Authority** (**CA**) is the ultimate authority as it holds the master key, also known as the root key, for signing all of the certificates that it gives the **Intermediary**, which then, in turn, issues the certificate to the requester.

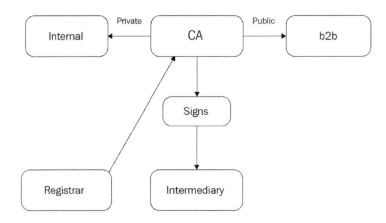

Figure 2.1 – CA Hierarchy

Let's look at the CA hierarchy shown in the preceding diagram in more depth:

- **Online CA**: An internal online CA is always up and running so that people in the company can request a certificate at any time of the day or night. This would not be the case in a government or top-security environment.

- **Offline CA**: An offline CA is for a military or secure environment where clearance and vetting must be completed before someone can be issued with a certificate. The CA is kept offline and locked up when it is not being used. It is switched off so that it cannot issue new certificates.

There are different types of CA:

- **Public CA**: A public CA is also known as a third-party CA and is commercially accepted as an authority for issuing public certificates. Examples include *Sectigo*, formerly known as *Comodo*, *Symantec*, *Go Daddy*, and more.

The benefit of using a third-party CA is that all of the management is carried out by them; once you purchase the certificate, all you have to do is install it. They keep an up-to-date **Certificate Revocation List (CRL)** where you can check whether your certificate is valid. A certificate that is not valid will not work if you are going to sell goods and services to other companies; this is known as a B2B transaction, which requires a public CA.

For example, I put gas in my car and go to pay for it. I give the attendant some monopoly money, but they refuse to take it; this would be the equivalent of a private CA. Businesses will not accept it as payment. I then go to the cash machine outside and withdraw $100 and I give this to the attendant; he smiles and accepts it and gives me some change. This is the equivalent of a public CA.

If you wish to trade and exchange certificates with other businesses, you need to get your certificate from a public CA. The certificate that follows has been issued to the Bank of Scotland from a public CA called DigiCert Global CA. You can see on the front of the certificate the purpose for use and also the dates that it is valid for. The X509 has an OID, which is basically the certificate's serial number – the same way that paper money has serial numbers:

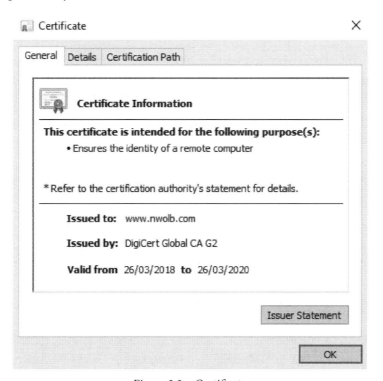

Figure 2.2 – Certificate

- **Private CA**: A private CA can only be used internally. However, although it is free, you must maintain the CA. Hopefully, your company has the skill set to do so.

- **Registration Authority (RA)**: The RA validates and accepts the incoming requests for certificates from users on the network and notifies the CA to issue the certificates. The certificates that are issued are known as X509 certificates.

- **Subordinate CA**: It could be the RA that issues certificates to users. In the CompTIA exam, the subordinate CA could be called an intermediary.

- **Certificate Pinning**: Certificate pinning prevents the compromising of the CA and the issuing of fraudulent X509 certificates. It prevents SSL man-in-the-middle attacks.

> Tip
>
> Certificate pinning prevents the compromising of the CA, certificate fraud, and SSL man-in-the-middle attacks.

Certificate Trust

Certificates have some form of trust where the certificate can check whether or not it is valid. We are going to look at different trust models. You need to ensure that you know when each is used:

- **Trust Anchor**: A trust anchor in a PKI environment is the root certificate from which the whole chain of trust is derived; this is the root CA.

- **Trust Model**: A trust model proves the authenticity of a certificate; there are two trust models:

    a. **Hierarchical Trust Model**: This uses a hierarchy from the root CA down to the intermediary (also known as a subordinate); this is the normal PKI model. An example can be seen in the certificate hierarchy diagram earlier in this chapter.

    b. **Bridge Trust Model**: The bridge trust model is peer-to-peer, where two separate PKI environments trust each other. The certificate authorities communicate with each other, allowing for cross certification. Sometimes, this is referred to as the trust model.

- **Certificate Chaining**: This chain of trust is used to verify the validity of a certificate as it includes details of the CRL. The chain normally has three layers, the certificate vendor, the vendor's CA, and the computer where the certificate is installed.

> **Tip**
> Certificate chaining shows the trust from the vendor, the vendor CA, and the computer. Fewer than three layers results in trust errors

Certificate Validity

Each time a certificate is used, the first thing that must happen is that it must be checked for validity. The following diagram shows the certificate validity process:

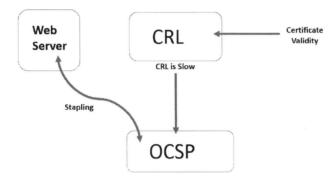

Figure 2.3 – Certificate validity

There are three separate processes that you must know thoroughly, and these are as follows:

- **Certificate Revocation List (CRL):** The first stage in checking whether a certificate is valid, no matter the scenario, is to check the CRL. If the X509 is in the CRL, it is no longer valid and will not be accepted. No matter how obscure the question posed in the exam, unless it is going slow or it is a web server looking for a faster lookup, it will be the CRL that provides certificate validity.

- **Online Certificate Status Protocol (OCSP):** Only when the CRL is going slow will the OCSP come into play. It is much faster than the CRL and can take a load from the CRL in a very busy environment.

- **OCSP Stapling/Certificate Stapling:** Certificate stapling, also known as OCSP stapling, is used when a web server bypasses the CRL to use the OCSP for a faster confirmation, irrespective of whether or not a certificate is valid.

> **Tip**
> Certificate validity can only be done by the CRL or OCSP. OCSP is used only when the CRL is going slow or has been replaced by the OCSP

Certificate Management Concepts

We are now going to look at the different ways in which certificates are managed in a PKI environment, starting with the request for a new certificate and ending with different certificate formats. You must learn all of this information thoroughly as these aspects are heavily tested:

- **Certificate Signing Request (CSR)**: This is the process of requesting a new certificate.

- **Key Escrow**: The key escrow holds the private keys for third parties and stores them in a **Hardware Security Module (HSM)**:

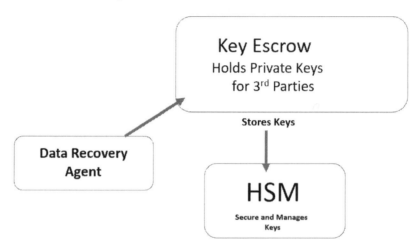

Figure 2.4 – Key escrow

- **Hardware Security Module (HSM)**: The HSM can be a piece of hardware attached to the server or a portable device that is attached to store the keys. See the preceding diagram for more on this. It stores and manages certificates.

- **Data Recovery Agent (DRA)**: If a user cannot access their data because their private key is corrupted, the DRA will recover the data. The DRA needs to get the private key from the key escrow.

- **Certificates**: There are two main certificate types: the *public key* and the *private key*. The public key is sent to third parties to encrypt the data, and the private key decrypts the data. If you think of the private key as your bank card, that's a thing you wouldn't give away. The public key is the deposit slip that is tied to your account. If you were in a room with 20 people who wanted to pay $20 into your account, you would definitely give them your deposit slip. You will always give your public key away because when you are encrypting data, you will always use the recipient's public key.

> **Tip**
>
> The **Data Recovery Agent (DRA)** needs a private key from the key escrow to recover data.

- **Object Identifier (OID)**: The OID on a certificate is similar to a serial number on a bank note. Bank notes are identified by their serial number. The certificate is identified by its OID.

- **Certificate Formats**: There are different certificate formats, and these are as follows:

Certificate type	Format	File extension
Private	P12	.pfx
Public	P7B	.cer
PEM	Base64 format	.pem
DER	Extension for PEM	.der

Figure 2.5 – Certificate format and file extensions

Types of Certificates

As a security professional, you will be responsible for purchasing new certificates, and therefore, you must learn the certificate types thoroughly to ensure that you make the correct purchases. We will start with the self-signed certificate, which can roll out with applications such as Microsoft Exchange Server or Skype, and finish with extended validation where the certificate has a high level of trust:

- **Self-Signed Certificate**: A self-signed certificate is issued by the same entity that is using it. However, it does not have a CRL and cannot be validated or trusted.

- **Wildcard**: For a wildcard certificate for a domain called `securityplus. training`, the wildcard certification would be `*.securityplus.training` and could be used for the domain and a subdomain. For example, in the `securityplus.training` domain, there are two servers called `web` and `mail`. The wildcard certification is `*.securityplus.training` and, when installed, it would work for the **Fully Qualified Domain Names (FQDNs)** of both of these—`web.securityplus.training` and `mail.securityplus. training`. A wildcard can be used for multiple servers in the same domain.

- **Domain Validation**: A **Domain-Validated (DV)** certificate is an X.509 certificate that proves the ownership of a domain name.

- **Subject Alternative Name (SAN)**: An SAN certificate can be used on multiple domain names, such as abc.com or xyz.com. You can also insert other information into an SAN certificate, such as an IP address.

- **Code Signing**: Code-signing certificates are used to digitally sign software so that its authenticity is guaranteed.

- **Computer/Machine**: A computer or machine certificate is used to identify a computer within a domain.

- **User**: A user certificate provides authenticity to a user for the applications that they use.

- **Extended Validation**: Extended validation certificates provide a higher level of trust in identifying the entity that is using the certificate. It would normally be used in the financial arena. You may have seen it in action where the background of the URL turns green, as shown in the following screenshot:

Figure 2.6 – Extended validation

Companies applying for the extended validation certificate would have to provide more detailed information about the company.

Tip

A wildcard certificate can be installed on multiple public facing websites as a cheaper option. A self-signed certificate can be installed on internal facing websites as a cheaper option.

Asymmetric and Symmetric Encryption

There are two main types of encryption that use certificates, and these are asymmetric and symmetric. We need to learn about each thoroughly. Let's start by understanding what encryption is. Please remember that you are taking plaintext and changing it into ciphertext.

Encryption Explained

Encryption is where we take plaintext that can be easily read and convert it into ciphertext that cannot be easily read:

- **Substitution Cipher**: Julius Caesar, who died in 44 BC, invented the first substitution cipher, where he moved each letter of the alphabet three places one way or another. This way, he could make his military plans unreadable if they had been intercepted. What he forgot about was that most people in those days could not read! This was called ROT 13, after the thirteen-letter rotation, and is now known as the Caesar cipher. For example, if I take the word ECHO and move each letter on thirteen places to the right in the alphabet sequence, you will get the word RPUB—that would be difficult for someone to read. To decrypt, you would roll back 13 spaces.

- **ROT 13**: ROT 13 is a variation of the Caesar cipher. As there are 26 letters in the alphabet, we are rotating the letters 13 times. The key to ROT 13 would be as follows:

Letter	A	B	C	D	E	F	G	H	I	J	K	L	M
ROT 13	N	O	P	Q	R	S	T	U	V	W	X	Y	Z
Letter	N	O	P	Q	R	S	T	U	V	W	X	Y	Z
ROT 13	A	B	C	D	E	F	G	H	I	J	K	L	M

Figure 2.7 – Caesar Cipher ROT 13 table

When receiving the message, GVZR SBE GRN, then we would apply ROT 13, but instead of going forward 13 places to decipher, we would simply go back 13 places, and the message would be TIME FOR TEA. From the preceding table, select a letter from the top and then the corresponding ROT 13 equivalent below it for both encryption and decryption.

There are two types of encryption that use certificates: asymmetric and symmetric. Let's look at each of these in turn:

- **Symmetric Encryption**: Symmetric encryption only uses one key, which is known as the private or shared key. The same key encrypts and decrypts the data. The danger of symmetric encryption is that if the key is stolen, the attacker gets the keys to the kingdom. The main reason for using symmetric encryption is that it can encrypt large amounts of data very quickly. The Security+ exam does not focus on key exchange, because it only uses one key, but instead focuses on which is the fastest or strongest symmetric key, and which is used for the encryption of large amounts of data. The symmetric encryptions are DES 56 bit, 3DES 168 bit, AES 256 bit, Twofish 128 bit, and Blowfish 64 bit. The smaller the key, the faster it is, but the larger the key, the more secure it is. It also uses block cipher where the data is transferred in blocks making it faster.

  Diffie Hellman (DH): When symmetric data is in transit, it is protected by Diffie Hellman, whose main purpose is to create a secure tunnel for symmetric data to pass through. It does not encrypt data, but creates a secure tunnel.

- **Asymmetric Encryption**: Asymmetric encryption uses two keys—a private key and a public key—and is also known as a PKI, complete with its CA and intermediary authorities. The Security+ exam tests the use of both the private and public keys very thoroughly. I have created the following diagram to help you understand the purpose of each key. See *Figure 2.8* below.

The first stage in encryption is the key exchange. You will always keep your private key and give away your public key. You will always use the recipient's public key to encrypt:

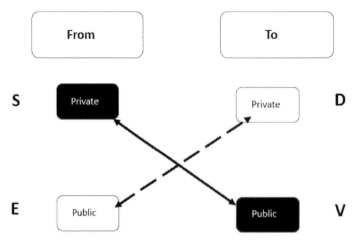

Figure 2.8 – Key exchange

In the preceding diagram, there are two different key pairs: the black key pair and the white key pair. These work together. Remember: the private key is your bank card; you will always retain it, but the public key is your deposit slip; you will give it away so that people can pay money into your account. The person who is sending the data is on the **From** side, and the person receiving the data is on the **To** side. A good way to remember the labels would be to think of South-East on the left-hand side and Distinguished-Visitor on the right. These labels stand for the following:

- **S**: Sign (digital signature)
- **E**: Encryption
- **D**: Decryption
- **V**: Validation

For example, Bob wants to encrypt data and send it to Carol. How is this done? Let's look at the following diagram. We can see that Bob owns the black key pair and Carol owns the white key pair. The first thing that needs to happen before encryption can happen is that they exchange public keys:

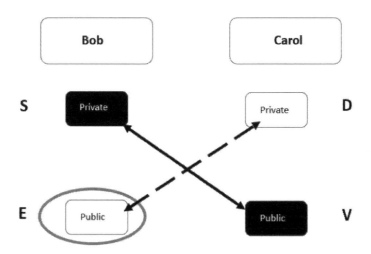

Figure 2.9 – Encryption

You can see under the column for **Bob** that he has his private key, which he will always keep, and the public key that Carol has given him. In the preceding diagram, you can see the label **E**, for encryption. Therefore, Bob uses Carol's public key to encrypt the data. Then, under **Carol**, you can see the letter **D**, for decryption. Therefore, when the encrypted data arrives, Carol uses the other half of the white key pair, the private key, to decrypt the data.

> **Tip**
> Your private key, or a key pair, is never installed on another server. You always retain the private key just like your bank card. You give the public key away or install on another server.

Digital Signatures Explained

When we send an email or document to someone, it could be intercepted in transit and altered. Your email address could be spoofed, and someone could send an email as if it was from you, but there is no guarantee of integrity. We sign the email or document with our private key and it is validated by our public key.

The first stage in digital signatures is to exchange public keys, the same principle as encryption. For example, George wants to send Mary an email and he wants to ensure that it has not been altered in transit:

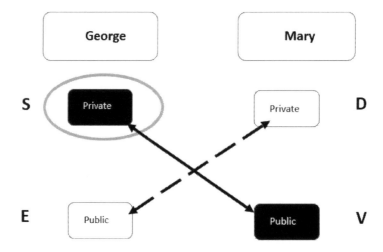

Figure 2.10 – Digital signature

In *Figure 2.10*, you can see that George is going to sign the email with his private key when he sends it to Mary, and she then validates it with the public key that George has already given to her. When the email has been validated, she knows that the email has not been tampered with. It could be read in transit, but not tampered with.

When people are asked to sign contracts, they sometimes use a third-party provider that asks them to digitally sign the contract. This then makes the contract valid as the digital signature proves the identity of the signatory.

Then there's non-repudiation. When I complete a digital signature, I am using my private key, which I should never give away to sign the email or document, proving that it has come from me. Non-repudiation means that I cannot deny that it was me who signed the document. I could not say it was done by someone else. In the early 6th century, King Arthur would send messages to his knights on a parchment scroll and then would put his wax seal on the scroll to prove it came from him. The digital signature in modern life is doing the same – it is proving who it came from. The digital signature creates a one-way hash of the entire document, so it also provides integrity similar to hashing.

> **Tip**
> Encryption uses the recipients' public key, where a digital signature used the sender's private key.

Cryptography Algorithms and Their Characteristics

If we look at symmetric and asymmetric keys, they use a cipher that has a number of bits attached to it—the lower the number of bits, the faster, and the higher the number of bits, the stronger and more secure it is.

For example, we have two people who are going to complete a challenge – they are Usain Bolt, who is DES, a 56-bit key, and we have King Arthur wearing armor, who has an RSA of 4,096 bits. The first part of the challenge is a 100-meter dash, in which Usain Bolt wins and King Arthur is held back by the weight of his armor, 90 meters behind. The second part of the challenge is a boxing match, and Usain keeps hitting King Arthur, who keeps laughing at him as he is being protected by his armor. Then, out of the blue, King Arthur lands a knockout blow to Usain. Since the challenge was for charity and the result was a draw, they are both happy.

Symmetric Algorithms

For the Security+ exam, you must know the characteristics of each of the symmetric algorithms, from when it is used to its key length. Remember, they will never ask you which key encrypts or decrypts, as the answer would always be the private key, also known as the shared key. Let's look at each of these characteristics in turn:

- **Advanced Encryption Standard (AES)**: AES comes in three key strengths: 128-, 192-, and 256-bits. AES is commonly used for L2TP/IPSec VPNs.

- **Data Encryption Standard (DES)**: DES groups data into 64-bit blocks, but for the purpose of the exam, it is seen as a 56-bit key, making it the fastest but weakest of the symmetric algorithms. This could be used for L2TP/IPSec VPNs, but is weaker than AES.

- **Triple DES (3DES)**: 3DES applies the DES key three times and is said to be a 168-bit key. This could be used for L2TP/IPSec VPNs but is weaker than AES.

- **Rivest Cipher 4 (RC4)**: RC4 is 40 bits and is used by WEP and is seen as a stream cipher.

- **Blowfish** and **Twofish**: Blowfish is a 64-bit key and Twofish is a 128-bit key, and both were originally designed for encryption with embedded systems. How can you remember which of these is faster as they have similar names? Easy. I have a pond with fish inside and I have a challenge with a guy called Tom. I need to catch two fish from the pond and he only needs to blow into the air. Guess what? He will win each time. Therefore, remember, Blowfish is faster than Twofish.

Asymmetric Algorithms

Asymmetric algorithms use a PKI environment as they use two keys: a private key and a public key. Let's now look at different asymmetric techniques.

Diffie Hellman (DH) does not encrypt data. Its main purpose is to create a secure session so that symmetric data can travel down it. The DH handshake is shown in the following diagram:

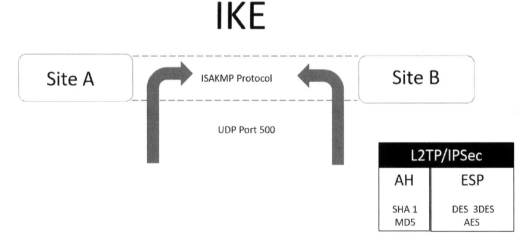

Figure 2.11 – DH handshake

DH creates the keys used in the **Internet Key Exchange** (**IKE**); it uses UDP port 500 to set up the secure session for the L2TP/IPSec VPN. Once the secure tunnel has been created, then the symmetric encrypted data flows down the tunnel.

- **Rivest**, **Shamir**, and **Adelman** (**RSA**): RSA is named after the three people who invented the algorithm. The keys were the first private and public key pairs, and they start at 1,024, 2,046, 3,072, and 4,096 bits. They are used for encryption and digital signatures.

- **Digital Signature Algorithm** (**DSA**): DSA keys are used for digital signatures; they start at 512 bits, but their 1,024-bit and 2,046-bit keys are faster than RSA for digital signatures.

- **Elliptic Curve Cryptography** (**ECC**): ECC is a small, fast key that is used for encryption in small mobile devices. However, AES-256 is used in military mobile cell phones. It uses less processing than other encryptions.

- **Ephemeral Keys**: Ephemeral keys are short-lived keys. They are used for a single session, and there are two of them:

a. **Diffie Hellman Ephemeral** (**DHE**)

b. **Elliptic Curve Diffie Hellman Ephemeral** (**ECDHE**)

- **Pretty Good Privacy** (**PGP**): PGP is used between two users to set up an asymmetric encryption and digital signatures. For PGP to operate, you need a private and public key pair. The first stage in using PGP is to exchange the keys. It uses RSA keys.

- **GnuPG**: GnuPG is a free version of OpenPGP; it is also known as PGP. It uses RSA keys.

> Tip
> PGP is used for encryption between two people. S/MIME is used for digital signature between two people

Symmetric versus Asymmetric Analogy

If we think of encryption as playing table tennis where each person has just one bat and the pace is extremely fast, this is similar to symmetric encryption as it uses one key. Then, if we change the game and we give the players two bats, the first bat to stop the ball and the second bat to hit the ball back, this would be much slower. The same can be said for encryption; asymmetric encryption is much more secure as it has two keys and uses DH, an asymmetric technique for setting up a secure tunnel for the symmetric data. Symmetric encryption uses a block cipher and encrypts large blocks of data much faster than the asymmetric technique.

XOR Encryption

The binary operation **Exclusive OR (XOR)** is a binary operand from Boolean algebra. This operand will compare two bits and will produce one bit in return:

- Two bits that are same: 0

- Two bits that are different: 1

This is the opposite to binary. For example, we are going to use the word TREAD in ASCII format and then we are going to insert a key using the word HELLO so that we can complete an XOR operation. See the following diagram:

	T	R	E	A	D
XOR (Original Input)	01010100	01110010	01100101	01100001	01100100
Key	01101000	01100101	01101100	01101100	01101111
Output	00111100	00010111	00001001	00001101	00001011

Figure 2.12 – XOR

XOR encryption is commonly used with AES, several symmetric ciphers, and a one-time pad.

Key Stretching Algorithms

Key stretching is where you append a random set of characters to a password to increase the size of the password and its hash, ensuring that a brute-force attack needs more compute time to crack the password.

- **BCRYPT**: BCRYPT is a password-hashing algorithm based on the Blowfish cipher. It is used to salt the passwords. A random string is appended to the password to increase the password length to help increase the compute time for a brute-force attack.

- **PBKDF2**: PBKDF2 stores passwords with a random salt and with the password hash using HMAC. It then iterates, which forces the regeneration of every password and prevents any rainbow table attack.

> Tip
>
> Symmetric encryption is used to encrypt large amounts of data as they have small, fast keys and use block ciphers.

Cipher Modes

There are different cipher modes; most symmetric keys use a block cipher and can encrypt a large amount of data quicker than asymmetric encryption. Let's look at these in turn:

- **Stream Cipher**: A stream cipher is a method of encrypting text (to produce ciphertext) in which a cryptographic key and algorithm are applied to each binary digit in a data stream, one bit at a time. It is normally used by asymmetric encryption.

- **Block Cipher**: A block cipher is where a block of data is taken and then encrypted; for example, 128 bits of data may be encrypted at a time. This is the method used today as it is much faster than a stream cipher. It is used by symmetric encryption with the exception of RC4.

Stream versus Block Cipher Analogy

We have two teams of four people who have been tasked with unloading a five-ton lorry full of skittles and placing them in a room on the bottom floor of a building.

There are skittles in boxes and there are skittles that have been placed loose. One of the teams has loose skittles that need to be bagged and the other lorry has boxes of skittles. It is obvious that the team with boxes of skittles will win. The stream cipher is bagging the skittles, whereas the block cipher has boxes of skittles.

Modes of Operation

Modes of operation are how ciphers work to achieve encryption. Let's look at the different modes:

- **Initialization Vector (IV)**: This is a random value used as a secret key for data encryption. This number, also called a **nonce**, is employed only one time in any session. The IV length is usually comparable to the length of the encryption key or the block of the cipher in use. Sometimes, this is also known as a starter variable.

- **Cipher Block Chaining (CBC)**: CBC adds XOR to each plaintext block from the ciphertext block that was previously produced. The first plaintext block has an IV that you XOR, and you then encrypt that block of plaintext. Refer to the following diagram:

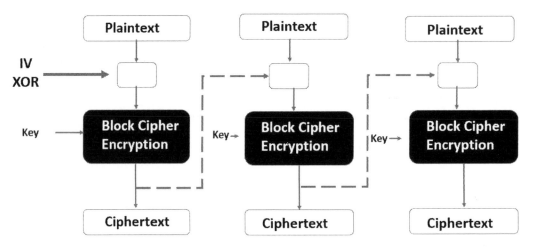

Figure 2.13 – Cipher Block Chaining

The next block of plaintext is XOR'd against the last encrypted block before you encrypt this block. When decrypting a ciphertext block, you need the XOR from the previous ciphertext block. If you are missing any blocks, then decryption cannot be done.

- **Electronic Code Book (ECB)**: ECB replaces each block of the clear text with the block of ciphertext. The same plaintext will result in the same ciphertext. The blocks are independent from the other blocks. CBC is much more secure.

- **Galois/Counter Mode (GCM)**: This is a block cipher mode of operation that uses universal hashing over a binary Galois field to provide authenticated encryption. It can be implemented in hardware and software to achieve high speeds with low cost and low latency.

- **Counter Mode** (**CTR**): CTR turns a block cipher into a stream cipher. It generates the next key stream block by encrypting successive values of a counter rather than an IV.

> **Tip**
> Stream cipher encrypts one bit at a time

Quantum Computing

Traditional computer chips use bits to store data in values of 1 where the bit is switched on, and a 0 value where the bit is switched off. Quantum computing uses qubits, which can be switched on or off at the same time or somewhere in between. This is known as a **superposition**.

A traditional computer trying to find the way from A to B could only try a single path at any one time until it found the path; however, quantum computing could try every path at the same time. Quantum computing will make cracking encryption much faster and, at this moment in time, Google has created a quantum computer that is 53 qubits, known as Sycamore, that made calculations in a few minutes that would have taken an earlier supercomputer 10,000 years to calculate. Post quantum computing could see a very powerful computer with massive qubits using Shor's algorithm to break PKI technology.

Blockchain and the Public Ledger

Blockchain was originally the technology that powered Bitcoin, but it has greater scope than that. It is a digital ledger of transactions and the data is secured by technology. Data is stored in batches called blocks that are distributed to many computers. Therefore, if you wanted to tamper with the blockchain, it would be impossible as you would have to change the data on every computer holding a copy. As they say, there is safety in numbers.

Blockchain can be used to store financial, medical, or land sale transactions. This data is chained together with a block of data holding both the hash for that block and the hash of the preceding block. To create a new block on the chain, the computer that wishes to add the block solves a cryptographic puzzle and sends the solution to the other computers participating on that blockchain. This is known as a proof of work. Once that has been verified by those computers on this network, a new block is added to the end of the chain. Should data in the chain be modified, a new block with the changes is added, referring to the amended block. Since the data is held by many computers, it makes it impossible to carry out fraudulent transactions as copies are held in multiple places.

Blockchain does not use intermediaries such as banks and financial institutions. Therefore, when someone presents data from the blockchain, it is known to be accurate and can be trusted. An example is where a brother and sister have been left a house in the will of one of their relatives and they want to ensure that they are the legal owners. They can follow each transaction in the blockchain from the purchase of the house, and the number of times it has been bought and sold, to prove that they are the legal owners.

Hashing and Data Integrity

Hashing is where the data inside a document is hashed using an algorithm, such as a **Secure Hash Algorithm Version 1 (SHA1)**, SHA2, SHA3, and MD5. This turns the data inside the file into a long text string known as a hash value; this is also known as a message digest.

While you are hashing the same data, if you copy a file and therefore have two files containing the same data, then hash them with the same hashing algorithm. It will always produce the same hash value. Let's look at the following examples on hashing and data integrity:

- **Verifying Integrity**: During forensic analysis, a scientist takes a copy of the data prior to investigation. To ensure that they have not tampered with it during investigation, they will hash the data before starting and then compare the hash to the data when finished. If the hash matches, then they know that the integrity of the data is intact.

- **One-Way Function**: For the purpose of the exam, hashing is a one-way function and cannot be reversed.

- **Digital Signatures**: Digital signatures are used to verify the integrity of an email so that you know it has not been tampered with in transit. The private certificate used to sign the email creates a one-way hash function, and when it arrives at its destination, the recipient has already been given a public key to verify that it has not been tampered with in transit. This will be covered in more depth later on in this book.

- **RIPEMD**: This is a 128-bit hashing function. RIPEMD has been replaced by RIPEMD-160, RIPEMD-256, and RIPEMD-320. For the purpose of the exam, you need to know that it can be used to hash data.

Comparing and Contrasting the Basic Concepts of Cryptography

In this section, we are going to outline the uses of different aspects of cryptography.

Asymmetric – PKI

Asymmetric keys are obtained from a CA. If you are selling products or services with external entities, then you need to obtain your X509s from a public CA, otherwise your internal certificates will not be accepted.

Asymmetric – Weak/Depreciated Algorithms

SSL should now be depreciated as it is weak; an example of an exploit is the POODLE attack, which is a man-in-the-middle attack that exploits the vulnerabilities of SSL 3.0 using CBC. Asymmetric algorithms should not be using a key whose strength is 2046 or lower. However, an SSL VPN is the only VPN that uses an SSL certificate and works with legacy clients.

Asymmetric – Ephemeral Keys

Ephemeral keys are short-lived keys that are used for a one-time only session. There are two types of ephemeral keys: **Diffie Hellman Ephemeral (DHE)** and **Elliptic Curve Diffie Hellman Ephemeral (ECDHE)**. The other keys, used for other asymmetric and symmetric encryption, are known as static keys, as they have about a two-year lifespan.

Symmetric Algorithm – Modes of Operation

Block cipher mode takes blocks of data depending on the key and encrypts that data in blocks—this makes the encryption of a large amount of data much faster.

In an L2TP/IPSec VPN tunnel, we have a choice of three different versions of symmetric encryption. The weakest is DES, which has a 56-bit key, followed by 3DES, which has a 168-bit key. The most secure is AES, as it can go from 128 bits up to 256 bits. Remember, symmetric encryption has only one key. It is much faster for encrypting a larger amount of data, but it needs DH, an asymmetric technique, to create a secure tunnel before it is used.

Symmetric Encryption – Streams versus Block Ciphers

Symmetric encryption uses a block cipher, where blocks of data are encrypted. The key size determines how large the block of data is. For example, if I use DES, then I can only encrypt blocks of 56 bits, whereas AES can encrypt blocks of data of up to 256 bits.

Asymmetric encryption encrypts one bit at a time. Therefore, it is slower but more secure than symmetric encryption as it uses a larger key size and uses two keys: public and private.

Symmetric Encryption – Confusion

Confusion massively changes the input to the output by putting it through a non-linear table created by the Symmetric Encryption – Secret Algorithm key.

A secret key is the piece of information that is used to encrypt and decrypt messages in symmetric encryption.

> **Tip**
> Ephemeral keys are for one-time use and they are of two types – DHE and ECDHE

Hashing Algorithms

A hashing algorithm takes the data from a document and generates a hexadecimal value from that input. If you take the same data and hash it with the same algorithm, it will generate the same hash. In the Security+ exam, the hashing algorithms are SHA-1, which is 160 bits, SHA-2, which is 256 bit, SHA-3, which is 512 bits, and MD5, which is 128 bits. Hashing is a one-way function to ensure that the integrity of the data is intact.

Crypto Service Provider

A crypto service provider is a software library. For example, Microsoft uses the Crypto API and has providers including the following:

- **Microsoft AES Cryptographic Provider**: This service provider provides support for the AES algorithm.

- **Microsoft DDS and DH/Channel Cryptographic Provider**: This supports hashing and data signing with DSS and key exchanging for DH.

Crypto Module

A crypto module is a combination of hardware and software that implements crypto functions such as digital signatures, encryption, random number generation, and decryption.

Protecting Data

One of the key functions of a security team is protecting a company's data, as it is difficult to put a price on lost data. Let's look at three types of data: at rest, in use, and in transit:

- **Data-at-Rest**: Data-at-rest is data that is not being used and is stored either on a hard drive or external storage. Let's look at the different devices:

  a. **Desktops and Laptops**: We could use Bitlocker, which is known in the Security+ exam as **Full Disk Encryption** (**FDE**). The desktop or laptop would need a TPM chip built into the motherboard. We could also use **Data Loss Prevention** (**DLP**) to prevent someone stealing the data with a USB drive. DLP works on a regular expression or a pattern match. Once that value has been matched, the data is blocked.

  b. **Tablets/Phones**: Tablets and phones will need **Full Device Encryption** (**FDE**) to encrypt the device so that data cannot be stolen.

  c. **USB or Removable Drive**: We can use **Full Disk Encryption** (**FDE**) so that if the drive is lost or stolen, the data is unreadable.

- **Data-in-Transit**: When purchasing items, we use TLS, SSL, or HTTPS to encrypt the session before we enter the credit card details. If we are remote users, we would use a VPN session to tunnel into the workplace to access data. TLS will be used to encrypt emails as they travel between mail servers.

- **Data-in-Use**: When we use memory on a device, it is in the **Random Access Memory** (**RAM**) or a faster block of memory called the CPU cache. We can protect this data by using full memory encryption.

Basic Cryptographic Terminologies

The Security+ exam is full of cryptographic terminologies, and in this section, we are going to start with obfuscation, which makes the code obscure. Try asking your family and friends to say the word *obfuscation* and watch them struggle. It is aptly named as the word itself is very obscure! You must know the terminology thoroughly.

Obfuscation

Obfuscation is the process where you take source code and make it look obscure, so that if it is stolen, it would not be understood. It is used to mask data.

Pseudo-Random Number Generator

Pseudo-Random Number Generator (PRNG) refers to an algorithm that uses mathematical formulas to produce sequences of random numbers. Random numbers can be used when generating data encryption keys.

Nonce

A nonce is an arbitrary number that can be used just once; it is often a random number.

Perfect Forward Secrecy

When a VPN makes a secure connection, a key exchange is made for each secure session, but it links to the server's private key. With perfect forward secrecy, there is no link between the session key and the server's private key. Therefore, even if the VPN server has been compromised, the attacker cannot use the server's private key to decrypt the session.

Security through Obscurity

The concept of security through obscurity is to prevent anyone from outside the organization from knowing the architecture or design of the system or any of its components. The internal people are aware of the weaknesses of the system, but you want to prevent an outside person from knowing anything about it. Obfuscation is a technique that makes stored source code unreadable.

Collision

If you hash the same data or password with the same hashing algorithm, then it will always create the same hash. Hashes are used to store passwords or digitally sign documents. A collision attack is where the attacker tries to match the hash; if the hash is matched, it is known as a collision, and this could compromise systems.

Steganography

Steganography is where a document, image, audio file, or video file can be hidden inside another document, image, audio file, or video file. The document, image, or file will be larger, and images will have a much lower resolution.

Homomorphic Encryption

Homomorphic Encryption allows an accountant to run calculations against data while it is still encrypted and could be used with data stored in the cloud.

Diffusion

Diffusion is a technique where you change one character of the input, which will change multiple bits of the output.

Implementation Decisions

In today's world, security administrators need to look at how the company operates to ensure it is more secure. Do they want to implement smart cards for multifactor authentication? Do they want to implement a VPN so that remote users can connect to the company securely? Do they need to implement a DLP template to ensure that sensitive data cannot be emailed from the company?

Once the company's vision has been decided, the security team needs to look at the algorithms that they need. Normally, this would be the strongest possible. However, we need to ensure that the server has enough processing power to deal with any increase in key length. We should not be using a key of fewer than 2,046 bits as this is too insecure.

Common Use Cases for Cryptography

In the Security+ exam, *use case* just means examples of when something is used. We are now going to look at examples of when different cryptography techniques are used.

Supporting Confidentiality

A company's data cannot be priced, and the disclosure of this data could cause grave danger to the company. If your competitors stole your secrets, they could beat you to the market and you would not get the rewards that you deserved. To prevent data from being accessed, we will encrypt the data to prevent it from being viewed and prevent any protocol analyzer from reading the packets. When people access the company's network from a remote location, they should use a L2TP/IPSec VPN tunnel, using AES as the encryption method to create a secure tunnel across the internet and to prevent man-in-the-middle attacks. Encryption could be coupled with mandatory access control to ensure that data is secure and kept confidential.

Supporting Integrity

There are two main reasons for ensuring integrity. The first would be to hash data stored on a file server so that we can prove whether or not the data has been tampered with. This could also be the case for a forensic examination of a laptop seized by the police – the forensic scientist could hash the data before the examination and then re-hash it at the end to prove that they had not tampered with the data. The hash values should match. Another method of proving integrity would be to digitally sign an email with your private key to prove to the recipient that it has not been tampered with in transit. Prior to this, you had to send them your public key to validate the email. This proves that the email has maintained its integrity and has not been tampered with in transit.

Supporting Non-Repudiation

When you digitally sign an email with your private key, you cannot deny that it was you, as there is only one private key; this is known as non-repudiation. When two separate parties decide to do a business deal together, they may use a third party to create a digital contract, but parties would log in to where the contract was stored. Once they digitally sign it, then it is legally binding.

Supporting Obfuscation

When companies store their source code, they use obfuscation to make it obscure so that it cannot be read by anyone who steals it. This is also known as security by obscurity, where you want to prevent third parties knowing about your IT systems and identifying any weaknesses in the system.

Low-Power Devices

Small **Internet of Things** (**IoT**) devices will need to use ECC for encryption, as it uses a small key – they do not have the processing power for conventional encryption.

High Resiliency

We should be using the most secure encryption algorithm to prevent the encryption key from being cracked by attackers. The more secure the encryption key, the longer and more processing power it will take to gain the encryption key. In an RSA encryption environment, we should use a key with at least 3,072 bits. We should also look at implementing accelerator cards to reduce the amount of latency on the encryption or decryption.

Supporting Authentication

A corporate environment should not use a single-factor username and password as they are not as secure as multifactor usernames and passwords. We should adopt at least two-factor authentication and use a smart card and PIN to make authentication more secure. Installing a RADIUS server adds an additional layer to authentication to ensure that authentication from the endpoints is more secure.

Resource versus Security Constraints

The more secure the encryption used and the higher the key length, the more processing power and memory the server will need. If there are not enough resources on the server, it could be vulnerable to a resource exhaustion attack, which causes the systems to hang or even crash; this is like a DoS attack. We must strike a balance between the hardware resources that the server has and the amount of processing power we use.

Practical Exercises

For these three practical exercises, you need a 2012/2016 server that is a domain controller.

If you are a home user and have access to a desktop with Windows 7, Windows 8.1, or Windows 10, and do not have a server, you can still complete the second exercise.

Practical Exercise 1 – Building a Certificate Server

To build a certificate server, follow these steps:

1. Log in to your 2012/2016 domain controller and open **Server Manager**.

2. Select **Manage**, followed by **Add Roles and Features**. Then, click **Next** three times.

3. On the **Select Server Roles** page, check the top box, **Active directory certificate server**. Select the **Add Features** button. Click **Next** three times. Check the **CA** box, then click **Next**, and then **Install**. This will take a few minutes. When finished, press **Close**.

4. On the **Server Manager** toolbar, double-click on the yellow triangle. This is a notification. In the post-deployment configuration wizard, double-click on the blue hyperlink, and then click **Configure active directory certificate service**. Click **Next**, and then, in the role services wizard, check the **CA** box. You need to wait a few seconds before the **Next** button comes alive. Press **Next** twice. In the **CA Type** wizard, select **Root CA** and then click **Next** three times. For the CA name under **Common name for this CA**, enter the name MyCA, click **Next** three times, and then click **Configure**. After it is configured, press **Close**.

5. On the **Server Manager** toolbar, press **Tools**, and then **CA**. Expand **MyCA** on the left- hand side, and then expand **Issued Certificates**, which should be blank, as no certificates have been issued. See the following screenshot:

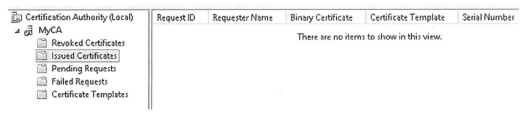

Figure 2.14 – Certificate server

Practical Exercise 2 – Encrypting Data with EFS and Stealing Certificates

To encrypt data with EFS and stealing certificates, perform the following steps:

1. Go to the desktop. Create a folder called test.

2. Inside the folder, create a text document called data.

3. Right-click the text document called data, and then select **Properties**.

4. On the **General** tab, click **Advanced**, and then check the box against **Encrypt content to secure data**. The data folder should turn green. This means it is encrypted with EFS.

5. Go to the **Start** button, type mmc, and then select the icon with the red suitcase.

6. Console 1 should open. Select **File | Add remove snap in**, select **Certificates**, select **Add**, click **Next**, and then **Finish**.

7. Expand **Certificates | Current User | Personal**. You should see an entry for an EFS certificate.

8. Right-click the certificate. Select **All tasks | Export**.

9. The certification export wizard appears. Press **Next**. On **Export Private Key**, select **Yes**, export the private key, and press **Next**. You will see that it is the P12 format. Press **Next**, check the **Password** box, enter the password `123` twice, and then press **Next**. In the file to export, call it `PrivKey` and save it to the desktop. Click **Next** and then **Finish**.

10. A box telling you the export was successful should appear.

11. Repeat the exercise and export the public key as `PubKey`.

12. You should notice the two files on the desktop. The public key has a `.cer` extension and looks like a certificate. The private has a `.pfx` extension and looks like a letter being inserted into an envelope.

Practical Exercise 3 – Revoking the EFS Certificate

To revoke the EFS certificate, perform the following steps:

1. Go to **Server Manager | Tools** and select **Certificate Authority**.

2. Expand **Issued Certificates** and you should see an EFS certificate.

3. Right-click the certificate and select **All Tasks**.

4. Revoke the certificate.

You will now notice that it has moved from **Issued Certificates** to **Revoked Certificates**.

Review Questions

Now it's time to check your knowledge. Answer the questions, and then check your answers, which can be found in the *Assessments* section at the end of the book:

1. What type of certificate does a CA have?

2. If I am going to use a CA internally, what type of CA should I use?

3. If I want to carry out B2B activity with third-party companies or sell products on the web, what type of CA should I use?

4. Why would I make my CA offline when not in use?

5. Who builds the CA or intermediary authorities?

6. Who signs X509 certificates?

7. What can I use to prevent my CA from being compromised and fraudulent certificates being issued?

8. If two entities want to set up a cross-certification, what must they set up first?

9. What type of trust model does PGP use?

10. How can I tell whether my certificate is valid?

11. If the CRL is going slow, what should I implement?

12. Explain certificate stapling/OCSP stapling.

13. What is the process of obtaining a new certificate?

14. What is the purpose of the key escrow?

15. What is the purpose of the HSM?

16. What is the purpose of the DRA and what does it need in order to complete its role effectively?

17. How can I identify each certificate?

18. What format is a private certificate and what file extension does it have?

19. What format is a public certificate and what file extension does it have?

20. What format is a PEM certificate?

21. What type of certificate can be used on multiple servers in the same domain?

22. What type of certificate can be used on multiple domains?

23. What should I do with my software to verify that it is original and not a fake copy?

24. What is the purpose of extended validation of an X509?

25. What type of cipher is the Caesar cipher and how does it work if it uses ROT 4?

26. What is encryption and what are the inputs and outputs called?

27. What type of encryption will be used to encrypt large amounts of data?

28. What is the purpose of DH?

29. What is the first stage in any encryption, no matter whether it is asymmetric or symmetric?

30. If Carol is encrypting data to send to Bob, what key will they each use?

31. If George encrypted data 4 years ago with an old CAC card, can he unencrypt the data with his new CAC card?

32. If Janet is digitally signing an email to send to John to prove that it has not been tampered with in transit, what key will they each use?

33. What two things does digitally signing an email provide?

34. What asymmetric encryption algorithm should I use to encrypt data on a smartphone?

35. What shall I use to encrypt a military mobile telephone?

36. Name two key-stretching algorithms.

37. What is the purpose of key stretching?

38. What is the difference between stream and block cipher modes, and which one will you use to encrypt large blocks of data?

39. What happens with cipher block chaining if I don't have all of the blocks?

40. If I want to ensure the integrity of data, what shall I use? Name two algorithms.

41. If I want to ensure the protection of data, what shall I use?

42. Is a hash a one-way or two-way function, and is it reversible?

43. What type of man-in-the-middle attack is SSL 3.0 (CBC) vulnerable to?

44. Explain why we would use **Diffie Hellman Ephemeral (DHE)** and **Elliptic Curve Diffie Hellman Ephemeral (ECDHE)**.

45. What are the strongest and weakest methods of encryption with an L2TP/IPSec VPN tunnel?

46. What is the name of the key used to ensure the security of communication between a computer and a server or a computer to another computer?

47. What should I do to protect data at rest on a laptop?

48. What should I do to protect data at rest on a tablet or smartphone?

49. What should I do to protect data at rest on a backend server?

50. What should I do to protect data at rest on a removable device, such as a USB flash drive or an external hard drive?

51. What two protocols could we use to protect data in transit?

52. How can you protect data in use?

53. What is the purpose of obfuscation?

54. What is the purpose of perfect forward secrecy?

55. What type of attack tries to find two hash values that match?

56. What is the purpose of rainbow tables?

57. Explain the concept of steganography.

58. What are the two purposes of **Data Loss Protection (DLP)**?

59. What is the purpose of salting a password?

3
Investigating Identity and Access Management

Controlling and allowing access to computer systems is a key duty of any security professional. We will look at the different types of access control so that you can select the best solution for your company and, in an examination, choose the best method for a given scenario.

In this chapter, we will look at different types of authentication, looking first at Identity and Access Management concepts.

We will cover the following exam objectives in this chapter:

- Understanding Identity and Access Management Concepts
- Implementing Authentication and Authorization Solutions
- Summarizing Authentication and Authorization Design Concepts
- Common Account Management Policies

Understanding Identity and Access Management Concepts

One of the first areas in IT security is giving someone access to the company's network to use resources for their job. There are four key elements to **Identify and Access Management (IAM)**, and these are identity, authentication, authorization, and accounting. Let's look at each of these in the order that they should be presented:

- **Identify**: Each person needs some form of identification so that they can prove who they are; this could be anything, ranging from a username to a smart card. It needs to be unique so that the person using that identity is accountable for its use.

- **Authentication**: The second part after proving your identity is to provide authentication for that identity. This can be done in many ways; for example, inserting a password or if you have a smart card, it would be a **Personal Identification Number (PIN)**.

- **Authorization**: Once the individual has been authenticated, they are given an access level based on their job role. This could also be known as their permission level to the system to which they have access.

- **Accounting**: Computer systems maintain a log of when users log in and log out, and accounting is the process of maintaining these log files. This could be the security log in a Windows desktop in Event Viewer or it could be a database on a AAA server that is responsible for authentication, authorization, and accounting. Examples of these are RADIUS and DIAMETER from Microsoft or TACACS+ from CISCO. These are described in more depth in *Chapter 8, Securing Wireless and Mobile Solutions*.

Identity Types

An **identify provider (IdP)** is an entity that can validate that the credentials that are presented are valid. The identify could be a certificate, token, or details such as a username or password. IdP is used by cloud providers who use federation services to validate the identity of a user. An example of this is that they would use SAML to pass credentials to the IdP to validate their identity.

Example: A user authenticates using a token from a provider such as OKTA. The cloud provider uses SAML to pass the credentials back to OKTA to verify the user's identity.

what is okta.

The following can be used when assessing a person's identity as it needs to be unique to them:

- **Username**: This is the account identity given to the user.

- **Attribute**: This is a unique variable that the user has in their account details, for example, an employee ID.

- **Smart Card**: A credit card token with a certificate embedded on a chip; it is used in conjunction with a pin.

- **Certification**: This is a digital certificate where two keys are generated, a public key and a private key. The private key is used for identity.

- **Token**: This is a digital token that can either be a SAML token used for federation services or a token used by **Open Authentication (OAuth)**.

- **SSH Keys**: These are typically used by an administrator using a secure remote connection to the server. First of all, a key pair, private and public keys, is generated. The public key is stored on the server, with the private key remaining on the administrator's desktop. **Example**: Using a tool such as OpenSSH, the `ssh-keygen -t` RSA command is used to generate a RSA public and private key pair on the administrator's desktop. The next step is to use `ssh-copy-id` to log in to the server and copy the public key across. This is added to the list of authorized keys on the server. While copying, the administrator may be asked to provide their process whereby the key is generated and copied across. An administrator will use the `ssh-root@server` and a user will use **username@server** to test the SSH keys.

Account management ranges from account creation on startup to its disablement when someone leaves the company. Fully understanding these concepts is crucial in obtaining the Security+ certification.

Account Types

Each user in a system needs an account to access the network in a Microsoft Active Directory environment. The user account has a **Security Identifier (SID)** linked to the account. When I create a user called `Ian`, they may have an SID of `1-5-1-2345678-345678`. When the account is deleted, the SID is gone, and a new SID is created.

For example, a member of the IT team has deleted a user account called `Ian`. It may have an SID of `SID 1-5-1-2345678-345678`, so he quickly creates another account called `Ian`, but this account cannot access resources as it has a new SID of `SID 1-5-1-2345678-3499999`. The first portion from left to right identifies the domain, and then the remainder is a serial number that is never reused.

There are various different types of user accounts and these are heavily tested in the Security+ exam; you must know when you would need each account:

- **User Account**: A user account, also known as a standard user account, has no real access. They cannot install software – they give users limited access to the computer systems. There are two types of user accounts – those that are local to the machine, and those that access a domain. A domain is another name for a large group of users.

- **Guest Account**: A guest account is a legacy account that was designed to give limited access to a single computer without the need to create a user account. It is normally disabled as it is no longer useful, and some administrators see it as a security risk.

- **Sponsored Guest Account**: A sponsored guest account is used for external speakers who may need access to the internet while delivering their presentation.

  Example: John Smith has been asked by Company A to deliver a presentation to company employees about a new pension plan. While he is delivering the presentation, he wants to show the latest share prices for the stock market. The finance department have asked the IT department to let John Smith access the company network to use the internet. The IT Director decided that the best course of action was to create a sponsored guest account that would allow John to have access to the company guest Wi-Fi.

  > **Tip**
  > A guest speaker should be allocated a sponsored guest account.

- **Privilege Account**: User accounts do not have rights, but privilege accounts have much higher access to the system and tend to be used by members of the IT team. Administrators are an example of privilege accounts.

- **Administrative Account**: An administrative account can install software and manage the configuration of a server or a computer. They also have the privileges to create, delete, and manage user accounts. An administrator should have two accounts – a user account for routine tasks, and then an administrator account to carry out their administrative duties.

- **Service Account**: When software is installed on a computer or server, it needs higher levels of privilege to run the software, but at the same time, we need a lower-level administrative account and the service account fits the bill. An example of this is an account to run an anti-virus application.

> **Tip**
> A service account is a type of administrator account used to run an application.

- **Shared Account**: When a group of people perform the same duties, such as members of customer services, they can use a shared account. If you need to set up monitoring or auditing to individual employees, you must eliminate the practice of using shared accounts.

  Example: A multinational corporation that has 100,000 employees has five members of the **Human Resources** (**HR**) team that receive and process email applications from potential employees. They all use a shared account called jobs@corporations.com and between them, they open and action the resumés that they receive.

  Mr. Grumpy was one of the people who applied for a job within the company and has complained to the **Chief Executive Officer** (**CEO**) because he was not happy with how his application was handled. The CEO wanted to know which of the HR employees was responsible, but could not identify the person responsible as all five members of the HR team were using a shared account. They all denied dealing with the application.

  > **Tip**
  > When you need to monitor or audit to an employee level, you must eliminate the use of shared accounts.

- **Generic Accounts**: Generic accounts are default administrative accounts created by manufacturers for devices ranging from baby alarms to smart ovens and smart TVs. They all have default usernames and passwords. If you surf the web for the device that you have purchased, it is very easy to find the credentials to hack that device. As cybercrime is increasing each day, we should rename the default account name and its associated password. Most people purchasing IoT devices are not aware of these accounts.

  Example: Baby monitors are getting more sophisticated and come with the ability to see and hear your baby from somewhere else in your home via a web browser. When the police have investigated such instances, they have found out that the baby monitors can be used to film children when they are asleep using the default user account and password. Most parents are unaware that this is possible.

> **Tip**
> If you do not change the default username and password for household devices, known as IoT, it is possible for a cybercriminal to hack into your home. This includes baby monitors, TVs, ovens, and refrigerators.

Let's now look at the different types of authentication.

Authentication Types

There are various types of authentication and in this section, we are going to look at these, starting with security tokens and devices. Let's first look at biometric controls, followed by identity management using certificates.

Security Tokens and Devices

There are different types of tokens that have different time limits. Let's look at the difference between the Time-Based One-Time Password and the HMAC-Based One-Time Password:

- **Time-Based One-Time Password** (**TOTP**): A TOTP requires time synchronization, because the password needs to be used in a very short period of time, normally between 30 and 60 seconds. In the following diagram, we can see the TOTP that has come to a phone. It can also come to a device similar to the RSA Secure ID token. TOTP could be used when you want to access secure cloud storage or your online bank account:

165323

Use with 30 seconds

Figure 3.1 – TOTP

- **HMAC-Based One-Time Password** (**HOTP**): An HOTP is similar to TOTP in that a one-time password is issued. The main distinguishing factor is that there is no restriction in terms of time, but you can only use this password once.

Next, we will look at certification-based authentication.

Certification-Based Authentication

Certificate-based authentication is very popular as it provides two-factor authentication, which makes it more secure than single-factor authentication, such as a username and password. We will now look at its various types:

- **Smart Card**: As previously mentioned in this book, a smart card looks like a credit card with a chip on it. The certificate is located on the chip itself and does not leave any trace (footprint) on the computer or laptop being used.

- **Common Access Card** (**CAC**): CACs are used by governmental and military personnel as they provide both authentication and identification as it has a picture of the user on it. They are similar to smart cards. On the front side of a CAC is a picture of the user with their service (Army, Navy, or Airforce), and the reverse side shows their blood group and their Geneva Convention Category. To view a CAC card, please go to `https://www.cac.mil/Common-Access-Card/`.

- **Personal Identity Verification** (**PIV**): This is very similar to the CAC, but is used by federal agencies rather than the military.

Let's now look at other types of authentication.

Port-Based Authentication

1EEE 802.1x is a port-based authentication protocol that is used when a device is connected to a switch or when a user authenticates to a wireless access point. Authentication is normally done by certificate.

> **Tip**
> Authentication with a password that has a short lifespan will be a TOTP.

Location-Based Authentication

Location can be added as an additional factor in authentication. Geofencing can be used to establish a region and can pinpoint whether or not you are in that region and if you are not, you will not be able to log in. This helps prevent fraud when someone from a foreign country attempts to log in to your systems and is used by many cloud providers. Let's look at some of these:

- **Context-Aware Location**: This can be used to block any attempt to login outside of the locations that have been determined as allowed regions. Geolocation can track your location by your IP address and the ISP that you are using.

- **Smart Phone Location Services**: This can be used to identify where your phone is located by using the **Global Positioning System (GPS)**, and if you do not want to be discovered, you should disable location services.

- **Impossible Travel Time**: This is a security feature used by cloud providers such as Microsoft with their Office 365 package to prevent fraud. If a person is located in Toronto and then 30 minutes later is deemed to be in Las Vegas, their attempt to log in will be blocked.

- **Risky Login**: This is another security feature used by cloud providers where they have a database of the devices used by each user. An email will be sent to the user when the system cannot identify the device used to log in. Only upon verification will access for the new device be permitted.

Miscellaneous Authentication Technologies

Each day there are different authentication technology methods, and we will look at some of these here:

- **SMS**: This is used as an additional layer of security where the user is authenticated and a SMS message is sent to the user's cell phone. They then insert the code and are authenticated. There is usually a time limit associated with its use.

- **Token Key**: Tokens can vary from a hardware device that received a one-time-password, that would normally last between 30-60 seconds, to the fob or card used to gain access to a building via a card reader.

- **Push Notification**: An email is sent to the user when access to their systems has been received by an unusual device; for example, if I access Dropbox from a friend's laptop.

- **Phone Call**: When someone has accessed a system, they may receive a phone call as an additional layer of security.

- **JavaScript Object Notation Web Token (JWT)**: JWT is an internet standard where the server signs a token with its private key and sends it to a user to prove who they are. It can also be used to digitally sign documents and email. It is used by **Open Authentication (OAuth)**. For example, it may be passed through an HTTP header to prove the identity of a user, sometimes known as a claim.

- **Static Codes**: These codes change after a period of time, like a PIN for a smart card. These are commonly used by broadband engineers.

- **Authentication Applications**: This could be using Kerberos, who completes a **Ticket Granting Ticket** (**TGT**) session that results in a ticket that can be exchanged to give access to applications. We could also use certificate-based authentication or, in the case of the cloud, use conditional access to gain access to applications.

Let's now learn how to implement authentication and authorization solutions in the next section.

Implementing Authentication and Authorization Solutions

In this section, we will look at the different types of authentication and authorization solutions that can be used. As an IT security professional, you will need good knowledge of these solutions. Let's start by looking at authentication management.

Authentication Management

There are different types of authentication management and we will look at each of these in turn:

- **Password Keys**: This looks like a USB device and works in conjunction with your password to provide multifactor authentication. An example of this is YubiKey. YubiKey is a **Federal Information Processing Standards** (**FIPS**) 140-2 validation that provides the highest-level **Authenticator Assurance Level 3** (**AAL3**) used for storing passwords.

- **Password Vaults**: Password vaults are stored locally on the device and store all of your passwords so that you don't need to remember them. The password vault uses AES-256 encryption, so it makes storage secure. A vault is only as secure as the master password that is used to protect the vault itself and normally employs multifactor authentication.

- **Trusted Platform Module** (**TPM**): TPM chips are normally built into the motherboard of a computer and they are used when you are using **Full Disk Encryption** (**FDE**). An example of FDE would be Bitlocker.

- **Hardware Security Module** (**HSM**): An HSM can be a removable device that can be attached to a computer or server via a USB connection. They are also used to store encryption keys, a key escrow who holds the private keys for third parties and stores them in an HSM.

- **Knowledge-Based Authentication** (**KBA**): This is normally used by banks, financial institutions, or email providers to identify someone when they want a password reset. There are two different types of KBA, dynamic and static, and they have their strengths and weaknesses:

  – **Static KBA**: These are questions that are common to the user. For example, "What is the name of your first school?" and these are deemed pretty weak.

  Example: In 2008, the Alaska Governor Sarah Palin's Yahoo account was hacked by entering the answers to "Where did you first meet your spouse?", followed by her date of birth and ZIP code.

  – **Dynamic KBA**: These are deemed to be more secure because they do not consist of questions provided beforehand.

  Example: A bank wants to confirm the identify of a customer and they ask the customer to name three direct debit mandates, the date, and the amount paid.

Authentication Protocols

Extensible Authentication Protocol (**EAP**) is an authentication framework allowing point-to-point connections. These are commonly used with wireless communication. Let's look at the various types of EAP:

- **Protected Extensible Authentication Protocol** (**PEAP**): The PEAP is a version of EAP that encapsulated the EAP data and made it more secure for WLANS.

- **EAP-FAST**. EAP-FAST, also known as **Flexible Authentication via Secure Tunneling**, developed by Cisco, does not use certificates, but protected access credentials instead. It is used in wireless networks.

- **EAP-TLS**: EAP-TLS needs X509 certificates installed on the endpoints for authentication.

- **EAP-TTLS**: EAP-TTLS needs the certificates to be installed on the server. It creates a tunnel for the users' credentials to travel through.

Authentication, Authorization, and Accounting (AAA) Servers

The two main AAA servers are Microsoft's **Remote Authentication Dial-In User Service (RADIUS)** and CISCO's **Terminal Access Controller Access-Control System Plus (TACACS+)**. Both of these servers provide authentication, authorization, and accounting. Let's look at each of these in turn:

- **RADIUS Server**: The RADIUS server is UDP-based, and it authenticates servers such as **Virtual Private Network (VPN)** servers, **Remote Access Services (RAS)** servers, and the 802.1x authenticating switch. Each of these are known as RADIUS clients, even though they are servers themselves. If I had a small company, I could outsource my remote access server and put in a RADIUS server that would check any remote-access policies and verify that authentication was allowed by contacting a domain controller.

- **RADIUS Clients**: RADIUS clients are VPN servers, RAS servers, and the 802.1x authentication switch. Every RADIUS client needs the secret key that is sometimes known as the session key or shared secret to join the RADIUS environment. RADIUS authentication communicates over the UDP port 1812. RADIUS accounting uses UDP Port 1813.

- **Diameter**: Diameter is the more modern version of RADIUS that works on TCP. For the exam, remember that Diameter is the AAA server that uses the EAP.

- **TACACS+**: This is the CISCO AAA server that used TCP, and uses TCP port 49 for authentication.

Remote Access Authentication

A **Virtual Private Network (VPN)** allows someone working remotely, either from a hotel room or home, to connect securely through the internet to the corporate network:

Figure 3.2 – VPN

Let's now look at remote access services:

- **Remote Access Services (RAS)**: RAS is a legacy protocol that pre-dated the VPN. The RAS client used modems and a dial-up network using telephone lines. It was very restricted in speed.

- **Authentication for VPN/RAS**: There are numerous methods of authentication used by VPN or RAS. We will look at these here:

  a. **Password Authentication Protocol (PAP)**: PAP should be avoided at all costs as the passwords are transmitted as clear text and can be easily captured.

  b. **Challenge Handshake Authentication Protocol (CHAP)**: CHAP was used to connect to an RAS server with a four-stage process:

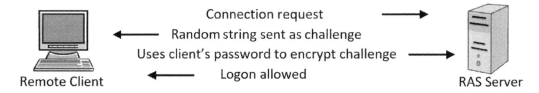

Figure 3.3 – Challenge Handshake Authentication Protocol

Let's understand this using the following four steps:

1. The client makes a connection request to the remote access server.

2. The RAS server replies with a challenge that is a random string.

3. The client uses their password as an encryption key to encrypt the challenge.

4. The RAS server encrypts the original challenge with the password stored for the user. If both values match, then the client is logged on.

- **MS CHAP/MSCHAP version 2**: MS CHAP/MSCHAP version 2 are Microsoft's versions of MS CHAP. MS CHAP has been superseded by MS CHAP v2 and can be used by both VPN and RAS.

Let's now look at access control schemes.

Access Control Schemes

The three main parts of access controls are identifying an individual, authenticating them when they insert a password or PIN, and then authorization, where an individual has different forms of access to different data:

- **Identification**: This is similar to everyone who has their own bank account. The account is identified by the account details on the bank card. Identification in a security environment may involve having a user account, a smart card, or maybe a fingerprint reader—this is unique to that individual.

- **Authentication**: Once the individual inserts their method of identification, they are then authenticated, for example, by inserting a password or a PIN.

- **Authorization**: This is the level of access you have to selective data. You are normally a member of certain groups; for example, a sales manager could access data from the sales group and then access data from the managers group. You will only be given the minimum amount of access required to perform your job. This is known as least privilege.

  Example: Someone working in finance will need a higher level of security clearance and will have to access different data than a person who dispatches an order in finished goods.

Let's now look at privilege access management.

Privilege Access Management

Privilege Access Management (**PAM**) is a solution that helps protect the privilege accounts within a domain, preventing attacks such as pass the hash, pass the ticket, and privilege escalation. It also gives visibility in terms of who is using privilege accounts and what tasks they are being used for. The setup for PAM is as follows:

Figure 3.4 – PAM diagram

The preceding ABC domain will hold the non-privilege account, and the bastion forest will hold the admin accounts. A bastion forest is a remote forest that has a very high level of security. The bastion forest works on a **Just Enough Administration** (**JEA**) approach by giving the administrator enough privileges to carry out a certain task.

Microsoft produced a JEA toolkit using Windows PowerShell so that each type of admin has a certain number of privileges for the tasks that they are allowed to carry out.

The company will use an identity management solution such as Microsoft Identify Management that holds the different policies for each type of privilege account.

Example: Fred is the SQL database administrator who wants to complete an update to the SQL database. In the following diagram, you can see that he first of all logs in to **Identity Manager** (**IM**) using **Multi-Factor Authentication** (**MFA**). IM looks at the policies that it holds relating to Fred's account and contacts the bastion domain that produced an admin Kerberos ticket that is then used to give Fred admin access to the SQL database to perform admin tasks:

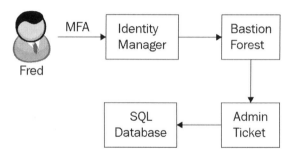

Figure 3.5 – Obtaining admin privileges

Admin privileges cannot be obtained for day-to-day tasks such as accessing the internet or sending emails.

Mandatory Access Control

Mandatory Access Control (**MAC**) is based on the classification level of the data.

MAC looks at how much damage they could cause to the interest of the nation. These are as follows:

- **Top Secret**: Highest level, exceptionally grave damage
- **Secret**: Causes serious damage
- **Confidential**: Causes damage
- **Restricted**: Undesirable effects

Examples of **Mandatory Access Control (MAC)** are as follows:

Data types	Classification
Nuclear energy project	Top Secret
Research and development	Secret
Ongoing legal issues	Confidential
Government payroll	Restricted

There are different roles associated with classifying, storing, and giving access to data, and these are as follows:

- **Owner**: This is the person who writes the data and determines the classification. For example, if they are writing a secret document, they will pitch it at that level, no higher.
- **Steward**: The steward is the person who is responsible for labeling the documents.
- **Custodian**: The custodian is the person who stores and manages classified data.
- **Security Administrator**: The security administrator is the person who gives access to classified data once clearance has been approved.

Discretionary Access Control

Discretionary access control involves **New Technology File System (NTFS)** file permissions, which are used in Microsoft operating systems. The user is only given the access that is required to perform their job. These could be classified as user-based or user-centric.

These permissions are shown in the following screenshot:

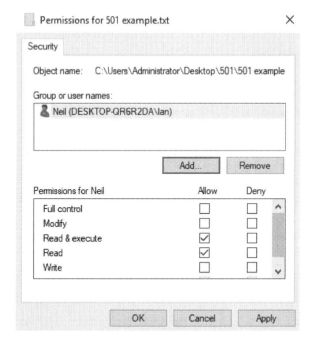

Figure 3.6 – DAC permissions

The permissions are as follows:

- **Full Control**: Full access.

- **Modify**: Change data, read, and read and execute.

- **Read and Execute**: Read the file and run a program if one is inside it.

- **List Folder Contents**: Expand a folder to see the subfolders inside it.

- **Read**: Read the contents.

- **Write**: Allows you to write to the file.

- **Special Permissions**: Allows granular access; for example, it breaks each of the previous permissions down to a more granular level.

- **Data Creator/Owner**: The person that creates the unclassified data is called the owner and they are responsible for checking who has access to that data.

Least Privilege

Least privilege is where you give someone only the most limited access required so that they can perform their job role; this is known as a "need to know" basis. The company will write a least privilege policy so that the administrators know how to manage it.

Linux Permissions (not SELinux)

Linux permissions come in a numerical format; the first number represents the owner, the second number represents the group, and the third number represents all other users:

- Permissions:

    a. **Owner**: First number

    b. **Group**: Second number

    c. **All Other Users**: Third number

- Numerical values:

    a. 4: Read (r)

    b. 2: Write (w)

    c. 1: Execute (x)

Unlike a Windows permission that will execute an application, the execute function in Linux allows you to view or search.

A permission of 6 would be read and write, a value of 2 would be write, and a value of 7 would be read, write, and execute. Some examples are as follows:

- **Example 1**: If I have 764 access to File A, this could be broken down as follows:

    a. **Owner**: Read, write, and execute

    b. **Group**: Read, write

    c. **All Other Users**: Read

- **Example 2**: Determine which of the following permissions to File B is the highest and which is the lowest:

    a. 776 File B, also shown as rwx rwx -rw

    b. 677 File B

    c. 777 File B

The highest would therefore be the third example.

Another way in which this can be shown in the exam is by using three sets of three dashes.

For example:

- Owner full control would be shown as `rwx --- ---`.
- Group full control `--- rwx ---`.
- User full control `--- --- rwx`.

You can also change permissions in Linux. If the permission to `File C` is 654 and we wish to change these permissions to give full control, we will run the `chmod 777 File C` command, which changes the permissions to `File C`.

Role-Based Access Control

This is a subset of duties within a department. An example would be two people within the finance department who only handle the petty cash. In IT terms, it could be that only two of the IT team administer the email server.

Rule-Based Access Control

In **Rule-Based Access Control** (**RBAC**), a rule is applied to all of the people within a department, for example, contractors will only have access between 8 a.m. and 5 p.m., and the help desk people will only be able to access Building 1, where their place of work is. It can be time-based or have some sort of restriction, but it applies to the whole department.

Attribute-Based Access Control

In **Attribute-Based Access Control** (**ABAC**), access is restricted based on an attribute in the account. John could be an executive and some data could be restricted to only those with the executive attribute. This is a user attribute from the directory services, such as a department or a location. You may wish to give different levels of control to different departments.

Group-Based Access

To control access to data, people may be put into groups to simplify access. An example would be if there were two people who worked in **Information Technology** (**IT**) who needed access to older IT data. These people are called Bill and Ben:

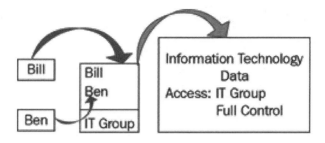

Figure 3.7 – Group-based access

Everyone in the sales team may have full control of the sales data by using group-based access, but you may need two new starters to have only read access. In this case, you would create a group called new starters and give those people inside that group only read permission to the data.

Summarizing Authentication and Authorization Design Concepts

We are going to look at authentication and authorization design concepts that are used by corporate environments. We are going to look at directory services, federation services, biometrics, and multifactor authentication. Let's look at each of these in turn.

Directory Services

Identity management in a corporate environment will use a directory database. This is a centralized database that will authenticate all domain users. We are going to look at Microsoft's Active Directory, where a protocol called the **Lightweight Directory Access Protocol** (**LDAP**) manages the users in groups. Let's look at how it works.

LDAP

Most companies have identity and access services through a directory that stores objects such as users and computers as X500 objects. These were developed by the **International Telecommunication Union** (**ITU**). These objects form what is called a distinguished name and are organized and stored by the LDAP.

There are only three values in X500 objects; these are DC (domain), **Organization Unit** (**OU**), and CN (anything else).

In this example, we have a domain called *Domain A* and an OU called *Sales*; this is where all of the sales department users and computers reside. We can see inside the Sales OU a computer called **Computer 1**:

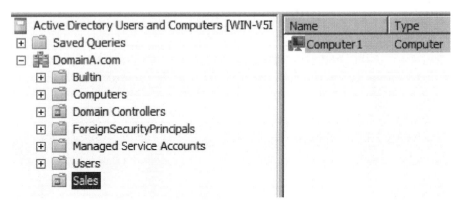

Figure 3.8 – Active Directory

When creating the X500 object, we start off with the object itself, **Computer 1**, and then continue up through the structure. As **Computer 1** is neither an OU nor a domain, we give it a value of CN. Then we move up the structure to **Sales**. As it is an OU, we give it that value. **Computer 1** is a CN, **Sales** is an OU, and the domain is divided into two portions, each having the value of DC. The distinguished name is here: **CN=Computer1, OU=Sales, DC=DomainA, DC=com**.

The way it is stored in the Active Directory can be viewed using a tool called **ADSI Edit**:

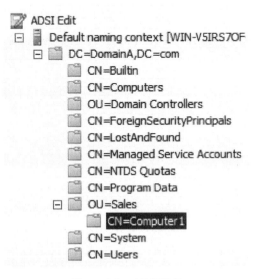

Figure 3.9 – ADSI Edit

LDAP is the active directory storeman responsible for storing the X500 objects. When the Active Directory is searched, then LDAP provides the information required. LDAPS is the secure version of LDAP.

Here are some examples.

- **Example 1**: If I want to know how many people are in the IT OU, I can search the Active Directory. LDAP provides the search and returns a reply saying that the IT department has 10 members.

- **Example 2**: I am searching the Active Directory for a user called Fred. Once again, LDAP finds the user. If you have 10,000 people in your domain, you will have them in different OUs to make it easier to find and manage them. However, if you need to find someone, this will still be difficult. That is why we need LDAP to perform the search. It saves time.

Kerberos

Kerberos is the Microsoft authentication protocol that was introduced with the release of Windows Server 2000. It is the only authentication protocol that uses tickets, **Updated Sequence Numbers** (**USN**), and is time stamped. The process of obtaining your service ticket is called a **Ticket Granting Ticket** (**TGT**) session. It is important that the times on all servers and computers are within 5 minutes of each other; time can be synchronized by using a time source such as the Atomic Time clock.

If Kerberos authentication fails, this is normally down to the user's computer or device time clock being out of sync with the domain controller by 5 minutes or more. A **Network Time Protocol** (**NTP**) server can be placed on your LAN to keep the domain computers and servers in sync with each other.

A TGT session is where a user sends their credentials (username and password, or it could be a smart card and PIN) to a domain controller that starts the authentication process and, when it has been confirmed, will send back a **Service Ticket** that has a 10-hour lifespan. This service ticket is encrypted and cannot be altered:

Figure 3.10 – TGT session

Single Sign-On/Mutual Authentication: Kerberos provides single sign-on as the user needs to log in only once. It then uses their **Service Ticket** to prove who they are. This is exchanged for a **Session Ticket**, with the server that they want to access resources on. In the example here, the user will use their service ticket for mutual authentication with an email server:

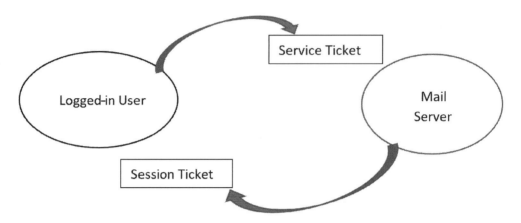

Figure 3.11 – Mutual authentication

The preceding diagram shows the logged-in user exchanging their encrypted **Service Ticket** with the mail server, which, in return, provides mutual authentication by returning a **Session Ticket**. The logged-in user checks that the session ticket's timestamp is within 5 minutes of that of the domain controller. This means that Kerberos can complete mutual authentication.

> **Important note**
>
> You need to remember that Kerberos is the only authentication protocol that uses tickets. It will also prevent replay attacks as it uses USN numbers and timestamps. It can also prevent pass-the-hash attacks.

NT Lan Manager (NTLM): NTLM is a legacy authentication protocol that stores passwords using the MD4 hash that is very easy to crack. It was susceptible to the pass-the-hash attack. It was last used in a production environment in the 1990s. Kerberos prevents pass-the-hash attacks as it uses an encrypted database.

Transitive Trust

Transitive trust is where you have a parent domain and maybe one or more child domains; these are called **trees**. Refer to the following diagram:

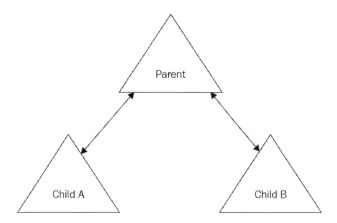

Figure 3.12 – Transitive trust

Between the **Parent** domain and each child domain is two-way transitive trust, where resources can be shared two ways. Because the **Parent** domain trusts both child domains A and B, it can be said that **Child A** transitively trusts **Child B** as long as the administrator in **Child B** wishes to give someone from **Child A** access to resources and vice versa. Think of a domain as being people from the same company.

> **Tip**
> When the exam mentions a third party in relation to third-party authentication, this can only mean federation services. Federation services require cookies to be enabled.

Federation Services

Federation services are used when two different companies want to authenticate between each other when they participate in a joint venture. Think of two car manufacturers wanting to produce the best car engine in the world. Both companies have experts on engines, but they want to work together to produce a super engine. The companies don't want to merge with one another; they want to retain their own identify and have their own management in place. These are known, to each other, as third parties.

Each of these companies will have their own directory database, for example, an active directory, that will only have users from their domain. Therefore, normal domain authentication will not work. Let's now look at the two different domains and their directory databases:

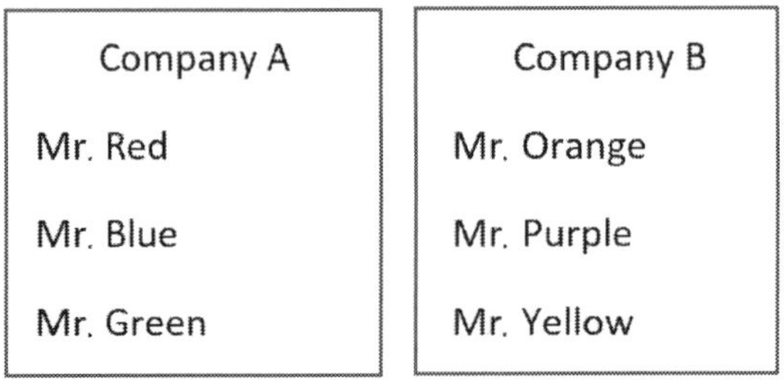

Company A	Company B
Mr. Red	Mr. Orange
Mr. Blue	Mr. Purple
Mr. Green	Mr. Yellow

Figure 3.13 – Directory databases

Company A has three users in its directory services – Mr. Red, Mr. Blue, and Mr. Green. Company B also has three users – Mr. Orange, Mr. Purple, and Mr. Yellow. This means that they can only change passwords for the people in their own domain.

If Mr. Orange was to try and access the Company A domain, he would need an account. Since he does not have an account, the security administrator from Company A has no way of providing authentication. He then needs to make an agreement with Company B to set up a federation trust where the people from the other domain would need to use alternative credentials instead of a username and password or a smart card and PIN. They use extended attributes.

User-Extended Attributes are extended attributes used by their directory services. They are, in addition to the basic attributes, comprising the following.

- Employee ID
- Email address

They both have decided that the extended attributes that they will use will be the user's email address. Because an email address is easy to find or guess, they will also need to use their domain password. This is known as a claim. When the exam talks about authentication using the phrase *third party* or extended attributes, think of federation services.

The two companies need to exchange the extended attribute information and require a special protocol to do that, so they use **Security Assertion Mark-up Language (SAML)** as it is XML-based authentication, which is used to pass the credentials between Company A and Company B. The companies are said to be peers of each other:

Figure 3.14 – SAML

Federation Services – Authentication: In this scenario, Mr. Yellow is going to authenticate himself with Company A so that he can access limited resources. He contacts **Company A** through a web browser, and it asks him for his Employee ID and password:

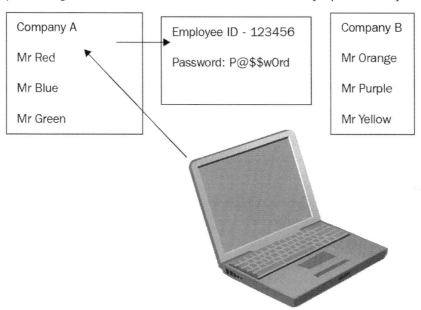

Figure 3.15 – Federation Services

Federation Services – Exchange of Extended Attributes: **Company A** now uses SAML to pass the authentication details of Mr. Yellow to Company B. Mr. Yellow's domain controller confirms that they are correct:

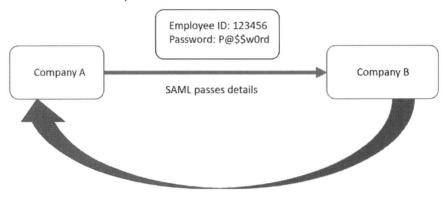

Figure 3.16 – Extended attributes sent to Company A using SAML

Once **Company B** confirms that Mr. Yellow's extended attributes are valid, the **Company A** domain controller sends a certificate to Mr. Yellow's laptop. This certificate is used next time for authentication. They could alternatively use cookies.

> **Tip**
> When the exam mentions authentication using extended attributes, this can only mean federation services. Cookies used for authentication would also be federation services.

Shibboleth

Shibboleth is an open source federation service product that uses SAML authentication. It would be used in a small federation service environment. Shibboleth can use cookies.

Single Sign-On (SSO)

SSO is used in a domain environment. This is where someone logs in to the domain and then can access several resources, such as the file or email server, without needing to input their credentials again. Think of it as an all-inclusive holiday, where you book into your hotel and the receptionist gives you a wristband that you produce when you want to consume food and drink. Federation services and Kerberos (Microsoft authentication protocol) are both good examples of SSO. You log in once and access all of your resources without needing to insert your credentials again.

Internet-Based Open Source Authentication

More and more people are accessing web-based applications and need an account to log in. However, applications hosting companies do not want to be responsible for the creation and management of the account accessing the application. They use OAuth to help them facilitate this:

- **OAuth 2.0**: OAuth 2.0 provides authorization to enable third-party applications to obtain limited access to a web service.

- **Open ID Connect**: Open ID Connect uses OAuth to allow users to log in to a web application without needing to manage the user's account. It allows users to authenticate by using their Google, Facebook, or Twitter account. For example, the Airbnb website that finds users accommodation allows you to sign up using your Google or Facebook account.

Biometrics

Biometrics is a method of authentication using an individual's characteristics, for example, using a fingerprint, as everyone's fingerprints are very different. In 1892, Inspector Eduardo Alvarez from Argentina made the first fingerprint identification in the case against Francisca Rojas, who murdered her two sons and cut her own throat in an attempt to place the blame on someone else, but the inspector proved that she was guilty.

We will now look at the types of biometrics:

- **Fingerprint Scanner**: Fingerprint scanners are now very common; for example, if you are going to the USA on holiday, when you go through customs, you are required to place all of your fingerprints in the scanner. Another use of a fingerprint scanner is when you are setting up your iPhone; you can set it up so that you press the home button to log in instead of using a password. Refer to the following screenshot:

Figure 3.17 – iPhone fingerprint scanner

> **Tip**
> Retina and iris scanners both look at an individual's eye and the scanners themselves are physical devices.

- **Retina Scanner**: With appropriate lighting our retina can be easily identified as the blood vessels of the retina absorb light more readily than the surrounding tissue.

- **Iris Scanner**: Most countries have issued biometric passports where the person inserts their passport into the reader and a camera about 1.5 meters away confirms the identity of the user by scanning their iris.

- **Voice Recognition**: The voice patterns can be stored in a database and used for authentication.

- **Facial Recognition**: Facial recognition looks at the shape of the face and characteristics such as mouth, jaw, cheekbone, and nose. Light can be a factor when you use this software. There are much better versions of facial recognition, such as those that use infrared. You need to ensure that you are looking straight at the camera each time.

- **Vein**: Using blood vessels in the palm can be used as a biometric factor of authentication.

- **Gait Analysis**: Authentication can be used with low resolution video as your gait is the way that you walk.

Microsoft has released a facial recognition program called **Windows Hello**, which was released with Windows 10; this uses a special USB infrared camera. It being infrared is much better than other facial recognition programs that can have problems with light. Biometric errors are as follows:

- **False Acceptance Rate (FAR)**: FAR is what it says on the label. It accepts unauthorized users and allows them to gain access. This is known as a Type II error. Unauthorized users are **allowed**; look for the middle letter as an A.

- **False Rejection Rate (FRR)**: FRR is where legitimate users who should gain access are rejected and cannot get in. This is known as a Type I error. Authorized users are **rejected**; look for the middle letter as an R.

> **Exam Tip**
> When looking at FAR or FRR, remember to look at the middle letter. Authorized users are rejected, the middle letter in FRR is *R* for *reject*. Unauthorized users are allowed so we look for the middle letter being *A* therefore we get FAR. Remember *Authorized* that starts with *A* does not belong to FAR that has an *A* as the middle letter. A does not select A.

- **Crossover Error Rate (CER)**: This is where the FAR and FRR are equal. If you are going to purchase a biometric system, you need a system that has a low CER:

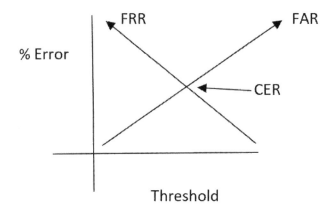

Figure 3.18 – Crossover error rate

- **Efficacy Rates**: When purchasing a biometric system, you would want one with a low efficacy rate. This can be measured by looking at the CER point. If it is lower down the graph, then there are fewer errors, but if it is at the top of the graph, this indicates multiple errors and could prove more difficult to support. If this was the case, you would change your biometric system. You will need a device with a low efficacy rate and a CER of less than 5%.

Authentication Factors

There are different authentication factors that range from something you know, for example, a password, to something you are using, for example, an iris scanner. The following are the different authentication factors:

- **Multi-Factor Authentication**: These factors are grouped into different types and the number of factors is the number of different groups being used. For example, if you have a smart card, this is something you have and the card's PIN is something you know; this means it is a dual factor, but the smart card and PIN is also known as multi-factor. So, multi-factor could also be more than two different factors; it just means multiple factors.

- **Something You Know**: This would be a username, password, PIN, or your date of birth; these are all something that you know. The one-time code that is delivered by an OTP/TOTP/HOTP device is also something that you know.

- **Something You Have**: This could be, for example, a secure token, key fob, or card. The hardware token is tamper-proof and sends a different PIN every 60 seconds. The key fob is similar to some cards that are placed close to a proximity card. Once you hear a beep, then the door opens. A smart card that could be used with a PIN could also be something you have. The OTP/TOTP/HOTP device that brings your single code is also seen as something you have:

Figure 3.19 – Hardware token and key fob used with a proximity card

- **Something You Are**: This is called biometric authentication. It is the trait of an individual that is used for authentication; for example, using an iris or retina, palm, fingerprint reader, or your voice.

- **Something You Do**: This would be swiping a card, inserting your signature, or maybe the way you walk (this is called your gait). It could also be the dwell time; for example, the speed that you type and how far in you press the keys.

- **Somewhere You Are**: This would be a location that you are in. Are you in London or Disneyland, Florida? This is a location-based policy.

Number of Factors – Examples

Let's look at combining different factors to determine a single factor, dual factor, or multifactor. Here are different factor examples:

- **Single Factor**: If I have a username, password, and PIN, then it is only single factor as they come from the same group.

- **Two Factor**: If you have a smart card and a PIN, this is two factors, also known as dual factor.

- **Multifactor**: This is where more than one factor can be used; for example, if you have a smart card, the card is something you have, inserting into the reader is something you do, and then the PIN is something you know.

> **Tip**
> The number of factors is determined by the different numbers of factor groups being mentioned.

Cloud Versus On-Premises Authentication

We will now look at the main differences between being authenticated in the cloud or on-premises.

On-Premises

The perimeter of on-premises is very easy to establish and much easier to control as we can use proximity cards, while guards on reception can also control access to the company. You are responsible for the security of your building and for securing access to your computer systems that can be deemed trusted systems. They will never go offline. We can apply multi-factor authentication by using smart card authentication.

In the Cloud

There may be a problem if you have no internet access as you will not be able to connect to the cloud. With the adoption of cloud computing, the security perimeter is no longer confined to the on-premises environment, but now extends outside of those parameters. Authentication within a cloud environment should adopt a zero-trust model, where every connection is deemed to be a hacker as we cannot see who is logging in. We could therefore use conditional access to prove who is the person logging in, using a series of *if-then* statements. These policies are enforced following a successful login. The three areas of conditional access are Signal, Decision, and Enforcement. Refer to the following diagram:

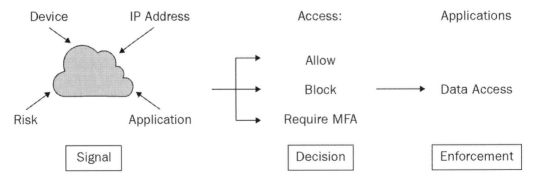

Figure 3.20 – Conditional access policy

- **Signal**: This could be a user or group, location, device, calculated risk, and the application that needs to be accessed.

- **Decision**: This could range from allow to block, or require **multifactor authentication (MFA)**

- **Enforcement**: Access to the application that has been approved.

Another security feature used by the cloud is risky logins. **Cloud Service Providers (CSPs)** have a central database of the devices that a person uses to log in. If the system deems that the device cannot be approved, it will notify the user of the risky login. If it is not approved, then user access will be blocked.

- **Example 1**: If a member of the finance team wants to access the payroll system, they may need to use MFA or access will be blocked.

- **Example 2**: If a member of finance has upgraded their computer, then a risky login would be notified to him by email. Before being allowed access to the payroll system, they would need to confirm that it was them using this new computer.

Let's now look at some common account management policies.

Common Account Management Policies

To ensure smooth account management, it is vital that company-wide policies are in place and that everyone within the company adheres to them otherwise chaos could ensue. Let's look at each of these policies in turn.

Account Creation

Multinational corporations will generate hundreds of accounts annually and need to have a standardized format. This is known as a standard naming convention. Account templates are copied and modified with the details of new employees. Some examples of standard naming conventions are as follows:

- First name, last name: *John.Smith*

- Last name, first name: *Smith.John*

- First initial, last name: *J.Smith*

If you have *John Smith* and *Jack Smith*, you would have two *J Smiths*. Therefore, you may also use a middle initial, *J A Smith*, or a number at the end, *J Smith1*, to make them unique.

All user accounts need to be unique so that each person is responsible for their own account. If you leave your computer logged on to the network while you go for a coffee and someone deletes data using your account, then you are held responsible. A good practice would be to lock your screen while you are not at your desk to prevent this.

Without a standard naming convention, accounts would be created differently and cause chaos when you tried to find users in your directory service.

Employees Moving Departments

When employees move between departments, IT teams normally modify their account for the next department they move to; they don't generally get a new account. In the Security+ exam, when people move department, they are given new accounts and the old account remains active until it has been disabled.

Disabling an Account

There are a few times when the IT team will disable accounts as a good practice; let's look at the reasons for this:

- **Employee Leaving**: A good practice when someone leaves the company is that human resources provide the employee with an exit interview to find out the reasons that they are leaving. The final step is that the IT team should disable their accounts and reset their passwords. These steps keep their email and certificate settings so that encrypted data can still be accessed and they can no longer access the network. If you delete the account, then you lose all of this.

- **Extended Absence Period**: When an employee is away from a company for a month or more, then it may be prudent to disable the account so that it cannot be accessed. It could well be that the employee is on maternity/paternity leave, seconded to another company, on a long course, or taking a gap year to fulfill one of their dreams. This then means that, while they are away, the account cannot be hacked and can be reactivated once they return.

- **Guest Account**: Guest accounts are designed for temporary users but are seldom used; they are disabled to prevent them being hacked.

> Tip
> When an employee leaves a company, the first stage is that the account is disabled and not deleted. You will also reset the password so that the old account holder cannot use the account.

Account Recertification

Account recertification is a process where an auditor will review all of the user accounts. The auditor will have a matrix showing all of the active accounts and what privileges and access that they should have. If the auditor finds anything wrong, then they will report it to management, who will then either write a new account policy or make changes to the management of accounts using change management. For the purpose of the exam, the auditor should be looked at as a snitch; they will never take any action, but they will report their findings to management.

Account Maintenance

Account maintenance is ensuring that accounts are created in accordance with the standard naming convention, disabled when the employee initially leaves, and then deleted maybe 30 days later.

Account Monitoring

If you wish to find out when a user account has been granted a new set of privileges, then this can only be done via active monitoring of the accounts. This could be automated by using a **Security Information and Event Management** (**SIEM**) system that will create and alert you regarding changes to the system. You will not be alerted by a user account review as there could be 6-12 months between the review—you may need to know immediately.

> Tip
>
> If you want to know immediately when there is a change to a user account, such as it being given higher privileges, then you need active account monitoring or you need to set up a SIEM system.

Security Information and Event Management

Security Information and Event Management (**SIEM**). A SIEM system is used for real-time monitoring and can be used to aggregate, decipher, and normalize non-standard log formats; it can also filter out false positives. The only time that a SIEM system will not provide the correct information is when the wrong filters are used or where we scan the wrong host:

- **Account Management**: In a multinational corporation that may have in excess of 50,000 users, it is very important that account management policies are in place so that the directory service is kept up to date. Let's look at different account management tools and policies. A directory service query can be run against the system to discover accounts that have not been used for a certain period of time.

- **Account Expiry**: When companies employ temporary employees such as sub-contractors during the account creation phase, an expiry date will be enabled. This is to prevent someone from trying to gain access to the company network once their contract has expired. Once the account hits the expiry date, the account is automatically disabled:

Figure 3.21 – Account expiry

> **Tip**
>
> If a person moves to a new department, they get a new account. If their old account is still being used, then we should get an auditor who will perform a user account review.

- **Time and Day Restriction**: Time and day restriction is set up for each individual user as a company may have many different shift patterns and may not wish their employees to access their network outside of their working hours. This prevents users coming in at 3 a.m. when nobody else is on the company's premises and stealing data:

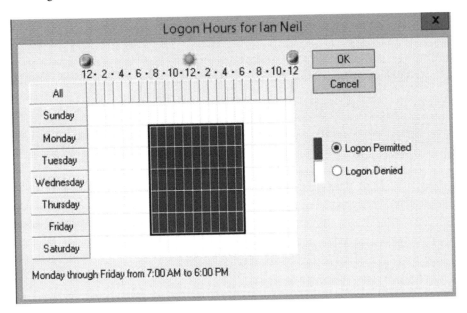

Figure 3.22 – Time and day restrictions

Example: A toy factory may employ university students to work prior to the busy Christmas period with three different shift patterns; 6 a.m. - 2 p.m., 2 - 10 p.m., and 10 p.m. - 6 a.m. Each employee will have a time and day restriction in place so that they can log in only for their individual shift times.

- **Account Lockout**: To prevent dictionary and brute-force attacks, account lockout is enforced so that maybe three or five attempts to enter the password are allowed. Once exceeded, the account is disabled. This prevents hackers guessing an account password.

> **Tip**
> If a time restriction is to be placed on a group of contractors, RBAC will be used. Time and day restrictions can only be used for individuals.

Group-Based Access Control

When a company has a large number of users, it is difficult to give each user access to the resources that they need in order to perform their job. Groups are created and they will contain all users in that department. For example, the sales group will then contain all of the people working in sales and the group will be used to allow access to resources such as a printer or file structure. If you decide to use group-based access control and you have new employees or interns, you may create another group for them with lower permissions.

For example, in a large corporation, there are 25 employees who work in marketing and require full access to the marketing file share. Next week, they will have three new interns start with the company, but they need only read access to the same share. We therefore do the following:

- A global group called marketing is created; all 25 employees are added to the group. The group is given full control access to the data.

- A global group called marketing interns is created; the three interns are added to the group. The group is given read access to the data.

> **Tip**
> If group-based access is used in the exam question, then the solution will be a group-based access solution.

Account Audits

An auditor will carry out a user account review periodically to ensure that old accounts are not being used after an employee either moves department or leaves the company. The auditor will also ensure that all employees have the correct number of permissions and privileges to carry out their jobs and that they don't have a higher level than required. Least privilege is giving the individual only the access that they require in order to perform their job.

Passwords

Passwords are one of the most common ways of authenticating a user; they are also the authentication factor that is most likely to be inserted incorrectly, maybe because they use uppercase and lowercase characters, numbers, and special characters not seen in programming. Some people may have the *Caps Lock* key reversed without knowing it.

When a password is inserted, it is shown as a row of dots, and therefore users cannot see their input. However, in the password box in Windows 10, you can press the eye icon to see the password that you have inserted. This reduces the risk of people being locked out.

Default/Administrator Password

An administrator should have two accounts, one for day-to-day work and the other for administrative tasks. If your company is using a device such as a wireless router, the default administrative username and password should be changed as they are normally posted on the internet and could be used for hacking your device/network.

Passwords – Group Policy

A group policy allows security administrators to create settings once and then push them out to all machines in their domain. This could cover maybe 5-10,000 machines. It reduces configuration errors and reduces the labor required to carry out the task. One portion of a group policy deals with passwords; please refer to the following screenshot:

Policy	Security Setting
Enforce password history	24 passwords remember
Maximum password age	42 days
Minimum password age	0 days
Minimum password length	0 characters
Password must meet complexity requirements	Disabled
Store passwords using reversible encryption	Disabled

Figure 3.23 – Password policies

Let's look at each of these, going from top to bottom:

- **Enforce Password History**: This prevents someone from just reusing the same password. The maximum number that can be remembered is 24 passwords, as set in the screenshot. This would then mean that, when I set my first password, it would then need another 24 passwords before I could use it again.

- **Password Reuse**: Password reuse is a term used in the exam that means the same as password history. They both prevent someone from reusing the same password. Password history would be used for a Windows operating system and password reuse for any other products. An example of this could be a smartphone or an email application.

- **Maximum Password Age**: This is the maximum number of days that a password can be used for before you are required to change it. The default is 42 days but, in a more secure environment, it could be lowered to maybe 21 days; this is really the maximum time that the password can be used. If it is set at 21 days, you could reset at any time before 21 days pass.

- **Minimum Password Age**: The minimum password age is to prevent someone from changing a password 25 times on the same day to enable them to come back to the original password. If you set the minimum password age to 2 days, then you could only change your password every 2 days.

- **Complex Passwords**: Complex passwords (sometimes known as strong passwords) are formatted by choosing three of the following four groups:

  a. **Lowercase**: For example, a, b, and c

  b. **Uppercase**: For example, A, B, and C

  c. **Numbers**: For example, 1, 2, and 3

  d. **Special Characters Not Used in Programming**: For example, $ and @

  If I choose the password P@$$w0rd, then it contains characters from all four groups, but it would be cracked very quickly as most password crackers replace the letter *o* with a zero and replace an *a* with the @ sign.

- **Store Passwords Using Reversible Encryption**: This is when a user needs to use their credentials to access a legacy (old) application; because it is storing them in reversible encryption, they could be stored in clear text—this is not good. Companies tend to have this option disabled at all times as it poses a security risk.

- **Account Lockout – Threshold**: This determines the number of times that a user can try a password before the system locks you out; companies normally set this value to three or five attempts.

> **Tip**
> When purchasing devices, you should always change the default password that the manufacturer has set up to prevent someone hacking your device.

Once you are locked out, your account is disabled:

Policy	Security Setting
Account lockout duration	30 minutes
Account lockout threshold	3 invalid logon attempts
Reset account lockout counter after	30 minutes

Figure 3.24 – Account lockout

> **Tip**
> Know the password options and types of password attacks thoroughly.

- **Account Lockout – Duration**: Both **Account Lockout Duration** and **Reset Account Lockout Counter After** should not be enabled. If these are disabled, the person locked out will have to contact the security administrator to have their password reset. This way, the administrator knows who keeps forgetting their password and will keep monitoring them.

Password Recovery

People can be locked out from time to time by forgetting their password. They can reset their passwords by going to a portal and selecting **Forgotten my password**, and then filling in personal details and having the password reset option send a code to their phone via SMS or by email.

Some desktop operating systems allow you to create a password reset disk so that you can save to an SD card or a USB drive; this is not normally used in a corporate environment.

Credential Management

The details of usernames and passwords that someone uses to access a network or an application are called credentials. Users will sometimes have more than one set of credentials to access their local network, and their Facebook, Hotmail, or Twitter account. It would be a serious security risk to use the same account and password for any two of these. Windows 10 has a Credential Manager that can store credentials in two categories – generic credentials and Windows 10. When you log in to an account and you check the **Remember Password** box, these details could be stored inside credential management to consolidate them. This can be for generic accounts used to access web portals or Windows 10 credentials:

Figure 3.25 – Credential Manager

Let's check out a practical exercise in the next section.

Practical Exercise – Password Policy

In this practical exercise, you need to prevent users from resetting their account by using the same password. The company should not allow users to change their password more than once every three days and these passwords need to be complex. A user must use a minimum of 12 passwords before they can reuse the original password. You need to prevent a hacker using more than five attempts at guessing a password:

1. On a Windows 10 desktop, type `gpedit.msc` or, on a domain controller, go to **Server Manager | Tools | Group Policy management**. Edit the **Default Domain Policy** field.

2. Under **Computer Configurations**, expand **Windows Settings**.

3. Select **Security Settings**.

4. Select **Account Policy**, and then select **Password Policy**.

5. Select **Password History** and enter `12` passwords remembered. Press **OK**.

6. Select **Minimum Password Age**. Enter `3` days, and then press **OK**.

7. Select **Password must meet complexity requirements**. Select the radio button, click **Enabled**, and then press **OK**.

8. Go back to **Account Policies** and select **Account Lockout Policies**.

9. Select **Account Lockout Threshold** and change the value to `5` invalid login attempts. Press **OK**.

Review Questions

Now it's time to check your knowledge. Answer these questions and check your answers, found in the *Assessment* section at the end of the book:

1. What is the most common form of authentication that is most likely to be entered incorrectly?

2. When I purchase a new wireless access point, what should I do first?

3. What is password history?

4. How can I prevent someone from reusing the same password?

5. Explain what format a complex password takes.

6. How can I prevent a hacker from inserting a password multiple times?

7. What type of factor authentication is a smart card?

8. How many factors is it if I have a password, PIN, and date of birth?

9. What is biometric authentication?

10. What authentication method can be used by two third parties that participate in a joint venture?

11. What is an XML-based authentication protocol?

12. What is Shibboleth?

13. What protocol is used to store and search for Active Directory objects?

14. What is the format of a distinguished name for a user called Fred who works in the IT department for a company with a domain called Company A that is a dotcom?

15. What authentication factor uses tickets, timestamps, and updated sequence numbers and is used to prevent replay attacks?

16. What is a **Ticket Granting Ticket (TGT)** session?

17. What is single sign-on? Give two examples.

18. How can I prevent a pass-the-hash attack?

19. Give an example of when you would use Open ID Connect.

20. Name two AAA servers and the ports associated with them.

21. What is used for accounting in an AAA server?

22. What is the purpose of a VPN solution?

23. Why should we never use PAP authentication?

24. What type of device is an iris scanner?

25. What could be two drawbacks of using facial recognition?

26. What is Type II in biometric authentication and why is it a security risk?

27. What is a time-limited password?

28. How many times can you use an HOTP password? Is there a time restriction associated with it?

29. How does a CAC differ from a smart card and who uses CAC?

30. What is a port-based authentication that authenticates both users and devices?

31. What type of account is a service account?

32. How many accounts should a system administrator for a multinational corporation have and why?

33. What do I need to do when I purchase a baby monitor and why?

34. What is a privilege account?

35. What is the drawback for security if the company uses shared accounts?

36. What is a default account? Is it a security risk?

37. The system administrator in a multination corporation creates a user account using an employee's first name and last name. Why are they doing this time after time?

38. What two actions do I need to complete when John Smith leaves the company?

39. What is account recertification?

40. What is the purpose of a user account review?

41. What can I implement to find out immediately when a user is placed in a group that may give them a higher level of privilege?

42. What will be the two possible outcomes if an auditor finds any working practices that do not confirm to the company policy?

43. If a contractor brings in five consultants for two months of mail server migration, how should I set up their accounts?

44. How can I ensure that the contractors in Question 44 can only access the company network from 9 a.m. - 5 p.m. daily?

45. If I have a company that has five consultants who work in different shift patterns, how can I set up their accounts so that each of them can only access the network during their individual shifts?

46. A brute-force attack cracks a password using all combinations of characters and will eventually crack a password. What can I do to prevent a brute-force attack?

47. The IT team have a global group called *IT Admin*; each member of the IT team are members of this group and therefore have full control access to the departmental data. Two new apprentices are joining the company and they need to have read access to the IT data. How can you achieve this with the minimum amount of administrative effort?

48. I have different login details and passwords to access Airbnb, Twitter, and Facebook, but I keep getting them mixed up and have locked myself out of these accounts from time to time. What can I implement on my Windows 10 laptop to help me?

49. I have moved departments, but the employees in my old department still use my old account for access; what should the company have done to prevent this from happening? What should their next action be?

50. What is the purpose of the `ssh-copy-id` command?

51. Describe the process of impossible time travel.

52. When I log in to my Dropbox account from my phone, I get an email asking me to confirm that this was a legal login. What have I been subjected to?

53. What is the purpose of a password vault and how secure is it?

54. What type of knowledge-based authentication would a bank normally use?

55. What is the difference between FAR and FRR?

56. What is a solution that helps protect privilege accounts?

57. What is the danger to households with IoT devices?

58. Why do cloud providers adopt a zero-trust model?

59. Which authentication model gives access to a computer system even though the wrong credentials are being used?

4
Exploring Virtualization and Cloud Concepts

In today's world, most businesses either use virtualization as it allows them to recover very quickly from a disaster or they have moved to the cloud to avoid spending a vast amount of money on equipment and disaster recovery. In this chapter, we are going to look at cloud concepts and virtualization, which will be broken down into the following topics:

- Overview of Cloud Computing
- Implementing Different Cloud Deployment Models
- Understand Cloud Computing Concepts
- Understanding Cloud Storage
- Selecting Cloud Security Controls
- Exploring the Virtual Network Environments

Overview of Cloud Computing

The demand for cloud computing has risen over the last few years as the workforce has been more mobile; the cloud solution is very cost-effective and maintains the high availability of systems. Before you decide to move to a **Cloud Service Provider (CSP)**, you need to ensure that you trust them 100%.

There are many good reasons why cloud computing has become popular:

- **Elasticity**: The cloud is like a pay-as-you-go model where one day you can increase resources and then the next day you can scale down the resources. You can even add more processor power, faster disks, more memory, or dual network cards whenever you want – there's no need to wait for delivery times, but the cost increases:

  Example 1: A toy firm is hiring 50 temporary workers from October onward to deal with the rush for toys at Christmas. If the toy company were not on the cloud, they would have to purchase another 50 desktops, but instead, they lease **Virtual Machines (VMs)** from a CSP. Once the Christmas rush has ended, the lease of their machines ends. You only pay for what you need.

  Example 2: An IT training company uses 12 laptops for the delivery of different courses. Each week the image changes and they have to roll it out 12 times – this is time-consuming. Images are stored in a library on a file server. When they move to the cloud, they just roll out one image and don't need to reimage each laptop. Today, they are delivering Word 2016, therefore they connect to cloud VM with an i5 processor with 4 GB of RAM for two days. They send an image to the **CSP**, which clones each desktop.

  The next week, in another location, they will deliver Skype for Business, so they use the same laptops and don't need to reimage them. They connect to the cloud to VMs with quad-core i7 processors with striped disk sets and 64 GB of RAM. The course is now for five days, so it is longer and more expensive. The image is uploaded to the CSP, which clones the machines, and the course is ready to go. As the course duration is longer and the machines have more resources, the CSP will bill for the resources used. They do not need to purchase the additional hardware and the setup is more cost-effective.

- **Scalability**: Scalability is the ability of a company to grow while maintaining a resilient infrastructure. The cloud enables a company to do so and grow without the worry of needing to make capital expenditure while doing so. It enables the company to grow faster than an on-premises company that needs to invest more money into bricks and mortar. As the cloud allows elasticity, it goes hand in hand with becoming scalable. As your company grows, the cloud provider can allow you to lease more resources. If at any time you want to reduce the amount of resources needed, the cloud provider can do that too.

  Example: Company A is a newly formed business that has hit the marketplace running; there is a need for the company to rapidly expand and open new offices in Chicago and London, as sales in those locations are astronomically high. Normally, when a new site is opened, it needs to invest $100,000 in IT equipment, so the company has turned to a CSP for the new equipment. They will lease the offices until sufficient sales have been made to invest in purchasing a property. All of the employees will have laptops and high-speed fiber broadband. The network infrastructure will be cloud-based, therefore there is no need to purchase physical servers that would have reduced their cash flow. Cash flow is maintained, even though new equipment has been provided.

- **No Capital Expenditure (CAPEX)**: When you move your infrastructure to the cloud, there is no capital expenditure; normally, IT resources have a maximum lifespan of 3–5 years. As technology keeps moving and hardware becomes obsolete, this means they may have to find $75–300,000 every five years just for hardware.

  Example: A company is looking to upgrade their desktops and servers with the cost of hardware being $250,000 and a disposal fee of $25,000 in five years' time. If they move to the cloud, it is going to cost them $60,000 a year. However, they don't need to find the whole $250,000 in one lump sum as the CSP will update their hardware perpetually so that the hardware will never be obsolete. It will also help the company maintain a better cash flow, as capital expenditure is not required. The price is 1.8% higher per year, which could be justified as there are no maintenance fees or disaster recovery sites required, making it very cost-effective. The CSP deals with maintenance and disaster recovery as part of the cloud plan.

- **Location-Independent**: As you are accessing the cloud through a browser, it is location-independent, therefore it offers faster recovery if your premises have a disaster.

  Example: One of your company offices is located in Northern California and recently was burned down by a wildfire; however, since your data and infrastructure are cloud-based, you can operate quickly from another location as long as you have internet access. If you had a traditional network, the infrastructure would have been burned down, your desktops would have been gone, and it could take a week or two to get back to an operational state.

- **Regional Storage of Data**: The cloud is regulated, therefore data from a country must be stored within that region as laws on data compliance can change from region to region.

- **No Maintenance Fees**: The CSP provides ongoing maintenance, so when the cloud contract is signed there are no hidden costs.

- **No Disaster Recovery Site Required**: The CSP provides 99.999% availability of its IT systems, therefore, once your data is in the cloud, there is no requirement for a disaster recovery site as the CSP provides that as part of the contract.

> **Exam tip**
> Private cloud = single tenant
> Public cloud = multitenant
> Community cloud = same industry, and sharing resources

Implementing Different Cloud Deployment Models

We will first look at the different cloud models and their characteristics. The most common cloud model is the public cloud, so let's start with that:

- **Public Cloud**: This is the most common model, where the CSP provides cloud services for multiple tenants. This is like being one of many people who rent an apartment in an apartment block. Just like in the public cloud, none of the tenants owns their apartment:

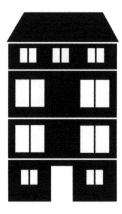

Figure 4.1 – Public cloud

Example: A small company does not want to invest $50,000 in IT systems, so they purchase their cloud package from a cloud provider where they and another company are hosted by the cloud provider. This is similar to someone renting one apartment in a block from a landlord – you lease but do not own the apartment. This is a multitenant environment where the cloud provider has multiple companies on the same virtual host.

- **Private Cloud**: A private cloud is where a company purchases all of its hardware. This gives them more control than other cloud models. They normally host their own cloud because they do not want to share resources with anyone else, but at the same time, their workforce has all of the mobile benefits of the cloud. However, larger companies might let the CSP provide all of the resources, but they will not be hosted in the same environment as everyone else: they will be separate. It is similar to someone buying a house because they want privacy. The private cloud needs isolation from other companies, which is why it is known as single-tenant:

Figure 4.2 – Private cloud

Example: An insurance company wants its sales staff to be in a cloud environment where they can access resources from anywhere, whether they are at home, at a customer's site, or in a hotel room. The problem they have is that they do not wish to share resources with other cloud tenants. Therefore, they purchase the hardware and their IT team hosts its own private cloud. The benefit of this is that the sales team can access any resources they want at any time of day or night. It is known as single-tenant but, like owning your own home, they buy the equipment.

- **Community Cloud**: The community cloud is where companies from the same industry collectively pay for a bespoke application to be written, and the cloud provider manufacturers host it:

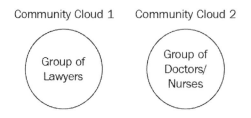

Figure 4.3 – Community cloud

In the preceding diagram, you can see lawyers on the left-hand side, and on the right-hand side is a group of medical people – doctors and nurses. The lawyers cannot share the same software package as the medical people, since they have different requirements. Therefore, **Community Cloud 1** is for lawyers who have brainstormed and financed the perfect legal application, which is hosted in the cloud – this is private to them. **Community Cloud 2** is for a group of medical people. It could be two hospitals that have designed and shared the cost of making the perfect medical software package, which is hosted by the CSP.

Example: There is no application that can provide all of the functionality required for pawnbrokers to list the assets that have been pawned with the payment made against each asset. There is no application that can track assets that have not been reclaimed and that need to be sold in the shops and on the internet. Three of the largest pawnbroking companies enter into a business venture in which they get together and design the perfect application to enable their companies to be more efficient and save labor costs over time. The cloud provider creates this application and hosts it. This saves them the costs of purchasing new hardware. The cloud provider will also back up the data each night and guarantee 99.99% availability of the systems. This is known as a community cloud as the application is no good to anyone other than a pawnbroker.

- **Hybrid Cloud**: Companies that decide not to host their company in the cloud are known as on-premises, but during their peak time they may expand into the cloud. This is known as **cloud bursting**. A mixture of both on-premises and the cloud is known as a hybrid model:

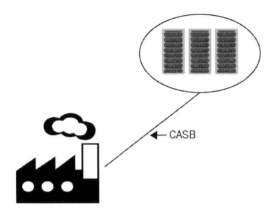

Figure 4.4 – Hybrid cloud

In the bottom left-hand corner of the preceding figure, we have a brick factory. This is known as on-premises, as the company owns a brick-and-mortar building. In the top-right corner are servers in the cloud. The **Cloud Access Security Broker (CASB)** enforces the company's policies between the on-premises situation and the cloud.

Understanding Cloud Service Models

There are different types of cloud services, and these are very heavily tested in the Security+ exam; therefore, we will show screenshots of the types of offerings. We will first look at infrastructure as a service, which is the model that you may have more control over.

Infrastructure as a Service (IaaS)

If you think of a network infrastructure, you think of desktops, servers, firewalls, routers, and switches – the hardware devices for a network. When you purchase these devices, they have a default factory setting and these settings need to be configured. Desktops are bare-bones, meaning that they have no operating system installed. IaaS is the same; you need to preconfigure these devices, install an operating system, and maintain the patch management. See the pricing (as of writing this book) for IaaS in the screenshot that follows:

Example pricing for popular products

App Service	Virtual Machines	Azure SQL Database
Compute	Compute	Databases
Quickly create powerful cloud apps for web and mobile	Provision Windows and Linux virtual machines in seconds	Managed relational SQL Database as a service
Starting from	Starting from	Starting from
$0.013 /hour	**$0.008** /hour	**$0.021** /hour
Free for the first 12 months	Free for the first 12 months	250GB free for the first 12 months

Blob storage	Azure Kubernetes Service (AKS)	Functions
Storage	Containers	Compute
REST-based object storage for unstructured data	Simplify the deployment, management, and operations of Kubernetes	Process events with serverless code
Starting from	Pay only for virtual machines. Starting from	Starting from
$0.002 /GB	**$0.008** /hour	**$0.20** /million executions
5GB free for the first 12 months	Free for the first 12 months	1 million requests per month always free

Figure 4.5 – Microsoft's IaaS offering (July 2018)

Distributive Allocation

When you decide to use an IaaS model or IaaS models, you may install a virtual load balancer to provide a distributive allocation of some of your server capacity. A load balancer will allocate the load across multiple servers to ensure that no single server is overburdened.

> **Exam tip**
> IaaS is where you will install the operating system and patch it. This is the service under IaaS you have more control over. The private cloud is the cloud model that gives you more control.

Software as a Service (SaaS)

This is where the CSP hosts a bespoke software application that is accessed through a web server. Let's look at three examples of this: Goldmine, Salesforce, and Office 365.

Example 1: GoldMine is a SaaS package, that is, a **Customer Relationship Management (CRM)** package, which is used by companies that sell products and services. It will host lists of their customers, with contact numbers and addresses:

WHAT'S INCLUDED	SUBSCRIPTION
Contact management	YES
Email linking	YES
Web and mobile device access	OPTIONAL
Sales forecasting and opportunity management	YES
Marketing list management and group emails	YES
Integration for Constant Contact campaign downloads	YES
Customer service management	YES
Real time dashboards	YES
Customize fields	YES

Figure 4.6 – Goldmine – SaaS

Example 2: Salesforce is an internationally used software package employed by sales teams to show a sales forecast over a period of time. It will allow salespeople to enter potential sales leads, categorize them, and hold any correspondence between the parties:

Figure 4.7 – Salesforce – SaaS

Example 3: Office 365 is a Microsoft product where the packages range from email to various Office applications that are all hosted in the cloud. Each user has a 1 TB storage space. The premium package (as of the writing of this book) comes with Skype, Exchange for email, and SharePoint, which is a document management system:

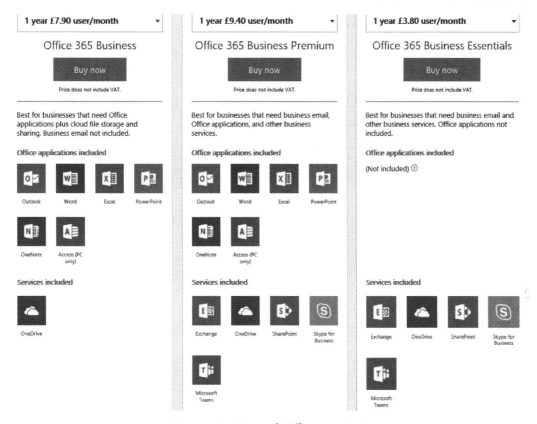

Figure 4.8 – Microsoft Office 365 – SaaS

Exam tip

SaaS is a bespoke vendor application that cannot be modified and you use it with a pay-per-use model, as a subscription, and you cannot migrate any applications or services to any SaaS environment.

Platform as a Service (PaaS)

This provides the environment for developers to create applications; an example of this is Microsoft Azure. The platform provides a set of services to support the development and operation of applications, rolling them out to iOS, Android devices, as well as Windows devices. You could migrate your bespoke software applications under PaaS. Bespoke means customized.

Security as a Service (SECaaS)

SECaaS provides **Identity and Access Management** (**IAM**), which provides identity management that allows people to have secure access to applications from anywhere at any time. The following screenshot shows Okta providing secure web authentication into Google Apps:

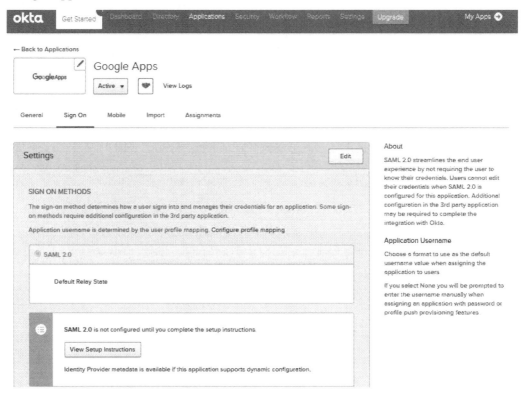

Figure 4.9 – Okta security as a service (SECaaS) for Google Apps

The user in the preceding screenshot needs to validate their identity and has presented a SAML token from Okta, the **identity provider** (**IdP**).

Anything as a Service (XaaS)

Anything as a Service (**XaaS**) describes a multitude of other cloud services that are available, such as **Network as a Service** (**NaaS**), providing network resources; **Desktop as a Service** (**DaaS**); **Backup as a Service** (**BaaS**); and many more. As new services appear, they will fall under the category of XaaS.

Understanding Cloud Computing Concepts

In this section, we are going to look at different cloud computing concepts that may appear in the CompTIA Security+ exam. Make sure that you are familiar with them:

- **Cloud Service Provider** (**CSP**): CSPs are entities that resell cloud services to customers. They can provide infrastructure, software, VMs, and other services that a customer needs. **Managed Cloud Service Providers** (**MCSP**) will also take over the day-to-day running of your cloud as they have the expertise to do so.

- **Managed Security Service Provider** (**MSSP**): An MSSP will maintain the security environment for companies that will include enterprise firewalls, intrusion prevention and detection systems, and SIEM systems. They have a very highly skilled workforce who will take this headache away from a company. At `https://wizardcyber.com/blog/managed-security-service-provider/` is an article about choosing an MSSP.

- **Fog Computing**: Fog computing complements cloud computing by processing data from IoT devices. It allows you to analyze the data before committing it to the cloud. The data is put in a location between the device and the cloud. It brings cloud computing nearer to the sensor; it also reduces the cost of data moving back and forth between the device and the cloud. We can use 4G/5G, Wi-Fi, or Zigbee. It also reduces latency as it prioritizes the traffic, and this can be important for life support systems. This can help healthcare applications process data more quickly as it is much closer to the device, and they are not transmitting data back and forth between the device and cloud.

Example: An alert from the sensor of a life support system is sent to the cloud and then to the clinician, but with fog computing, which is closer to the sensor, it can reduce the latency as the clinician is alerted much more quickly:

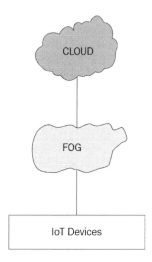

Figure 4.10 – Fog computing

- **Edge Computing**: All the processing of data storage is closer to the sensors rather than being thousands of miles away on a server at a data center.

- **Thin Client**: A thin client is a client that has limited resources that are insufficient to run applications. It connects to a server and processes the application on its resources.

- **Containers**: A container allows the isolation of an application and its files and libraries so that they are not dependent on anything else. It allows software developers to deploy applications seamlessly across various environments. Containers are used by **Platform as a Service (PaaS)** products.

  Example: Microsoft's version of Docker runs on Linux but allows application containers on Linux, Windows, and "macOS".

- **Microservices/API**: This allows you to define individual services that can then be connected by using an application program interface. They are loosely coupled and can be reused when creating applications.

- **Infrastructure as Code**: This is where you manage your computer infrastructure with configuration files rather than by a physical method. This is very common with cloud technologies making it easier to set up computers and roll out patches. This ensures that each computer has the same setup, in contrast with the human errors that may be encountered when setting up a computer manually. An example would be setting up your infrastructure using PowerShell and using **Desired State Configuration** (**DSC**) to ensure that there is no deviation from the required setting. You can use PowerShell scripts to create VMs, firewalls, and load balancers. Let's look at a few more examples:

    a. **Software-Defined Network (SDN)**: Traditional networks route packets via a hardware router and are decentralized; however, in today's networks, more and more people are using virtualization, including cloud providers. A SDN is where packets are routed through a controller rather than traditional routers, which improves performance. It has three different planes: the control plane prioritizes the traffic, the data plane does switching and routing, and the management plane deals with monitoring the traffic. An overview of SDN can be found at https://www.cisco.com/c/en_au/solutions/software-defined-networking/overview.html.

    b. **Software-Defined Visibility (SDV)**: This gives you visibility of the network traffic use. It can collect and aggregate the data on the network traffic and provide good reports to the network administrators.

- **Serverless Architecture**: This is where you will use the Backend as a Service, where a third-party vendor hosts your applications as a pay-as-you-go model based on the compute time that you use. You will lease servers or data storage from them.

- **Services Integration**: This is where the provision of several business services is combined with different IT services and are integrated to provide a single solution for a business.

- **Resource Policies**: These are policies that state what access level or actions someone has to a particular resource.

- **Transit Gateway**: This is a network hub that acts as a regional virtual router to interconnect **virtual private clouds** (**VPC**) and VPN connections.

- **Virtualization**: In a cloud environment the infrastructure is built on a virtual environment. The storage for these machines normally comes from a **Storage Area Network** (**SAN**). Virtualization is explained at the end of this chapter. The benefits of using VMs in the cloud are that you can increase and decrease resources at the drop of a hat. It will only take your cloud provider a few minutes to spin up additional machines. Snapshots can be used to roll the VMs back to a previous configuration.

Understanding Cloud Storage Concepts

Cloud storage utilizes SAN for the virtual components used in a cloud network. A SAN is a hardware device that contains a large number of fast disks, such as **Solid-State Drives** (**SSDs**), and is isolated from the LAN as it has its own network servers. The disks are set up with some form of redundancy, such as RAID 5, so that the storage space is redundant. Each switch and storage system on the SAN must be interconnected, and the physical interconnections must support bandwidth levels that can adequately handle peak data activities. There are two connection types:

- **Fiber Channel**: Fast but expensive, as it needs fiber channel switches and fiber cables, which are expensive.

- **iSCSi Connector**: Runs **Small Computer System Interface** (**SCSI**) commands over Ethernet, and can connect through normal Ethernet switches and still offer good speed. This is a much cheaper option. The servers that use SAN storage are diskless but use the SAN storage as if they had disks installed, but you need very fast connection speeds so that the server does not suffer from performance issues.

Example: In the following diagram, Server 1 is a virtual host, and it needs another 200 TB of disk space to host more VMs, but it has no physical disk slots available. It connects to the SAN using Ethernet and Ethernet switches; this connector is known as an iSCSi connector:

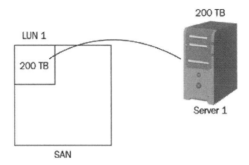

Figure 4.11 – SAN

The SAN allocates 200 TB by giving it a **Logical Unit Number** (**LUN**). This is known as |an **iSCSi target**. Server 1, which has been allocated the space, is known as the **iSCSi initiator**. Server 1 is diskless but still sets up the disk space using disk management as if it were a physical disk. To prevent latency, the connection between Server 1 and the SAN must be fast. Server 1 could be a virtual host that holds many VMs. It is vital that this server is fully patched at all times.

It is quite common to use cloud storage to hold your data, from the iCloud service provided by Apple, Google Drive provided by Google, OneDrive provided by Microsoft, or Dropbox provided by Dropbox, Inc. This storage resides on a SAN inside a data center. The consumer versions of cloud storage allow you to have limited storage space, but offer to sell you a business version or additional storage by charging a monthly subscription fee. Let's understand cloud storage by looking at the following diagram:

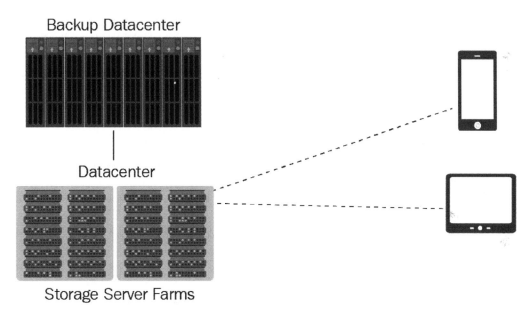

Figure 4.12 – Cloud storage

In the preceding diagram, you can see on the left-hand side a data center that has a vast amount of storage servers in a configuration called a **server farm**. The data center is a secure location where your data resides, but the data must stay within your world region. The Security+ exam may see it as different countries rather than world regions. The data center has a backup data center to provide redundancy. The storage on these servers is likely to be diskless SAN storage.

Cloud providers provide **Binary Large OBject (BLOB)** storage that can be used as a large storage area for a database or large amounts of binary or text data. It can be also used for images that can be used by a browser or video and audio files for streaming video or gaming.

Selecting Cloud Security Controls

To ensure that the cloud environment is as secure as possible, there are many controls that need to be in place. Let's look at some of these controls.

High Availability Access Zones

In a global Azure environment, there are Azure regions. Inside each region, there are high availability zones. These zones are physical locations that may hold two or more data centers and provide high availability within their zone. They are independent from each other with their own networks. Inside each network, they have their own power and **Heating Ventilation and Air Conditioning (HVAC)** systems that regulate their own cooling using hot and cold aisles. Applications can be distributed across multiple zones so that if one zone fails, the application is still available.

Resource Policies

These are policies that state what access level or actions someone has to a particular resource. This is crucial for resource management and audit. We need to apply the principle of least privilege.

Secret Management

This is a secure application, and it could be called a vault where the keys, tokens, passwords, and SSH keys used by privileged accounts are stored. It could be a vault that is heavily encrypted to protect these items. Microsoft uses RSA 2048-bit keys to protect Azure secret management.

Integration and Auditing

Integration is the process of how data is being handled from input to output. A cloud auditor is responsible for ensuring that the policies and controls that the cloud provider has put in place are being adopted. They will test that these controls and the system integration are working as expected. They will be an independent third party. Some of these controls may include the following:

- Encryption Levels
- Access Control Lists
- Privilege Account Use
- Password Policies
- Anti-Phishing Protection
- Data Loss Prevention Controls

Storage

It is vital that the data held in cloud storage is highly available, and that only those who are authorized can access the data. Let's look at permissions, encryption, replication, and high availability:

- **Permissions**: Users have a storage identity and are put into different storage groups that have different rights.

- **Encryption**: With cloud storage, you may need to have more than one type of encryption. You would use symmetric encryption as there will be a large amount of data; normally, AES-256 will be used. Microsoft uses RSA 2048 -bit encryption for blob storage. You will also need encryption for data in transit, such as TLS or SSL. Microsoft uses **Transport Data Encryption** (**TDE**) to access resources in the cloud using RSA 2048 or 3072 -bit encryption.

- **Replication**: In the cloud, multiple copies of your data are always held for redundancy. This is in case there are power or hardware failures or environmental disasters such as hurricanes. The data cannot be located outside of the region where it is created. There are four different types of replication:

  a. **Local Redundant Storage** (**LRS**): Three copies of your data are replicated at a single physical location. Not good for high availability. It is the cheapest solution, but if the power goes then everything has gone.

b. **Zone Redundant Storage (ZRS)**: Data is replicated between three separate zones within your region. It should be used in your primary region; however, if a disaster affects the region then you have no access to data.

c. **GEO Redundant Storage (GRS)**: Three copies of your data are replicated in a single physical location in the primary region using LRS, then one copy is replicated to a single location in a secondary region.

d. **GEO Zone Redundant Storage (GZRS)**: Data is replicated between three separate zones within your primary region, then one copy is replicated to a single location in a secondary region.

- **High Availability**: High availability ensures that copies of your data are held in different locations. An example of this could be a backup data center, as shown in *Figure 4.12* earlier in this chapter. Using storage regions with three different zones by using ZRS, and replicating to other secondary regions such as GRS and GZRS, also provide high availability.

Networks

In a cloud environment, you must ensure that your networks and VMs are protected against any attack. In this section, we will look at virtual networks, public and private subnets, segmentation, and API inspection and integration. Let's look at each of these in turn:

- **Virtual Private Cloud (VPC)**: A VPC is a virtual network that consists of shared resources with a public cloud, where the VMs for one company are isolated from the resources of another company. This is part of IaaS. These separate VPCs can be isolated using public and private networks or segmentation.

- **Public and Private Subnets**: Our cloud environment needs to be broken down into public subnets that can access the internet directly or private subnets that have to go through a NAT gateway and then an internet gateway to access the internet; see the following figure. Let's look at the private subnets first:

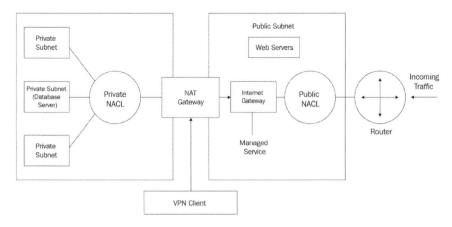

Figure 4.13 – Public and Private Subnets

- **Private Subnets**: Our VPC contains three private subnets. Each of these subnets has its own CIDR IP address range and cannot connect directly to the internet. They must go through the NAT gateway, which in turn uses the internet gateway to access the internet. In each of the subnets, a default route with an IP address of 0.0.0.0 must be directed to go to the internet gateway. If routing tables do not know where to send traffic, they follow the default route. Client VMs and database servers would be stored in the private subnet. The private subnet will use one of the following IP address ranges:

```
10.0.0.0
172.16.x.x - 172.31.x.x
192.168.0.0
```

All other IP address ranges, except the APIPA 169.254.x.x, are public addresses. Private subnets will hold the domain infrastructure, such as domain controllers, mail servers, and database servers that you don't want to communicate directly with the internet.

- **NAT Gateway**: This allows the private subnets to communicate with other cloud services and the internet, but hides the internal network from internet users. The NAT gateway has the **Network Access Control List** (**NACL**) for the private subnets.

- **Public Subnets**: Resources on the public subnet can connect directly to the internet. Therefore, public-facing web servers will be placed within this subnet. The public subnet will have a NAT gateway for communicating with the private subnets, an internet gateway, and a managed service to connect to the internet.

- **VPN Connection**: To create a secure connection to your VPC, you can connect a VPN using L2TP/IPsec to the public interface of the NAT gateway.

- **Segmentation**: The security of services that are permitted to access or be accessible from other zones has a strict set of rules controlling this traffic. These rules are enforced by the IP address ranges of each subnet. Within a private subnet, VLANs can be used to carry out departmental isolation.

- **API inspection and integration**: **Representational State Transfer**, known as **REST**, refers to a new way to write web service APIs so that different languages can be transported using HTTP.

Compute

These are the resources that a computer needs to function effectively. Let's look at resources that affect cloud computing:

- **Security Groups**: A compute security group profile is allocated by using a security group template that also states the cloud account, the location of the resource, and the security rules.

- **Dynamic Resource Allocation**: This uses virtualization technology to upgrade and downscale the cloud resources as the demand grows or falls.

- **Instance Awareness**: We must monitor VM instances so that an attacker cannot place an unmanaged VM that would lead to VM sprawl and then ultimately VM escape. We must use tools like a **Network Intrusion Detection System** (**NIDS**) to detect new instances, and the IT team must maintain a list of managed VMs.

- **VPC Endpoint**: This allows you to create a private connection between your VPC and another cloud service without crossing over the internet.

- **Container Security**: This is the implementation of security tools and policies that ensures that your container is working as it was intended.

Solutions

These are the services that are required to secure our cloud environment. Let's look at each of them in turn:

- **Cloud Access Security Broker** (**CASB**): The CASB enforces the company's policies between the on-premises situation and the cloud. There is no group policy in the cloud.

- **Application Security**: This is using products such as Cloud WAF and **Runtime Application Self-Protection (RASP)** to protect against a zero-day attack, covered in *Chapter 9, Identifying Threats, Attacks, and Vulnerabilities*.

- **Next Generation Secure Web Gateway (SWG)**: An SWG acts like a reverse proxy, content filter, and an inline NIPS. An example of this is Netskope, which provides advanced web security with advanced data and threat protection with the following features: Cloud Security, Remote Data Access, Managed Cloud Applications, Monitor and Assess, Control Cloud Applications, Acceptable Use, Protect Against Threats, and Protect Data Everywhere.

  More details can be found at `https://www.digitalmarketplace.service.gov.uk/g-cloud/services/986853436243688`.

- **Firewall Considerations in a Cloud Environment**: The reason that we need a good firewall is to block incoming traffic and put up a barrier to protect the internal cloud resources against hackers or malware. The cloud firewalls tend to be Web Application Firewalls. The best cloud firewalls in 2020 were CloudFlare and Amazon Cloud Service Firewall. The top 20 are shown at `https://www.techradar.com/uk/best/cloud-firewall`. Let's look at firewall considerations.

  a. **Cost**: An example of cost as a consideration would be CloudFlare that has a free version with limited features. At the time of publishing, the pro version is $20 per month, the business version is $200, and the enterprise version is **Price on Application (POA)**. Each of the plans has additional features that can be added to that price. The enterprise solution is for customers with business-critical applications.

  b. **Need for Segmentation**: The cloud environment uses a Zero-Trust model where each individual needs to provide their identity and location to gain access to the cloud environment. The firewall controls access to each of the cloud regions and zones.

  c. **Interconnection OSI Layers**: A network firewall works on Layer 3 of the OSI controlling IP traffic, but most of the cloud firewalls are Web Application Firewalls working at Layer 7 of the OSI.

  d. **Cloud Native Controls versus Third-Party Solutions**: Vendors such as Microsoft and **Amazon Web Services (AWS)** have their own tools, such as **Azure Resource Manager (ARM)** and AWS Cloud Formation. These tools make managing Microsoft and AWS cloud resources easy. Using third-party tools adds more flexibility.

Let's explore the different virtual network environments in the next section.

Exploring the Virtual Network Environments

A virtual network is very similar to a physical network in many ways but, for the Security+ exam, we must know the concept of virtualization. To be able to host a virtual environment, we must install a hypervisor on a computer hosting the VMs. A hypervisor is software that runs on a virtual host that lets the host run virtual machines. There are two different types of hypervisor:

- **Type 1 Hypervisor**: This is an enterprise version that can be installed on a computer without an operating system, called bare metal. Examples are VMWare ESX, Microsoft's Hyper-V, or Zen, which is used by AWS.

- **Type 2 Hypervisor**: This needs an operating system, such as Server 2016 or Windows 10, and then the hypervisor is installed like an application. An example of a Type 2 hypervisor is Oracle's VM VirtualBox or Microsoft's virtual machine as a product.

The main server in a virtual environment is called a host, and the VMs that it hosts are called guests. This is very similar to a party where the person holding the party is a host and the people attending the party are called guests. There are various different components of virtualization:

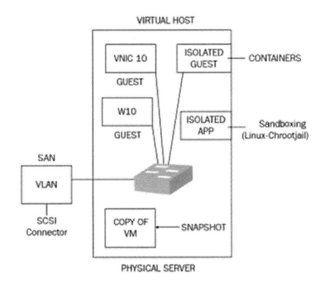

Figure 4.14 – Virtual host

Now, we will look at each of the components:

- **Host**: The host may hold 100 VMs and therefore the main resources that the host needs are storage that normally uses a SAN, memory, and processor cores. These can be increased through time and so the host is scalable (it can grow).

- **Guest**: Windows 10 is an example of a guest machine and it needs the same amount of resources as a physical Windows 10 machine. The benefit of using a guest machine is you can replace it in a disaster recovery situation within a couple of minutes. The following screenshot shows a virtual host with two guest machines, running Server 2016 and Windows 10:

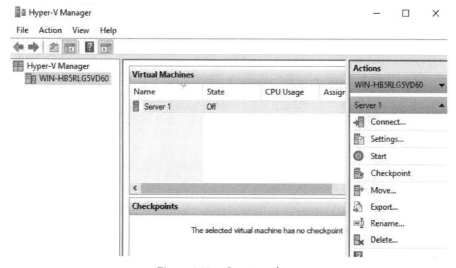

Figure 4.15 – Guest machines

- **Containers**: An isolated guest machine is known as a container. The best virtual container is called Docker. It is vendor neutral and will allow you to run applications that have autonomy. This means that they are easy to transfer between different hosts.

- **Virtual Switch**: Although a virtual switch can act like a switch connecting all of the machines, it can also create three different types of network: internet, external, and private. For each external network, the host needs a physical network card. Therefore, if you have two external networks, the host needs a minimum of two physical network cards. An internal network can create VLANs within this network:

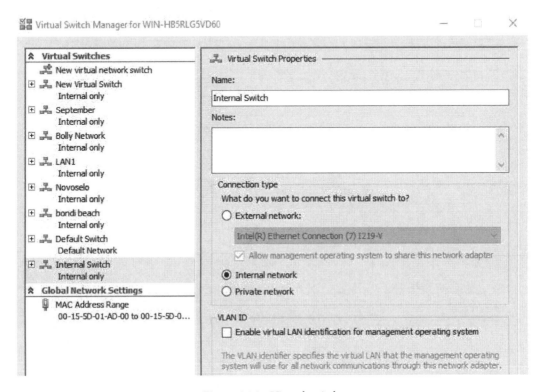

Figure 4.16 – Virtual switch

- **Sandboxing**: Sandboxing is where an application is placed in its own VM for patching and testing, or because it is a dangerous application that you don't want to roam across your network. In a Linux environment, this is known as a chroot jail.

- **Snapshot**: This is like taking a picture with a camera—whatever the virtual machine's setting is at that time is what you capture. You might take a snapshot before you carry out a major upgrade of a VM so that, if anything goes wrong, you can roll the machine setting back to the original. You can roll back to a previous setting within seconds. If you have spent an hour upgrading and patching a VM, you may snapshot it afterward to save the settings. Please see the following, a snapshot for Server 2016; Microsoft calls it a snapshot in Server 2008 but calls it a checkpoint from Server 2012 R2 onward, but it is basically a snapshot:

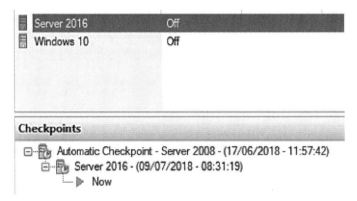

Figure 4.17 – Snapshot

- **System Sprawl**: This is where the virtual host is running out of resources or is overutilizing resources. This could end up with the host crashing and taking out the virtual network. A way to avoid this is to use thin provisioning; this means only allocating the minimum amount of resources that your VM needs, gently increasing the resources required. The IT administrator should also produce a daily report on the usage of VMs so any increase can be identified.

- **VM Sprawl**: This is where an unmanaged VM has been placed on your network. Because the IT administrator doesn't know it is there, it will not be patched and, therefore, over a period of time it will become vulnerable and could be used for a VM escape attack.

  Sprawl Avoidance: One of the best ways to protect against VM sprawl is to have robust security policies for adding VMs to the network and use either a NIDS or Nmap to detect new hosts.

- **VM Escape**: VM escape is where an attacker gains access to a VM, then attacks either the host machine that holds all of the VMs, the hypervisor, or any of the other VMs.

    a. **VM Escape Protection**: One of the best ways to protect against VM escape is to ensure that the patches on the hypervisor and all VMs are always up to date. Ensure that guest privileges are low. The servers hosting the critical services should have redundancy and not be on a single host so that if one host is attacked, all of the critical services are set up as a single point of failure. We also need a snapshot for all servers and need to use VM migration so another copy is held in another location. We could also place a HIPS inside each VM to protect against an attack.

Review Questions

Now it's time to check your knowledge. Answer the questions, and then check your answers, which can be found in the *Assessments* section at the end of the book:

1. In a cloud environment, what is elasticity?
2. In which cloud environment would I install the software and then have to update the patches?
3. What cloud model would I not be allowed to migrate to?
4. What is the major benefit of using a public cloud?
5. What is a cloud single-tenant model?
6. What is a cloud multitenant model?
7. Describe how a community cloud operates.
8. Who is responsible for the disaster recovery of hardware in a cloud environment?
9. What is a **Cloud Access Security Broker (CASB)**?
10. What model is it if you own the premises and all of the IT infrastructure resides there?
11. What is a hybrid cloud model?
12. What is distributive allocation?

13. What type of model deals with identity management?

14. Where will a diskless virtual host access its storage?

15. If you have a virtual switch that resides on a SAN, what connector will you use for a VLAN?

16. What type of disks does a SAN use?

17. What is the machine that holds a number of VMs called?

18. What is a guest, and what can you use as a rollback option?

19. In a virtual environment, what is sandboxing and how does it relate to chroot jail?

20. Which is faster for data recovery: a snapshot or a backup tape?

21. What is a Type 1 hypervisor?

22. What is a Type 2 hypervisor?

23. Why does HVAC produce availability for a data center?

24. What do you call the cloud model where people from the same industry share resources and the cost of the cloud model?

25. What is an example of cloud storage for a personal user?

26. Explain the functionality of fog computing.

27. What is edge computing?

28. What are containers?

29. What is infrastructure as code?

30. Describe services integration.

31. What are cloud resource policies?

32. What is system sprawl, and what is a way to prevent it?

33. What is the best way to protect against VM escape?

34. What is a cloud region, and how can it provide redundancy?

35. What is secret management, and what encryption levels protect the secret management key?

36. Explain the main difference between LRS and ZRS. Which one is the cheapest?

37. Why would a VPC use private and public subnets?

38. What type of resources would be held on a public subnet?

39. What type of resources would be held on a private subnet?

40. How would someone connect to a VPC?

41. Where should a default route be pointing for a device within a private subnet, and what is its purpose?

42. Why might a third-party cloud solution be better than a cloud-native solutions?

Section 2: Monitoring the Security Infrastructure

In this section, you will gain knowledge of different types of penetration testing and scanning concepts that are crucial to security professionals. You will explore security protocol use cases, understand different network components, and also learn to secure your wireless and mobile solutions.

This section comprises the following chapters:

- *Chapter 5, Monitoring, Scanning, and Penetration Testing*
- *Chapter 6, Understanding Secure and Insecure Protocols*
- *Chapter 7, Delving into Network and Security Concepts*
- *Chapter 8, Securing Wireless and Mobile Solutions*

5
Monitoring, Scanning, and Penetration Testing

One of the most important roles of a security professional is to keep the company's environment safe from attack and so, in this chapter, we are going to look at monitoring, scanning, and penetration testing.

In this chapter, we will cover the following topics:

- Penetration Testing Concepts
- Passive and Active Reconnaissance
- Exercise Types
- Vulnerability Scanning Concepts
- Syslog/Security Information and Event Management
- Threat Hunting

Penetration Testing Concepts

A penetration test is an intrusive test where a third party has been authorized to carry out an attack on a company's network to identify weaknesses. The intrusive tests used by them can cause damage to your systems.

Penetration testing is commonly known as pen testing. Pen testers are given different amounts of information, including the following:

- **Black Box**: Black box pen testers work in an unknown environment and are given no information on the company. They will carry out an initial exploitation looking for vulnerabilities.

- **Gray Box**: Gray box pen testers work in a partially known environment as they are given limited information.

- **White Box**: White box pen testers work in a known environment. One of the purposes of a white box pen tester is to test applications in a sandbox so that when they are released, they do not have any vulnerabilities. They know everything about a system or application as they have access to an application's source code.

Example: A pen tester is about to carry out a pen test but has not been given any information on the system. As they arrive at the company, the IT manager offers them a cup of coffee and then gives them the Local Admin account of server 1. What type of pen test is this?

Answer: It is a gray box, as he has been given some information.

Rules of Engagement (ROE)

Before any pen testing commences, the following information needs to be established:

- **Client Contact Details**: Details of a person within the company who has authorized the pen test, also with their contact details, so that they can be updated periodically on the progress of the test. They should agree to a time and date to start the pen test.

- **Scope**: The type of test, whether it is black, gray, or white, and what action is allowed to be taken if a vulnerability has been found. For example, do we notify the customer of the vulnerability or has the customer given permission to exploit it as far as it can go? This may be intrusive.

- **IT Team Notification**: If this is an announced pen test, we should let the IT team know the IP addresses of the pen testers. This will allow the IT team to differentiate between live attacks and the pen testers.

- **Data Handling**: The rules of how the pen testers will handle **Personally identifiable information (PII)** and sensitive information that they acquire: do they keep copies on their computers, and what levels of encryption should they use for storage.

- **Web Applications**: Pen testing on web applications is conducted in a sandbox rather than affect the customer's potential sales on the production website.

- **Regular Client Meeting**: Depending on the length of the pen test, regular meetings should be conducted with the client, giving them real-time updates of the progress being made. The client will then inform the pen testers if their IT team has identified any breaches of security.

> **Exam Tip**
> A white box pen tester has all the information he needs, including the source code.

- **Cleanup**: This is the process to restore the environment back to the original state. The pen testers may be asked to provide details of vulnerabilities to the IT team so that they can secure their environment.

- **Bug Bounty**: This is a process where corporations or software vendors reward the testers who find vulnerabilities in their environment, especially those affecting the security of their environments. Large corporations should have this in place. The pen tester will be asked to look for the same software vulnerabilities as the bug bounty program.

Network Exploitation Techniques

As the pen testers carry out their testing, they may incorporate techniques used by attackers. Let's look at these here:

- **Pivoting**: A pivoting attack is when an attacker gains access to a desktop computer inside a company, which they then use to launch and attack another computer or server.

- **Lateral Movement**: This is where attackers move around your network looking for resources to exploit in an effort to avoid detection. This digs deeper into your network in a search.

- **Persistence**: This is an attack over an extended period of time.

- **Escalation of Privilege**: Escalation of privilege is where an attacker exploits a weakness in a system so that they can gain a higher level of privileges on it.

> **Exam Tip**
> A pivot is gaining access to one computer so that an attack can then be launched on a computer running a critical service.

Let's now look at passive and active reconnaissance.

Passive and Active Reconnaissance

In the CompTIA Security+ exam, they measure the types of reconnaissance that could be used by an attacker. Let's first look at active and passive reconnaissance and then the tools that can be used to carry out these activities:

- **Active Reconnaissance**: Active reconnaissance is where someone actively tries to gain information about the system. For example, an attacker finds a username left on one of the corporate desktops; they then ring up the active directory team, pretending to be that person and requests a password reset. This is active reconnaissance, as they have carried out an action.

- **Passive Reconnaissance**: Passive reconnaissance is where an attacker is constantly gathering information, without the victim's knowledge. For example, an attacker is sitting in a coffee shop when they realize that two members of Company A's security team are having lunch. The attacker listens to every word that is said, and the security team is unaware of the eavesdropping. This is passive reconnaissance.

Reconnaissance Tools

The following tools can be used for reconnaissance:

- **Drones**: Drones can be used for passive reconnaissance as they can have cameras, including thermal imaging, and can collect useful information. However, they also could be armed and used to cause destruction. In this case, drones constitute active reconnaissance.

- **War Flying**: This could also use a drone with a laptop or a **Personal Digital Assistant** (**PDA**) so that they can map out wireless networks, and they could also have Bluetooth and cellular capability. This is passive reconnaissance as it maps out the networks.

- **War Driving**: War driving is where someone drives around in a car mapping out wireless access points, including those that could be vulnerable. This is passive reconnaissance.

- **Footprinting**: Footprinting is the process that hackers would use to map out all of the connections to a specific computer looking for remote access capabilities, open ports, services, and vulnerabilities.

- **Open Source Intelligence (OSINT)**: This is intelligence collected legally from the public domain, such as social media or websites on the internet. It is used in law enforcement and business intelligence to help identify the source of attacks. It is only used for non-sensitive data.

> **Exam tip**
>
> Lateral movement is used by attackers to make their detection by security teams much harder.

Let's now look at the different types of exercise in the next section.

Exercise Types

Team exercises are similar to pen testing, but they use friendly IT professionals to participate in the different teams. The teams are red, blue, green, white, and purple. Let's look at each of these in turn:

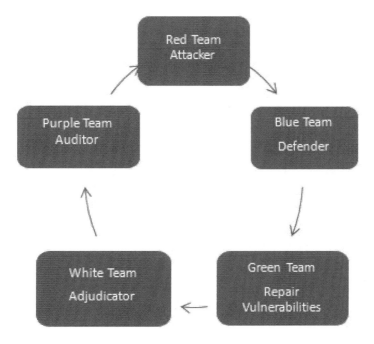

Figure 5.1 – Exercise teams

Here is a brief overview of the different teams:

- **Red Team**: The red team mimics an attacker, and they try to find vulnerabilities within your company. They quite often use social engineering and phishing as part of their attacks.

- **Blue Team**: The blue team looks to discover security vulnerabilities within the company and take action to mitigate them so that the company is secure.

- **White Team**: The white team organizes and judges cybersecurity exercises based on the information given. They set the rules of engagement and details of the exercise. If they find that the red team has created a vulnerability that is serious, they will stop the exercise immediately. They score the blue team's effort based on information from the red and green teams. They look at the reports regarding accuracy and ensure that any countermeasures are suitable.

- **Green Team**: The green team is trained to be an attacker, but has a defensive posture, and their focus is on repairing vulnerabilities as quickly as possible.

- **Purple Team**: The purple team can carry out the role of both the blue and red teams. By combining these teams, they can discover the threat actors' tactics. These guys could be auditors or external consultants.

> **Exam tip**
> White teams set up the rules of engagement and judge cyber security events, ensuring reports are accurate and that countermeasures are suitable.

We will now look at the different vulnerability scanning concepts in the next section.

Vulnerability Scanning Concepts

A vulnerability scanner is a passive scanner that identifies vulnerabilities or weaknesses in a system. For example, there could be a missing update for the operating system, anti-virus solutions, or account vulnerabilities. Microsoft has a vulnerability scanning tool called **Microsoft Baseline Security Analyzer** (**MBSA**), but there are many more in the marketplace.

A Zero-Day exploit cannot be traced by a vulnerability scanner; the exploit has not yet been identified and has no updates or patches available. Let's look at the type of output a vulnerability scanner could produce:

- **Common Vulnerabilities and Exposure (CVE): Massachusetts Institute of Technology Research & Engineering (MITRE)** is a non-profit, government funded organization working out of Bedford Massachusetts that looks at different attack vectors. They produced the **Common Vulnerability and Exposure (CVE)** list, which looks at computer flaws. Each flaw has an ID. Please look at the following URL for more information: `https://www.cvedetails.com/`.

- **Common Vulnerabilities Scoring System (CVSS)**: CVSS is built into many vulnerability scanners and indicates the severity of vulnerabilities. The security team can use this output to identify which vulnerabilities need to be dealt with first. Always deal with the critical event first. The scores and ratings are shown here:

Score	Rating
Critical	9.0-10.0
High	7.0-8.9
Medium	4.0-6.9
Low	0.1-3.9

- **False Positive**: A false positive is where the scan believes that there is a vulnerability but when you physically check, it is not there.

- **False Negative**: A false negative, on the other hand, is more dangerous. There is a vulnerability, but the scanner does not detect it. An example of a false negative is a Zero-Day exploit that is attacking the system without there being a way of detecting it.

- **True Positive**: This is where the results of the system scan agree with the manual inspection.

- **Log Reviews**: Following a vulnerability scan, it is important to review the log files that will list any potential vulnerabilities. The security team should ensure that these are addressed immediately.

> **Exam tip**
> When looking at CVSS events, always deal with the critical events first.

Credentialed versus Non-Credentialed Scans

There are two types of vulnerability scans – credentialed and non-credentialed. Let's look at these in turn:

- **Credentialed Scan**: A credentialed scan is a much more powerful version of the vulnerability scanner. It has higher privileges than a non-credentialed scan. It provides more accurate information, and it can scan documents, audit files, check certificates, and account information. It can tell you what accounts have a vulnerability, for example, those with non-expiring passwords.

- **Non-Credentialed Scan**: A non-credentialed scan has lower privileges than the credentialed scan. It will identify vulnerabilities that an attacker would easily find. We should fix the vulnerabilities found with a non-credentialed scan first, as this is what the hacker will see when they enter your network.

  Example: An administrator runs a non-credentialed scan on the network and finds that there are three missing patches. The scan does not provide many details on these missing patches. The administrator installs the missing patches to keep the systems up to date as they can only operate on the information produced for them.

Intrusive versus Non-Intrusive Vulnerability Scans

There are two types of vulnerability scans; one does not cause harm and the other can. Let's look at the differences here:

- **Non-Intrusive Scans**: These are passive and merely report vulnerabilities. They do not cause damage to your system.

- **Intrusive Scans**: An intrusive vulnerability scan can cause damage as they try to exploit the vulnerability and should be used in a sandbox and not on your live production system. The main difference between the intrusive scan and a pen test is that the person running the intrusive scan has more knowledge of the system than the pen tester.

Exam tip
A credentialed scan can produce more information and can audit the network.
A non-credentialed scan is primitive and can only find missing patches
or updates. It has fewer permissions than a credentialed scan.

Other Types of Scans That Can Be Performed

There are different types of scans apart from those listed in the previous section. Let's look at each of these in turn:

- **Network Scans**: These scans look at computers and devices on your network and help identify weaknesses in their security. They scan the whole network looking for nodes that are not fully patched or have open ports.

- **Application Scans**: Before applications are released, coding experts are employed to perform regression testing that will check whether your code is written properly. The best type of analysis is dynamic analysis, as it evaluates the program in real time. After this, the white box pen tester ensures that there are no weaknesses in the application.

- **Web Application Scans**: There are many sophisticated web application scanners due to the movement of my companies to the cloud. They crawl through a website as if they are a search engine looking for vulnerabilities. There are automated to look for vulnerabilities, such as cross-site scripting and SQL injection.

- **Configuring Review**: Configuration compliance scanners and desired state configuration in PowerShell ensure that no deviations are made to the security configuration of a system.

Penetration Testing versus Vulnerability Scanning

A penetration test is more intrusive as it tries to fully exploit the vulnerabilities that it finds and could cause damage to IT systems, whereas most vulnerability scanners are non-intrusive, as they scan for vulnerabilities. Even a credentialed scan only scans the registry/permissions and finds missing patches and vulnerabilities. It is informational and does not exploit the system, and therefore is less likely to cause damage to systems. Running a vulnerability scan can be done at the drop of a hat and is much cheaper than organizing a pen test.

Syslog/Security Information and Event Management

The systems on a network produce a massive amount of information in log files and most of them will be related to errors or possible attacks. They will require a real-time solution to correlate these events so that the security team can be alerted immediately. Let's look at the role that the SIEM and syslog server play.

Security Information and Event Management (SIEM) is regarded as an IT best practice, used by regulated industries as a whole, to fulfill security and audit compliance regulations, for example, HIPAA, GDPR, SOX, and PCI DSS. SIEM supports IT teams by consolidating event log values through the correlation, aggregation, normalizing standard, and non-standard log formats; it can also filter out false positives.

The only time that an SIEM system will not provide the correct information is when the wrong filters are used or the wrong host is monitored. In these cases, a false positive will be produced.

A **System Logging (Syslog)** protocol server is used to collect data from multiple sources and store them in a single location, such as an event logging database. Legitimate data can be filtered out, thereby reducing the amount of data held. The SIEM can benefit from the filtered data as searching becomes easier. The data between the syslog server and the SIEM system is encrypted.

The different aspects of a SIEM system is shown in the following diagram:

Figure 5.2 – SIEM cycle

Let's now look at the different aspects of a SIEM system:

- **Log Collectors**: SIEM have built-in log collector tools that can collect information from both syslog server and multiple other servers. An agent is placed on the device that can collect log information, parse the data into a better structure, and then pass it to the SIEM server for aggregation.

- **Log Aggregation**: The SIEM system can correlate and aggregate events so that duplicates are ruled out and a better understanding of the events occurring on the network are achieved to help identify potential attacks.

- **Log Forensics**: The log files can be used to find evidence for the forensics team to help them identity an attack.

- **Event Reporting**: A SIEM system has a dashboard and collects reports that can be reviewed on a regular basis to ensure that the policies have been enforced and that the company is compliant. It will also highlight whether or not the SIEM system is effective and working properly. False positives may arise because the wrong input filters are being used or the wrong hosts monitored.

- **Detect Threats**: From the events, the SIEM system can detects threats on the network and immediately forward the information pertaining to these threats to the security team.

- **Alert Security Breaches**: After receiving the detection of potential threats, the security team verifies whether the security breaches have taken place. It will then take the necessary action to stop the breach and prevent it from happening again.

Let's look at other functions that a SIEM server can carry out:

- **Real-Time Monitoring**: The SIEM can monitor in real time and therefore alert the security teams immediately as any event is discovered. This helps to protect your working environment.

- **Time Synchronization**: The SIEM system is reliant on all of the hosts that it collects and correlates data from in order to be in sync with each other. The time needs to be synchronized between all collection points. A **Network Time Protocol** (**NTP**) would be used to facilitate this. Otherwise, the events that are correlated may not be in the right order if the computer time clocks are out of synch.

- **Packet Capture**: The SIEM system has the ability to capture packets and analyze them to identify threats as soon as they reach your network. The security team can then be alerted immediately.

- **Data Inputs**: The SIEM system collects a massive amount of data from various sources, such as:

Intrusion detection systems	Desktop events
Firewall logs	Server events
Network packets	Antivirus events
Application servers	Database logs
Switches logs	Router logs

- **User Behavior Analysis** (**UBA**): This is based on the interaction of a user that focuses on their identity and the data that they would normally access in a normal day. It tracks the devices that the user normally uses and the servers that they normally visit. If you look at the behavior of one person, you may not identity attacks, but if you apply UBA to a whole company then you start to identify potential attackers as they deviate from normal patterns.

- **Security Monitoring**: This is a real-time protection and event monitoring system that correlates the security events from multiple resources, identifies a breach, and helps the security team to prevent the breach.

In the next section, we will look at **Security Orchestration, Automation, and Response** (**SOAR**) in detail.

Security Orchestration, Automation, and Response

SOAR is an automated tool that integrates all of your security processes and tools in a central location. As an automated process that is faster that humans searching for evidence of attacks, it helps reduce the **mean time to detect** (**MTTD**) and accelerates the time to respond to events.

This will produce faster alert information for the security operations team, where the human entities can take further action to keep the company safe. Let's look at the workflow in the following diagram:

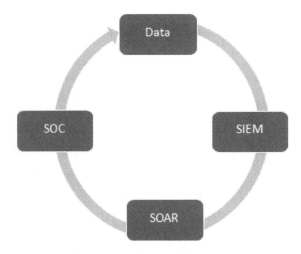

Figure 5.3 – Security integration

As you can see in the preceding diagram, we first of all sort the raw data. The data would then be sent to a syslog server and then arrive at the SIEM server. The SIEM server would then correlate the events with the SOAR tools, which in turn alert the SOC team.

Threat Hunting

Threat hunting is a dynamic process of seeking out cybersecurity threats inside your network from attackers and malware threats. According to the Security Intelligence website, an average cybercriminal can spend 191 days inside your network before being discovered. Please look at this article at the following link for more information: `https://securityintelligence.com/a-beginners-guide-to-threat-hunting/`.

Let's now look at the process of threat hunting so that we can understand it better. We will look at intelligence fusion, threat feeds, advisories and bulletins, and manoeuvre:

- **Intelligence Fusion**: Open source intelligence is available on the internet from various places such as vendor blogs, researchers, and websites such as *security week*. Please visit this URL for further details: `https://www.securityweek.com/virus-threats`. Companies such as *Crowdstrike* produce open source intelligence reports. Please refer to their 2020 report, which is available here: `https://go.crowdstrike.com/crowdstrike-2020-overwatch-threat-hunting-report-thank-you.html`. From these resources, you will have a better idea of the current threats and what you will be looking for.

- **Threat Feeds**: Open source threat feeds provide the latest information. Please look at the best resources for threat feeds listed on the *logz* website at the following URL: `https://logz.io/blog/open-source-threat-intelligence-feeds/`.

- **Advisories and Bulletins**: Advisories and security bulletins provide good advice on how to keep your company safe. The advisories tend to be government funded agencies. Bulletins tend to be released by vendors or private companies. Please look at the bulletin from the OPC foundation at the following link: `https://opcfoundation.org/SecurityBulletins/OPC%20Foundation%20Security%20Bulletin%20CVE-2017-12070.pdf`.

  Example: Let's look at two advisories, one in the US and the other in the UK. The *Cyber Security and Infrastructure Agency*, which is part of *US Government Homeland Security*, informs the public about threats. This helps you to protect your company. Please refer to *Alert (AA20-245A)* at `https://us-cert.cisa.gov/ncas/alerts/aa20-245a`. In the UK, the *National Cyber Security Centre* lists advisories at the following URL: `https://www.ncsc.gov.uk/section/keep-up-to-date/reports-advisories`.

- **Manoeuvre**: When you are going to carry out threat hunting, you first of all need to gain as much information from open source intelligence, feeds, advisories, and bulletins so that you know what you are looking for. You must also know your environment and how the applications and processes interact with each other so that you can identify what is not a threat. You must adopt the mindset of being an attacker and look for evidence of cyber attacks, but also look for any vulnerabilities from your research so that they can be secured.

Practical Exercise – Running a Credentialed Vulnerability Scanner

The **Microsoft Baseline Security Analyzer** (**MBSA**) is an example of a vulnerability scanner, but you must realize that there are others.

In this exercise, we are going to download the MBSA tool and run it against our local computer to look for vulnerabilities:

1. Go to Google and search for the *Microsoft Baseline Security Analyzer* tool. You can just enter MBSA and Google will find it.

2. Click on MBSASetup-x64-EN. The MBSA Setup wizard appears. Click **Next**, as shown in the following screenshot:

Figure 5.4 – MBSA setup page

3. Click on **I accept the license agreement** and then click **Next**:

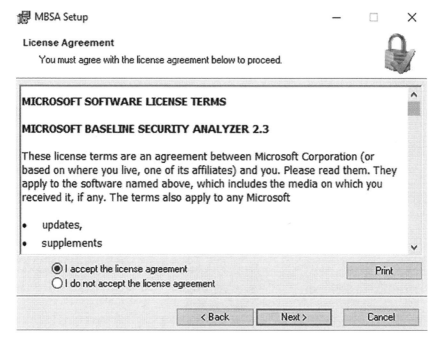

Figure 5.5 – Accepting the agreement

4. On the destination folder page, click **Next**.

5. On the **Start Installation** page, click **Install**. Then, the **Installation Progress** page will appear, as follows:

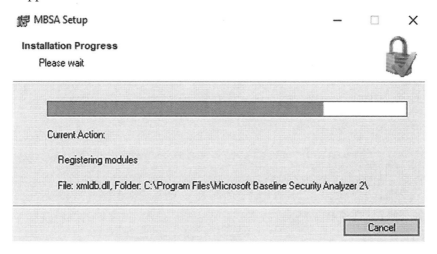

Figure 5.6 – Installation progress

6.   Then, the setup will conclude. Click **OK**:

Figure 5.7 – Installation complete

7.   A shortcut is placed on the desktop. Double-click it. The UAC prompt appears; click **Yes**:

Figure 5.8 – MBSA shortcut

8.   The MBSA Management console appears. Click **Scan a computer**, and then, in the bottom-right corner, click **Start Scan**:

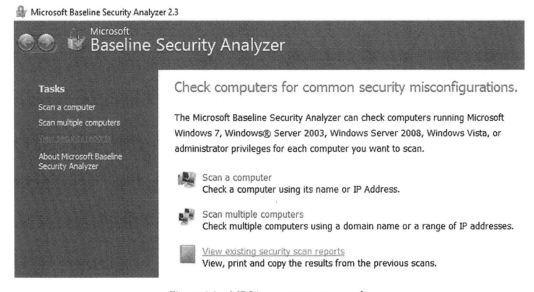

Figure 5.9 – MBSA management console

9. The scan starts and downloads security update information from Microsoft. As it compares computer updates against the latest updates for Windows 10, this will take about 10-15 minutes:

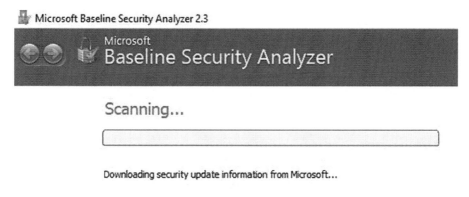

Figure 5.10 – Obtaining security updates from Microsoft

10. The scan results page appears. You will notice that the default is **Score (worst first)**:

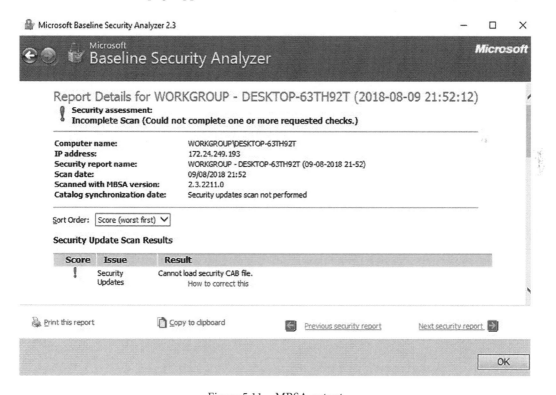

Figure 5.11 – MBSA output

11. Scroll down and you will see that the MBSA is a vulnerability scanner that is used as a credentialed scan, and that it produces some good results. However, it is passive and informational, and did not try to exploit the computer at all:

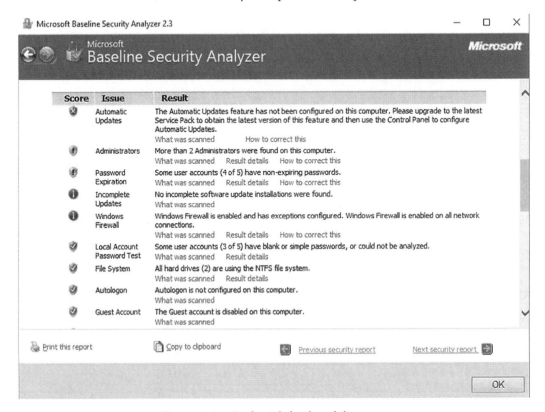

Figure 5.12 – Credentialed vulnerability scan

You can now see whether or not you have any vulnerabilities on your computer. There are hyperlinks below each item listed, giving you information on how to update your vulnerabilities.

Review Questions

Now it's time to check your knowledge. Answer the questions, and then check your answers, which can be found in the *Assessments* section at the end of the book:

1. Which pen tester would be given source code?

2. Why would a shared account pose a problem to monitoring?

3. Which pen tester would be given no access prior to the test but, at the last minute, is given a diagram of the desktops?

4. What needs to be established prior to a pen test commencing?

5. While carrying out an unannounced pen test, how does the tester know if the internal security team are on to him?

6. What is the scope of rules of engagement?

7. If the pen test has been announced to the IT team, what information should they give regarding the test prior to the test starting?

8. What is the main difference between a credentialed and a non-credentialed vulnerability scan?

9. At what phase of a pen test does the tester return the systems back to the original state or inform the IT team of vulnerabilities that need patching?

10. What is OSINT? Is it legal?

11. What is the purpose of the red team?

12. What is the purpose of the blue team?

13. What is the purpose of the white team?

14. What is the purpose of the purple team?

15. When evaluating CVSS scores, which vulnerabilities should you deal with first?

16. Describe a false positive.

17. What is a true positive?

18. What is the difference between intrusive and non-intrusive scans?

19. What is regression testing and who will carry it out?

20. When would dynamic analysis be carried out?

21. What is a syslog server and what purpose does it serve?

22. Why does a SIEM server rely on synchronized time clocks between all of the servers and devices that it collects data from?

23. What is the purpose of threat hunting?

6
Understanding Secure and Insecure Protocols

In this chapter, we will be looking at secure protocols and their uses, known as **use cases**. We will also cover insecure protocols, as you need to know their functions so that you know which secure protocol is the most suitable one to replace it with. The topics discussed in this chapter appear very often in the Security+ exam.

In this chapter, we are going to cover the following topics:

- Introduction to Protocols
- Insecure Protocols and Their Use Cases
- Secure Protocols and Their Use Cases
- Additional Use Cases and Their Protocols

Introduction to Protocols

Protocol refers to the rules required by different applications for the exchange of data, where the application can perform actions such as running commands on remote systems, sending and receiving emails, and downloading files from the internet. Each application has a special port number that it uses for communication. You can think of ports as being TV channels: if we want to watch sport, we go to the sports channels; if we want to watch the news, we go to the news channel. Applications are the same – if we want to send an email, we use an email application – and they all have a distinct port number for each communication mode.

There are two types of ports: **Transmission Control Protocol** (**TCP**) and **User Datagram Protocol** (**UDP**). The main difference between the two is that TCP is connection-oriented as it uses a three-way handshake, and UDP is faster but less reliable as it is connectionless. The following diagram shows the three-way handshake:

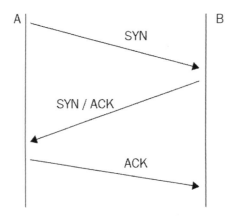

Figure 6.1 – Three-way handshake

In a three-way handshake, the first packet that is sent is called a **SYN** packet, where the sending host informs the receiving host of the number of its next packet. The receiving host sends a **SYN/ACK** packet, where it says what its next packet is. The **ACK** packet acknowledges both kinds of packets, and then the data is sent. The data is sent in chunks, and when it is received, an acknowledgment is sent that tells the sending host to send more packets. Once all of the data is sent, a three-way handshake confirms that all of the data is intact and the session closes.

In a UDP session, the application is responsible for ensuring that everything is received, and because a three-way handshake is not used, the connection is faster but less reliable. You would use UDP for streaming video and gaming, where speed is paramount.

Insecure Protocols and Their Use Cases

In this section, we are going to look in detail at the different *insecure protocols* and their use cases.

Insecure Protocols			
Protocol	**UDP**	**Port**	**Use Case**
File Transfer Protocol (FTP)		21	File transfer – passive FTP
Telnet		23	Run commands on remote hosts
Simple Mail Transport Protocol (SMTP)		25	Transport mail between Mail Servers
Domain Name System (DNS)		53	Host name resolution
	TCP/UDP	53	Zone transfer
		53	Name queries
Dynamic Host Configuration Protocol (DHCP)	UDP	67/68	Automatic IP address allocation
Trivial File Transfer Protocol (TFTP)	UDP	69	File transfer using UDP
Hypertext Transport Protocol (HTTP)		80	Web browser
Post Office Protocol 3		110	Pull mail from mail server, no copy left on mail server
Network Time Protocol (NTP)		123	Time synchronization
NETBIOS	UDP	137-139	NETBIOS to IP address resolution
Internet Message Access Protocol (IMAP 4)		143	Pulls mail from mail server
Simple Network Management Protocol (SNMP)	UDP	161	Notifies the status and creates reports on network devices
Lightweight Directory Access Protocol (LDAP)		389	Stores X500 objects, searches Directory services for users and groups and other information

Let's look at each of them:

- **FTP**: Transferring files is a common function. When we purchase an e-book, it is immediately available to download onto our Kindle. If I wish to upload files to a web server, I would use FTP on port 20, but the more common use is to download files using port 21, which is known as **Passive FTP**. The downside of using FTP is that the transfer is done using clear text, so a packet sniffer could view the information. It could be replaced by secure protocols such as SFTP or FTPS.

- **Telnet**: This is a protocol that was first used in 1973 to run remote commands on devices such as routers. Unfortunately, the session is in clear text and therefore not secure. If you want to know whether port 25 is open on a mail server called **Mail1**, you could run `telnet Mail1 25`. It is no longer used as it is insecure, but it may be tested. SSH is a secure protocol that replaced Telnet.

- **DHCP**: This allocates IP addresses dynamically to computers. If a computer cannot obtain an IP address, then either there is a faulty cable or there are no more IP addresses in the database, leading to resource exhaustion.

- **TFTP**: This is the UDP version of a file transfer; it is faster than FTP as it does not use a three-way handshake, but it is not secure as the files are transferred in clear text. It is used when user authentication is not required. It can be used to **Pre-boot eXecution Environment** (PXE) boot workstations prior to reimaging them.

- **HTTP**: This is used to access websites, no matter whether you are using Internet Explorer, Chrome, Firefox, or Microsoft Edge.

- **NTP**: This ensures that the clock times of all computers and servers are synchronized – here are a couple of examples of its use:

  Example 1: Kerberos needs the times for all of the clients and servers to be within 5 minutes of each other or users may not be able to log in or access resources.

  Example 2: SIEM servers collect logs and events from multiple servers and computers across the network. If the times are not synchronized, then the events cannot be put in chronological order.

- **SNMP**: Each network device has an agent installed and is programmed so that if a trigger is met, the SNMP management console is notified. SNMP can monitor the status of network devices and provide reports if required.

- **LDAP**: This is the insecure version of LDAP that creates, stores, and manages objects in a directory service.

There are different types of email protocols; some are web-based and some use the MAPI client on the desktop. Let's look at the insecure versions:

- **SMTP**: This is used to transfer files between different mail servers and is used for outbound emails.

- **Post Office Protocol 3 (POP3)**: This is an email client that pulls email from the mail server, but when the email is downloaded, it does not retain a copy on the mail server itself. It is not commonly used but is tested in the Security+ exam. There is also a secure version of POP3.

- **Internet Message Access Protocol Version 4 (IMAP4)**: A mail client that also pulls emails from the mail server, but it has more functionality than POP3 as a copy of the message is retained on the mail server. It can also provide tasks, calendars, and journaling. There is also a secure version of IMAP.

There are two types of **Name Resolution**: hostname resolution, which is the most common, and NETBIOS, which is a legacy name resolution that is very rarely used.

The most common form of name resolution is hostname resolution, where a database of hostnames for IP addresses called a DNS uses a flat file called the `hosts` file:

- **DNS**: This is a hierarchical naming system that takes a hostname and resolves it to an IP address. I don't need to know the actual IP address. If I want to go to the Microsoft website, I know that I need to enter `www.microsoft.com` in my web browser and it will take me there. If I had a user called Ian in a domain called `securityplus.training`, the hostname portion would be Ian and the **Fully Qualified Domain Name (FQDN)** would be `ian.securityplus.training`. The record types for the DNS database are as follows:

   a. **A**: IPv4 host

   b. **AAAA**: IPv6 host

   c. **CNAME**: Alias

   d. **MX**: Mail server

   e. **SRV Records**: Finds services such as a domain controller

For example, say a user would like to visit the website `ianneil501.com`; to get there, they would enter `www.ianneil501.com` in their web browser:

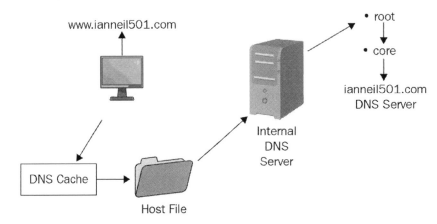

Figure 6.2 – DNS name resolution

Hostname resolution adopts a strict process and takes the first entry for the hostname no matter whether it is right or wrong—this is a pitfall of the process. In the preceding example, the DNS cache is empty, so it would move onto the `hosts` file located on the local computer and then the DNS server.

If you needed to view the DNS cache, you would run the `ipconfig/displaydns` command, and if you wanted to clear the DNS cache, you would run the `ipconfig/flushdns` command. Let's look at this process, starting with the DNS cache:

a. **DNS Cache**: This stores recently resolved names; attackers will attempt to poison the DNS cache by putting in incorrect entries to divert you to an alternative illegitimate server. DNSSEC helps prevent DNS poisoning.

b. **The Hosts File**: This is a flat file where entries are manually inserted and read from top to bottom. The first entry is always taken, whether right or wrong. The purpose of a host file is that if one user needs to go to a server called Sneaky Beaky, you would put an entry for the Sneaky Beaky server in their local `hosts` file that would allow them to go there. If you put the entry in the DNS server, that would allow anyone to find that server.

c. **DNS Server**: This normally maintains only the hostnames for your domain. It needs to complete a referral process through the root server of the internet, which is represented by a dot. The `nslookup` command is used to verify DNS entries held by the DNS server.

d. **Root Server**: The root server refers requests to the `.com` server, which in turn refers requests to the authoritative DNS server for the `ianneil501.com` domain (in our previous example), which then replies with the IP address of the website.

e. **Caching the Reply**: A copy of the name resolution is placed in the DNS cache for future use.

- **NETBIOS**: This is a Microsoft legacy naming convention that has a flat namespace that can have a maximum of 15 characters with a service identifier. Each computer name has three separate entries in its database, called *WINS*, and it uses a flat file called the `LMHosts` file. The entry for PC1 as a WINS database would be as follows:

PC1 <00>: `<00>` represents the workstation service.

PC2 <03>: `<03>` represents the messenger service.

PC3 <20>: `<20>` represents the server service.

In the past, when companies wanted meetings, such as a sales meeting, a date was set and the salespeople kept their schedule open, traveled to the location of the meeting the night before, and booked themselves into a hotel. This was very costly and time-consuming; nowadays, we use **Videoconferencing**, where everyone can attend the meeting, they do not have to travel, and can free their schedule more easily, making them more productive. In the Security+ exam, we need to be able to understand which protocols are used for such videoconferences:

- **Real-Time Protocol (RTP)**: Once **Session Initiation Protocol (SIP)** has established a session, RTP transfers the video-conferencing traffic. RTP can be replaced by the secure version, SRTP.

- **Media Gateway**: This allows different methods of video and voice to communicate with each other; for example, if you use an XMPP gateway, you can connect Jabber clients to a Skype session.

> **Exam tip**
> Both Kerberos and SIEM systems are reliant upon an NTP server to synchronize times between the nodes on a network.

Secure Protocols and Their Use Cases

In this section, we are going to look in detail at the various *secure protocols* and their use cases. The Security+ exam wants you to select the correct secure protocol for a given scenario to make your environment secure.

As most protocols use TCP ports, I will only mention the UDP ports, and therefore you can assume that if something is not labeled UDP, it is TCP. We will look at the secure protocols and their use cases:

Secure Protocols			
Protocol	UDP	Port	Use Case
Secure Shell (SSH)		22	Secure remote access
Secure Copy Protocol (SCP)		22	Secure copy to UNIX/LINUX
SSH File Transfer Protocol (SFTP)		22	Secure FTP download
DNSSEC	TCP/UDP	53	Secure DNS traffic
Kerberos		88	Secure authentication
Simple Network Management Protocol Version 3 (SNMP v3)	UDP	162	Secure status and reports of network devices
Lightweight Directory Access Protocol Secure (LDAPS)		389	Manages directory service information securely
Hypertext Transport Protocol Secure (HTTPS)		443	Secure Web Browser
Transport Layer Security (TLS)/Secure Socket Layer (SSL)		443	Secure Data in Transit
Internet Protocol Security (IPSec)	UDP	500	Secure session for VPN or between two hosts
Secure Simple Mail Transfer Protocol (SMTPS)		587	Secure SMTP
Secure Internet Message Access Protocol (IMAP 4)		993	Secure IMAP4
Secure Post Office Protocol 3		995	Secure POP3
Secure/Multipurpose Internet Mail Extensions (S/MIME)		993	Encrypt or digitally sign email
File Transfer Protocol Secure (FTPS)		989/990	Download large files securely
Remote Desktop Protocol (RDP)		3389	Microsoft remote access
Session Initiated Protocol (SIP)		5060/61	Connects internet-based calls
Secure Real Time Protocol (SRTP)		5061	Secure voice traffic

Let's look at each of them:

- **SSH**: This was invented to replace Telnet so that commands could be run securely; it is commonly used when you want remote access to network devices. It can be used as a command-line tool or in a **Graphical User Interface (GUI)**, but it is not browser-based.

- **SCP**: This is used to transfer files securely between hosts in a Linux environment.

- **SFTP**: This allows us to encrypt authentication and download files securely so that they cannot be tampered with. It is secure as it is packaged with SSH.

- **DNSSEC**: To prevent someone from gaining access to DNS records, DNSSEC was introduced to protect DNS traffic. Each DNS record is digitally signed, creating an RRSIG record to protect against attacks, guaranteeing you that they are valid and their integrity has been maintained. This prevents DNS poisoning.

- **Kerberos**: Kerberos is the authentication system used to log in to directory services and uses tickets for authentication. The user completes a session, called a **Ticket Granting Ticket (TGT)** session, and obtains a 10-hour service ticket. When the user tries to access email, their computer exchanges their encrypted service ticket for a session ticket, meaning the authentication is mutual and secure. All computers must have their time synchronized to be within 5 minutes of the domain controller's time. This replaces the insecure NTLM authentication and protects against pass-the-hash attacks.

  Each update to a directory service object is done by giving the change an **Updated Sequence Number (USN)**. For example, if one change is USN 23, the change after that must be USN 24, and it is stamped with the time it happens, which is known as *being timestamped*. Kerberos prevents replay attacks, where an interception is performed and information is altered and replayed at a later time. As the timestamps and USNs become out of sequence in such cases, the traffic is rejected.

- **SNMP v3**: SNMP v3 is the secure version of SNMP, as it authenticates and encrypts data packets. Each network device has an agent installed and is programmed so that if a trigger is met, the SNMP management console is notified. SNMP can monitor the status of network devices and provide reports if required.

- **LDAPS**: When objects are created in directory services, they are securely managed by LDAPS. LDAPS creates and stores objects in X500 format and uses three parameters: DC for domain, OU for organization unit, and CN for anything else. If I have a computer called **Computer 1** in an organizational unit called **Sales** in a domain called `DomainA.com`, the distinguished name would be `CN=Computer1`, `OU=Sales`, `DC=DomainA`, `DC=com`. Because the domain is in two portions separated by a dot, there will be two DC components. The following screenshot is from **ADSI Edit** and shows how it is sorted:

Figure 6.3 – ADSI Edit

When a systems administrator has 10,000 users and needs to find one of them, they use the search facility and LDAP brings back the result of the search.

- **HTTPS**: This can be used to secure a web page but is more commonly used when making a purchase on a website, where you will be diverted to a secure server that uses HTTPS so that your session is secure and you can then enter your credit or debit card details. It can also be used for webmail and to complete web forms securely.

- **TLS**: TLS is used to protect data in transit and is an upgraded version of SSL that is used to encrypt communications on the internet, such as email or internet faxing, and transfer data securely. It can be used in a web browser. When you start using secure email, the change from insecure email is done using the `STARTTLS` command.

- **IPSec**: IPSec can be used with L2TP/IPSec to provide a VPN session. An IPSec packet is in two separate portions: an **Authenticated Header** (**AH**) and then an **Encapsulated Security Payload** (**ESP**).

The header is hashed by using SHA1, which is 160 bit, or MD5, which is 128 bit, to confirm the integrity of the packet. The encapsulated payload is the data and it is encrypted by DES (56 bit), 3DES (168 bit), or AES (128, 192, or 256 bit). These are symmetric encryptions using block ciphers and are used to encrypt large amounts of data:

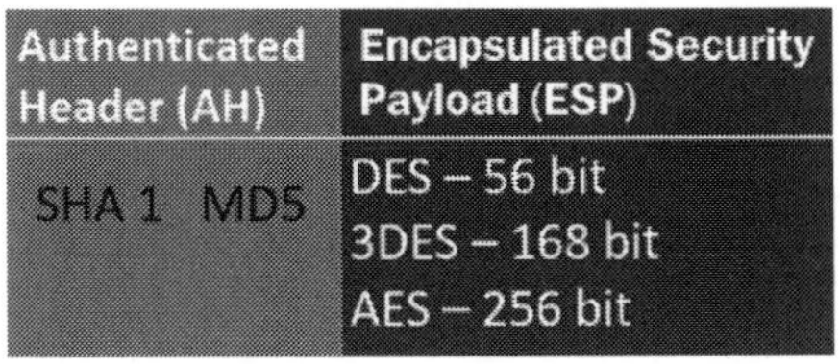

Authenticated Header (AH)	Encapsulated Security Payload (ESP)
SHA 1 MD5	DES – 56 bit 3DES – 168 bit AES – 256 bit

Figure 6.4 – IPSec packet

IPSec can be used to create a secure session between two hosts on a network and it has two different modes:

a. **Tunnel Mode**: This is used with L2TP/IPSec VPNs, where both the header and the payload are encrypted. It's normally used externally.

b. **Transport Mode**: This is used between two servers or hosts on an internal network, where only the payload is encrypted.

> **Exam tip**
> IPSec can be used in tunnel mode with L2TP/IPSec and in transport mode between servers in a local area network.

- **SMTPS**: This is secure SMTP and it uses TLS for encryption. It uses the `STARTTLS` command, which secures email.

- **IMAP 4**: This is an email client that has the ability to manage tasks and diaries.

- **Secure Post Office Protocol 3**: This is a legacy email client that does not leave copies of messages on the mail server.

- **S/MIME**: This uses **Public Key Infrastructure** (**PKI**) to either encrypt emails or digitally sign emails to prove the integrity of the message. It is very cumbersome as it requires each user to exchange their public key with others and does not scale very well.

- **FTPS**: This protocol is used to transfer large files securely, as it uses TLS to set up a secure tunnel before downloading the files, and this makes it faster. FTPS has two different modes:

  a. **Implicit Mode**: This negotiates a secure session using TCP port 990 for the control channel and 998 for the data channel.

  b. **Explicit Mode**: This is known as FTPES, where the client must request security; if they do not, the session will be refused.

- **RDP**: A Microsoft product that allows you to run a secure remote access session on a Windows desktop or server. When you set up remote access using RDP, the service obtaining the session needs to allow access for incoming remote sessions and then place the users into a remote desktop user group. If these two actions are not taken, it will not work. As most routers are CISCO products, RDP cannot be used to remotely access a router or any other networking device—only Microsoft products.

- **SIP**: This allows people all over the internet, and those with VoIP, to communicate using their computers, tablets, and smartphones. An example of this would be a secretary receiving a Skype call for their boss: SIP allows them to put the caller on hold, speak with their boss, and, if needs be, put the caller through.

- **SRTP**: This is used to secure video-conferencing traffic—it normally uses TCP port 5061. Voice traffic can be placed in its own VLAN to separate it from the rest of the network, therefore guaranteeing bandwidth.

> **Exam tip**
> You must know the purposes of the secure protocols and their associated ports.

Additional Use Cases and Their Protocols

In this section, we are going to look at additional use cases for subscription services, routing, switching, and Active Directory.

Subscription Services and Their Protocols

In the past, the traditional method for purchasing application software was to purchase the application on a DVD from a local store or wait 3-4 days for it to be delivered from Amazon. At that time, you would have to pay $300–$400 for the software. With the advent and evolution of the cloud, you can now obtain your applications through subscription services, where you pay a monthly fee and can download the application immediately.

Two examples of this are as follows:

- **Office 365**: Office 365 is from Microsoft, where you not only get email services, but you also get Skype, SharePoint, and Office applications.

- **Adobe Acrobat Pro**: Adobe Acrobat Pro is one of the premier applications that allows you to create and modify PDF files.

Routing and Its Protocols

The purpose of a router is to connect networks together, whether they are internal subnets or external networks, and route packets between them. A router sits at Layer 3 of the OSI reference model, where the data packets are known as IP packets, as Layer 3 of the OSI deals with IP addressing and delivery. If we look at the following figure, we can see five different routers that connect networks between **New York**, **Dublin**, **Paris**, **London**, and **Edinburgh**:

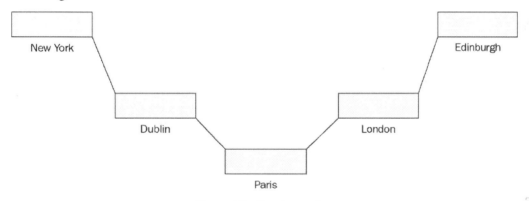

Figure 6.5 – Routing packets

If we think of these routers as post offices delivering mail, it may make it easier to understand. If mail arrives at the Paris post office, the people working there have two sacks, one for Dublin and the other for London; they just need to know where to send the mail next. They cannot have sacks for every destination in the world; it is just not feasible:

- **Example 1**: If mail arrives at the Paris post office and is destined for Edinburgh, the post office staff knows that they just need to put the mail in the London sack. Once the mail arrives in London, there will be two different sacks, one destined for Edinburgh and the other destined for Paris. The workers know to place the mail for Edinburgh in the Edinburgh sack.

- **Example 2**: If mail arrives at the Paris post office and is destined for New York, they know to place it in the Dublin sack. Once the mail arrives in Dublin, it is placed in the New York sack.

Routing packets is no more difficult than moving mail around the world; the router has many routes in a routing table and knows the next hop for packet delivery. Several protocols are used in the management and control of IP packets going through the router:

- **Access Control List (ACL)**: The router will have to allow rules at the top of the ACL, but the last rule is to deny all. It can restrict traffic based on IP addresses, protocols, and port numbers. If traffic that is not on the list arrives, then the last rule of denial will apply—this is known as **Implicit Deny**.

- **SSH**: SSH is used to remotely access the router and run commands securely.

> **Exam tip**
>
> A client might not obtain an IP address from a DHCP server due to network connectivity issues or resource exhaustion, where there are no IP addresses left to lease.

Switching and Its Protocols

A switch is an internal device that connects all of the users in a local area network so that they can communicate with each other. A computer connects to a wall jack into a patch panel, and then from the patch panel to the switch:

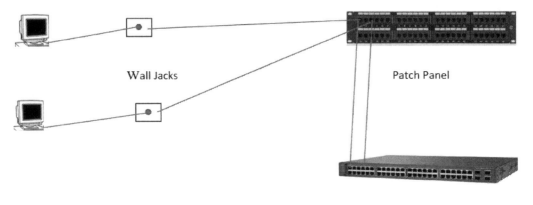

Figure 6.6 – Connecting to a switch

Let's look at the functionality and protocols used by a switch:

- **802.1x**: A managed switch is called 802.1x, where the switch identifies and authenticates devices connecting to the switch and blocks rogue devices, such as rogue access points, without the need to switch the port off. It controls the flow of traffic from wireless to wired communication and can work in conjunction with a **Remote Authentication Dial-In User Service** (**RADIUS**) server for authentication. Each device has an X509 certificate for identification.

- **Port Security**: Port security is where a port in a switch is switched off to prevent someone from plugging their laptop into a wall jack.

- **Flood Guard**: A flood guard is used in a switch to prevent **Media Access Control** (**MAC**) flooding, where the switch is flooded with a high volume of fake MAC addresses; this prevents **distributed denial-of-service** (**DDoS**) attacks.

- **VLAN**: VLANs can be set up on a switch to segment network traffic. For example, if the finance department wanted to be isolated from other departments within the local area network, a VLAN could be created. The VLAN tag must be set up; otherwise, the switch will not know where to send the traffic. You may also put machines that could be used for electronic bank transfers or credit card payments into their own VLAN for better security.

- **Spanning Tree Protocol** (**STP**): When more than one switch is connected, you may have redundant paths, and this causes looping that provides broadcast traffic. STP has an algorithm that sets up some ports to forward, listen, or block traffic to prevent looping.

Active Directory (Directory Services) and Its Protocols

Microsoft's Active Directory is a very common directory service, and we are going to look at the components and protocols used by it:

- **LDAP**: When objects are created in Active Directory, it is done by completing a wizard, then LDAP stores them as X500 objects. Therefore, it is the Active Directory store person. For example, LDAP is the same as a shopkeeper who sells shoes. When a delivery arrives, the shoes are unloaded and stored at the back of the shop. When a customer arrives and cannot see the size they want, they ask the shopkeeper, who goes to the storeroom to find the shoes. When a systems administrator opens up a wizard in Active Directory and creates a user account, LDAP creates and stores objects in X500 format. If the administrator has 10,000 users and needs to find a user, they use the search facility and LDAP brings back the result of the search.

- **LDAPS**: LDAPS performs the same function as LDAP; however, LDAP is not secure and is vulnerable to LDAP injection attacks, where an attacker tries to gain information from the directory service. Using LDAPS encrypts the session using SSL/TLS—this is known as LDAP over SSL—making it secure.

- **Kerberos**: Kerberos is the authentication system used to log in to Active Directory and uses tickets for authentication.

Review Questions

Now it's time to check your knowledge. Answer the questions, and then check your answers, which can be found in the Assessments section at the end of the book:

1. What is the authentication protocol that uses tickets and prevents replay attacks?

2. Describe how IPSec tunnel mode works.

3. Describe how IPSec transport mode works.

4. If an IT administrator uses Telnet to run remote commands on a router, which secure protocol can it be replaced with?

5. What is the purpose of a router?

6. What is the purpose of a switch?

7. What type of service is Spotify?

8. Explain how port security works.

9. Describe how a managed switch with 802.1x works.

10. What are the three portions of a distinguished name and the order that they come in?

11. Which protocol can I use to prevent DNS poisoning?

12. What are the two reasons why a computer might not receive an IP address from a DHCP server?

13. What type of server would both an SIEM server and a Microsoft domain controller benefit from having installed on their network?

14. If two companies rented offices on the same floor of a building, what could the building administrator implement to isolate them from each other?

15. What is the purpose of STP?

16. If a network administrator wanted to collect the statuses and reports of network devices, what secure protocol could they use?

17. If a network administrator wants to set up a VPN, what is the most secure protocol that they can use?

18. Which secure protocol can be used to prevent a pass-the-hash attack?

19. Which protocol protects data in transit?

20. Which protocol can be used to digitally sign an email between two people?

21. Which protocol can be used to secure video conferencing?

22. Which protocol allows a user to put a Skype session on hold, speak to another person, and then come back to the first caller?

23. A system administrator is managing a directory service using a protocol that uses TCP port 389. What protocol are they using and which protocol can be used to carry out the same task securely?

24. Say I use the `nbtstat -an` command and the output shows me the following:

    `IAN <00>`

    `IAN <20>`

    What naming convention is used and what format is being shown?

25. What protocol can be used to transfer large files remotely?

7
Delving into Network and Security Concepts

There are many network components and topologies (layouts) that we need to know about in order to maintain a secure environment. We are going to look at each of these in turn. We need to know how each device is configured and which device is the most appropriate to use in different scenarios.

In this chapter, we will look at the following topics:

- Installing and Configuring Network Components
- Remote Access Capabilities
- Secure Network Architecture Concepts
- Network Reconnaissance and Discovery
- Forensic Tools
- IP Addressing

Installing and Configuring Network Components

There are many different network components and we are going to look at each of these. For the Security+ exam, we need to know which device can be used in different scenarios, so let's first of all look at firewalls that prevent unauthorized access and then the other devices.

Firewall

A firewall prevents unauthorized access to the corporate network, and in the Security+ exam, we tend to use a back-to-back configuration, as shown here:

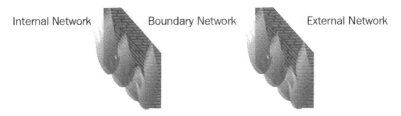

Figure 7.1 – Back-to-back firewall configuration

You can see that each of these firewalls is not letting traffic pass through them; this is because we need to open only the ports that we need. If the firewall on the right is traversed, then the firewall on the left will hopefully prevent access to the internal network, known as the **Local Area Network** (**LAN**). To enable applications to pass through the firewall, we must open the port number for each application. Each application has a different port number. If you think of someone who wants to watch the news, the Democrats watch CNN on channel 21 and the Republicans will watch Fox News on channel 29. Each TV program has a different channel number.

If we want to enable internet access, we should make an exception to the **Hypertext Transfer Protocol** (**HTTP**) on TCP port 80. This is the port number that each web server uses for communication and it does not matter whether they use Internet Explorer, Microsoft Edge, Google Chrome, or Firefox. Each of these applications uses TCP port 80 for web traffic.

The directions of ports are outbound, coming from the internal network and going to the external network, or inbound, coming from the external network and going to the internal network. If we opened only the outbound port for port 80, the request would go out, but the incoming response would be prevented.

The main purpose of a firewall is to prevent unauthorized access to the network. The default setting is to block all traffic allowed by exception. There are many different firewalls:

- **Host-Based Firewall**: This is an application firewall that is built into desktop operating systems, such as the Windows 10 operating system:

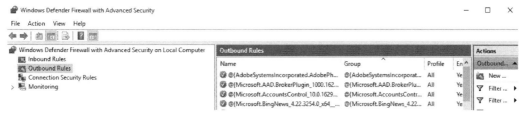

Figure 7.2 – Host-based firewall

As the host-based firewall is an application on a desktop, it is vulnerable to attack. If someone disables the service running the Windows firewall service, then the firewall is disabled, and the computer becomes vulnerable. The following screenshot shows the firewall service in a **Running** state:

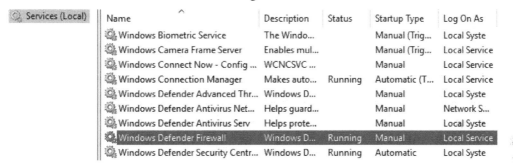

Figure 7.3 – Windows Firewall service

- **Network-Based Firewall**: This is a hardware appliance that keeps the network safe. It is vital that only the ports required are open. One of the configurations is the back-to-back configuration, where two layers of firewall are rolled out (see *Figure 7.1*). The network-based firewall is placed at the edge of the network to prevent unauthorized access.

- **Stateful Firewall**: This looks deep at the application and its traffic to see whether it is allowed through. For example, a packet arrives with the Get<webpage> command, and since the Get verb in HTTP is the request to view a web page, the traffic is allowed. However, if the HTTP verbs use the PUT verb, which could be used to deface the web page, it is blocked. If HEAD is used, it tries to pull down the website header information and it is also blocked. The stateful firewall knows the size of each packet and will block traffic that is not the size that it should be.

- **Stateless Firewall**: The stateless firewall could also be called a *packet-filtering firewall*. It only looks at whether the packet is permitted and never looks in depth at the packet format.

- **Web Application Firewall** (**WAF**): The WAF is placed on a web server and its role is to protect web-based applications running on the web server.

- **Unified Threat Management Firewall** (**UTM**): The UTM is a multipurpose firewall: it does malware, content, and URL filtering. It is known as an all-in-one security appliance.

- **Next Generation Firewall** (**NGFW**): This is a firewall that is application aware. It has cloud threat intelligence and the capabilities of an intrusion prevention system.

- **Open Source versus Proprietary**: An open source firewall is cheaper than a proprietary one and may have a limited number of licenses. Knowledge of the open source firewall is available to anyone, whereas a proprietary firewall is more expensive but may give better protection. There is no vendor support with open source.

> **Exam tip**
>
> A UTM firewall is an all-in-one security appliance that acts as a firewall and does content and URL filtering. It can also inspect malware.

Network Address Translation Gateway

Network Address Translation (**NAT**) is where a request from a private internal IP address is translated to an external public IP address, hiding the internal network from external attack (refer to *Figure 7.4*):

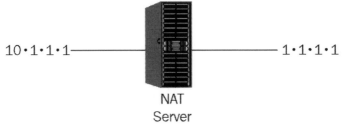

Figure 7.4 – NAT

A NAT could be set up to hide an R&D network as a competitor may try to steal your new ideas and get them to market before you. A NAT could be set up on a firewall or a NAT server and is also used to protect a cloud VPC.

Router

A router is a device that connects two different networks together when setting up a host machine; it is known as the *default gateway*. It is used by your company to give you access to other networks, for example, the internet. It has a routing table built into it, so it knows which route can be used to deliver network packets. The router is the IP equivalent of a post office sending letters around the world, but instead of letters, IP packets are being transported.

Quality of Service (**QOS**) ensures that applications have the amount of bandwidth they need to operate when there is limited network bandwidth.

Access Control List – Network Devices

The **Access Control List** (**ACL**) for network devices must not be confused with the ACL for files and folders; they are totally different. Two network devices that use the ACL are firewalls and routers. The ACL prevents access by using port numbers, application names, or IP addresses. When you install a new firewall or router, there are no rules, except the last rule of deny all. The default for either a router or firewall is to block all access allowed by creating exceptions by configuring allow rules for the traffic you want to allow through. If there are no allow rules, the last rule of deny applies. This is called an **Implicit Deny**.

Example: John has been doing some online shopping and bought a pair of shoes, but he cannot download the new book that he bought. He has used HTTP to gain access to a website, and then gone to the secure server for payment, using HTTPS for purchases to protect his credit card details. However, when trying to download the book, the traffic is being blocked by the firewall. The ACL allows TCP port 80 (HTTP) and TCP port 443 (HTTPS), but there is no allow rule for the FTP that uses TCP port 21:

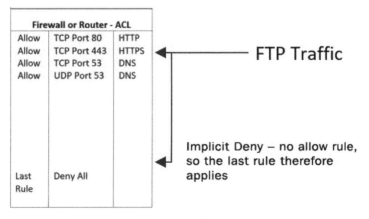

Figure 7.5 – Implicit Deny

As there is a no allow rule on the firewall for FTP traffic, when the FTP traffic arrives, it is checked against the allow rules, and if there is no matching rule, it then drops down to the last rule, denying all traffic. This is known as Implicit Deny. Although the example is for a firewall, an ACL is used by the router. Both devices are filtering incoming traffic.

Switch

A switch is an internal device that connects all users in a LAN. The switch has a table listing the MAC addresses of the host connected to it:

Figure 7.6 – Switch

Once the switch has been installed, it builds up a routing table; each host is identified by their MAC address. The switch delivers the packet only to the host that requires the packet. Switches can be stacked when there are more than 48 users connected to the network:

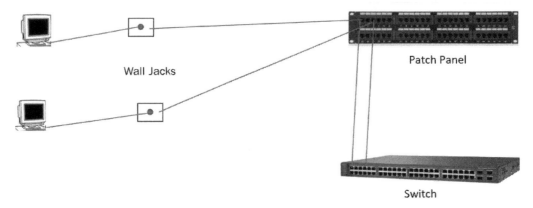

Figure 7.7 – Network connections

A computer has an Ethernet cable that plugs into a wall jack, and then the wall jack is connected to the patch panel by cables that are laid under floors or above ceilings. A user cannot see them. From the patch panel, there is a cable that goes into one port on the switch. The Ethernet cabling is placed inside a conduit to protect the cable. It is very easy to plug a cable into a wall jack. Therefore, the network administrator must place security for each of these ports on the switch.

There are two types, 802.1x and port security and other protection that can be configured:

- **Port Security**: When anyone, authorized or not, plugs their Ethernet cable into the wall jack, the switch allows all the traffic. The only way to protect this port is to enable port security where the port is turned off. This is not a good practice as you are limiting the functionality of the switch.

- **802.1x**: When a network administrator uses 802.1x port security, the device itself is authenticated by a certificate before a connection is made. It will prevent an unauthorized device from connecting and allow an authorized device to connect. The benefit of 802.1x over port security is that none of the ports on the switch have been disabled and the switch has full functionality.

- The others are as follows:

  – **Loop Protection**: When two or more switches are joined together, they can create loops that create broadcast storms. We need to use the **Spanning Tree Protocol (STP)** to prevent this from happening by forwarding, listening, or blocking on some ports.

  – **Bridge Protocol Data Units** (**BPDU**): These are frames that contain information about the STP. A BPDU attack will try and spoof the root bridge so that the STP is recalculated. A BPDU Guard enables the STP to stop such attempts.

  – **MAC Filtering**: Every device that has a network interface, whether it is wired or wireless, has a unique address on its network interface called the **Media Access Control** (**MAC**) address. If one MAC address is added to the MAC filtering list, then all other devices wishing to use the wireless access point must be added to the MAC filtering list or they will be blocked:

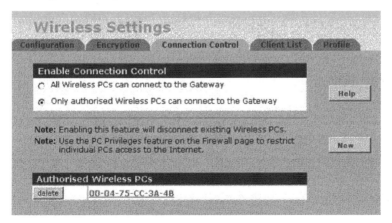

Figure 7.8 – MAC filtering

> **Exam tip**
> If you want to prevent someone from plugging their laptop into a reception area, we will use port security to shut that port down. But if you want to prevent a rogue server or a wireless access point from connecting to the network, we will use 802.1x port security, which authenticates the device.

Tap/Port Mirror

A tap or a port mirror (also known as *port spanning*) is set up on a port of a switch so that when the data arrives at that port, a splitter sends a copy to another device for later investigation, or it is sent to a sensor that will investigate the traffic and, if need be, inform the **Network Intrusion Detection System** (**NIDS**) of changes in traffic patterns.

Aggregation Switches

Link aggregation allows you to connect multiple switches together so that they work as a single logical unit and prevent looping:

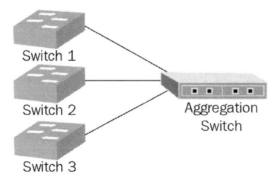

Figure 7.9 – Aggregation switch

This is used for fast recovery if one link fails.

Honeypot

When security teams are trying to find out the attack methods that hackers are using, they set up a website similar to the legitimate website with lower security, known as a **honeypot**. When the attack commences, the security team monitors the attack methods so that they can prevent future attacks. Another reason a honeypot is set up is as a decoy so that the real web server is not attacked. A group of honeypots is called a honeynet.

> **Exam tip**
> A honeypot can be used to examine the attack methods that hackers use.

Proxy Server

A proxy server is a server that controls requests from clients seeking resources on the internet or an external network. Think of it as a go-between that makes requests on behalf of the client, ensuring that anyone outside of your network does not know the details of the requesting host. The proxy server maintains a log file of every request, and so can track a user's internet usage.

The flow of data is from internal to external, and so is known as a **forward proxy**:

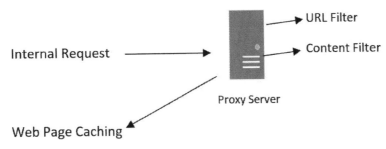

Figure 7.10 – Forward proxy

It has three main functions: URL filter, content filter, and web page caching:

- **URL Filter**: When a user goes to a website, they type the URL, for example, www. nfl.com. Companies may not want their employees going to Facebook or Twitter during working hours, so these websites are placed on the default block page. The URL filter checks the default block page to see whether there is a website that should be blocked. You will get a warning stating that the page is blocked and you cannot access it. Additionally, your attempt to access it will be logged.

- **Content Filter**: Looks at the content on the requested web page. It will block the request if the site involves gambling or inappropriate content.

- **Web Page Caching**: Most companies within the same industry tend to go to certain websites related to their line of business, or at lunchtimes people look at the sport results. Each time they go to the internet, a session is opened through the firewall. This allows an unsecured session to be seen and also consumes bandwidth. A more secure way of doing this is to have a proxy server cache the pages, but they need to ensure that the frequency of caching ensures that the content is relevant. You could never cache the stock market as the price fluctuates second by second.

The purpose of caching is to reduce the bandwidth being used and also make the access to web pages faster as they are actually obtaining content from their **LAN**. There are different types of caching:

a. **Active Caching**: The IT team sets up jobs to cache web pages; for example, they cache www.nfl.com at 3 a.m. local time to ensure it has the latest results.

b. **Caching**: When new web pages are being requested (as long as they are not blocked by a filter), the pages are fetched and submitted to the requesting host and a copy is then placed in the cache. That way, the second time it is requested, it is retrieved from the cache.

c. **Transparent Cache**: This intercepts the request by the host to use HTTP TCP port 80 and forwards it to the proxy without modifying the requested web page. Refer to *Figure 7.11* here:

Transparent Proxy

Transparent HTTP Proxy   ☒   Enable transport mode to forward all requests for destination Port 80 to the proxy server.

Transparent proxy mode works without an additional configuration being necessary on clients.

Figure 7.11 – Transparent proxy

d. **Non-Transparent Cache**: The non-transparent proxy needs the proxy setting to be configured on the client computer to allow access through TCP port 8080:

Figure 7.12 – Non-transparent proxy

There are two types of forward proxy servers and these are as follows:

- **Application Proxy**: This deals with requests on behalf of another server. It could be, for example, a page within an online shop that loads its content and displays data from another location outside of the shop.

- **Reverse Proxy**: The flow of traffic from a reverse proxy is incoming traffic from the internet coming into your company network. The reverse proxy is placed in a boundary network called the *screened subnet*. It performs the authentication and decryption of a secure session to enable it to filter the incoming traffic.

  Example: If a company sets up a webinar through Skype or another video conference application, they can invite potential customers. All of the conferencing requests will pass through a reverse proxy that authenticates them and redirects their session to the relevant Skype server.

Jump Servers

A jump server, also known as a jump host or jump box, is a hardened host that could be used as an intermediary device or as a gateway for administrators who would then connect to other servers for remote administration. It would only have secure remote access tools installed. It could be used to SSH into the screened subnet or an Azure public network.

Load Balancer

A network load balancer is a device that is used when there is a high volume of traffic coming into the company's network or web server. It can be used to control access to web servers, video conferencing, or email.

The web traffic, shown in *Figure 7.13*, comes into the load balancer from the **Virtual IP address (VIP)** on the frontend and is sent to one of the web servers in the server farm:

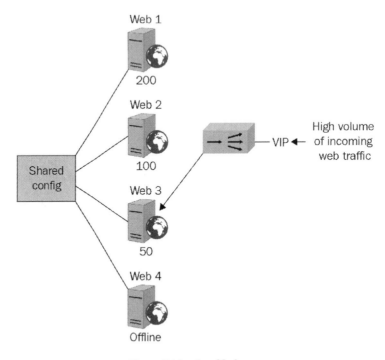

Figure 7.13 – Load balancer

Let's now look at the scheduling of load balancers.

Load Balancer Scheduling

Scheduling is how the load is distributed by the load balancer, let's look at these options in turn:

- **Least Utilized Host**: The benefits of a load balancer are that it knows the status of all of the web servers in the server farms and knows which web servers are the least utilized by using a scheduling algorithm.

  Example: The load balancer (see *Figure 7.13*) has selected to send the request to Web 3, which has the least number of requests (50), and Web 4 will not be considered as it is currently offline. A user requesting three different pages may obtain them from different web servers but may not know this as the load balancer is optimizing the delivery of the web pages to the user.

- **Affinity**: When the load balancer is set to **Affinity**, the request is sent to the same web server based on the requester's IP address. This is also known as *persistence* or a *sticky session*, where the load balancer uses the same server for the session.

- **DNS Round Robin**: While using DNS round robin, when the request comes in, the load balancer contacts the DNS server and rotates the request based on the lowest IP address first. It rotates around Web 1, Web 2, and Web 3, and then keeps the sequence going by going back to Web 1 on a rotational basis:

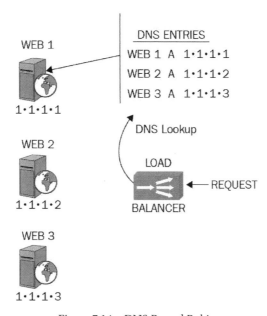

Figure 7.14 – DNS Round Robin

Next, we will look at the configurations for load balancers.

Load Balancer Configurations

There are many ways to set up a load balancer and we are going to look at each of these in turn:

- **Active/Active**: With active/active load balancers, the load balancers act like an array, dealing with the traffic together as they are both active. They cache the requests. If someone comes back for a second time to look at a web page, they will get the same load balancer that dealt with their first request. The downside is that since they are working close to full capacity, should one fail, then it will look as if the load balancers are going much slower. This is due to one load balancer dealing with the workload of two.

- **Active/Passive**: With active/passive load balancers, you have a pair of load balancers. The active node is fulfilling load balancing duties and the passive node is listening and monitoring the active node. Should the active node fail, then the passive node will take over, giving you redundancy.

Remote Access Capabilities

With the increased use of cloud technology and remote sales workforces, there has been an increase in employees who require remote access capabilities. At the time of writing this book, the majority of companies are working from home using remote access due to the COVID-19 pandemic. Let's look at the different types of remote access technologies in this section.

There are times when people who are working remotely need to access the company's network to access resources. There are two main types of remote access: the old-fashioned remote access server, using a modem, and the more modern **Virtual Private Network (VPN)** solutions. Let's look at these in turn:

- **Remote Access Server (RAS)**: A legacy server where dial-up networking is used, which is expensive as you need to pay the same cost as a telephone call. The server is located in the company network and the client has the software installed to allow communication. Each side has a modem that converts the digital communications in the computer to analog communication that can be transmitted over telephone lines. The speed of the modem is up to 56 Kbps – this makes the communication very slow. If you use dial-up networking to access the internet, the pages would load very slowly and look like a map. This is why it has been discontinued.

- **Virtual Private Network (VPN)**: This is located in the company's network and the client has a software to allow the connection, but it utilizes the internet; this makes it cheaper to use. Most hotels offer free Wi-Fi, and the sessions can be free. The downside is that the internet is the public highway, and a secure tunnel is used to protect against attack. The main tunneling protocols are as follows:

    a. **L2TP/IPSec**: This is the most secure tunneling protocol that can use certification, Kerberos authentication, or a preshared key. L2TP/IPSec provides both a secure tunnel and authentication.

    b. **Secure Socket Layer (SSL) VPN**: This works on legacy systems and uses SSL certificates for authentication. A newer version is TLS VPN.

    c. **HTML 5 VPN**: This is a VPN, similar to the SSL VPN, as it uses certificates for authentication. It is very easy to set up and you just need an HTML5-compatible browser such as Opera, Edge, Firefox, or Safari. There have been issues with this VPN as it is very slow.

A VPN creates a tunnel across the internet, normally from home or a remote site to your work. We need to look at the L2TP/IPSec tunnel that works at Layer 3 of the OSI Reference Model, where IPSec is used to encrypt the data. An IPSec packet is formed of two different portions:

- **AH**: The **Authenticated Header** (**AH**) consists of either SHA-1 (160 bits) or MD5 (128 bits) hashing protocols, which ensure that the packet header has not been tampered with in transit.
- **ESP**: The **Encapsulated Security Payload** (**ESP**) uses either DES (56 bits), 3DES (168 bits), or AES (256 bits). These are all symmetric encryption protocols, which means that they can transfer data much faster.

IPSec

IPSec can be used to create a secure session between a client computer and a server. For example, you may have the financial data on a financial server. All members of the finance team will have IPSec tunnels created between their desktops and the financial server. This will prevent anyone using a packet sniffer from stealing data from the financial server or any session across the network. This is known as **IPSec Transport Mode**. It encrypts on the payload.

IPSec can also be used as a VPN protocol as part of the L2TP/IPSec tunneling protocol that is used by major vendors who create VPN solutions, such as Cisco, Microsoft, Sonic Wall, or Checkpoint. This is known as **IPSec Tunnel Mode**. It encrypts both the header and the payload.

IPSec – Handshake

The first stage of an IPSec session is to create a secure tunnel. This is known as a **security association**. In the Security+ exam, this is called **Internet Key Exchange** (**IKE**). **Diffie Hellman** is used to set up a secure tunnel before the data:

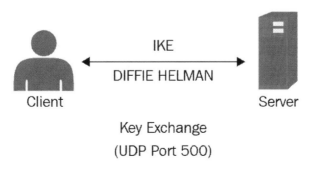

Figure 7.15 – Internet Key Exchange

The IKE phase of the IPSec session is using Diffie Hellman over UDP port 500 to create what is known as **quick mode**. This creates a secure session so that the data can flow through it.

The second phase is where the data is encrypted with DES, 3DES, or AES. AES provides the most secure VPN session as it uses 128, 192, or 256 bits. There are two different IPSec modes:

- **Tunnel Mode**: Tunnel mode is where the IPSec session is used across the internet as part of the L2TP/IPSec tunnel. During tunnel mode, the AH and the ESP are both encrypted.

- **Transport Mode**: Transport mode is where the IPSec tunnel is created with an internal network using client/server-to-server communication. During transport mode, only the ESP is encrypted.

VPN Concentrator

The purpose of the VPN concentrator is to set up the secure tunnel during the IKE phase. It needs to create a full IPSec tunnel. This is normally where you have a site-to-site VPN. See the next topic.

Site-to-Site VPN

A site-to-site VPN is where you have two different sites, each with a VPN concentrator at each site, and it acts as a leased line. A site-to-site VPN can act like a point to point connection between two sites. The session is set to **Always On**, as opposed to dial on demand:

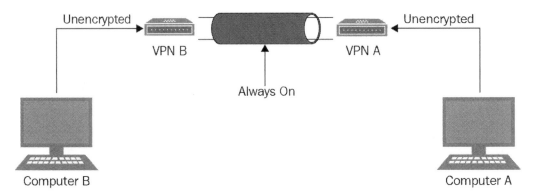

Figure 7.16 – Site-to-site VPN

VPN Always On versus On-Demand

There are two main session types:

- The first is `on-demand`, where a remote worker initiates a VPN session from home or a remote location, and when they finish the session, the connection is dropped.

- The second is where a site-to-site VPN is set up and the session is known as `always on`, where the session is permanent. It is point to point between two sites.

SSL VPNs

An SSL VPN is a VPN that can be used with a web browser that uses an SSL certificate for the encryption. It has been replaced in recent times with **Transport Layer Security (TLS)**, which is a more modern version of SSL. In the Security+ exam, an SSL VPN is normally used for legacy VPNs that don't support L2TP/IPSec and use an SSL certificate.

Exam tip

SSL VPNs are the only VPN to use an SSL certificate, and only need a web browser to make a connection. The SSL certificate could also be replaced by the more secure TLS certificate.

Split Tunneling

Split tunneling is where a secure VPN session is connected (this is the blue tunnel shown in the following diagram), and then the user opens an unsecured session that would allow the hacker to come in through the unsecured session and gain access to your company's network:

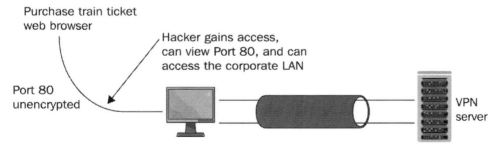

Figure 7.17 – Split tunnel

Example: John connects his L2TP/IPSec session into the company network and then he realizes that he needs a train ticket for tomorrow. Instead of dropping the secure session and then going to the rail website, he leaves it connected. Once he opens up his web browser, he is using HTTP on TCP port 80, which is unsecured. This means that, while he has the web browser open, a hacker could access his desktop and use the secure tunnel to gain access to the company network.

> **Exam tip**
> A VPN should always set up a full tunnel. No other form of tunneling, such as split tunneling, should be used.

Remote Support

We are going to look at different types of remote support, and the 'go to' version of secure remote access is **Secure Shell (SSH)**. We will start by looking at SSH:

- **SSH**: It replaces telnet, which sent passwords in clear text. Before you can start, you need to install the SSH keys on the network devices or servers. First of all, we procure a key pair, and private and public keys are generated. The public key is stored on the server, with the private key remaining on the administrator's desktop. SSH is available in the command line and **Graphical User Interface (GUI)**. We can also use SSH with a username and password or, in a Microsoft environment, we would use Kerberos to produce a ticket.

    Example: Using a tool such as OpenSSH, the `ssh-keygen -t` RSA command generates a public and private RSA key pair on the administrator's desktop. The next step is to use the `ssh-copy-id` command to log in to the server and copy the public key across. This is added to the list of authorized key files on the server. While copying, the administrator may be asked to provide their credentials. If you are connecting to a host for the first time, you will get the following message:

    ```
    Number of key(s) added:1
    Now try logging into the machine, with ssh 'username@<ip
    address>' and check to make sure that only the key(s) you
    wanted is added.
    ```

    If an administrator is logging in for the first time, he will use the `ssh-root@ server` command.

- **PowerShell**: Another version of remote support is Microsoft's PowerShell, which will allow remote access to another machine. On the remote target, we would run the PowerShell command, `Enable-PSRemoting -Force`. This command would allow for remote management, and then we would use the command `Enter-PSSession -ComputerName <hostname>`. PowerShell could be used for lateral movement across a network.

- **Remote Desktop Protocol (RDP) Server**: RDP allows you to securely connect to a computer running a Windows operating system.

- **Jump Server**: A jump server allows administrators a connection, who then, in turn, use SSH or RDP for remote administration.

Secure Network Architecture Concepts

We are going to look at secure network architecture and we will begin by looking at network appliances, starting with software-defined networks.

Software-Defined Network

Traditional networks route packets via a hardware router and are decentralized. However, in today's networks, more and more people are using virtualization, including cloud providers. A **Software-Defined Network** (**SDN**) is where packets are routed through a controller rather than traditional routers, which improves performance.

Securing networks and protecting them is vital to protecting a company's assets. We use different zones and topologies, network separation and segmentation, and install firewalls to prevent unauthorized access to the network.

First of all, let's look at the different zones and topologies. There are three main zones: LAN, WAN, and screened subnet:

- **Local Area Network** (**LAN**): A secure network with very fast links and a web server, called the *intranet*, that holds internal-only information, such as classified data, manufacturing price lists, or the internal forms library.

- **Screened Subnet**: A boundary layer between the LAN and the WAN that holds information that companies may want people from the internet to access. You may put your email server in the screened subnet, but never a domain controller. The web server inside the screened subnet is called the *extranet*, which requires a username and password to access the site. It could be used by a distributor that logs in to get a newly released price list.

- **Wide Area Network (WAN)**: Open to the public and not a safe place, as it is freely accessible, the web server inside the WAN is the internet. The internet is an example of a WAN, and any data traversing the internet needs to be encrypted. It covers a very large geographic area, and the links tend to be slower than the LAN and screened subnet.

Example: A store sells designer sneakers at $230. However, the shop's owner purchases them from the manufacturer by placing orders on the extranet server. Access to the extranet web server is via a unique username and password, and the price the shop purchases the sneakers at is $125, allowing for a profit of $105. On the intranet, the web server has the manufacturing price of the sneakers, which are made in China, for a mere $5 a pair:

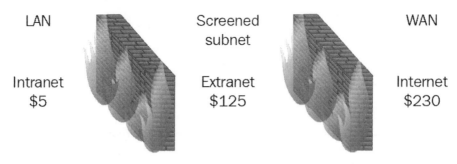

LAN	Screened subnet	WAN
Intranet $5	Extranet $125	Internet $230

Figure 7.18 – Network zones

From this information, you should ask yourself three simple questions:

- What would happen if the customer knew that the shop owner was making a profit of $105? They would definitely want a discount.

- What would happen if the shop owner discovered the manufacturing price was $5? They would also like a discount.

- What would happen if the customer found out that their designer sneakers were made for $5? They may decide not to purchase them as they are really cheap sneakers in disguise and, through social media, the manufacturer would lose market share.

You can see why data in a LAN needs to be secure and not freely available to the general public.

Network Segmentation

Cybercrime is rife and is the largest growing criminal industry. In today's world, most businesses are interconnected and use the internet. Maintaining the security and integrity of data, including research and development, is paramount. We need to be able to isolate, segment, or segregate our network, both physically and virtually. Let's look at the options we have:

- **Physical Segmentation/Separation**: If we have data, such as email or a web server, that we want people to be able to access from the internet, whether it be a customer or one of our salespeople, we will physically separate it from our LAN by placing it in the screened subnet, which is a boundary layer, so that users accessing this data do not need to come into our secure LAN. You would never place a domain controller or a database server in the screened subnet.

- **Air Gaps**: Another physical method is to create air gaps between some systems that we use internally to separate confidential systems from normal systems:

  Example 1: The US Department of Defense has two distinct networks:

  The **Secret Internet Protocol Router Network (SIPRNet)**, where classified data, such as top secret or secret documentation, is accessed, and the **Non-classified Internet Protocol Router Network (NIPRNet)**, where unclassified data is held. These two private networks have air gaps between them so that a desktop from the NIPRNet cannot access the SIPRNet, or vice versa.

  Example 2: In a finance department, there is one computer that would be used to make electronic payments, such as **Bankers' Automated Clearing System (BACS)** or **Clearing House Automated Payments System (CHAPS)** transfers, and this machine would not be accessible by everyone in that finance department. Therefore, it would be isolated from the other departmental machines. This is also an example of an air gap.

- **Logical Separation – VLAN**: There is sometimes a need to create a separate logical network within the LAN to segment a department from the rest of the internal network. The device that connects all of the internal computers is called a switch, but within a switch we have the ability to create a **Virtual Local Area Network (VLAN)**. If you look at *Figure 7.19*, you can see a switch with two separate VLANs:

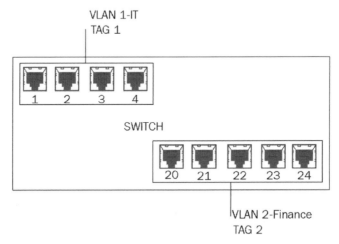

Figure 7.19 – Two VLANs

A VLAN is created by using the software on the switch where you can bond a number of ports to work together as a separate logical network. If you look at *Figure 7.19*, you can see that port numbers 1-4 have been used to create a VLAN for the IT department, and then ports 20-24 have been used to create another VLAN for the finance department. Although both of these departments are on an internal device, creating the VLANs isolates them from other VLANs and the company's network. An important factor is that a VLAN tag is set up so that when traffic arrives at the switch, it knows where to send it.

- **East-West Traffic**: This is where traffic moves laterally between servers within a data center. North-South traffic moves outside of the data center.

- **Zero-Trust**: A zero-trust network is used when no traffic is authorized; they have zero-trust. They must then validate or verify who they are before accessing resources. The cloud uses zero-trust.

- **Virtualization**: If we create a virtual network, we can isolate the users on that network from other users on the same virtual network using VLANs. On a virtual host, I can create many different isolated virtual networks. Virtualization is covered in *Chapter 6, Understanding Cloud Models and Virtualization*.

Next, we will look at intrusion prevention systems.

Intrusion Prevention System

An **Intrusion Prevention Systems (IPS)** protects the network against attacks. There are of two types. The first type is the **Network Intrusion Prevention System (NIPS)**, which can only operate on your network and cannot work inside a host. The second is called the **Host Intrusion Prevention System (HIPS)**, and it operates inside a host machine and cannot operate on the network.

An NIPS is an internal network device whose role is to prevent access to the network, and it is placed on the perimeter of your network behind your firewall. Think of NIPS as John Wick with a big gun whose job it is to shoot the bad guys; he is your network protection.

Intrusion Detection System

The **Intrusion-Detection System (IDS)** is the same as the IPS. There is the HIDS, which only works on a host, and the NIDS, which only works on the network. Think of the IDS as Sherlock Holmes, the famous detective. His job is to find different traffic patterns on the network and then inform John Wick, the NIPS, who will then remove them from the network.

> **Exam tip**
> NIPS has the capability to detect as well as protect if there are no NIDS on your network. To protect a virtual machine from attack, you will install an HIPS.

Modes of Detection

There are three modes of detection used by the NIPS/NIDS. For the purpose of the exam, you must know them thoroughly:

- **Signature-Based**: This works off a database of known exploits and cannot identify new patterns. If the database is not up to date, it will not operate efficiently.

- **Anomaly-Based**: This starts off the same as the signature-based mode of detection, with the known-exploits database, but with the ability to identify new variants.

- **Heuristic/ Behavioral-Based**: Instead of trying to match known variants, the heuristic/behavioral-based mode of detection starts off with a baseline and matches traffic patterns against the baseline. This is also known as **anomaly-based**.

> **Exam tip**
> Anomaly-based NIPS/NIDS detect new patterns and are much more efficient than signature-based, systems which can only work with known variants.

Modes of Operation

There are different modes of operation for the sensors of the NIPS/NIDS:

- **Inline**: The NIPS will be placed on, or very near to, the firewall as an additional layer of security. When the NIPS has been set up in inline mode, the flow of traffic goes through the NIPS. This is known as *in-band*.

- **Passive**: The traffic does not go through the NIPS. This mode is normally used by the NIDS as it detects changes in traffic patterns in the local network. This is known as *out-of-band*. Sensors and collectors forward alerts to the NIDS.

When sensors are placed inside the network, they can only detect traffic once it is inside your network and has passed through your firewall. If you wish to detect attacks before they come into your network, the sensor must be placed on the network external to the firewall.

Sensor/Collector

A sensor/collector can be a device, tap, or firewall log whose purpose is to alert the NIDS of any changes in traffic patterns within the network. If you place your first sensor on the internet side of your network, it will scan all of the traffic from the internet.

Monitoring Data

When we use analytics (how we analyze the data) to examine the information provided, it is based on rules that are set inside the IPS/IDS. However, no system is foolproof. They try their best but sometimes provide outcomes that are different to those expected. There are two different types:

- **False Positive**: The NIDS/NIPS has decided, based on the information gathered, that an attack is taking place. However, when the network administrator investigates it, they find that there is no attack.

- **False Negative**: The NIDS/NIPS is not updated, and attacks have been taking place without detection.

> **Exam tip**
> A false positive is a false alarm; however, a false negative doesn't detect anything while you are being attacked.

- **True Positive**: The monitoring system and the manual inspection agree.

Network Access Control

If you have a Windows desktop or laptop and you go away on holiday for 2-3 weeks, when you come back, your device may need multiple updates.

After a remote client has authenticated, **network access control** (**NAC**) checks that the device being used is fully patched. See *Figure 7.20*:

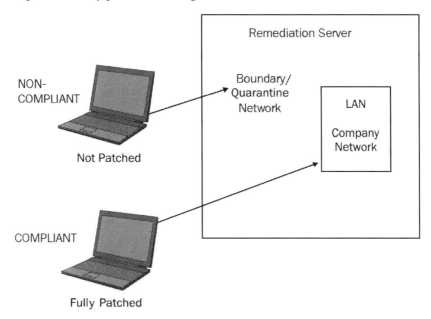

Figure 7.20 – NAC

When the user is authenticated, the **Health Authority** (**HAuth**) checks against the registry of the client device to ensure that it is fully patched. A fully patched machine is deemed compliant and allowed access to the LAN. In the preceding diagram, the bottom laptop is compliant. If the device is not fully patched, it is deemed non-compliant and is redirected to a boundary network, which could also be known as a *quarantine network*. The components of NAC are as follows:

- **Host Health Checks**: The HAuth checks the health of the incoming device to ensure that it is fully patched.

- **Compliant/Non-Compliant Device**: A device that is fully patched is compliant, but a device that has missing patches is deemed non-compliant.

- **Agents**: Each device has an agent installed so that the HAuth can carry out health checks. The two types of agents are as follows:

  a. **Permanent**: The agent is installed on the host.

  b. **Dissolvable**: A dissolvable agent is known as temporary and agentless and is installed for a single use.

- **Remediation Server**: This sits on the boundary or quarantine network. When the non-compliant machine is connected to the boundary network, it can obtain the missing updates from the remediation server. Once the device is fully patched, it is then allowed to access the LAN.

The Domain Name System

The most common form of name resolution is hostname resolution. It is a database of hostnames and the IP addresses that they are allocated.

Domain Name System (DNS) is a hierarchical naming system that takes a hostname and resolves it to an IP address. This means that I don't need to know the actual IP address. of a website to visit it If I want to go to the Microsoft website, I know that I need to enter `www.microsoft.com` in my web browser and it will take me there. If I have a user called *Ian* in a domain called `ianneil501.com`, the hostname portion would be `Ian` and the **Fully-Qualified Domain Name (FQDN)** would be `ian.ianneil501.com`. Records in the DNS database are as follows:

- **A**: IPv4 host
- **AAAA**: IPv6 host
- **CNAME**: Alias
- **MX**: Mail server
- **SRV records**: Finds services such as a domain controller

Example: A user would like to visit the website of `http://ianneil501.com`. To get there, they would enter `www.ianneil501.com` in their web browser as per *Figure 7.21*. The hostname resolution follows a strict process:

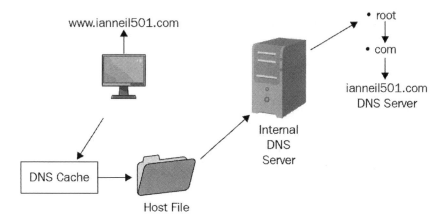

Figure 7.21 – Hostname resolution

In *Figure 7.21*, the hostname resolution adopts a strict process and takes the first entry for that hostname, irrespective of whether it is right or wrong—this is a pitfall of the process. Let's look at this process, starting with the DNS cache:

- **DNS Cache**: Stores recently resolved names. If the cache is empty, attackers will attempt to poison the DNS cache by putting in wrong entries to divert you to a server where they can attack you.

  In the preceding example, the DNS cache is empty, so it would move onto the host file located on the local computer. If you need to view the DNS cache, you would run the `ipconfig /displaydns` command, and if you wanted to clear the DNS cache, you would run the `ipconfig /flushdns` command.

- **Hosts File**: This is a flat file where entries are manually inserted and read from the top to the bottom. It takes the first entry, whether right or wrong. The purpose of a host file is that if one user needs to go to a server called **Sneaky Beaky**, I would put an entry for that server in their localhosts file that would allow them to go there. If I put the entry in the DNS server, that would allow anyone to find that server. In the preceding example, the hosts file is empty, so name resolution would move to the DNS server, whose IP address is in the local computer's network card.

- **DNS Server**: This normally maintains only the hostnames for your domain and would then need to complete a referral process through the root server of the internet, which is represented by a dot.

- **Root Server**: The root server would then refer the request to the `.com` server, which in turn refers the request to the authoritative DNS server for the `ianneil501.com` domain, which would then reply with the IP address of the website.

- **Cache the Reply**: A copy of the name resolution is placed in the DNS cache for future use.

DNS Poisoning

When DNS resolution occurs, the first place that is checked is the DNS cache on the local machine. After that, it goes to the hosts file and then onto the DNS server. DNS poisoning is the process of putting bad entries into the DNS cache, diverting requests to a fraudulent website that has been made to look like the legitimate website (see *Figure 7.22*):

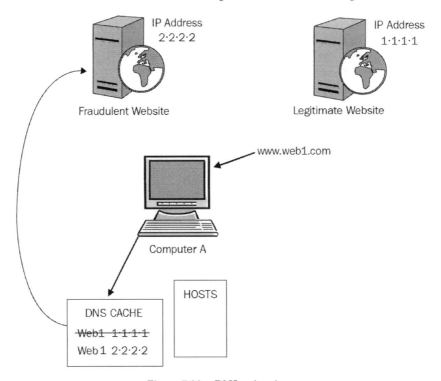

Figure 7.22 – DNS poisoning

If we look at *Figure 7.22*, **Computer A** has already visited the legitimate website, called **Web 1**, and its proper IP address of `1.1.1.1` has been placed in its DNS cache. When DNS resolution is performed, the DNS cache is searched first, followed by the hosts file, followed by the internal DNS server.

The attacker has now deleted the entry for **Web 1** and inserted their entry for **Web 1** with an IP address of 2.2.2.2. Now, when the user enters the www.web1.com URL, the only entry in the DNS cache is **Web 1** 2.2.2.2 and the user is diverted to a website that looks like the legitimate website. When they enter their card details to make a purchase, their account is emptied.

DNSSEC

To prevent someone from gaining access to DNS records, DNSSEC was introduced to protect the DNS traffic. Each DNS record is digitally signed, creating an *RRSIG* record to protect against attacks, assuring you that they are valid, and that their integrity has been maintained.

> **Exam tip**
> DNSSEC produces an RRSIG record for each host.

Network Reconnaissance and Discovery

Command-line tools are used every day by security professionals for network discovery and reconnaissance. Therefore, for the Security+ exam, you must be familiar with them, and so I have provided a screenshot for many of them. We are going to see when we would use each of them in turn:

- **Fingerprinting**: This is the process of capturing your network traffic, and mapping all of the network devices, protocols, and IP address ranges so that they have information that will help an attacker get an idea of how your network is laid out.

- **Footprinting**: This is looking at the network topology and gathering as much information as you can, such as email addresses. They will identify vulnerabilities within a company that can be used as an attack vector.

- **Internet Control Message Protocol (ICMP)**: ICMP brings back the replies when you use command-line tools. Therefore, if you block incoming ICMP connections on the network firewall, none of the tools will work externally.

- **Ping**: Ping is used to test connectivity to another host. In the following screenshot, you can see that we have pinged the hostname, `ianneil501.com`, and we have received four replies. The **Total Time to Live (TTL)** is a maximum of `128` seconds; in this case, it is `47` seconds—see the following screenshot:

```
C:\WINDOWS\system32>ping ianneil501.com

Pinging ianneil501.com [46.30.213.45] with 32 bytes of data:
Reply from 46.30.213.45: bytes=32 time=42ms TTL=47
Reply from 46.30.213.45: bytes=32 time=44ms TTL=47
Reply from 46.30.213.45: bytes=32 time=42ms TTL=47
Reply from 46.30.213.45: bytes=32 time=43ms TTL=47

Ping statistics for 46.30.213.45:
    Packets: Sent = 4, Received = 4, Lost = 0 (0% loss),
Approximate round trip times in milli-seconds:
    Minimum = 42ms, Maximum = 44ms, Average = 42ms
```

Figure 7.23 – Ping

- **Continuous Ping**: Continuous ping uses the `ping -t` command and is used for diagnostic testing. Normally, we run `ping -t` when we cannot connect and then, once we can connect, we will get replies. See the following screenshot:

```
C:\WINDOWS\system32>ping -t www.ianneil501.com

Pinging www.ianneil501.com [46.30.213.45] with 32 bytes of data:
Reply from 46.30.213.45: bytes=32 time=42ms TTL=47
Reply from 46.30.213.45: bytes=32 time=43ms TTL=47
Reply from 46.30.213.45: bytes=32 time=41ms TTL=47
Reply from 46.30.213.45: bytes=32 time=41ms TTL=47
Reply from 46.30.213.45: bytes=32 time=47ms TTL=47
Reply from 46.30.213.45: bytes=32 time=49ms TTL=47
Reply from 46.30.213.45: bytes=32 time=45ms TTL=47
Reply from 46.30.213.45: bytes=32 time=43ms TTL=47
Reply from 46.30.213.45: bytes=32 time=44ms TTL=47
Reply from 46.30.213.45: bytes=32 time=46ms TTL=47
Reply from 46.30.213.45: bytes=32 time=42ms TTL=47
Reply from 46.30.213.45: bytes=32 time=43ms TTL=47
Reply from 46.30.213.45: bytes=32 time=42ms TTL=47
Reply from 46.30.213.45: bytes=32 time=43ms TTL=47
Reply from 46.30.213.45: bytes=32 time=43ms TTL=47
Reply from 46.30.213.45: bytes=32 time=41ms TTL=47
Reply from 46.30.213.45: bytes=32 time=46ms TTL=47
```

Figure 7.24 – Continuous ping

- **Hping**: This tool can be used as a TCP/IP packet assembler and analyzer. It allows you to test the security of your network devices, such as firewall rules and open ports, and analyzes network traffic, including packet formats and traceroute.

- **Tracert/Traceroute**: This shows the route taken from a computer to a website. It can show any latency traveling through a particular router. It is like traffic going into a city center; the closer the traffic is to the center, the slower it is. It shows information for a maximum of 30 hops:

```
C:\WINDOWS\system32>tracert www.ianneil501.com

Tracing route to www.ianneil501.com [46.30.213.45]
over a maximum of 30 hops:

  1    <1 ms    <1 ms    <1 ms  192.168.0.254
  2     1 ms     1 ms     1 ms  209.134-31-62.static.virginmediabusiness.co.uk [62.31.134.209]
  3     *         *         *    Request timed out.
  4    20 ms    19 ms    17 ms  perr-core-2a-ae16-0.network.virginmedia.net [62.253.138.245]
  5     *         *         *    Request timed out.
  6    29 ms    26 ms    26 ms  86.85-254-62.static.virginmediabusiness.co.uk [62.254.85.86]
  7    34 ms    33 ms    32 ms  ldn-b1-link.telia.net [213.248.84.25]
  8    30 ms    27 ms    26 ms  ldn-bb4-link.telia.net [62.115.143.26]
  9    42 ms    41 ms    37 ms  hbg-bb4-link.telia.net [62.115.122.160]
 10    46 ms    42 ms    49 ms  kbn-bb4-link.telia.net [213.155.135.121]
 11    53 ms    52 ms    45 ms  kbn-b3-link.telia.net [62.115.114.69]
 12    43 ms    43 ms    43 ms  onecom-ic-307407-kbn-horsk-i1.c.telia.net [62.115.47.242]
 13    43 ms    42 ms    44 ms  ae1-200.dr3-cph3.pub.network.one.com [46.30.210.17]
 14    43 ms    50 ms    43 ms  xe-0-2-0-200.ar1.pub.webpod1-cph3.one.com [46.30.210.31]
 15    41 ms    41 ms    41 ms  webcluster46.webpod1-cph3.one.com [46.30.213.45]
```

Figure 7.25 – Tracert

- **Pathping**: This has the functionality of both `ping packets` and `tracert`. It also calculates statistics after the trace, showing the packet loss at each router it passes through:

```
0  WIN-HB5RLG5VD60.Domain.local [100.120.39.46]
1  100.120.39.1
2  r-1-43-234-77.ff.avast.com [77.234.43.1]
3  10.27.0.18
4  border4.ae15.avast-30.lon007.pnap.net [212.118.253.133]
5  core3.tge0-3-0-3-bbnet2.lon003.pnap.net [212.118.240.102]
6  107.6.86.150
7  173.231.129.66
8  195.66.226.81
9  a184-28-198-144.deploy.static.akamaitechnologies.com [184.28.198.144]

Computing statistics for 225 seconds...
            Source to Here   This Node/Link
Hop  RTT    Lost/Sent = Pct  Lost/Sent = Pct  Address
  0                                            100.120.39.46
                              0/ 100 =   0%    |
  1   21ms    0/ 100 =  0%    0/ 100 =   0%    100.120.39.1
                              0/ 100 =   0%    |
  2   23ms    0/ 100 =  0%    0/ 100 =   0%    r-1-43-234-77.ff.avast.com [77.234.43.1]
                              0/ 100 =   0%    |
  3   ---    100/ 100 =100%  100/ 100 =100%   10.27.0.18
                              0/ 100 =   0%    |
  4   ---    100/ 100 =100%  100/ 100 =100%   border4.ae15.avast-30.lon007.pnap.net [212.118.253.133]
                              0/ 100 =   0%    |
  5   23ms    0/ 100 =  0%    0/ 100 =   0%   core3.tge0-3-0-3-bbnet2.lon003.pnap.net [212.118.240.102]
                              0/ 100 =   0%    |
  6   23ms    0/ 100 =  0%    0/ 100 =   0%   107.6.86.150
                              0/ 100 =   0%    |
  7   ---    100/ 100 =100%  100/ 100 =100%   173.231.129.66
                              0/ 100 =   0%    |
  8   ---    100/ 100 =100%  100/ 100 =100%   195.66.226.81
                              0/ 100 =   0%    |
  9   23ms    0/ 100 =  0%    0/ 100 =   0%   a184-28-198-144.deploy.static.akamaitechnologies.com [184.28.198.144]
```

Figure 7.26 – Pathping

- **Netstat**: Netstat is used to see the established connections and the listening ports. It can also let you know what services are running a computer. If you reboot the computer, all of the established ports will disappear. Refer to the following screenshot:

```
C:\WINDOWS\system32>NETSTAT

Active Connections

  Proto  Local Address          Foreign Address        State
  TCP    127.0.0.1:5939         DESKTOP-QR6R2DA:49758   ESTABLISHED
  TCP    127.0.0.1:7778         DESKTOP-QR6R2DA:49793   ESTABLISHED
  TCP    127.0.0.1:49669        DESKTOP-QR6R2DA:49670   ESTABLISHED
  TCP    127.0.0.1:49670        DESKTOP-QR6R2DA:49669   ESTABLISHED
  TCP    127.0.0.1:49758        DESKTOP-QR6R2DA:5939    ESTABLISHED
  TCP    127.0.0.1:49793        DESKTOP-QR6R2DA:7778    ESTABLISHED
  TCP    127.0.0.1:49794        DESKTOP-QR6R2DA:49795   ESTABLISHED
  TCP    127.0.0.1:49795        DESKTOP-QR6R2DA:49794   ESTABLISHED
  TCP    192.168.0.118:49672    r-54-45-234-77:https    CLOSE_WAIT
  TCP    192.168.0.118:49677    DE-HAM-PLS-R012:5938    ESTABLISHED
  TCP    192.168.0.118:49748    ams10-004:http          ESTABLISHED
  TCP    192.168.0.118:49753    40.67.255.199:https     ESTABLISHED
```

Figure 7.27 – Netstat

> **Exam tip**
>
> Netstat shows the established and listening port, but if you reboot the
> computer, the established connections disappear.

- **Nslookup**: Nslookup is a diagnostic tool for verifying the IP address of a hostname
  in the DNS server database. We can also use the `set type=MX` command, which
  brings back the DNS details on all mail servers in the domain. See the following
  screenshot:

```
C:\Users\Administrator>nslookup www.ianneil501.com
Server:  cache2.service.virginmedia.net
Address:  194.168.8.100

Non-authoritative answer:
Name:    www.ianneil501.com
Addresses:  2a02:2350:5:100:8b40:0:7611:8566
          46.30.213.45
```

Figure 7.28 – Nslookup

- **Dig**: Dig is the equivalent of `nslookup` in a Linux/Unix environment. As we can see in the following screenshot, the IP address of Google is `216.58.220.110`:

```
[root@centos7 ~]# dig google.com

; <<>> DiG 9.9.4-RedHat-9.9.4-29.el7_2.3 <<>> google.com
;; global options: +cmd
;; Got answer:
;; ->>HEADER<<- opcode: QUERY, status: NOERROR, id: 32702
;; flags: qr rd ra; QUERY: 1, ANSWER: 1, AUTHORITY: 0, ADDITIONAL: 1

;; OPT PSEUDOSECTION:
; EDNS: version: 0, flags:; MBZ: 0005 , udp: 4000
;; QUESTION SECTION:
;google.com.                    IN      A

;; ANSWER SECTION:
google.com.             5       IN      A       216.58.220.110

;; Query time: 27 msec
;; SERVER: 192.168.12.2#53(192.168.220.2)
;; WHEN: Tue Sep 04 11:18:22 AEST 2018
;; MSG SIZE  rcvd: 55
```

Figure 7.29 – Dig

- **Address Resolution Protocol** (**ARP**): ARP is used to translate the IP address to a MAC address; the `arp -a` command shows the ARP cache. An attacker could use ARPSpoof, ARPoison, and Ettercap to poison your ARP cache. These tools could be used to create ARP broadcasts by sending unsolicited ARP replies. Please read the article at `https://openmaniak.com/ettercap_arp.php`. We can prevent ARP poisoning by using `arp-s` to add a static entry to the ARP cache, or we could detect it by capturing packets on your network using Wireshark:

```
C:\Users\Administrator>arp -a

Interface: 172.18.27.177 --- 0x7
  Internet Address      Physical Address      Type
  172.18.27.191         ff-ff-ff-ff-ff-ff     static
  224.0.0.22            01-00-5e-00-00-16     static
  224.0.0.251           01-00-5e-00-00-fb     static
  224.0.0.252           01-00-5e-00-00-fc     static
  239.255.255.250       01-00-5e-7f-ff-fa     static
  255.255.255.255       ff-ff-ff-ff-ff-ff     static

Interface: 192.168.0.118 --- 0xe
  Internet Address      Physical Address      Type
  192.168.0.134         20-47-ed-97-3b-3a     dynamic
  192.168.0.158         20-47-ed-c9-54-1a     dynamic
  192.168.0.159         20-47-ed-2a-27-42     dynamic
  192.168.0.163         30-59-b7-7e-c3-23     dynamic
  192.168.0.250         d0-bf-9c-45-b2-be     dynamic
  192.168.0.254         64-12-25-5a-06-c1     dynamic
  192.168.0.255         ff-ff-ff-ff-ff-ff     static
  224.0.0.22            01-00-5e-00-00-16     static
  224.0.0.251           01-00-5e-00-00-fb     static
  224.0.0.252           01-00-5e-00-00-fc     static
  239.255.255.250       01-00-5e-7f-ff-fa     static
  255.255.255.255       ff-ff-ff-ff-ff-ff     static
```

Figure 7.30 – ARP cache

- **ipconfig/ip/ifconfig**: These commands show the IP configuration. The Windows version is `ipconfig`, but Unix/Linux can use `ip` or `ifconfig`.

  The `ipconfig /displaydns` command is run in the following screenshot, and it shows the DNS cache on a computer:

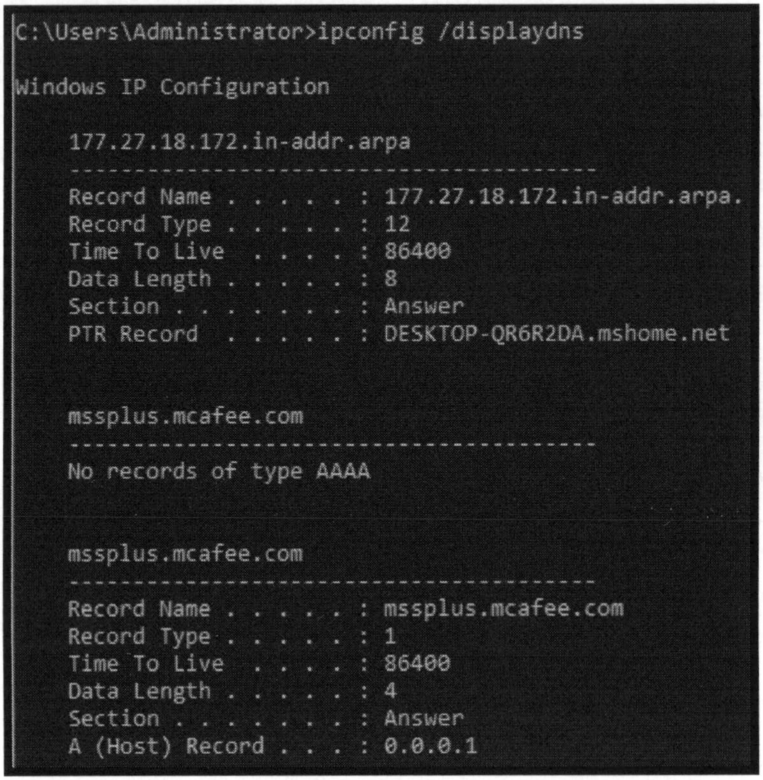

```
C:\Users\Administrator>ipconfig /displaydns

Windows IP Configuration

    177.27.18.172.in-addr.arpa
    ----------------------------------------
    Record Name . . . . . : 177.27.18.172.in-addr.arpa.
    Record Type . . . . . : 12
    Time To Live  . . . . : 86400
    Data Length . . . . . : 8
    Section . . . . . . . : Answer
    PTR Record  . . . . . : DESKTOP-QR6R2DA.mshome.net


    mssplus.mcafee.com
    ----------------------------------------
    No records of type AAAA


    mssplus.mcafee.com
    ----------------------------------------
    Record Name . . . . . : mssplus.mcafee.com
    Record Type . . . . . : 1
    Time To Live  . . . . : 86400
    Data Length . . . . . : 4
    Section . . . . . . . : Answer
    A (Host) Record . . . : 0.0.0.1
```

Figure 7.31 – DNS cache

- **ipconfig /flushdns**: This is used to clear out all entries in the DNS cache. See the following screenshot:

```
C:\Users\Administrator>ipconfig /flushdns

Windows IP Configuration

Successfully flushed the DNS Resolver Cache.

C:\Users\Administrator>
```

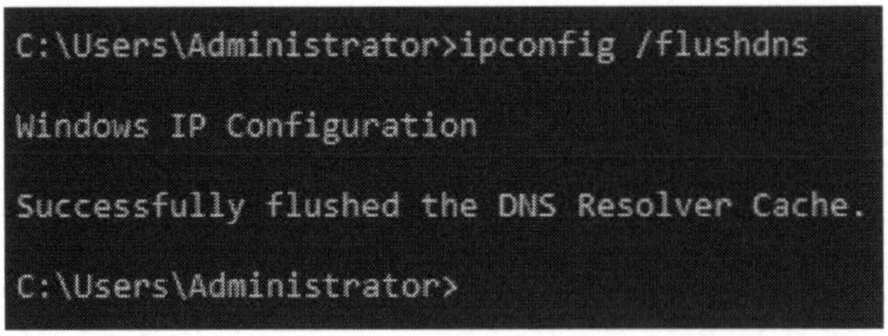

Figure 7.32 – Clearing the DNS cache

- **tcpdump**: This is used by Linux/Unix as a packet sniffer command.

  `tcpdump -i eth0` shows information on the first Ethernet adapter, as shown in the following screenshot:

```
# tcpdump -i eth0
tcpdump: verbose output suppressed, use -v or -vv for full protocol decode
listening on eth0, link-type EN10MB (Ethernet), capture size 65535 bytes
11:33:31.976358 IP 172.16.25.126.ssh > 172.16.25.125.apwi-rxspooler: Flags [P.], seq 3500440357
:3500440553, ack 3652628334, win 18760, length 196
11:33:31.976603 IP 172.16.25.125.apwi-rxspooler > 172.16.25.126.ssh: Flags [.], ack 196, win 64
487, length 0
11:33:31.977243 ARP, Request who-has tecmint.com tell 172.16.25.126, length 28
11:33:31.977359 ARP, Reply tecmint.com is-at 00:14:5e:67:26:1d (oui Unknown), length 46
11:33:31.977367 IP 172.16.25.126.54807 > tecmint.com: 4240+ PTR? 125.25.16.172.in-addr.arpa. (4
4)
11:33:31.977599 IP tecmint.com > 172.16.25.126.54807: 4240 NXDomain 0/1/0 (121)
11:33:31.977742 IP 172.16.25.126.44519 > tecmint.com: 40988+ PTR? 126.25.16.172.in-addr.arpa. (
44)
11:33:32.028747 IP 172.16.20.33.netbios-ns > 172.16.31.255.netbios-ns: NBT UDP PACKET(137): QUE
RY; REQUEST; BROADCAST
11:33:32.112045 IP 172.16.21.153.netbios-ns > 172.16.31.255.netbios-ns: NBT UDP PACKET(137): QU
ERY; REQUEST; BROADCAST
11:33:32.115606 IP 172.16.21.144.netbios-ns > 172.16.31.255.netbios-ns: NBT UDP PACKET(137): QU
ERY; REQUEST; BROADCAST
```

Figure 7.33 – tcpdump

- **Nmap**: Nmap is a free and open source network mapper that can be used to create an inventory of all of the devices on your network and can be used for banner grabbing.

- **Netcat**: Netcat, or nc, is a utility for showing network connections in a Linux/Unix environment. In the following screenshot, the `netcat -z` command is being used to scan ports `78-80`, and from this you can see that ports `78` and `79` are closed, but port `80`, being used by HTTP, is open. The `-v` switch means verbose and shows all the information. Refer to the following screenshot:

```
$ netcat -z -v ianneil501.com 78-80

nc: connect to ianneil501.com port 78 (tcp) failed: connection refused
nc: connect to ianneil501.com port 79 (tcp) failed: connection refused

Connection to ianneil501.com port 80 (tcp/html) succeeded!
```

Figure 7.34 – Netcat

- **IP Scanners**: The following screenshot shows the Angry IP scanners that can scan all IP addresses in a given range. The green icon shows that the IP address is active and responding, blue is active but not responding, and the red icon shows that it is inactive. Open ports are also shown:

Figure 7.35 – Angry IP

- **Curl**: This is a command-line tool used to transfer data. It can also be used in banner grabbing; this is fetching remote banner information from web servers. -s is silent and -I fetches the HTTP headers.

  Example: curl -s -I 192.168.24.21 will then fetch the HTTP headers and the output might look like this:

```
HTTP/1.1 200 OK
Date:  Fri 16 Oct 2020 17:30:12 GMT
Server Apache/2.2.8 (Ubuntu) DAV/2
X-Powered-By PHP/5.2.4-2ubuntu5.24
Content-Type:  text/html
```

- **The Harvester**: This is a passive tool that comes with Kali Linux and we can use it to harvest the email addresses of an organization.

Example: I want to search for the email addresses of a domain called mydomain. com, with a maximum search of 500 entries, and I want to have my source for searching as the google search engine. I would run the following syntax:

```
theharvester -d mydomain.com -l 500 -b google
```

- **Sn1per**: This is a pen test reconnaissance tool that can be used for automated tests. This tool can be used by pen testers, bug bounty researchers, and security teams. It can look for vulnerabilities in your network, open ports, it can diagnose DNS, issues it has Nmap capabilities, and it can find application weaknesses.

- **Scanless**: This is a port scanner that has the ability to be anonymous so that the scan cannot be traced back to your IP address.

- **Dnsenum**: This tool can identify DNS records, such as MX, mail exchange servers, NS, and host A records for a domain. This way, an attacker has an idea of how large your organization is and if it is worth attacking. The internal team can also run it to see what information is available to attackers.

- **Nessus**: This is a remote scanning tool that can highlight vulnerabilities that can be exploited by hackers.

- **Cuckoo**: This tool creates a sandbox that can be used for analyzing files for malware inspection.

- **HIDS/HIPS**: HIDS/HIPS are both used inside host computers; the HIDS is used to detect attacks, and the HIPS is used to protect the computer against attacks. Both have filters set up to choose an alert type to filter. Look at the following screenshot, where we are setting a filter for insecure SSH connection attempts:

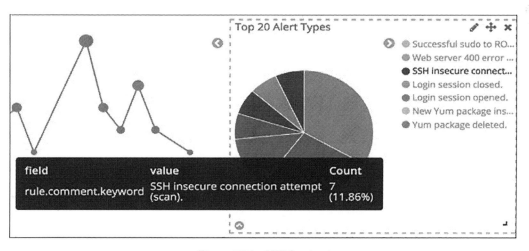

Figure 7.36 – HIDS output

- **Anti-virus/Advanced Malware Tools**: There are quite a few anti-virus/anti-malware tools that will scan the computer on a regular basis and then produce reports. The following screenshot shows a list of viruses that have been quarantined. The AVG free anti-virus software has quarantined the four viruses so that they cannot cause any damage:

Figure 7.37 – Quarantined viruses

- **File Integrity Checker**: Microsoft has a **System File Checker** (**SFC**) that can replace corrupted files by replacing them with a copy held in a compressed folder with system32. You run it with the sfc /scannow command, as shown in the following screenshot:

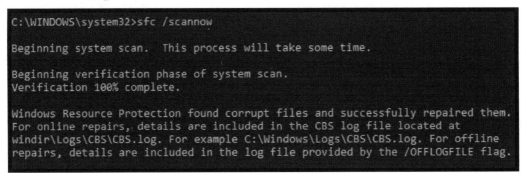

Figure 7.38 – System file checker

- **File Checksum Integrity Verifier** (**FCIV**): This is a Microsoft utility that can check the hash value of system files to ensure that there has been no tampering.

- **File Manipulation**: In a Linux environment you may want to look deeper into different files, including the log files that are produced. Let's look at some manual tools that an administrator could use, starting with Cat:

  a. **Concatenate (Cat)**: The `cat` command in Linux can be used to create files, view files, and also concatenate a number of files into another file. To create a new file called `sportsfile`, we use the following syntax:

  ```
  cat > sportsfile
  ```

  You can also concatenate the contents of three files and combine them in an output file using the following syntax:

  ```
  cat file1.txt file2.txt file3.txt | sort > samplefile.txt
  ```

  b. **Head**: The most important file in Linux is the `/var/log/messages` file, which shows system events such as a shutdown and reboot. We can use the `head` command to check the top 10 messages from that log using the following syntax:

  ```
  head /var/log/messages -n 10
  ```

  c. **Tail**: We can use the `tail` command to view the last 10 messages in the `/var/log/messages` log file using the following syntax:

  ```
  tail /var/log/messages -n 10
  ```

  d. **Grep**: This command is used to search text and log files for specific values. For example, if we wanted to search a file called **telephone numbers** for the number `236237`, we would use the following syntax:

  ```
  grep -f 236237 telephonenumbers.txt
  ```

  e. If we want to search a whole directory for the word `project`, we can use the following syntax:

  ```
  grep -r project
  ```

  f. **chmod**: This command is used to change the permission level, for example:

  ```
  chmod 766
  ```

Where the owner has `rwx`, the group has `rw-` and the others have `rw-`.

g. **Logger**: You can use logger to add a message to the local system log file or to a remote syslog server. We want the name of the local machine and a message of *today we found a phishing attack* to be added to the syslog server whose IP address is `1.1.1.1` at end of the `/var/log/syslog` file using the following syntax:

```
logger -n 1.1.1.1 'hostname' today we found a phishing
attack
```

- **Protocol Analyzer**: A protocol analyzer, such as Wireshark, can capture the traffic flowing through the network, including passwords in clear text and any commands being sent to network-based applications. A protocol analyzer can identify the three-way handshake between two hosts and the verbs being used with applications, such as the HTML GET verb for fetching a web page. But if we see the PUT or HEAD verb, we would recognize this as an attack.

Example: Someone within the company is not working as they should be and has been surfing the web, and the manager has called you in as the security administrator to gather evidence. You decide that a protocol analyzer or packet sniffer is the best tool for tracking the information. You run a Wireshark session and capture visits to the NFL website. When you analyze the trace, you notice that the request is using the HTTP GET verb. This is the request for a page on www. nfl.com. In the following screenshot, we are looking at an article entitled *Josh Hobbs and Mike Glennon drawing trade interest*. The URL is https://www.nfl. com/news/josh-dobbs-mike-glennon-drawing-trade-interest-0ap3000000952209:

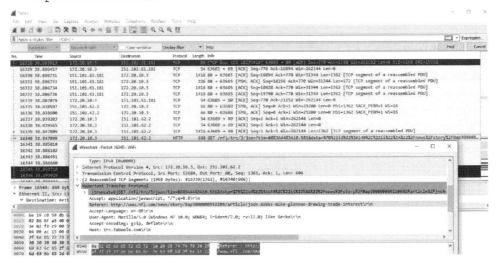

Figure 7.39 – Protocol analyzer

A protocol analyzer can also be referred to as a *packet sniffer* in the CompTIA Security+ exam.

- **tcpreplay**: This is an open source tool that can be used to analyze .pcap files generated by either Wireshark or tcpdump and then replay the traffic and send it to the NIPS to see whether it detects it.

Exploitation Frameworks

Exploitation framework tools, such as the open source Metasploit Framework, can develop and execute exploit code against a remote target computer. This can be used to harden your IT systems before they are attacked. They use information from the National Vulnerability Database, that is comprised of **Common Vulnerabilities and Exposures (CVE)** and uses the **Common Vulnerability Scoring System (CVSS)**, to show the level of severity of each of the vulnerabilities.

Forensic Tools

A forensics team may need to use tools to copy data or check the hash values to prove to the judge that the data has not been tampered with during the investigation. When a criminal's laptop arrives at the police station, the first thing a forensics team will do is to take a system image or a computer or a forensic copy of a removal drive. Let's look at some of the tools to begin with by cloning a disk:

- **How to Clone a Disk Using Third-Party Software**: In a Windows 10 environment, it is possible to capture a system image using the backup tools, but many IT security professionals prefer to use a third-party imaging product such as Acronis. Please read the following article at https://www.acronis.com/en-us/products/disk-director-home/. Another alternative is Clonezilla. Please read the article at https://clonezilla.org/

- **How to Clone a Disk Using the 'dd' Command**: When the forensics team are going to investigate an image on a desktop or laptop, the dd command can be used to clone a disk or copy a folder in a Linux/Unix environment. Here are two examples, the first to copy an entire hard drive, and the second to copy and deploy an image.

  In an SCSI environment, the first disk is known as /dev/sda, the second as/dev/sdb, and so on. If the first disk has two partitions, these will be sda1 and sda2.

  The if command represents the input file and the of command represents the output file.

- **Copy Entire Hard Disk**: We are going to copy the first SCSI disk to the third SCSI disk. The syntax we need is as follows:

```
dd if = /dev/sda of = /dev/sdb
```

- **Create an Image**: We are going to make a disk image of /dev/sda. We would use the following syntax:

```
dd if=/dev/sda of=~/sdadisk.img
```

- **Deploy an Image**: We are going to deploy the preceding image onto the /dev/sdb disk. We would use the following syntax:

```
dd if=sdadisk.img of=/dev/sdb.
```

- **Hashing**: The forensics examiner might use a hashing tool such as MD5, SHA1, or SHA256 to hash the data before or after the investigation. If the hash values match, then the data is said to have integrity.

- **Using the 'dcfldd' Command to Check File Hashes**: The dcfldd command is an enhanced version of the dd command and can be used to obtain forensic information such as the hash of the drive. This can be stored in the hashlog.txt file. In the following example, we are going to get the hash of the second partition on the second SCSI drive:

```
dcfldd if=/dev/sdb2 of=/media/disk/test_image.dd
hash=md5, sha1 hashlog=/media/disk/hashlog.txt
```

- **Capturing System Memory – Dump Files**: When a computer system crashes (commonly known as the *blue screen of death*), all of the content of the memory is saved in a dump file (.dmp). These dump files can be analyzed by using a tool such as *Blue Screen Review*. A Linux version would be memdump.

- **WinHex**: This can be used on any version of Windows operating systems to help forensics teams find evidence. It is a hexadecimal editor that can be used to find deleted or lost data and recover data from a corrupt drive: https://www.x-ways.net/winhex/index-m.html.

- **FTK imager**: This can be used to collect copies of data without making changes to the original evidence: https://marketing.accessdata.com/ftkimager4.2.0.

- **Autopsy**: This can be used to analyze hard drives, smartphones, and media cards. It has a built-in translator to translate foreign languages into English.

- **Password Crackers**: Password crackers, such as the Cain portion of Cain and Able or LOphtcrack, can be used to crack the passwords and create password hashes. In the Security+ exam, when you see names in clear text followed by hashes, the hash is a hash of the password.

IP Addressing

Everyone using the TCP/IP protocol for connectivity and every device has a unique IP address. In this section, we are going to look at the differences between the two types of IP addresses: IP version 4 and IP version 6.

IP Version 4

There are public addresses that you can lease, and private addresses that are free but can only be used internally. If you have a banger car, you can drive it around a private piece of land all day long, but as soon as you put it on a public road without any insurance, if you were caught by the police, they would impound the car. Private IP addresses can operate internally, but the routers on the internet will drop any private IP packets.

There are three private IP address ranges:

- **Class A**: The first number on the left starts with 1-126, although 127 is technically a Class A address. We cannot allocate it to a host as it is used for diagnostic testing.

- **Class B**: The range is `172.16.x.x` to `172.31.x.x`. It is only a partial address range.

- **Class C**: The range is `192.168.x.x`, and is the complete address range.

Each IP version 4 client needs an IP address and a subnet mask whose job is to determine whether the packet delivery is local or remote. If the packet is for a remote address, then the client needs to be configured with a default gateway – the router interface on the LAN. If the client does not have a default gateway, then it is restricted to communicating on the local network.

Subnet Mask

The subnet mask is used to divide IP addresses into blocks so that different subnets have their own IP address range. When using classful IP addressing, the default masks are as follows:

Class A: 255.0.0.0

Class B: 255.255.0.0

Class C: 255.255.255.0

The subnet mask can also tell whether the packet delivery is local or remote. If it is remote, it will send the packet to the default gateway.

CIDR Mask

With IP version 4 addresses, there are 4 octets each of 8 bits, making it 32-bit IP addressing. CIDR masks can be used in the same way as the subnet mask to divide networks into IP address ranges. If I have a CIDR mask of /24, that means I then have 24 bits for the network and 8 bits for hosts:

- /8 is the same as 255.0.0.0, as it uses 8 bits from the left.
- /16 is the same as 255.255.0.0, as it uses 16 bits from the left.
- /24 is the same as 255.255.255.0, as it uses 24 bits from the left.

Cloud providers allocate CIDR blocks in both IP version 4 and IP version 6 for each different **Virtual Private Clouds (VPC)**.

DHCP

The automatic way of allocating IP addresses is to use a server called the **Dynamic Host Configuration Protocol (DHCP)** server. This is a server with a database of IP addresses that can allocate to requesting hosts. There is a four-stage process, and it is known as D-O-R-A.

IP Version 4 – Lease Process

IP version 4 observes the following steps to perform the lease:

1. **Discover**: When the client boots up, it sends a broadcast to find a DHCP server and can be identified by inserting its **Media Access Control** (**MAC**) address into the broadcast packet.

2. **Offer**: If the client is lucky enough to find a DHCP server, it then receives an offer packet from the DHCP server. If there are two DHCP servers, it will receive two offers.

3. **Request**: The client replies back to the DHCP server that it wants to obtain the address from.

4. **Acknowledgment**: The final packet from the DHCP server is the acknowledgment that included the IP address, subnet mask, default gateway, and DNS address.

5. **Command line**: To release and renew an IP address using the command line, we would run the `ipconfig /release` command and then the `ipconfig/renew` command.

IP Version 4 Lease Process – Troubleshooting

A DHCP client will not always obtain an IP address because maybe it cannot connect to the DHCP server. Another reason is that the address pool is exhausted. In these cases, the local machine will allocate an **Automated Private IP Address** (**APIPA**), starting with `169.254.x.x`. This is an excellent aid to troubleshooting, as it lets the network engineer know that the client cannot contact the DHCP server.

There are many reasons why this happens, so let's look at the DHCP process:

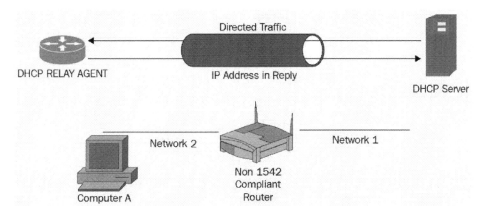

Figure 7.40 – DHCP process across subnets

If the DHCP client is on another subnet, it can cause some problems:

- **RFC-1542-Compliant Router**: A device that connects different networks and subnets together. DHCP-broadcast traffic will pass through an RFC-1542-compliant router, but in *Figure 7.40*, the router is not an RFC-1542-compliant router, and so broadcast traffic from Computer A will not get to the DHCP server, and an APIPA address will be allocated that will prevent the client from obtaining network resources.

- **Opening Ports**: If the router is a not an RFC-1542-compliant router, you could open UDP ports 67 and 68 by setting allow rules on the ACL of the router, otherwise the DHCP broadcast will suffer from an Implicit Deny.

- **DHCP Relay Agent**: A DHCP relay agent is programmed with the IP address of the DHCP server. Therefore, it contacts the server using unicast and not broadcast traffic. The DHCP relay agent acts as a set of ears listening for DHCP discover requests. It then acts as a proxy and obtains an IP address from the DHCP server to return to the requesting client.

- **DHCP Snooping**: DHCP snooping prevents a rogue DHCP server from allocating IP addresses to a host on your network.

> **Exam tip**
> If you cannot get an IP address from a DHCP server, this is because of network connectivity or resource exhaustion. When this happens, you will get an APIPA address starting with 169.254.x.x.

IP Version 6 Addressing

IP version 6 addresses are in a colon-hexadecimal format and comprise 8 blocks of 4 digits, making it a 128-bit address. The first 64 bits from the left-hand side are the routing or network portion, and the last 64 bits will be used for the host. Using IP version 6 reduces that number of entries into a routing table and this will make routing more efficient. However, on the downside, companies would have to convert all of their network applications and devices to be IP version 6-compatible.

There are different address ranges, and the main four points are as follows:

- **Public**: The public addresses, just like the IP version 4 addresses, can be used externally. They start on the right-hand side with values of 2001, 2002, or 2003. An example is 2001:ABCD:0000:0000:0000:0000:1230:0ABC.

- **Link Local**: Link local addresses are like the APIPA IP version 4 address. They are restricted to one subnet and start with `fe80`.

- **Unique Local**: Unique local addresses are sometimes known as site-local addresses. They are restricted to a site and start with either `fc00` or `fd00`. A site is a number of IP subnets.

- **Simplify – Removing Leading Zeros**: An IP version 6 address can be simplified by removing leading zeros and replacing a number of blocks of `0000` with a double colon. Here are two examples:

Example 1: We have an IP version 6 address of `2001:ABCD:0000:0000:0000:0000:1230:0ABC` that we want to simplify. In this case, we will remove only the leading zeros:

```
2001:ABCD:0000:0000:0000:0000:1230:0ABC
2001:ABCD::1230:ABC
```

You will notice that we have replaced four blocks of zeros with double colons. We need to count the remaining blocks and, since there are four, we know that four blocks are missing.

Example 2: We have an IP version 6 address of `2001:ABCD:0000:0000:ABCD:0000:1230:0ABC` that we want to simplify. In this case, we will remove only the leading zeros:

```
2001:ABCD:0000:0000:ABCD:0000:1230:0ABC
2001:ABCD::ABCD:0:1230:ABC
```

You will notice that this is trickier as there are blocks of zeros in two places, but we replace the first blocks of zeros with the double colons, and then, if we have further blocks of zeros, we replace each of these with `:0:`. In the example, we count only six blocks, so we know we have only two blocks of zeros.

> **Exam tip**
> Cloud providers allocate IP addresses for VPC by using different CIDR blocks for each network.

Review Questions

Now it's time to check your knowledge. Answer the questions, and then check your answers, which can be found in the *Assessments* section at the end of the book:

1. What is the purpose of a web application firewall and where is it normally placed?

2. What is Implicit Deny and which two devices does it affect?

3. What is the firewall that does content filtering, URL filtering, and malware inspection?

4. Which network device connects two networks together?

5. Which type of internal device connects users on the same network?

6. Which type of device hides the internal network from hackers on the internet?

7. What is an inline NIPS?

8. Which type of IPS protects virtual machines from attack?

9. Which type of IPS is placed behind the firewall as an additional layer of security?

10. If I don't have a NIDS on my network, which device can passively monitor network traffic?

11. What is the difference between a signature and anomaly-based NIDS?

12. What is the passive device that sits on your internal network?

13. If I receive an alert that server 1 has a virus and I inspect the server and there are no viruses, what is this known as?

14. How can I prevent someone from accessing a medical center's network by plugging their laptop into a port in the waiting room?

15. How can I prevent someone from plugging a rogue access point into my network?

16. How do 802.1x and port security differ? Which one gives me more functionality?

17. Which is the purpose of web caching on a proxy server?

18. What is the purpose of a VPN?

19. What happens in the IKE phase of a VPN session?

20. What is the purpose of a VPN concentrator?

21. What is the most secure VPN tunneling protocol?

22. What modes would you use in a L2TP/IPSec tunnel over the internet and then internally?

23. Which VPN session type would you use on a site-to-site VPN?

24. What network device should you use to manage a high volume of web traffic?

25. What type of network is used by a virtual network so that the route requests are forwarded to a controller?

26. What is the purpose of a screened subnet and what type of web server is located there?

27. If I want to find out what attack methods a potential hacker is using, what do I need to set up?

28. What is the purpose of network access control? Name the two agents that it uses.

29. What type of device can be used to automate the collection of log files across many different devices?

30. If I wanted to back up data to a backup device but, at the same time, prevent someone from deleting the data, what device do I need to use?

31. Explain the port mirror process and name another device that could be used for the same process?

32. What type of records are created by DNSSEC?

33. What are the two portions of an IPSec packet?

34. How can I tell whether my laptop fails to get an IP address from a DHCP server?

35. What type of IP address is 2001:123A:0000:0000:ABC0:00AB:0DCS:0023 and how can we simplify it?

36. What is the benefit of an HTML 5 VPN?

37. What mode is an L2TP/IPSec VPN if it encrypts both the header and the payload?

38. What is the purpose of a jump server?

39. What is load balancing persistence or affinity?

40. What is the downside to using two load balancers in an active/active mode?

41. Three different groups of workers are in an open plan office and they are all connected to the same physical switch. What can be done to isolate them from each other?

42. How does East-West traffic operate?

43. What is a zero-trust network and where is it likely to be used?

44. Why would someone use Angry IP?

45. When can I use `curl` or `nmap`?

46. When would someone use the Harvester tool?

47. How can an attacker find the DNS records from your domain?

48. Why would I use the scanless tool?

49. What tools can I use as a sandbox to analyze files for malware?

50. What is the purpose of DHCP snooping?

51. What are the two main reason why I would receive an APIPA address of `169.254.1.1`?

8
Securing Wireless and Mobile Solutions

Over the past 5 years, there has been an increased use of wireless devices, both in the workplace and in hotels and coffee shops. The demand is so high that if your hotel does not provide Wi-Fi, then your bookings may decrease. As wireless has increased, so have the mobile devices, ranging from IoT, smart phones, and tablets to laptops. Today's security professionals need to have a good fundamental knowledge of security for both mobile devices and wireless solutions. This is what we will be covering in this chapter.

In this chapter, we will cover the following topics:

- Implementing Wireless Security
- Understanding Secure Mobile Solutions

Implementing Wireless Security

Wireless communication is now part of everyday life, from using 4G/5G on your mobile phone to access the internet or using Bluetooth to listen to your music as you walk down the road. However, if your wireless device is insecure, this can lead to data loss and maybe someone stealing funds from your bank account.

Let's first look at the different types of wireless networks:

- **WLAN**: A **Wireless Local Area Network** (**WLAN**) is an internal corporate wireless network that sits in your Local Area Network. Normally, in a WLAN, you would use WPA2 Enterprise, the corporate version of wireless with CCMP, the strongest wireless encryption as it uses AES encryption.

- **Guest**: A guest wireless network is a wireless network separate from your WLAN where visitors can access the internet; it may be used for training purposes. The guest wireless network can be used by members of staff to access the internet during their lunchtimes.

- **Infrastructure**: An infrastructure wireless network is where devices connect to a wireless network using a **Wireless Access Point** (**WAP**).

- **Ad Hoc**: An ad hoc network is where wireless connectivity is enabled between two devices without a WAP.

- **Wireless Scanner/Analyzer**: This is good for troubleshooting wireless connectivity and collecting SSID information from packets going to the WAP.

> **Exam tip**
> A guest wireless network gives visitors access to the internet and could also be used by employees at lunchtime.

In the following section, we will look at WAP controllers.

Wireless Access Point Controllers

Whether you are a home or a business user, you will need to set up your WAP in order to provide an IP address and internet connectivity to the devices using the WAP. Let's look at the two different types of controllers.

- **Fat Controllers**: A fat controller is a standalone WAP, similar to that used at home. It has its own pool of DHCP addresses, and all configurations for the wireless network are installed on the WAP.

- **Thin Controllers**: A thin controller allows multiple WAPs to be controlled remotely by a single controller; this is ideal in a corporate environment where there are quite a few WAPs.

> **Exam tip**
> A thin controller is used to manage multiple WAPs remotely.

Securing Access to Your WAP

Without the use of encryption, there are some simple methods for securing access to your WAP:

- **Default Username and Password**: When you install a WAP, it has a default username and password, both being set to *admin or password*, in lowercase. One of the first steps is to change both of these and then set up an encryption method. The admin password is known as the *master password* and should be protected by encrypting it with Counter Mode with **Cipher Block Chaining Message Authentication Code Protocol** (**CCMP**), which is the strongest as it uses AES 128-bit for encryption in WPA2 and 256-bit for encryption in WPA3.

- **Disable the Security Set Identifier (SSID)**: The name of the wireless network is known as the SSID. The default setting for the SSID is called *default*. One of your first steps is to change this. You could protect the wireless network by disabling the SSID so that it is not broadcast. In *Figure 8.1*, the SSID is still enabled. The administrator should check the box next to **Disable Broadcast SSID**:

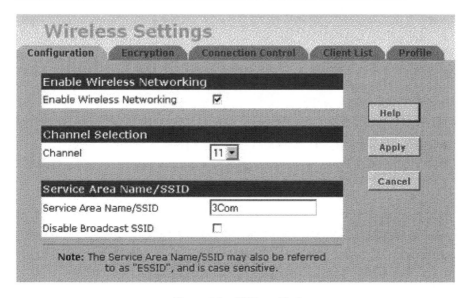

Figure 8.1 – SSID enabled

- **Discovering the Disabled SSID**: A Wi-Fi analyzer, sometimes called a wireless sniffer or a wireless scanner, has the ability to extract the SSID from a packet going to the WAP. An SSID decloak device can magically capture the SSID from a WAP. To protect the WAP, we must use encryption.

- **MAC Filtering**: To control access to a WAP, we insert the **Media Access Control** (**MAC**) address into MAC filtering, and then only those devices with a MAC address will be allowed access. A MAC address is a unique address that every device has embedded into it. If you think of it, why did they not call it MAC addition, because that is basically what you are doing?

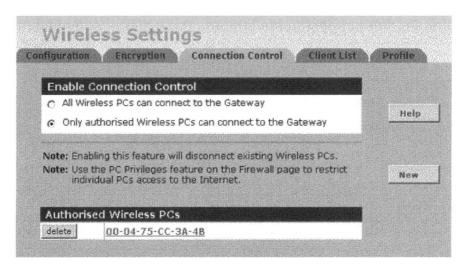

Figure 8.2 – MAC filtering

In the following section, we will look at the different wireless bands.

Wireless Bandwidth/Band Selection

There are different wireless standards, and we need to know the limitations of each. The band selection is also known as the frequency:

Standard	Frequency	Speed	Remarks
802.11 a	5 GHz	54 Mbps	5 GHz channel bandwidth is 40 MHz
802.11 b	2.4 GHz	11 Mbps	2.4 GHz channel bandwidth is 20 MHz
802.11 g	2.4 GHz	54 Mbps	
802.11 n	2.4 GHz/5Hz	150 Mbps	MIMO - multiple input multiple output and travels the furthest distance

Wireless Channels

In the Security+ exam, the wireless channels go from *channel 1* up to *channel 11*, and the device placement should be as follows:

- **Channel 1**: Your first wireless device
- **Channel 11**: Your second wireless device
- **Channel 6**: Your third wireless device

We place the device's channels as far apart as possible to prevent the overlap of adjacent channels and interference. Wireless devices can suffer interference from elevators, baby monitors, cordless phones, metal racking, and load-bearing walls, to name but a few things.

Wireless Antenna Types

WAP uses antennas to operate. There are three main antenna types:

- **Omnidirectional**: Omnidirectional antennas provide the most coverage as they transmit over 360 degrees.
- **Directional**: Directional antennas transmit only in one direction. Therefore, if the antenna is pointing in the wrong direction, there will be no connection to the wireless network.
- **Yagi**: A Yagi fin is an antenna that can transmit in two directions. Therefore, it is suitable for placement between two buildings.

Wireless Coverage

One of the security implications of having a wireless network is to ensure that wireless networks will have coverage. This will give access to resources in a timely fashion without the coverage being extended outside of the companies' boundaries where it could be hacked.

Let's look at options that need to be considered before setting up a wireless network:

- **Site Survey**: Before we install a wireless network, we need to complete a site survey so that we identify what could cause interference with the wireless network. In certain areas, we may need an extra WAP because of potential interference with the network. If we install a wireless network and it does not function properly or runs at a slow speed, then we have not carried out a thorough site survey.

- **WAP Placement**: There are many things that could interfere with or prevent your wireless network from working, and these include load-bearing walls, cordless phones, microwaves, elevators, metal frames, metal doors, and radio waves.

- **Heat Map**: A heat map shows your wireless coverage. The red and orange areas indicate good coverage, but the blue areas indicate poor coverage:

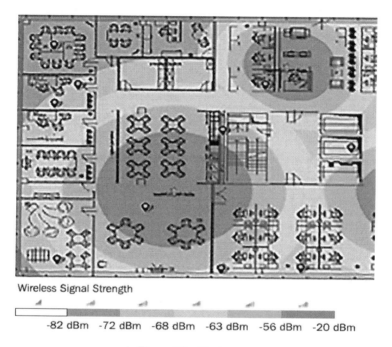

Wireless Signal Strength

-82 dBm   -72 dBm   -68 dBm   -63 dBm   -56 dBm   -20 dBm

Figure 8.3 – Heat map

The heat map could also show green as poor coverage and it can help you identify where you have channel overlap.

- **Low-Power Directional Antennas**: If the wireless network goes outside of the boundary of a company's network, it may be hacked or attacked. To prevent these attacks, we turn down the power of the WAP and this reduces the distance of the wireless network coverage.

- **Wireless Speed Slow**: If the speed of the wireless network is very slow, we may be too far away from the WAP or the connection may be saturated as a result of downloading large files.

> **Exam tip**
> If my newly installed WLAN is not fully functional, we may not have carried out the site survey properly or placed it incorrectly.

Wireless – Open System Authentication

If we want to set up a wireless network for the general public to access without any encryption or any passwords, we could use Open System Authentication, but users would have to access the WAP at their own risk.

Wireless Encryption

Wireless networks need to be secure and they can be secured by using encryption. Let's look at the types of wireless encryption.

- **Wired Equivalent Privacy (WEP)**: WEP is the weakest form of wireless security, with a 40-bit key that is very easy to crack.

- **Wi-Fi Protected Access (WPA)**: WPA replaced WEP as it uses the **Temporal Key Integrity Protocol** (**TKIP**), which was designed to be more secure than WEP. WPA is backward compatible with WEP, and TKIP is backward compatible with legacy wireless encryption.

Wi-Fi Protected Access Version 2 (WPA2)

Let's look at the different types of WPA 2:

- **Wi-Fi Protected Access Version 2 (WPA2)**: This is much stronger than WPA as it uses Counter Mode with the Cipher Block Chaining Message Authentication Code Protocol. This is the strongest version of WPA2 as it uses AES for authentication.

- **WPA2-Pre-Shared Key (WPA2–PSK)**: WPA2-PSK was introduced for the home user who does not have an enterprise setup. The home user enters the password of the wireless router to gain access to the home network; this is very common nowadays.

- **WPA2-Enterprise**: WPA2-Enterprise is a corporate version of WPA2 where a RADIUS server combines with 802.1x, using certificates for authentication. It is used in a centralized domain environment.

- **WPA2-TKIP**: WPA2-TKIP could be used for backward compatibility with legacy systems. However, TKIP was replaced by a more secure CCMP that is not backward compatible.

- **WPA2-CCMP**: WPA2-CCMP (Counter Mode with Cipher Block Chaining Message Authentication Code Protocol) is the strongest version of WPA2 as it uses AES for authentication.

- **WPA2-WPS**: When we access our wireless network or gaming console, we may use WPS, where the password is already stored and all you need to do is to press the button to get connected to the wireless network. This could be the victim of a brute-force attack.

Wi-Fi Protected Access Version 3 (WPA3)

Let's now look at WPA3 and its features, which replaced WPA2. At the time of writing, this is 15 years old.

Wi-Fi Protected Access Version 3 (**WPA 3**) was released in 2018 to address the weaknesses in WPA2 and uses a much stronger 256-bit Galois/Counter Mode Protocol (GCMP-256) for encryption. There are two versions, *WPA3-Personal* for home users, and *WPA3-Enterprise* for corporate users.

Let's look at some of the features of WPA3:

- **Protected Management Frames** (**PMF**): This can provide multicast transmission and has the ability to protect wireless packets against **Initialization Vector** (**IV**) attacks where the attacker tries to capture the encryption keys.

- **Simultaneous Authentication of Equals** (**SAE**): SAE is used with WPA3-Personal and replaces the WPA2-PSK. SAE uses a very secure Diffie Hellman handshake, called dragonfly, and protects against brute-force attacks. It uses **Perfect Forward Secrecy** (**PFS**), which ensures that your session keys cannot be compromised and is immune to offline attacks.

- **Wi-Fi Easy Connect**: This makes it very easy to connect IoT devices, such as a smartphone, by simply using a QR code.

- **WPA3-Enterprise**: WPA3 has an enterprise version that supports 256-bit AES, whereas, WPA2 only supported 128 bits, making it suitable for the government and finance departments. It uses **Elliptic-Curve Diffie Hellman Ephemeral** (**ECDHE**) for the initial handshake.

- **WPA3-Personal**: This uses SAE, which means that users can use passwords that are easier to remember. It also uses PFS, which means the traffic is secure even if the password has been compromised. It is easier to connect IoT devices.

- **Wi-Fi Enhanced Open**: This is an enhancement of WPA2 open authentication, where it uses encryption for open authentication. It can be used in public areas such as hotels, cafés, and airports, where no password is required, and this prevents eavesdropping as it uses PMF.

Wireless Captive Portals

When you join the wireless network at the airport, you are connected to the free Wi-Fi, yet you cannot access the internet right away. It redirects you to a captive portal so that you can provide additional validation of who you are, normally through an email address or your Facebook or Google account information. You could also need to agree to the terms of their AUP. You can also accept to pay their premium subscription, thereby giving you a faster connection.

Wireless Attacks

There are three main types of attacks relating to wireless networks:

- **Evil Twin**: An evil twin is when there is another WAP that looks like the legitimate WAP but it has no security. This is designed to lure you into using this WAP and is where your traffic will be captured.

- **Wireless Disassociation Attack**: This type of attack comes under the realm of a **Denial of Service (DoS)** attack. A de-authentication frame is sent to the wireless user so that their connection to the WAP drops.

- **Rogue Access Point**: A rogue access point is where an additional access point is joined to your corporate network, yet again with no security, so as to lure users into connecting to it. This can be prevented by installing 802.1x-managed switches where all devices connecting to the network are authenticated.

Wireless Authentication Protocols

There are numerous wireless authentication protocols:

- **Extensible Authentication Protocol (EAP)**: EAP is an authentication framework allowing point-to-point connections. The WAP will send authentication information. The client will use this information so that only they can communicate with one another. There are different types, so let's look at a few of these here:

  a. **Protected Extensible Authentication Protocol (PEAP)**: The PEAP is a version of EAP that encapsulated the EAP data and made it more secure for WLANs.

  b. **EAP-FAST**: EAP-FAST, developed by Cisco, is used in wireless networks and point-to-point connections to perform session authentication. It replaced LEAP, which was insecure.

c. **EAP-TLS**: EAP-TLS is the most secure version of wireless authentication as it requires a X509 certification from its local CA installed on the client that is stored in the **Trusted Platform Module (TPM)** chip.

d. **EAP-TTLS**: EAP-TTLS uses two phases; the first is to set up a secure session with the server, utilizing certificates that are seamless to the client, which will then use a protocol such as MS-CHAP to complete the session. It is designed to connect older legacy systems.

- **IEEE 802.1x**: IEEE 802.1x is transparent to users as it uses certificates and can be used in conjunction with a RADIUS server for enterprise networks.

- **RADIUS Federation**: A RADIUS federation is a federation service where access to the network is gained by using WAPs. It has nothing to do with a RADIUS server; this is a misconception by test takers. They think that a RADIUS federation is related to RADIUS authentication. It is merely a label.

Example: Two different universities decide to have a joint venture for finance and mathematics. They decide on using federation services for authentication so that when the students go to the third-party university and connect to the network through a WAP, this makes it a RADIUS federation. If they connected via an Ethernet cable, it would just be federation services.

In the following section, we will look at how we can securely deploy mobile devices.

Deploying Mobile Devices Securely

Mobile devices are now used in our everyday lives and they pose problems for security teams as they are very portable and extremely easy to steal. In this section, we will look at some of the problems that you may face as a security professional. But first, let's look at mobile device management.

Mobile Device Management

Mobile Device Management (MDM) sets policies for the installation and protection of mobile devices. For example, they may prevent the camera from being used on mobile devices and could also prevent a smartphone from being able to send/receive texts. You can set password policies on the password length, or remote wipe for lost or stolen devices, where the device is rolled back to the factory setup.

Bring Your Own Device

Bring Your Own Device (BYOD) is where an employee is encouraged to bring in their own device so that they can use it for work. Although this may save the employer money, it also has its pitfalls. BYOD needs two policies to be effective, but I will break the onboarding/offboarding into separate parts:

- **Acceptable Use Policy (AUP)**: An AUP outlines what the employee can do with the device during the working day. For example, they will not be allowed to play games or surf their personal email. If this is not acceptable, then the BYOD falls at the first hurdle and employees cannot bring their devices to work.

- **Onboarding Policy**: The onboarding policy would ensure that the device coming into the company's network is fully patched and secure before being attached to the network.

- **Offboarding Policy**: The offboarding policy covers things such as handing back the company's data, as this could pose a problem. If the device owner does not agree, you may have to take them to court to get your data back. Some companies use storage segmentation, also known as *containerization*, where they insert a storage card where the business data would be stored. During offboarding, the employee would simply be asked to hand back the card.

  Example 1: A new employee has brought their mobile device into the company and within 30 minutes, one of the file servers has caught a virus. The security team tracks the source of the virus to the mobile device. How could this have been avoided? It's simple – the onboarding policy has not been carried out properly; if it had been, the virus would have been removed before connecting the device.

  Example 2: John, a member of the sales team, who has been using his tablet for BYOD, has just won the National Lottery and decided to leave the company. During the offboarding phase, he was asked to reset his tablet to its factory settings to ensure that the data was deleted. John has refused to do this as he has personal data and music files on the tablet. The company have called the local police and accused him of stealing their data. John informed the police officer that this is his personal device with his own data, and he produced a copy of the sales receipt for the device. The police officer was powerless and could do nothing further. The company would have to take John to court and prove that the data was theirs. John is now traveling the world, leaving the company with a further headache; they cannot take John to court because they don't know which country he is in. If they had used storage segmentation and asked John for the storage card on exit, this scenario would never have occurred.

Choose Your Own Device

Choose Your Own Device (**CYOD**) avoids problems of ownership because the company has a variety of tablets, phones, and laptops. When a new employee comes along, they merely choose one of these devices from a list. When they leave the company and offboard, the devices are taken from them as they belong to the company. The acceptable use policy would state that the devices can only store company data as they are corporate-owned devices.

Corporate-Owned Personally-Enabled

Corporate-Owned Personally-Enabled (**COPE**) is where the company purchases the device, such as a tablet, phone, or laptop, and allows the employee to use it for personal use. This is a much better solution for the company than BYOD. However, the IT team can limit what applications run on the devices as they are corporate-owned. Some countries' laws prohibit the wiping of personal devices. With COPE, however, since the company owns the device, they have every right to wipe it remotely if it is lost or stolen.

Exam tip

With CYOD or COPE, there will only be a limited choice of devices and this is much easier to support than BYOD, which could involve thousands of devices.

In the following section, we will look at different mobile device connection methods.

Mobile Device Connection Methods

There are various different connection methods for mobile devices:

- **Cellular**: This is where tablets and phones are using 3G, 4G, or 5G to connect to their provider without needing any other devices. Cellular connections are encrypted to prevent anyone seeing who is logging on or stealing your data. The problem that cellular faces is that, if there are no masts nearby and the device has a setting of no service, they will not work.

- **Hotspot**: A hotspot is a physical location where people can connect to so that they can access the internet. It is possible to turn your cellular phone into a hotspot.

- **Global Positioning System** (**GPS**): GPS uses three satellites in the Earth's orbit to measure the distance between two points.

- **Radio-frequency identification** (**RFID**): This uses radio frequency to identify electromagnetic fields in a tag to track assets. It is commonly used in shops as the tags are attached to high value assets to prevent theft. When the asset leaves the store, an alarm goes off.

- **Wi-Fi**: Connecting to a WAP is a common method of gaining access to the internet. The connection needs to be encrypted to prevent man-in-the-middle attacks. Some wireless providers have hotspots in major cities and airports so that their customers can connect. If we use a WAP, this is known as an infrastructure setup, and if we connect two wireless devices together without an access point, this is known as ad hoc. Wi-Fi direct is where two devices connect to one another, and one acts like an access point.

- **Bluetooth**: You may see someone walking down the street with a piece of gray plastic on one of their ears and they seem to be talking to themselves, but they are using their phone with a Bluetooth connection. Most Bluetooth devices have a range of about 10 meters. The devices are paired using a code to connect and provide a **personal area connection** (**PAN**). For example, Ian is driving and has his phone set to hands-free. As he is driving, he receives a phone call from a friend and he has him on loudspeaker; this is an example of using Bluetooth. It is commonly used for headsets.

- **Near-Field Communication** (**NFC**): NFC is normally used to make a wireless payment when the card must be within 4 cm of the card reader. You should store your NFC-enabled card inside an aluminum pouch or wallet to prevent someone standing very close to you from skimming your card.

> **Exam tip**
> NFC is used for contactless payments within 4 cm of the card.

- **Infrared**: An infrared device is purely line-of-sight and has a maximum range of about 1 meter. This can be used to print from your laptop to an infrared printer. Infrared connections are not encrypted, but you could see an attacker as they need to be within 1 meter.

- **USB**: Some mobile devices can be tethered to a USB dongle to gain access to the internet. A flash USB device can be used to transfer data between devices, as it is self-installing, and the security teams tend to use group policy to prevent data from being stolen by removable devices or use **Data Loss Prevention** (**DLP**).

- **Secure Satellite Communications (SATCOM):** The **secure satellite communications (SATCOM)** equipment used by the US military is currently undergoing impressive capacity and performance advances. There is a dish at one location that connects point to point with a dish in another location. At the same time, it faces increasing security threats on several fronts:

Figure 8.4 – SATCOM

Let's now move on to the different types of mobile device concepts and the role each of them plays.

Mobile Device Management Concepts

Mobile Device Management (MDM) is a management console that allows security administrators to control, secure, and enforce policies on smartphones, tablets, and other endpoint devices. You can prevent smartphones from sending text messages or using the camera. It sets up the authentication method, including the length of the password. Let's look at the different aspects of MDM:

- **Unified Endpoint Management (UEM):** This provides management of the hardware, for example, desktops, printer, tablets, smartphones, and IoT devices ensuring that they are patches similar to **network access control (NAC)**. It can control the security and applications running on the devices and can determine which devices have been subject to jailbreaking and rooting and will block them.

An example of this is Microsoft Intune. Details can be found at `https://www.microsoft.com/en-gb/microsoft-365/enterprise-mobility-security/microsoft-intune`.

- **Mobile Application Management (MAM)**: This allows a security team to tie down an application's security before it is allocated to any personnel. It controls access to company applications and data and can restrict the exfiltration of data from the company applications.

Mobile devices are very small and very easy to steal. Therefore, we need to look at how we can prevent someone from accessing the data even if the device's host has been lost or stolen. We will first look at screen locks and passwords, followed by biometrics, and then context-aware authentication:

- **Screen Locks**: Screen locks are activated once the mobile device has not been accessed for a period of time. Then, after it is locked, the user gets a number of attempts to insert the PIN before the device is disabled.

- **Passwords and PINs**: Some mobile devices, such as smartphones, are very easy to steal and you can conceal them by putting them in a pocket. It is crucial that strong passwords and PINs with six or more characters are used. This makes decoding them more difficult and can lead to the device being disabled.

  Example: An iPhone gives you six attempts to log in, and after that it will disable the login for 1 minute. If you then fail on the seventh attempt, it locks you out for a further 2 minutes. If you continue to input the wrong PIN, you get locked out for 60 minutes on your ninth attempt.

  > **Exam tip**
  > Mobile devices need screen locks and strong passwords to protect them.

- **Biometrics**: Mobile devices can use biometrics, such as fingerprint or facial recognition. Apple uses Touch ID and Microsoft uses Windows Hello.

- **Context-Aware Authentication**: Context-aware security is location-based. It checks the country from where the request for authentication is being made. This is extremely important if you are using a zero-trust model.

  Example: Mary, a financial director based in London, is using context-aware authentication. For the authentication to be successful, the user must be Mary, the time has to be between 9 a.m. and 5 p.m., Monday to Friday, and she needs to be in London. If not all of these criteria are met, then authentication fails.

Device Management

Corporate devices need to be controlled so that employees cannot simply connect to an app store and download every application that they wish. For example, allowing games on corporate devices would have an adverse impact on productivity and security. We are now going to look at the downloads, applications, and content managers, and their characteristics, followed by remote wipe:

- **Download Manager**: The download manager controls the number of connections and the speed of downloading onto a mobile device.

- **Application Management**: Application management uses whitelists to control which applications are allowed to be installed onto the mobile device.

- **Content Management**: Content management stores business data in a secure area of the device in an encrypted format to protect it against attacks. It prevents confidential or business data from being shared with external users.

- **Remote Wipe**: When a mobile device has been lost or stolen, it can be remote wiped. The device will revert to its factory settings and the data will no longer be available.

> **Exam tip**
> Geo-tracking will tell you the location of a stolen device.

Device Protection

Mobile devices are very easy to lose or steal, so we must have some way of finding those devices; we are going to look at the differences between geofencing, geolocation, and using cable locks:

- **Geofencing**: Geofencing uses the **Global Positioning System** (**GPS**) or RFID to define geographical boundaries. Once the device is taken past the defined boundaries, the security team will be alerted.

- **Geolocation**: Geolocation uses GPS to give the actual location of a mobile device. This is used when you lose your iPad and then you use your iPhone to determine its location. This can be very useful if you lose or drop a device.

- **Cable Locks**: Cable locks on laptops and tablets prevent them from being stolen.

> **Exam tip**
> Geofencing prevents mobile devices from being removed from the company's premises.

Device Data

To protect the data that is stored on a device, we should implement **Full Device Encryption (FDE)**. The device requires a **Trusted Platform Module (TPM)** chip to store the encryption keys.

Example: A salesperson has just received a new company laptop where the operating system has been hardened. The device uses Bitlocker encryption, where the whole drive is encrypted to protect the data stored on the hard drive. In the Security+ exam, this is known as FDE.

Keeping your company data separate from personal data on a BYOD is very important. Let's look at two options for doing this:

- **Containerization**: This gives organizations the ability to deploy and manage corporate content securely in an encrypted space on the device. All corporate resources, such as proprietary applications, corporate emails, calendars, and contacts, reside within this managed space. We could also place an application inside a virtual machine to segregate it from the laptop.

- **Storage Segmentation**: This is where an external device is connected to a laptop, for example, a USB flash drive or **Secure Digital (SD)** card. This allows the data on storage segmentation to be separate from any application or data already on the device.

Example: If you are using your own smartphone as a BYOD but your company has asked you to separate the business data that they give you from your personal data, for example, pictures of family and friends that you already have stored on the phone, the easiest way to do this is to install an SD card on the phone where you will store the company data. This makes offboarding your data pretty easy; all you would have to do is eject the SD card and surrender it to the company.

Mobile Device Enforcement and Monitoring

There are many different tools and features that roll out with mobile devices. As a security professional, you need to know the security threats that they pose. Some of the features that a security professional should be well-versed in are mentioned here:

- **Network Access Control**: Network access control ensures that mobile devices that connect to your network are fully patched and compliant before obtaining access to the internal network

- **Firmware Over-The-Air (OTA) Updates**: Firmware is a software that is installed on a small, read-only memory chip on a hardware device and is used to control the hardware running on the device. Firmware OTA updates are pushed out periodically by the vendor, ensuring that the mobile device is secure. An example is when the mobile device vendor sends a notification that there is a software update; this will include a firmware update.

- **Custom Firmware – Android Rooting**: Custom firmware downloads are used so that you can root your mobile device. This means that you are going to give yourself a higher level of permissions on that device and remove the vendor's security.

> **Exam tip**
> Rooting and jailbreaking remove the vendor restrictions on a mobile device to allow unsupported software to be installed.

- **Carrier Unlocking**: Carrier unlocking is where a mobile device is no longer tied to the original carrier. This will allow you to use your device with any provider.

- **Jailbreaking**: Jailbreaking is similar to rooting, only this time the operating system is Apple's iOS – this allows you to run unauthorized software on Apple devices and remove device security restrictions placed on the device. You can still access the Apple App Store even though jailbreaking has been carried out.

- **Rooting**: Rooting is similar to jailbreaking, except it is for an Android device.

- **Third-Party App Stores**: There is a danger of downloading apps from third-party app stores as there is no guarantee of the quality of the app being installed. This could pose a security risk. Later, you could find that it had embedded monitoring software.

- **Sideloading**: Sideloading is having an application package in .apk format and then installing it on a mobile device. This is useful for developers who want to trial third-party apps, but also allow unauthorized software to run on a mobile device.

- **SE Android**: Android devices have a Knox container that allows you to segment business data separate from personal data. SE Android will prevent applications outside of the Knox container from accessing resources inside the Knox container.

- **USB On-The-Go** (**USB OTG**): USB OTG allows USB devices plugged into tablets and smartphones to act as a host for other USB devices. Apple does not allow USB OTG. Attaching USB devices can pose security problems as it makes it easy to steal information.

- **Camera Use**: Smartphones and tablets roll out with very good quality camera and video recorders whose media can be circulated on social media within seconds. This poses a security risk to companies, as trade secrets could be stolen very easily. Research and development departments ban the use of personal smartphones in the workplace. MDM polices may disable the cameras on company-owned smartphones.

- **Recording Microphones**: Smartphones and tablets can record conversations with their built-in microphones. They could be used to take notes, but they could also be used to tape conversations or record the proceedings of a confidential meeting.

- **Short Message Service** (**SMS**): This is known as text messaging and has become a common method of communication. These messages can be sent between two people in a room without other people in the room knowing about their communication. These text messages could be used to launch an attack.

- **Multimedia Messaging Service** (**MMS**): This is a way to send pictures as attachments, similar to sending SMS messages.

- **Rich Communication Service** (**RCS**): This is an enhancement to SMS and is used in Facebook and WhatsApp to send messages so that you can see the read receipts. You can also send pictures and video.

- **GPS Tagging**: When you take a photograph, GPS tagging inputs the location where the photograph was taken. Most modern smartphones do this by default.

- **Payment Methods**: Smartphones allow credit card details to be stored locally so that the phone can be used to make contactless payments using near-field communications. If this is a BYOD, it needs to be carefully monitored as someone could leave the company with a company credit card and continue to use it. MDM may prevent the payment function by disabling this tool in the mobile device management policies.

- **Wi-Fi Direct/Ad Hoc**: The Wi-Fi direct wireless network allows two Wi-Fi devices to connect to each other without requiring a WAP. It is single-path and therefore cannot be used for internet sharing. An ad hoc wireless network is where two wireless devices can connect with a WAP, but it is multipath and can share an internet connection with someone else.

- **Tethering**: Tethering is where a GPS-enabled smartphone can be attached to a mobile device to provide internet access. Microsoft's Windows 10 is capable of tethering. The danger of this is if someone uses a laptop to connect to the company's network and then tethers to the internet, it could result in split tunneling. This is where a user has a secure session via VPN to the corporate LAN, and then opens up a web browser with an insecure session that could be hacked and gives the attacker a gateway to a secure session to your LAN. MDM must ensure that this does not happen. When tethering, to ensure security, we must only create one session at one time.

- **Push Notification Services**: Can be used to inform the device owner that an email or a text has arrived. For example, if someone sends you a message to your LinkedIn account, a push notification can tell you that you have a new message.

Review Questions

Now it's time to check your knowledge. Answer the questions, and then check your answers, which can be found in the *Assessments* section at the end of the book:

1. What two groups of people might use a guest wireless network?

2. What is the difference between fat and thin wireless controllers?

3. What is the WAP master password, and how would you protect it?

4. What two things can a Wi-Fi Analyzer perform?

5. What is the purpose of MAC filtering?

6. Why should you place your first WAP on channel 1, your second WAP on channel 11, and your third WAP on channel 6?

7. Why would an engineer carry out a site survey prior to installing a wireless network?

8. Would you go to your online banking if you are in a hotel that uses Open Authentication?

9. What is the weakest version of wireless encryption?

10. If a friend comes to visit me in my house and asks for the wireless password, what am I giving them?

11. What is the most secure version of WPA2?

12. When using WPA3-Personal, what replaces the pre-shared key?

13. When using a WPA3 wireless, what replaces WPA2-Open Authentication?

14. What is the most secure version of wireless?

15. How do I access a wireless network if I use WPS and what type of attack is it vulnerable against?

16. What is the purpose of a captive portal for a wireless network?

17. What benefit does WPA3 bring to IoT devices?

18. What needs to be installed on the endpoint if you are going to use EAP-TLS for wireless authentication?

19. If a user installs pirate software on their corporate laptop, which policy have they violated?

20. What would be the benefit to first-line support if the company were to adopt CYOD instead of BYOD?

21. If I am staying in a hotel and their Wi-Fi is not working, how can I get access to the internet?

22. If my cell phone has been lost or stolen, what should be done using MDM?

23. What three things should I do to protect the data stored on my smartphone?

24. If a company has suffered several thefts of company laptops, what could you use to prevent further thefts?

25. How can we keep company data separate from personal data on a cell phone that is being used as a BYOD device so that offboarding is easy to achieve?

26. What is the purpose of using SE Android?

27. What is a wireless short-range payment type?

Section 3: Protecting the Security Environment

In this section, you will learn to identify the different types of malware and virus and take the appropriate action to protect against them. You will look at the importance of policies and regulatory frameworks in reducing the risk. Next, you will learn about secure coding techniques, quality control, and testing. Finally, you will discover incident response procedures and learn how to apply mitigation techniques or controls to secure an environment.

This section comprises the following chapters:

- *Chapter 9, Identifying Threats, Attacks, and Vulnerabilities*
- *Chapter 10, Governance, Risk, and Compliance*
- *Chapter 11, Managing Application Security*
- *Chapter 12, Dealing with Incident Response Procedures*

9

Identifying Threats, Attacks, and Vulnerabilities

As a security professional, you must be fully aware of the different types of attacks that your company could be subjected to. The different attacks range from different types of malware that employees may come across to social engineering, where the attacker will contact them directly and try to exploit their personal vulnerability. We will then look at the different types of threat actors and their characteristics. And finally, we will look at password exploitation and other advanced attacks.

In this chapter, we will cover the following topics:

- Virus and Malware Attacks
- Social Engineering Attacks
- Threat Actors
- Advanced Attacks

Let's start by looking at virus and malware attacks.

Virus and Malware Attacks

In today's world, viruses and malware are rife; there are many different variants, and we will look at each of these in turn:

- **Virus**: A virus is a program that embeds itself in another program and can be executed in many different ways; for example, by clicking on a link on a web page, or by opening up an email attachment. Once it has been activated, it replicates itself, going from host to host. A lot of viruses use port 1900.

- **Polymorphic Virus**: This virus mutates as it spreads so that it is difficult to detect. The hash value changes as it mutates and it may cause a program error if not found.

- **Potentially Unwanted Programs (PUPs)**: These are programs that are downloaded with other programs and they tend to use resources and slow your computer down. Installing *Malwarebytes* would alert you to them being installed.

- **Fileless Virus**: This virus runs in memory and is very hard to identify as it piggybacks itself onto other programs, phishing attacks, or applications, such as Word. This could be prevented by *McAfee Behavior Analysis*, which detects programs that execute at the same time as the legitimate software.

- **Command and Control Malware**: This is malware that takes over the complete computer and can then be used to steal data, reboot, or shut down the computer or perform a **Distributed Denial-of-Service (DDoS)** attack on your network. It can be launched via a phishing attack or downloaded malware.

- **Ransomware**: Ransomware involves the attacker encrypting the files on a user's computer and then displaying a link asking for money to release the files. Another example of ransomware is when you download a free program, and it says that you have problems with your computer, so you need to purchase the full version of the software. This is quite subtle.

> **Tip**
> Remember, the rule of thumb is that if you have to part with money, then it is ransomware.

An example of this is shown in *Figure 9.1*:

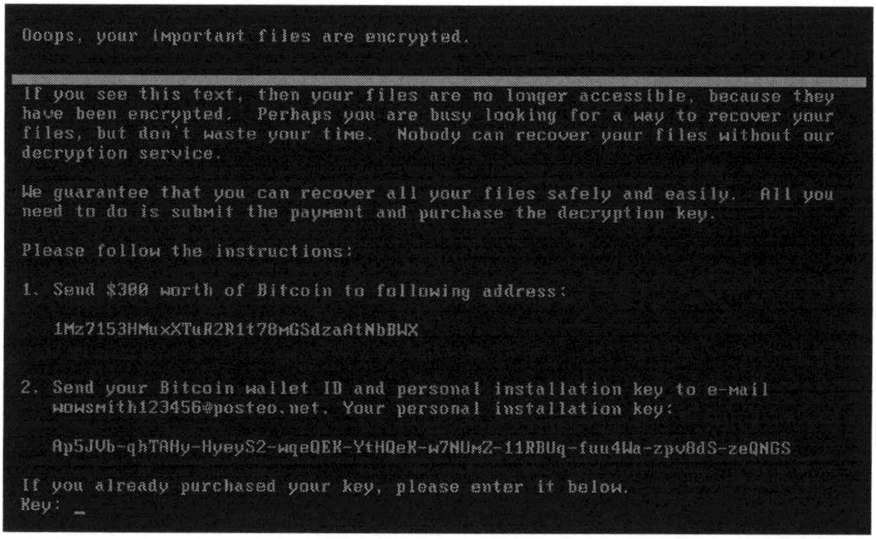

```
Ooops, your important files are encrypted.

If you see this text, then your files are no longer accessible, because they
have been encrypted. Perhaps you are busy looking for a way to recover your
files, but don't waste your time. Nobody can recover your files without our
decryption service.

We guarantee that you can recover all your files safely and easily. All you
need to do is submit the payment and purchase the decryption key.

Please follow the instructions:

1. Send $300 worth of Bitcoin to following address:

   1Mz7153HMuxXTuR2R1t78mGSdzaAtNbBWX

2. Send your Bitcoin wallet ID and personal installation key to e-mail
   wowsmith123456@posteo.net. Your personal installation key:

   Ap5JVb-qhTAHy-HyeyS2-wqeQEK-YtHQeK-w7NUmZ-11RBUq-fuu4Wa-zpvBdS-zeQNGS

If you already purchased your key, please enter it below.
Key: _
```

Figure 9.1 – Ransomware

- **Crypto-Malware**: Crypto-malware is a type of ransomware that encrypts data, and it tries to stay in your system for as long as possible without being detected. Once enough data has been encrypted, an ultimatum is given to pay a ransom or the decryption key will be deleted by a certain date.

- **Worm**: A worm is a program that replicates itself to spread to other computers, exploiting security weaknesses. Common ports for worms are `1098`, `4444`, and those in the `5000` range.

  Example: The *Nimda* virus was released in September 2001. Its name is *admin* spelt backward and refers to a file called `admin.dll`. When it runs, it continues to propagate itself. The main target of Nimda was Microsoft's IIS web server and file servers. It would create a **Denial-of-Service (DoS)** attack and its job was to simply slow networks down to a halt. When it accessed a server, it would run down mapped network drives of everyone connected to the server, and then it rewrote the system files so that they had an EML extension. Once it had totally destroyed a machine, a huge white envelope appeared on the desktop. This meant that it would no longer function.

- **Trojan**: Trojans are known for being embedded in programs that you download. They try to exploit `system32.exe` and then run a DLL file to attack the operating system kernel. This is the management part of the operating system. The Trojan will try to find password information and set up an SMTP engine that uses a random port to send those details to the attacker:

```
Trojan.BHO.H File C:\WINDOWS\SysWOW64\fezegepo.dll
Trojan.Vundo File C:\WINDOWS\system32\fezegepo.dll
```

- **Remote Access Trojan** (**RAT**): An RAT is a program that sends login details to the attacker to enable them to take full control of the computer.

   Example: *Gh0st RAT* is a RAT that was originally designed by threat actors in China. A user clicks on a link and a dropper program called `server.exe` installs Gh0st RAT with `svchost.dll`, which then allows the attacker to take control of the computer. It can then log keystrokes, download and upload files, and run webcam and microphone feeds.

- **Rootkit**: A rootkit is a program that could install itself in the system BIOS, and no matter how many times the operating system is reinstalled, it keeps coming back. A Linux rootkit uses the Bash shell to launch itself.

- **Backdoor**: A backdoor is a piece of software or a computer system that is created by program developers in case someone locks themselves out of the program; they are generally undocumented. Attackers use these to gain access to systems.

- **Logic Bomb**: A logic bomb is a virus that is triggered by either an action or at a specific date; for example, the Fourth of July or Christmas Day. This could be based on time, running a `.bat/cmd` file, a script, or using a task scheduler.

- **Keylogger**: The main idea behind keyloggers is to track and log keystrokes. You can install a keylogger by putting it on a very small, thin USB drive at the rear of a desktop computer.

- **Adware**: Adware is an unwanted program that keeps popping up with unwanted advertisements. One way to stop adware is to enable a pop-up blocker.

- **Spyware**: This is renowned for slowing down computers as it uses your computer's processing power and RAM resources to continually track what you are doing on your computer and sends the information to a third party. A good spy is covert and collects information, and spyware is no different.

- **Botnet**: A bot is a program that infects and takes control of a computer. The name is derived from the words *robot* and *network*. A botnet is a collection of bots that have been set up for malicious purposes, normally to carry out a DoS attack.

We will look at social engineering attacks in the next section.

Social Engineering Attacks

Social engineering attacks are based on the exploitation of someone's personality; they could be referred to as *hacking the human*. There are various types of social engineering attacks. Let's look at each of them in turn, starting with phishing/spear phishing:

- **Phishing and Spear Phishing**: Phishing attacks are carried out by emailing someone, requesting that they need to complete the attached form, perhaps as there is a problem with their bank account. Such forms ask for personal details that could later be used for identity fraud. Such emails often look as though they have come from a legitimate body, so users are fooled into carrying out the instructions they contain. **Spear phishing** is a phishing attack that targets a group of people:

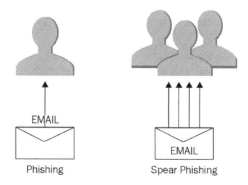

Figure 9.2 – Phishing attack

- **Credential Harvesting**: This is an attack that is normally done using a phishing attack, where it states that some details on your account are incorrect and it gives you a hyperlink to resolve the situation. When you click on the link, it gives you a fake web page to log in to. That way, your account details can be collected.

- **Whaling**: A whaling attack is an attack that targets either a **Chief Executive Officer** (**CEO**) or a high-level executive. CEOs and high-level executives have intense days, so they might action what *looks* like a minor request quickly so that they can move on to their next task, but end up being attacked.

- **Vishing**: A vishing attack involves the use of a VoIP phone, another telephone, a modem, or someone leaving a voicemail to try and extort information.

- **SMiShing**: This attack is basically phishing but uses SMS text messages. They will ask you either to visit a website or call a phone number that turns out to be a premium rate call.

  Example: You get a text message that your Facebook account needs to be validated. When you click on the link, you are asked for your password or the website downloads a virus.

- **Pretexting**: This is where the attacker makes up a scenario asking for details to confirm someone's identity. This could then lead to identity theft.

  Example: Someone pretends to be from Netflix saying that there has been suspicious activity on your account. They ask you to confirm whether or not it was you and could you please confirm your account details.

- **Elicit Information**: This is where the attacker will try and get you to provide information; for example, using a false statement in the hope that you will correct the statements. Another way is *flattery*. For example, they give you compliments to build up your ego in the hope that you will boast and provide more information. *Bracketing* is another method.

  Example: The hacker wants to know how many motion sensors there are in one part of the building. The attacker says to the security guard, *"I bet the security in this building is pretty good. I bet you have about four motion detectors in the lobby"*, and the security guard says, *"You are very close, but we actually have seven"*.

  > **Exam tip**
  > Eliciting information is where the attacker says a statement in the hope that you will correct them and provide them with accurate information.

- **Identity Theft**: This is where someone steals your **Personally Identifiable Information** (**PII**) to commit fraud or take control of one of your accounts. You should not throw pieces of information away or you could have an attacker carry out dumpster diving. Pretexting and phishing are other ways in which your information can be collected. Types of identity theft include the following:

  a. Opening bank accounts, taking out loans, or getting credit cards

  b. Obtaining passports or driving licenses

  c. Ordering goods in your name

  d. Taking over your existing accounts

  e. Taking out mobile phone contracts

- **Invoice Scams**: This is where criminals obtain details of genuine invoices and they submit them for payment but change the bank details. When the finance team look at invoices, they look at purchase orders and invoice details as well as the product, but seldom look at the bank details of the person being paid.

- **Spam Over Instant Messaging (SPIM)/SMiShing**: This is sending spam messages via instant messaging or SMS. SmiShing is using SMS text messages to attack someone.

- **Tailgating**: Tailgating is when someone opens a door using their ID badge and then someone follows them in before the door closes. This can be especially effective if the person going through first is a middle-aged man and the tailgating person is a pretty lady. They may be old school and keep the door open for the lady. A mantrap will prevent this.

- **Piggybacking**: This is similar to tailgating, except they have permission from an employee. They may pretend to be a hospital porter so that an employee allows them access. This could also be where they seem to be struggling with a huge box and they get an employee to hold the door open while they gain access.

- **Impersonation**: Impersonation can involve someone putting on a uniform—of a traffic warden or police officer, for example. Imagine you are driving down the street and get flagged down by a police officer, who is holding something that looks like a speed gun. Another form of impersonation is that someone pretends to be from the help desk asking you for information about your department or tells you that you need to change your password because of problems with the IT systems.

- **Reconnaissance**: There are two types of reconnaissance: *passive* and *active*. *Passive* reconnaissance is where the attacker researches your company and collects information that will be used at a later stage. *Active* reconnaissance is where the attacker interacts with the user or their desktop; for example, if someone has your username and tries to reset the password, that would be active reconnaissance if they go to your run command or alter your registry.

- **Influence Campaigns**: These campaigns are a social engineering attack to influence people from countries all over the world. There are two main types: *social media* and *hybrid warfare*. Let's look at each of these in turn:

  a. **Social Media**: All over the world, social media has been used to influence voters in forthcoming elections. Facebook and Twitter have been used extensively with many election campaigns.

b. **Hybrid Warfare**: Normally carried out by state actors to influence the balance of power in a country by using military, political, economic, or civil means, and conceivably running a campaign to spread disinformation. Refer to the following diagram:

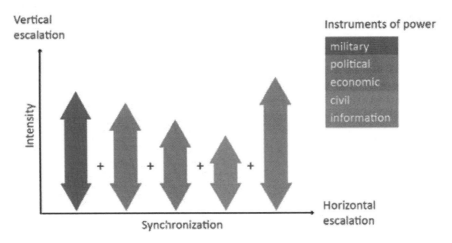

Figure 9.3 – Hybrid warfare

Example 1: In May 2014, *CyberBerkut*, a Russian hacker group, exploited cyber vulnerabilities in the network of the *Ukrainian National Election Commission* to undermine the credibility of the elections.

Example 2: The deep sectarian, ethnic, and economic divisions in Syrian society were exploited by both Iran and ISIS with a view to achieving their strategic objectives.

- **Dumpster Diving**: Dumpster diving is when someone removes the trash from your trash can in the hope of finding a letter that holds PII that can be used later to commit fraud. The best way to prevent this is to shred all mail that has PII before you dispose of it. A new type of dumpster diving has emerged where the attacker steals information from your recycle bin, or they steal information from removable media such as USB drives that you have on your desk.

- **Shoulder Surfing**: Shoulder surfing involves a person standing behind someone who's using a computer so that they can see sensitive information. Another example is someone using an ATM machine while the person behind them is using their smartphone to video the transaction. This is effective as the victim is concentrating on withdrawing their money and is not aware that they are being watched.

- **Hoax**: The jdbgmgr.exe virus hoax in 2002 involved email spam that advised computer users to delete a file named jdbgmgr.exe because it was a computer virus that looked like a cute little bear. This bear was found in the system 32 folder and this meant that people were deleting their actual system files. This is the equivalent of opening up your car hood and removing all of the leads and spark plugs. Another example of a hoax would be purchasing fake anti-virus software that does not work.

- **Watering Hole Attack**: Companies in the same industry visit very similar websites. Therefore, attackers identify a website that people in a particular industry are likely to visit and then infect it with a virus. This is effective as the people targeted have often been using the website for years and trust its content.

- **Pharming**: This is a DNS redirection attack where either the DNS cache has been poisoned or an entry is placed in your hosts file.

- **Authority**: An email may be sent out by someone of a higher authority, such as the CEO or HR manager, ordering you to complete a form that can be accessed by clicking on a link. See the following email. This is effective because nobody wants to defy the CEO:

> From: Ian Neil (CEO)
>
> To: All Staff
>
> Subject: UPDATE YOUR FINANCIAL DETAILS
>
> Dear All,
>
> The finance team are moving to a new finance application and have told me that personnel within the company have not updated their bank details. You need to click on this link and update your details: http://update.details.wehackyou.com.
>
> Failure to do so by the end of play today will result in disciplinary action against those individuals that do not comply.
>
> Kind Regards,
>
> Ian Neil
>
> Chief Executive Officer

- **Intimidation**: An example of intimidation is someone pretending to be someone of high authority, for example, a policeman. They then threaten an individual, telling them that they will be in trouble if they don't do as they are told. This is effective because victims of this kind of attack are made to believe that they have no other choice but to do as they are asked.

> **Tip**
> An email from your CEO, a high-level executive, or the HR manager telling you to fill in a form or click on a link, is an authority attack.

- **Urgency**: An example of an urgency attack is someone arriving at a reception desk and demanding access quickly. They could target a new receptionist, who may get flustered and let them in. Another good example is a "fireman" demanding access to the server room before the building burns down. This is effective because the receptionist panics, believing that there is actually a fire.

> **Tip**
> Allowing a fireman into your server room is an urgency attack.

- **Scarcity**: An example of this kind of attack is trying to panic you into making a snap decision. An example is where you want to rent a hotel room for a weekend away; you and 10 friends pick a hotel and go onto the website and it says *Only one room left!* in red. You purchase the last room, and so do 10 of your friends, and guess what? There is still only one room left!

  Example: A personal secretary receives a phone call from someone claiming to be in charge of domain names while the CEO is at a conference. The caller tells the secretary that they are calling to renew the domain name and that it must be done in the next 30 minutes or else the company will lose the domain name. They state that the renewal will be $45. The secretary knows that the company website and email addresses cannot operate without the domain name. This attack is effective because the secretary cannot disturb the CEO during an important meeting, so they purchase the domain name renewal. It may well be 3-4 months before the renewal date.

- **Familiarity and Trust**: In preparation for these attacks, hackers make themselves familiar to their victims; they come around a lot bringing with them boxes of chocolates and eventually they become trusted. At that point, they can begin working their way inside a company, for example, gaining access to areas of the company that they should not be able to access. This is effective as they become part of the furniture and nobody questions their actions.

- **Consensus**: People like to be accepted by their peers and co-workers. An attacker might ask for some information and state that they obtained it last week from a co-worker and just need an update on it. This works as the person supplying the information does not want to be seen as acting differently from other members of the team. Sometimes, this is referred to as *social proof*.

We will look at threat actors in the next section.

Threat Actors

A threat actor is another name for a hacker or attacker who is likely to attack your company; they all have different attributes. They will investigate your company from the outside, looking for details on social media and search engines. Let's now look at threat actor types:

- **Hackers**: There are three different types of hackers, so let's now look at each of these in turn:

  a. **Black Hat**: The black hat hacker has no information because they are not authorized by the company.

  b. **Gray Hat**: The gray hat hacker is provided with limited information from the company as they may be participating in the bug bounty program.

  c. **White Hat**: The white hat hacker is a former black hat hacker who is employed by the company to test applications for flaws and vulnerabilities before its release. They have all of the information that they need, including the source code.

- **Hacktivist**: A hacktivist is an external threat actor who defaces your website or breaks into your computer or network. They are politically motivated and seek social change. Their motivation is that they want to bring awareness to their cause by gaining more press coverage.

- **Shadow IT**: This is where people plug their own computers and devices into your network without consent. These devices may not be patched over a period of time and become vulnerable. This may result in a threat actor gaining access to your network via this system and this may lead to pivoting.

- **Competitor**: A competitor is another company in the same industry as your company who tries to steal your trade secrets and cause damage to your production system to prevent you from getting products to market. They will hope to get these products before you to capture a higher market share.

> **Tip**
> A competitor is a threat actor who will try and steal a company's trade secrets or sabotage your production systems to gain a competitive edge in the marketplace.

- **Script Kiddie**: A script kiddie is a person who does not have high technical knowledge and uses script and code that they find to make an attack against your company. Their motivation is that they want to be seen as a famous hacker and gain notoriety. They have no preference in terms of who they attack; they just want to be noticed. They will purchase tools from the dark web.

- **State Actors**: A state actor is another country that poses a threat to your country; their motivation is that they want to undermine your nation. They are well-organized and well-funded. An example of this is someone interfering with your country's election process.

- **Advanced Persistent Threat (APT)**: An APT is an external threat that tries to steal data from your network, but they are there for an extremely long period of time. They are very sophisticated and could be funded by a foreign government.

- **Criminal Syndicates**: Criminal syndicates target companies mainly to steal money. They either want to blackmail you into paying a ransom for the return of your data, or they threaten to make that information public by publishing it on the internet or selling it to one of your competitors. They have people working for them who have a high level of sophistication and their motivation is financial wealth.

- **Insider Threat**: An insider threat is a disgruntled employee who might have been overlooked for promotion and their relationship with their company has gone sour. They are also known as *malicious insider threats* and are the most difficult to protect yourself from as they are already on your network.

In this section, we discussed the different types of threat actors. Now, let's look at the different types of advanced attacks in the next section.

Advanced Attacks

In this section, we will be looking at advanced attacks, starting with types of password attacks.

Password Attacks

The two most common password attacks are *dictionary* attacks and *brute-force* attacks. Let's look at these in turn:

- **Dictionary Attack**: For a dictionary attack, we could start by using all of the words in the Oxford English Dictionary and use them to try and crack passwords, but misspelled names or passwords with special characters such as $ or % can't be cracked, as they don't appear in the dictionary.

  Which of the following passwords would a dictionary attack crack?

  a. `elasticity`

  b. `el@ST1city`

  c. `fred123`

  d. `blueberry`

  It would crack `elasticity` and `blueberry`, but `el@ST1city` features numbers and characters not in a dictionary. Therefore, it will fail. It wouldn't crack `fred123` either as it contains numbers.

- **Brute-Force Attack**: A brute-force attack runs through all of the different combinations of letters and characters and will eventually crack a given password. The length of the password may slow down such an attack, but it will eventually be cracked. This is the fastest type of password cracker and will crack all different combinations. Salting a password with randomized characters will only slow a brute-force attack down. There are two types of brute-force attacks:

  a. **Online mode**: The attacker must use the same login interface as the user's application.

  b. **Offline mode**: The attacker steals the password file first, and then tries to crack each user's password offline. They cannot be detected and so have unlimited attempts at cracking the password.

  Which of the following passwords would a brute-force attack crack?

  a. `elasticity@abc123`

  b. `el@ST1city`

  c. `fred12redrafg`

  d. `blueberryicecream12345`

  It would crack them all – eventually.

- **Hybrid Attack**: A hybrid attack is a combination of both a dictionary attack and a brute-force attack.

- **Spraying Attack**: The hacker first of all searches the internet for people who work within an organization and sees whether they can work out the standard naming convention. They then look at online resources, such as *Facebook*, *Twitter*, and *LinkedIn*, to find the names of as many employees and apply the standard naming convention. When they have the standard naming convention, they apply this to each employee name that they find. They then use a tool such as Kali Linux and spray the password, which means using the most common passwords one at a time against the list of employees in the hope that one matches.

- **Plaintext/Unencrypted**: These passwords can be cracked by a brute-force attack.

- **Account Lockout**: Account lockout refers to the number of attempts a user can make to insert their password before being locked out of the system. If I set the account lockout at three attempts, it will stop both dictionary and brute-force attacks.

- **Minimum Number of Characters**: Should account lockout not be an option, the best way to prevent the password from being cracked is by **salting** or **key stretching**, where randomized characters are inserted into the password. This will prevent a dictionary attack, but will only slow down a brute-force attack.

> **Tip**
> Setting account lockout at a low value will prevent a brute-force attack.

- **Login Errors**: Inserting an incorrect password because you rushed inserting it or have *Caps Lock* on/off will create password errors. If we look at certificates, smart cards, **Time based One Time Password** (**TOTP**), and passwords, passwords are the most likely to be inserted incorrectly.

- **Weak Implementations**: Weak implementations of passwords are as follows:

  a. Using the most common passwords

  b. A low number of characters (fewer than seven characters)

  c. Simple passwords such as 123456 or abcdef

  d. Default passwords for devices

These are very easy to guess using a password cracker. `Password` is the most common password to be used. The following list shows some of the most common passwords over the years:

- `123456`

- `Password`

- `123456789`

- `qwerty`

- `letmein`

- `iloveyou`

- `abc123`

- `football`

Physical Attacks

In this section, we will look at different types of physical attacks. We will first look at USB devices and cables, followed by card cloning, also known as *skimming*:

- **Malicious USB Cable**: These cables could look like a Lightning cable, but they have a Wi-Fi chip built into one of the sockets. These cables act as if they were a mouse and keyboard. An attacker can use a nearby smartphone to run malicious commands on the device.

- **Malicious USB Drive**: An attacker leaves a malicious USB drive in a place where an employee might find it. The person finding the drive inserts it into their computer to identify the owner, but instead opens a file that run a malicious code that could give the attacker control over their computer. Normally, there is only one file visible that is a shortcut to a malicious program. Click on the shortcut and you will be infected. Watch this *Trend Micro* video for more information: `https://www.youtube.com/watch?v=0hs8rc2u5ak`.

- **Card Cloning**: This attack can also be called *skimming*, and this is where a credit card has been put through a card cloning machine. The most common places for these devices are ATM machines, or when you pay the bill at a restaurant. To prevent this, you need to ensure when you use an ATM machine that you pull the card reader to ensure that another device is not placed in there. In a restaurant, ensure that the server doesn't make an excuse to get a card payment machine and leave with your card. Make sure that the card does not leave your sight.

- **Supply Chain Attacks**: Most large companies have a very secure environment. Therefore, hackers will look at those companies that supply software or maybe computer hardware or services to that company. Large organizations must ensure that their supply chains have the same security standards, otherwise the supply chain could be compromised and that could lead to a breach in their security. Companies normally don't think about getting attacked by the legitimate software that they purchase. The supply chain could attack them by installing software updates. As an example, Target once suffered a supply chain attack launched by maintenance engineers for their HVAC system.

- **Cloud versus On-Premise Attacks**: Most on-premise companies have perimeter fencing, CCTV, security guards on the gates, and restricted areas of the building. This makes it difficult to hack. In the cloud environment, they use a zero-trust model, where every user or device needs to identify themselves, sometimes even having to provide their location before they can access resources.

- **Artificial Intelligence**: This is where you have a machine that is programmed to think like a human and not like a robot. This is known as machine learning. Let's look at two types of attacks using artificial intelligence:

  a. **Tainted Training Data for Machine Learning**: Instead of the machine being programmed to carry out work, it can be tainted and taught to ignore certain attacks. Machine learning is used here to program the device not to detect some forms of attack.

  b. **Security of Machine Learning Algorithms**: Machine learning can help the cybersecurity team identify patterns and thereby help identify attacks. They can analyze malicious patterns in encrypted data to help identify attacks, rather than decrypt the data.

On-Path Attacks

On-path attacks are interception attacks where the attacker places themselves between two entities, normally a web browser and a web server. They normally modify the communications to either collect information or impersonate the other entity. The following section lists different types of on-path attacks:

- **Man-in-the-Middle (MITM) Attack**: An MITM attack is where the attacker intercepts traffic going between two hosts and then changes the information in the packets in real time. A MITM can inject false information between the two hosts. See *Figure 9.4*, where Mary is contacting Carol, but John is the man in the middle and changes the conversation as it moves back and forth:

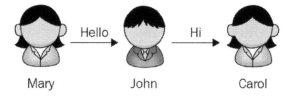

Figure 9.4 – On-path – MITM

Example: A hacker is imitating the conversations of two parties to gain access to funds. The attacker intercepts a public key and with that, can put in their own credentials to trick the people on both sides into believing that they are talking to each other in a secure environment. While online shopping from home or a mobile device, victims think that they are buying goods from a legitimate source, but instead their money is being stolen.

- **Man-in-the Browser (MITB) Attack**: An MITB attack is where a malicious plugin or script has been downloaded and the browser has been compromised. It acts like a trojan, meaning that when you next carry out online banking, it steals your online banking details.

- **Padding Oracle on Downgraded Legacy Encryption (POODLE)**: A POODLE attack is a man-in-the-middle attack that exploits the use of SSL 3.0 on legacy systems. This is extremely insecure. The weakness happens with the SSL 3.0 browser, which uses a cipher or a block cipher in CBC mode. A downgrade attack is when you abandon a higher level of security for an older, low-level security system. In this case, we are downgrading the computer's browser to an older version of the browser's SSL 3.0 using a **Chain Block Cipher (CBC)**.

- **Replay Attack**: A replay attack is an MITM attack that intercepts data but replays it at a later date. Kerberos, a Microsoft authentication protocol, can prevent this as each entry has updated sequence numbers and timestamps. For example, when communication takes place between two hosts on a Windows network that uses Kerberos authentication, data is being transmitted, with USN 7 appearing and then USN 10 appearing. The receiving host will then realize the data is not as it should be. When USN and USN 8 or USN 9 are received the next day, they will be rejected as being out of sequence, thereby preventing the replay attack.

- **Session Replay Attacks**: When a user visits a website, a session ID is set up between the user and the web server. This information can be stored in a cookie and is present in the traffic going between the user and the website. The attacker can steal a cookie or can use a protocol analyzer and capture the session ID from the http packets. They can now impersonate the user when accessing the website. This can be prevented by using encrypted HTTP traffic and the session ID will be inside the encrypted traffic.

> **Exam tip**
> A POODLE attack is an MITM downgrade attack using SSL 3.0 in CBC mode.

Network Attacks

In this section, we will look at different types of network attacks:

- **DoS Attack**: A DoS attack is where the victim's machine
  or network is flooded with a high volume of requests from another host so that
  it is not available for any other hosts to use. A common method is to use `SYN` flood
  attacks, where the first two parts of the three-way handshake occur, and the victim
  holds a session waiting for an `ACK` that never comes.

> **Tip**
> A DoS network attack comes from a single IP address, whereas a DDoS
> network attack emanates from multiple IP addresses.

- **DDoS attack**: There are different types of DDoS attacks and we are going to look at
  the **network**, **application**, and **Operational Technology** (**OT**) attacks. Let's look at
  each of these in turn:

  a. **Network**: A DDoS network attack is where a botnet is set up to flood a victim's
     system with an enormous amount of traffic so that it is taken down. Refer to
     Figure 9.5. If a stateful firewall were to be used to prevent a network DDoS attack,
     it would prevent the traffic from entering your network:

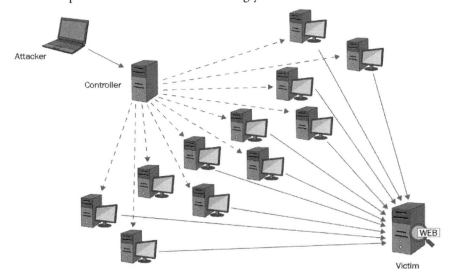

Figure 9.5 – DDoS attack

b. **Application**: This is where the DDoS tries to flood a particular application, and the number of packets is known as **requests per second (rps)**. This is where specially crafted packets are sent to the application so that it cannot cope with the volume.

c. **OT**: This can be the hardware or software that controls devices used in video surveillance. In the past, these devices worked in an air-gapped environment as CCTV, but nowadays there are interconnected video surveillance solutions and these are now being targeted by a DDoS attack so that they fail and leave a company vulnerable.

- **Amplification Attack**: A DNS amplification is a DDoS attack in which the attacker exploits vulnerabilities in DNS servers to turn initially small queries into much larger payloads, which are then used to bring down the victim's servers. An example of this would be a *smurf* attack, where a directed IP broadcast is sent to a border router with the victim getting the resultant replies.

> **Exam tip**
> Kerberos prevents replay attacks as it uses updated sequence numbers and timestamps.

- **Zero-Day Attack**: A zero-day attack is when an exploit is found but, at that time, there is no solution to prevent it, so the attackers attack more, unless you have previously taken a baseline. If you look at *Figure 9.6*, you will see the timeline of a zero-day attack:

Figure 9.6 – Zero-day exploit

It takes two or more days for a solution to prevent it. No anti-virus program, SIEM, NIDS, or NIPS will be able to stop a zero-day attack. This is because vendors don't have the ability to detect it that day itself. Vendors will be waiting for an update.

The only way to detect a zero-day exploit is when you have previously taken a baseline of your computer, and then you can check the changes since the baseline; this will identify a zero-day exploit. If you have no previous baseline, then you will not detect it.

- **Pivoting**: This is where an attacker gains access to the network via a vulnerable host. It then attacks a critical server, such as a domain controller or a database server. In a virtual world, this would be called **VM Escape**.

- **Pass-the-Hash Attack**: Older operating systems such as Windows NT 4.0 stored the password locally and it was hashed with MD4. Attackers used to use a rainbow table to complete a hash collision attack. You could prevent pass-the-hash attacks by disabling NTLM. NTLM was replaced by Active Directory using Kerberos authentication, where the passwords are stored in encrypted data. This is the best method for preventing pass-the-hash attacks.

> **Important note**
> A zero-day virus cannot be traced or discovered by any security device, as it may take up to 5 days before a patch or update is released. It can be detected by comparing baselines.

- **ARP Poisoning**: **Address Resolution Protocol** (**ARP**) operates at *Layer 2* of the OSI reference model and operates using **Media Access Control** (**MAC**) addresses. ARP poisoning is an attack that must be done locally and can redirect you to another website similar to DNS poisoning. The best way to prevent ARP poisoning is to use `arp -s` to insert static entries into the ARP cache. ARP broadcasting sends unsolicited ARP replies to the victim. ARP spoofing allows an attacker to intercept data frames on a network, modify traffic, or stop all traffic.

- **MAC Spoofing Attack**: MAC spoofing is the theft of the MAC address of another networked device, which is then used to gain access to the network; for example, a wireless access point that uses MAC filtering.

- **MAC Flooding**: This is where an attacker floods a switch with Ethernet packets so that it consumes the limited memory that a switch has. This can be prevented by using an 802.1x managed switch with an AAA server.

- **MAC Cloning/Spoofing**: This is used when you want to pretend to be a different device, so you can connect to a network device or bypass the security on a captive portal.

- **IP Spoofing**: IP spoofing is the modification of an **Internet Protocol** (**IP**) packet using a fake IP address to mask the identity of the sender. This prevents the attacker from being traced when they carry out a malicious attack.

- **Privilege Escalation**: A privilege escalation attack is where an attacker wants to grant themselves more permissions than they are entitled to. With a higher level of privilege, they will be able to run unauthorized code or make changes to the IT infrastructure. They may try to use someone else's account to access the Active Directory and allocate themselves a higher level of privilege.

  Example: John, an administrator, leaves his laptop unattended when his boss urgently asks him to go into their office. Mary, who is a normal user, goes into John's laptop, clicks on the shortcut to the directory service, and makes herself a member of the administrator's group. When John comes back, he does not realize anything has happened, as his laptop seems the same as when he left it.

Application/Programming Attacks

Programming attacks use scripts or overload the characters or integers expected. Let's look at these in turn:

- **SSL Striping**: This is an attack where the attackers carry out an SSL downgrade attack, where they manage to bypass the certificate-based protection and turn the session into an HTTP attack. This is where they can now capture data such as credit card numbers.

- **Resource Exhaustion**: This is where an attack on an application consumes all of the available memory and CPU cores. It could also be where all of the IP addresses have been allocated on an DHCP server.

- **Dynamic Link Library (DLL) Injection**: This is a technique used for running code within the address space of another process by forcing it to load a DLL. This makes the application run differently from how it was designed to. For example, you could install a malware DLL in another process.

- **Cross-Site Request Forgery (XSRF)**: This is known as XSRF, or CSRF. The attacker could carry out this attack by using a cookie to pretend to be the user, or the user could click on a like or share button. The user has to be authenticated to the web server.

- **Cross-Site Scripting (XSS)**: XSS is when a user injects malicious code into another user's browser. It uses both HTML tags and JavaScript. The following is a very simple server-side script to display the latest comments:

```
print "<html>"
print "Latest comment:" print database.latestComment
print "</html>"
```

The attacker could alter the comment to have HTML tags for a script, as follows:

```
<html>
Latest comment:
<script>    (Javascript code is placed here)        </script>
</html>
```

When the user loads the page into the browser, it will now launch the JavaScript and then the attack will be successful. Here are some examples using JavaScript.

Example 1: *JavaScript – Creating a Money Variable*: JavaScript can use the `var` command, which means **variable**. An example would be to set a variable for money, and then allocate it a value of `300.00`. As you can see, we used `var` for the variable and then use `money` as its label. In the next row, we use the `money` variable and give it a value of `300.00`:

```
<script type="text/javascript">
<!—
var money; money = 300.00;
//-->
</script>
```

Example 2: *JavaScript – Setting the Day of the Month*: We will use JavaScript to set the day of the month. You will notice the JavaScript code between `<html>` tags: `<script>` to start the script and `<\script>` to end the script. The `var` command is very common in JavaScript:

```
<!DOCTYPE html>
<html>
<body>
<p>Click the button to display the date after changing the day of the month. </p>
<button onclick="myFunction()">Try it</button>
<p id="demo"></p>
<script>
function myFunction() {
var d = new Date(); d.setDate (15);
document.getElementById("demo").innerHTML = d;
}
</script>
</body>
</html>
```

An XSS attack can be identified by looking for the `var` command and for a variable with `<html>` `tags` `<script>` and `</script>`. Scripts with `var` are likely to be JavaScript. This is a very popular exam topic.

- **XML Injection**: XML is a language similar to HTML that is used with web data. The attacker will try and manipulate the XML script to carry out attacks. It is interoperable with Java and an XML injection attack is similar to XSS above. It can also be used to replace variables in the script.

Example: Equivalent XML Payload:

```
<?xmlversion="1.0"encoding="UTF-8"?><root><query>a'%3E%3C
script%3Ealert(,123')%3C/script%3E</query></root>8
```

If you look at line two from `'%3E%3Cscript%` through to `script%3E<`, data is inserted into the XML script similar to XSS. You can prevent an XML injection attack by using input validation.

- **Buffer Overflow**: A buffer overflow occurs when a program tries to store more data than it can hold in a temporary memory storage area. Writing outside the allocated memory into the adjacent memory can corrupt the data, crash the program, or cause the execution of malicious code, which could allow an attacker to modify the target process address space:

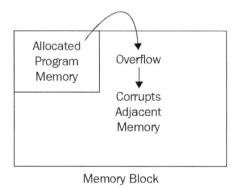

Memory Block

Figure 9.7 – Buffer overflow

In the example here, we are going to set up a buffer to be a maximum of 64 characters, and then we are going to use `strcpy` to copy strings of data. A string of data is used to represent a number of text characters. The problem that arises is that `strcpy` cannot limit the size of characters being copied. In the example here, if the string of data is longer than 64 characters, then a buffer overflow will occur:

```
int fun (char data [256]) {
int I
```

```
char tmp [64]; strcpy (tmp, data);
}
```

The buffer overflow could cause a memory leak, where the application consumes all available memory.

- **Integer Overflow**: An integer overflow is a condition that occurs when the result of an arithmetic operation, such as multiplication or addition, exceeds the maximum size of the integer type used to store it.

- **SQL Injection Attack**: When you use a SQL database, you can run queries against the SQL database using Transact-SQL. An example would be, if I want to know the customers that I have in my SQL database, I can run the following Transact-SQL query: `Select* from Customers`. This will display all of the customers in my SQL database. A SQL injection attack is where the SQL command is modified to gain information from the database by ending the statement with `1=1`. Since one equals one, the statement is true, and information will be acquired.

  A stored procedure is a pre-written SQL script that might ask you for a list of all customers who have purchased items over $1,000 in the last 7 days. When this is written, it is saved as a stored procedure called *ABC*. When I run the ABC stored procedure, it will give me all of the information I require, and an attacker won't be able to modify the script inside. This is the best way to stop a SQL injection attack. The other way is to use input validation, which is not as effective.

> **Exam tip**
>
> `strcpy` could create a buffer overflow as it cannot limit the amount of characters.

- **Improper Error Handling**: Applications have a tendency to create errors and the applications themselves do not validate the information returned in errors. Web servers host applications where the frontend is the web server, and the backend is a SQL database that can hold credit card information. Attackers can use *fuzzing*, where they send random input to an application with the hope that they can get good information from the errors, such as the server IP address. They can also insert commands into SQL scripts. To prevent this, we can use input validation, and in the SQL server we can use a sealed script called a *stored procedure*, which is much better than input validation.

- **Input Validation**: Input validation is where data is entered either using a web page or wizard; both are set up to only accept data in the correct format within a range of minimum and maximum values. Have you ever completed a web form quickly and maybe put your zip code into another field? This results in an error in the form and it fails to process the submit button. The web form then has a list at the top, in red, of the incorrect parameters, with a red star next to each of them. Once you have corrected the entries, the form will accept these and submit them. Input validation can prevent SQL injection, buffer overflow, and integer overflow attacks.

- **LDAP Injection Attack**: LDAP is used to manage a directory service using X500 objects, such as cn, ou, and dc. In an LDAP injection attack, an attacker inserts data into an LDAP statement. This can be prevented by using input validation, which is why Microsoft uses wizards to input data into Active Directory.

  Example: In the following example, a query is constructed to validate a user's credentials for the purpose of logging in:

  String filter = "(&(USER = " + user_name + ") (PASSWORD = " + user_password + "))";

  To log in, a user would provide their user credentials and this filter above would be used to validate your credentials. An attacker would create specially crafted input for the variable username, such as Ian Neil (&), and any value for the password. The finished query will become
  (&(USER = ianneil)(&))(PASSWORD = pass)).

  Only the first portion of this query is processed by the LDAP server (&(USER = ianneil)(&), which always evaluates to true, allowing the attacker to gain access to the system without needing to provide valid user credentials.

- **PowerShell**: PowerShell can perform tasks in a Windows environment. Each command is known as a cmdlet and can be saved to a script with a .ps1 extension. PowerShell comprises a noun and a verb; for example, Get-Help will show you the help commands.

If I want to see what services are running on a computer, I can run the `get-service` command, which will show me all of the services running. See *Figure 9.8*:

```
Windows PowerShell
Copyright (C) Microsoft Corporation. All rights reserved.


PS C:\Users\Administrator.WIN-HB5RLG5VD60> get-service


Status   Name                DisplayName
------   ----                -----------
Running  AdobeARMservice     Adobe Acrobat Update Service
Running  AdobeUpdateService  AdobeUpdateService
Running  AGMService          Adobe Genuine Monitor Service
Running  AGSService          Adobe Genuine Software Integrity Se...
Stopped  AJRouter            AllJoyn Router Service
Stopped  ALG                 Application Layer Gateway Service
Stopped  AppIDSvc            Application Identity
Running  Appinfo             Application Information
Running  AppMgmt             Application Management
Stopped  AppReadiness        App Readiness
Stopped  AppVClient          Microsoft App-V Client
Running  AppXSvc             AppX Deployment Service (AppXSVC)
Stopped  AssignedAccessM...  AssignedAccessManager Service
Running  AudioEndpointBu...  Windows Audio Endpoint Builder
Running  Audiosrv            Windows Audio
Running  AVG Antivirus       AVG Antivirus
Running  AVG Firewall        AVG Firewall Service
Running  AVG Tools           AVG Tools
Running  avgbIDSAgent        avgbIDSAgent
Running  AvgWscReporter      AvgWscReporter
Stopped  AxInstSV            ActiveX Installer (AxInstSV)
Stopped  BcastDVRUserSer...  GameDVR and Broadcast User Service_...
Stopped  BDESVC              BitLocker Drive Encryption Service
Running  BFE                 Base Filtering Engine
```

Figure 9.8 – The get-service command

If we only want to find the Windows services, we can use the `get-service -name win*` command. See *Figure 9.9*:

```
PS C:\Users\Administrator.WIN-HB5RLG5VD60> get-service -name win*

Status   Name              DisplayName
------   ----              -----------
Stopped  WinDefend         Windows Defender Antivirus Service
Running  WinHttpAutoProx...  WinHTTP Web Proxy Auto-Discovery Se...
Running  Winmgmt           Windows Management Instrumentation
Stopped  WinRM             Windows Remote Management (WS-Manag...
```

Figure 9.9 – The filter get-service command

We can filter the first command by inserting a pipe and then using a `where` statement. We can use the following commands: `-lt` for less than; `-gt` for greater than; `-eq` for equals; and `-ne` for not equals.

In the next example, if we want to see the services that are stopped, we could use `get-service | Where-object {$_. status -eq stopped}`, instead of using -eq stopped, you could use -ne running. The `$` is a variable, and then we use the `Status` column header. Refer to the following *Figure 9.10*:

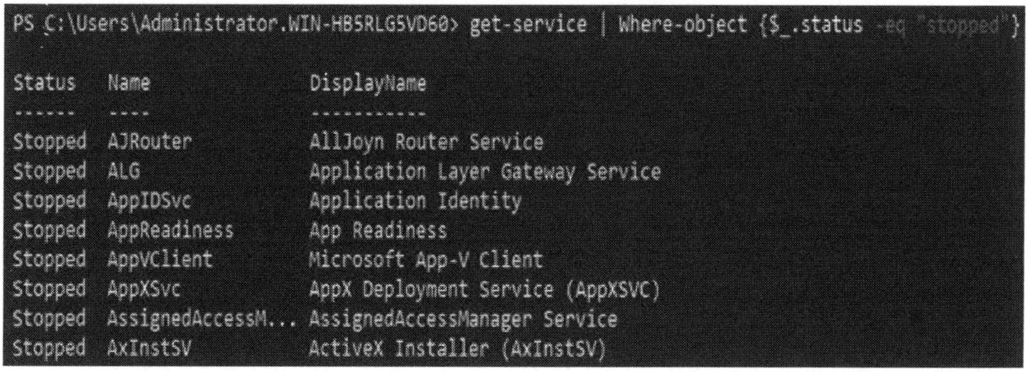

```
PS C:\Users\Administrator.WIN-HB5RLG5VD60> get-service | Where-object {$_.status -eq "stopped"}

Status    Name              DisplayName
------    ----              -----------
Stopped   AJRouter          AllJoyn Router Service
Stopped   ALG               Application Layer Gateway Service
Stopped   AppIDSvc          Application Identity
Stopped   AppReadiness      App Readiness
Stopped   AppVClient        Microsoft App-V Client
Stopped   AppXSvc           AppX Deployment Service (AppXSVC)
Stopped   AssignedAccessM... AssignedAccessManager Service
Stopped   AxInstSV          ActiveX Installer (AxInstSV)
```

Figure 9.10 – Services stopped

PowerShell has many different modules that can be used for remote access as well as for use by attackers. These attacks have been on the increase. It has been used for the following attacks:

a. Injecting malware directly into memory

b. Used to run macros

c. Lateral movement attacks

Please read the following article on these attacks: `https://securityintelligence.com/an-increase-in-powershell-attacks-observations-from-ibm-x-force-iris/`.

We should ensure that we use the following command to stop someone running a PowerShell command on a server or desktop:

```
Set-ExecutionPolicy Restricted
```

We should use the latest version of PowerShell as this is the most secure.

- **Python**: Python is a powerful scripting language used by administrators of websites and are vulnerable to backdoor attacks. Please read the following article, where Python was used to steal SSH keys: `https://hub.packtpub.com/python-libraries-removed-from-pypi-caught-stealing-ssh-and-gpg-keys/`.

- **Bourne Again Shell (Bash)**: In a Linux system, we use the Bash shell to run commands and run executables and automated tasks. Shellshock was a Bash shell vulnerability that allowed attackers to obtain remote access to many web servers: `https://en.wikipedia.org/wiki/Shellshock_(software_bug)`.

- **Macros**: Macros are disabled by default in Microsoft Office. These are a series of actions that you want to carry out that are normally used with Word or Excel and they use Microsoft's Visual Basic for Applications scripting language. Macros can be launched through phishing emails. Beware of emails saying **Confidential Information** or for invoices for unknown purchases. You can go into a Word document and select **File | Options | Trust Center | Trust Centre Settings | Disable all macros with notifications** to ensure that macros won't run. A good anti-virus software will also prevent macros from running. Please read the following article on Office macro attacks: `https://www.cynet.com/attack-techniques-hands-on/office-macro-attacks/`.

Hijacking-Related Attacks

In this section, we will look at attacks where a hacker hijacks either a device, cookie, or piece of software. Let's look at these in turn:

- **Bluejacking**: Bluejacking is where an attacker takes control of a Bluetooth device such as a phone. They are then able to make phone calls and send text messages.

- **Bluesnarfing**: Once again, an attacker hijacks a Bluetooth phone, but in this scenario, they extract contact details and any sensitive information.

> **Tip**
> Input validation could prevent SQL injection, buffer overflow, and integer overflow attacks.

- **Session Hijacking**: When you visit a website, your desktop can store your browsing information in a file called a *cookie*. This is a security risk as it can be used to identify you. For example, the second time you visit a website, it may say **Good Morning, Mr Smith** at the top. If someone copies your cookie and places it on their machine, the website will also see them as Mr. Smith. This is known as **Session hijacking**.

- **Domain Hijacking**: Domain hijacking is when someone tries to change the domain registration of a domain with the internet authorities so that they can control it for profit. For example, an attacker manages to re-register the domain name of a well-known company and can access the control panel with the original domain's company, *Hosting A*. They then take out a hosting package with *Hosting B*, where they copy over all of the files from *Hosting A* and move them into *Hosting B*. They then point the DNS records to *Hosting B*, where they can take sales from customers who believe they are trading with the original company.

- **URL Hijacking**: URL hijacking is a process in which a website is falsely removed from the results of a search engine and replaced by another web page that links to the remote page. Another form of this is **Typosquatting**.

- **URL Redirection**: This is where an attacker redirects you from a legitimate website to a fraudulent website. This can be done if you can hack the control panel for the domain. This can be prevented by keeping your software up to date, using a web application firewall, or using an automated website scanner that will find vulnerabilities.

- **Typosquatting**: When someone types the URL of a website into their browser, they may transpose two characters of the website name if they have typed it very quickly. Typosquatting is where an attacker creates websites with characters transposed to redirect a user's session to a fraudulent website. This is also known as **URL hijacking**.

> **Tip**
> A stored procedure could prevent a SQL injection attack as it is a pre-written script that is executed and cannot be altered when executed.

- **Clickjacking**: Clickjacking is a malicious technique for tricking a web user into clicking on an icon or link, the outcome of which is different from what the user perceives they are clicking on, thereby potentially revealing confidential information or taking control of their computer. An attacker establishes a malicious website that invisibly embeds the Facebook **Like** or **Share** button in a transparent iframe. When the victim clicks within the malicious site, the click is directed to the invisible **Like** or **Share** button.

Driver Manipulation

Device drivers allow an operating system such as Windows to talk to hardware devices such as printers. Sophisticated attackers may dive deep into device drivers and manipulate them so that they undermine the security on your computer. They could also take control of the audio and video of the computer, stop your anti-virus software from running, or your data could be exposed to someone else. There are two main driver manipulation techniques, and these are as follows:

- **Shimming**: A *shim* is a small library that transparently intercepts API calls and changes the arguments passed. They can also be used to run programs on different software platforms than they were developed for. Normally, it is used to help third-party software applications work with an operating system.

- **Refactoring**: Refactoring is the process of changing an application's code to avoid detection by anti-virus software while still retaining its attack functionality.

Cryptographic Attacks

There are a variety of cryptographic attacks, and we will now look at these in turn. You need to thoroughly know these for the Security+ exam. We will start with the *birthday attack* and finish with *key stretching*:

- **Birthday Attack**: The birthday paradox states that in a random gathering of 23 people, there is a 50% chance that two people will have the same birthday. If we store passwords as hashes, then all passwords that are the same will produce the same hash if we use the same hashing algorithm. The birthday paradox looks for collisions in hashes. If it finds two hashes of the same value, the attacker also knows that the password is the same.

- **Digital Signatures**: Digital signatures are susceptible to a birthday attack.

- **Rainbow Tables**: Rainbow tables are lists of pre-computed passwords with a corresponding hash. You can obtain free rainbow tables from the internet. Some larger rainbow tables are 690 GB in size. These tables speed up the cracking of passwords that have been hashed.

- **Collision Attack**: A collision attack on a cryptographic hash tries to find two inputs producing the same hash value; this is known as a **hash collision**.

- **Salting Passwords**: Salting password values is where a random set of characters is inserted into, or appended to, a password hash. This prevents duplicate passwords being stored and prevents rainbow tables and collision attacks. This also creates a longer password, slowing down brute-force attacks.

- **Key Stretching**: Key stretching is similar to salting a password by inserting random strings to prevent rainbow table and collision attacks. *Bcrypt* and *PBKDF2* can be used for key stretching. For example, a company has a password policy of not using complex passwords and has therefore suffered many attacks. To prevent this in future, they use Bcrypt to key stretch weak passwords, making them more difficult to crack. They could have introduced both complex passwords and key stretching to make passwords more secure.

Review Questions

Now it's time to check your knowledge. Answer the questions, and then check your answers, which can be found in the *Assessments* section at the end of the book:

1. If I install a freeware program that analyzes my computer and then finds 40,000 exploits and asks me to purchase the full version, what type of attack is this?

2. Describe how a fileless virus operates.

3. How does an attacker carry out credential harvesting?

4. How is pretexting used in an attack?

5. How does an invoice scam work?

6. How does an attacker carry out password spraying?

7. How does an attacker use a malicious USB drive?

8. How does artificial intelligence tainting help attackers?

9. When I go to a restaurant, how can I protect myself against card cloning?

10. What is an on-path attack?

11. Why is operational technology vulnerable to attack?

12. What is crypto-malware?

13. What type of virus replicates itself and uses either ports 4444 or 5000?

14. What type of virus inserts .dll into either the SysWOW64 or System32 folder?

15. What is an RAT?

16. What type of virus attacks the Windows/System32 folder on Windows, or the Bash shell on Linux?

17. How does a logic bomb virus work?

18. What is the purpose of a keylogger?

19. What is a botnet?

20. Explain a phishing attack.

21. How does spear phishing differ from a phishing attack?

22. What is a whaling attack?

23. What type of attack can include leaving voicemail?

24. What is tailgating?

25. What is social engineering?

26. What type of attack could involve dressing as a police officer?

27. What type of attack is it if a fireperson arrives and you let them into the server room to put out a fire?

28. What type of attack is it if I am in an ATM queue and someone has their phone to one side so that they can film the transaction?

29. What type of attack is distributing fake software?

30. What is a watering hole attack?

31. What type of attack is it if I receive an email from my company's CEO, telling me to complete the form attached by clicking on a link in the email?

32. One of my bosses asks me to give them information that one of my peers gave them last week. I am not too sure, but I give them the information. What type of attack is this?

33. What type of attack is a multiple SYN flood attack on a well-known website that takes it down?

34. Explain a man-in-the-middle attack.

35. How does a replay attack differ from a man-in-the-middle attack?

36. What type of attack is a man-in-the-middle attack using an SSL3.0 browser that uses a CBC?

37. What type of attack is a man-in-the-browser attack?

38. How can I prevent a replay attack in a Microsoft environment?

39. How can I prevent a pass-the-hash attack?

40. What type of attack uses HTML tags with JavaScript?

41. What type of exploit has no patches and cannot be detected by NIDS or NIPS?

42. What is domain hijacking?

43. What is bluejacking?

44. What is bluesnarfing?

45. What type of attack is a local attack and how can I prevent that attack?

46. For what type of attack would I use the strcpy tool?

47. What is an integer overflow attack?

48. What type of attack uses the phrase 1=1?

49. Name two methods for preventing the type of attack in question 38.

50. What type of attack is session hijacking?

51. If I misspell a website but still get there, what type of attack is this?

52. What type of attack would I use shimming or refactoring for?

53. What type of system is susceptible to a birthday attack?

54. What are rainbow tables?

55. How can I store passwords to prevent a dictionary attack?

56. Name two tools that can be used for key stretching.

57. What is the fastest password attack that can crack any password?

58. What is the only way to prevent a brute-force attack?

59. What can we do to slow down a brute-force attack?

60. What type of authentication is the most prone to errors?

61. What is an evil twin?

62. How can I prevent an attack by a rogue WAP?

63. I am trying to use the internet, but my wireless session keeps crashing, what type of attack is this?

64. How close does an attacker need to be for an NFC attack?

65. What is a pivot?

10
Governance, Risk, and Compliance

As a security professional, you need to understand that identifying and managing risks can help keep your company environment safe from various types of attacks. We will look at the importance of policies and regulatory frameworks for reducing the risk of successful attacks. We will look at different threats, vulnerabilities, and the roles that different threat actors play.

This chapter is broken down into the following sections:

- Risk Management Processes and Concepts
- Threat Actors, Vectors, and Intelligence Concepts
- The Importance of Policies to Organizational Security
- Regulations, Standards, and Frameworks
- Privacy and Sensitive Data Concepts

Risk Management Processes and Concepts

Risk is the probability that an event will happen – risk can also bring profit. For example, if you place a bet in roulette at a casino, then you could win money. It is, however, more likely that risk will result in financial loss. Companies will adopt a risk management strategy to reduce the risk they are exposed to; however, they may not be able to eliminate risk completely. In IT, new technology comes out every day and poses new risks to businesses, and therefore risk management is ever-evolving. The main components of risk management are assets, risks, threats, and vulnerabilities. Let's look at each of these, starting with assets:

- **Asset**: The first stage in risk management is the identification and classification of the asset. If the asset is a top-secret document, you will handle and store it differently than an asset that is unclassified and available for free on the internet.

  For example, if you had 1 kg of trash and you placed it outside your front door at night, you would be certain that in the morning it would still be there; however, if the asset was 1 kg of 24-carat gold and you left it outside your house at night, it would probably not be there in the morning.

- **Risk**: Risk is the probability that an event will occur, resulting in financial loss or loss of service.

- **Threat**: A threat is someone or something that wants to inflict loss on a company by exploiting vulnerabilities. It could be a hacker that wants to steal a company's data.

- **Vulnerability**: This is a weakness that helps an attacker exploit a system. It could be a weakness in a software package or a misconfiguration of a firewall.

Risk management processes and concepts need to be in place so that we can reduce the attack surface that's available for attackers. The first stage in risk assessment is to identify and classify the assets. How expensive or important the assets are will determine the amount that will be spent on protecting them. Let's now look at the different risk types.

> Exam Tip
> The first stage in risk assessment is to classify the asset. The classification will tell us how an asset is to be treated and handled.

Risk Types

Risk types can be broken down into six categories. Let's now look at each of these in turn, starting with external risks:

- **External**: There are many different threat actors, ranging from competitors and script kiddies to criminal syndicates and state actors. Their ability to attack depends on the level of sophistication of their tools, and this is very much dependent on how much funding they have. If it is a foreign government, they are well organized and well funded and have many assets at their disposal. There are also external environmental threats, such as fire and floods, and man-made threats, such as the accidental deletion of data or lasers.

- **Internal**: One type of internal threat is a malicious insider; that is, a threat actor who, for instance, has been overlooked for promotion or is not happy with their current salary. The other internal threat is human error, which is when data is accidentally deleted.

- **Legacy Systems**: The risk with legacy systems is that they might not have any vendor support because the vendor has deemed that the system has reached the end of its life and there will be no more patches. As technologies improve, so do the hacking tools, and the legacy systems may have limited or no protection against them.

- **Multiparty**: This is where a contractor wins a contract and then sub-contracts some of the parts of the contract to other companies, who in turn subcontract again. Sometimes that can mean many contractors being involved in a single contract, and if any of them becomes bankrupt, then they can no longer provide that service and cause disruption to the company. Another area of multiparty risk is social media, where you befriend people you have never met; they can then gather information from your private posts or infect them. Other parties could update your software with a vulnerability embedded into it, leaving you wide open to attack.

For example, say a contract is awarded to us to build a row of houses. Water, gas, electricity, and roads may be contracted out to other agencies. As you can see, many different parties would be involved, and we could be attacked by anyone working in the supply chain.

- **Intellectual Property (IP) Theft**: An IP theft would be copyright material, trade secrets, and patents being stolen by competitors. This would result in a loss of revenue. This data could be used in other countries where a legal route to recover your data or seek damages is impossible. We should use **Data Loss Protection (DLP)**, fingerprinting, or document management systems to protect against this.

- **Software Compliance/Licensing**: Software should only be purchased from reputable vendors to ensure that the software purchased is exactly what was ordered. Software purchased elsewhere may not be licensed, and this would lead to a regulatory fine, or the software itself may contain malware and attack you. One of the risks to your company is where the employees use more copies of the company-purchased software than the licenses that you purchase, sometimes for personal use.

> **Exam Tip**
>
> IP theft can lose you patents, secrets, and copyright material, and these can be taken to a country where you cannot mount a legal challenge. From there, they can manufacture your products.

Risk Management Strategies

In a risk treatment, the risk owner, who is the best person to classify an asset, looks at each individual risk; they (the risk owner) will then decide what action is best to reduce the risk to the company. The risk will then be included in the company's risk register so that it can be monitored. New risks should be recorded in the risk register immediately and the risk register should be reviewed every 6 months, because risks change as frequently as technology changes. Let's look at risk management strategies, starting with risk acceptance:

- **Risk Acceptance**: This entails evaluating the risk and then deciding not to take any action as you believe that the probability of it happening is very low or that the impact is low. For example, say I had company premises in Scotland and I was quoted $1,000 a year to insure the building against earthquakes. I would not take the insurance and would accept the risk as Scotland last had an earthquake in 1986, and the magnitude was 2.0, which means it was generally not felt.

- **Risk Transference**: Risk transference is where you decide that the risk is great and you want to offload the responsibility to a third party. For example, say I purchase a car and decide that there is a high risk of someone crashing into the car, so I take out car insurance to transfer the risk to the insurance company. The car is insured, but I am still the owner. Companies are now taking out cybersecurity insurance that would cover financial loss due to cyberattacks, legal fees due to lawsuits, and the ability to employ a private investigator to catch the criminal.

- **Risk Avoidance**: Risk avoidance is where the risk is deemed too high, so you decide to not carry out the task. For example, say you are standing at the edge of the Grand Canyon, looking down, and you can see the drop is about 1,200 feet. You are thinking of jumping down to the bottom without a parachute, but common sense kicks in and tells you that you are likely to die; therefore, you decide to adopt risk avoidance and not jump, as the risk is too high.

- **Risk Mitigation**: Risk mitigation is where you evaluate the risk and decide whether or not the risk as it stands will result in financial loss, loss of service, or being vulnerable to attack. For example, say you leave your home in the morning to go to work – if you leave the door open, someone will enter your property and take some of your personal possessions. You then adopt risk mitigation by closing and locking the door. Another example is if you purchase 50 new laptops for your company, with software installed, but there is no anti-virus software. There is a high risk that you could encounter a virus; therefore you decide to mitigate the risk by installing anti-virus software on all of the laptops. Risk mitigation is a technical control.

Risk Analysis

Risk analysis is the use of techniques to analyze risks so that you have an overall picture of the risks that your company may face. Let's look at each of these in turn, starting with the risk register:

> **Exam Tip**
> Insurance of any kind, whether it is for a car or for cybersecurity, is risk transference.

- **Risk Register**: When we look at the overall risk for a company, we use a risk register. This is a list of all of the risks that a company could face. The risk to the finance department with be assessed by the financial director, and IT-related risk would be looked at by the IT manager. Each department can identify the assets, classify them, and decide on the risk treatment. The financial director and IT manager are known as *risk owners* – they are responsible for the risk. The risk register must be updated on an annual basis to make it effective. The following table shows a sample risk register:

Ser	Date	Owner	Description	Probability	Impact	Severity	Treatment	Contingency	Action taken
1	01-05-2018	IT Manager	Loss of Switch	Low	High	High	Transfer. 2-hour fix SLA	Purchase spare switch	02-05-2018

Figure 10.1 – Risk Register

- **Risk Assessment Types**: There are two risk assessment types: *qualitative* and *quantitative*. Let's look at each of these in turn:

  a. **Qualitative Risk Analysis**: A qualitative risk analysis is where the risk is identified as a high, medium, or low risk.

  b. **Quantitative Risk Analysis**: A quantitative risk analysis is where you look at the high qualitative risks and give them a numeric value so that you can associate them with a cost for the risk. This is calculated by multiplying the probability with the impact of the risk. Sometimes probability is known as likelihood.

For example, say we are going to grade a risk and its probability from 1 to 9, with 1 being low and 9 being high. If we look at the impact of losing a mail server, the qualitative risk analysis would say that it is high, but the probability of losing it would be low:

Probability	Impact	Quantitative Risk
3	6	18

Figure 10.2 – Quantitative Risk

- **Risk Matrix/Heat Map**: A risk matrix is used to get a visual representation of the risks affecting a company. The heat map shows the severity of the situation, with the most severe risks being in red:

I	Very High	7	10	20	25
M	High	7	7	15	20
P	Medium	4	5	7	15
A	Low	4	1	1	3
C		Low	Medium	High	Very High
T			LIKELIHOOD		

Figure 10.3 – Risk Matrix

The areas in red would cause severe damage to the company, where pink would still mean a high risk. The lighter pink and green would mean a medium risk. The darker green and the very dark green would mean a low risk. This is a good way to present a risk analysis to senior management.

- **Risk Control Self-Assessment**: This is a process where all company employees decide to have a meeting or send out a survey. Management encourages the employees to evaluate existing risk controls so that they can decide whether the current risk controls are adequate and report back to the management. This is a bottom-up approach.

- **Risk Awareness**: This is the process of making all employees aware of risk and motivating them to take responsibility for looking at risks and making recommendations to management on how to reduce those risks.

- **Inherent Risk/Residual Risk**: Inherent risk is the raw risk, prior to any risk mitigation strategies being implemented. Residual risk is the amount of risk remaining after you mitigate the risk. Remember that you cannot eliminate a risk totally.

- **Control Risk**: This is where a risk control is measured after it has been in place for some time, to evaluate whether it is still effective.

- **Risk Appetite**: This is the amount of risk mitigation that a company is willing to do so that they can be compliant with current regulations and also be protected. Regulations that affect risk posture include EU **GDPR, Sarbanes-Oxley Act (SOX), Health Insurance Portability Accountability Act (HIPAA), Payment Card Industry (PCI)**, and **Data Security Standard (DSS)** regulations.

> **Exam Tip**
>
> Qualitative risk is about the severity of the risk – is it high, medium, or low?
> Quantitative risk is about a numerical value gained by multiplying probability
> (likelihood) with impact.

Calculating Loss

The following concepts can be used to calculate the actual loss of equipment throughout
the year and may be used to determine whether we need to take out additional insurance
against the loss of equipment:

- **Single Loss Expectancy (SLE)**: The SLE is to do with the loss of one item. For
  example, if my laptop is worth $1,000 and I lose it while traveling, then my SLE
  would be $1,000.

- **Annualized Rate of Occurrence (ARO)**: The ARO is the number of times that an
  item has been lost in a year. If an IT team loses six laptops in a year, the ARO would
  be six.

- **Annualized Loss Expectancy (ALE)**: The ALE is calculated by multiplying the SLE
  by the ARO – in the previous examples, we have $1,000 x 6 = $6,000. The ALE is the
  total loss in a year.

  For example, say a multinational corporation loses 300 laptops annually, and these
  laptops are valued at $850; would they take out an insurance policy to cover the
  costs of replacement if the insurance premiums were $21,250 monthly? The answer
  is no, because the cost of replacing them is the same as the cost of the insurance.
  They would take a risk on not losing 300 laptops next year. The calculations are
  as follows:

  a. ALE: SLE x ARO

  b. ALE: $850 x 300 = $225,000

  c. Monthly cost: $225,000/12 = $21,250

> **Exam Tip**
>
> ALE = SLE x ARO
> ARO = ALE/SLE
> SLE = ALE/ARO

Disasters

There are different types of disasters that pose a risk to companies. Let's look at these, starting with environmental threats:

- **Environmental Threat**: This threat is based on environmental factors, for example, the likelihood of a flood, hurricane, or tornado. If you live in Florida, there is a peak season for hurricanes from mid-August to October. However, if you live in Scotland, hurricanes are very infrequent, the last being Hurricane *Friedhelm* in 2011. Florida has a high risk of having a hurricane, whereas Scotland would be extremely low risk.

- **Man-Made Threat**: This is a human threat – it could be a malicious insider attack, where an employee deliberately deletes data, or it could just be an accidental deletion by an incompetent member of staff. Lasers and bombs are also man-made threats.

- **Internal Threat versus External Threat**: An internal risk could be a flood, power failure, or maybe internal structural damage to a building. An external risk could be threat actors or natural disasters such as an earthquake or hurricanes.

Business Impact Analysis Concepts

Business Impact Analysis (**BIA**) is the process of looking into disasters and calculating the loss of sales, regulatory fines, and the purchase of new equipment. BIA looks at financial loss following a disaster. Let's look at the concepts of BIA, starting with the single point of failure:

- **Single Point of Failure**: The single point of failure is any single component that would prevent a company from remaining operational. This is one of the most critical aspects of BIA.

- **Recovery Point Objective (RPO)**: The RPO is how long a company can last without its data before the lack of data starts to affect operations. This is also known as *acceptable downtime*; if a company agrees that it can be without data for 3 hours, then the RPO is 3 hours. If the IT systems in a company suffer a loss of service at 13:00, then the RPO would be 16:00. Any repair beyond that time would have an adverse impact on the business as the company cannot operate without its data beyond that point.

- **Recovery Time Objective (RTO)**: The RTO is the time that a company needs to be returned to an operational state. In the preceding RPO scenario, we would like the RTO to be before 16:00. If the RTO is beyond 16:00, then once again it has an adverse impact on the business.

> **Exam Tip**
> The most important factor that an auditor will look at when assessing BIA is the single point of failure. They will also take the RPO and RTO into consideration.

- **Mean Time to Repair (MTTR)**: The MTTR is the average amount of time it takes to repair a system. If my car breaks down at 14:00 and it was repaired at 16:00, the MTTR would be 2 hours.

- **Mean Time Between Failures (MTBF)**: The MTBF shows the reliability of a system. If I purchased a new car for $50,000 on January 1, then it breaks down on January 2, 4, 6, and 8, I would take it back to the garage as the MTBF would be pretty high. For $50,000, I want a car that is more reliable.

- **Disaster Recovery Plan (DRP)**: There are many different types of disasters and there needs to be a DRP for each of them to recover from a failure as quickly as possible. Any downtime will have a financial impact on a company. For more, information, please read *Chapter 12, Dealing with Incident Response Procedures*.

- **Functional Recovery Plans**: Functional recovery plans use structures, walk-throughs, tabletop exercises, and simulations. More details are in *Chapter 12, Dealing with Incident Response Procedures*.

- **Mission Essential Functions/Identification of Critical Systems**: When we look at BIA as a whole, we have to see what the company's mission-essential functions are; for example, an airline depends heavily on its website to sell airline tickets. If this was to fail, it would result in a loss of revenue. Critical systems for the airline would be the server that the website was placed on and its ability to contact a backend database server, such as SQL, that holds ticketing information, processes credit card transactions, and contains the order history for each customer.

  For example, what would be the mission-essential functions of a newspaper, and what would be its critical systems? Newspapers generate revenue not only via sales but more importantly by selling advertisement space in the paper. The mission-essential function would be the program that creates the advertisements, and the critical systems would be the server that the program resides upon, the database for processing payments, and the systems used to print the newspapers.

- **Site Risk Assessment**: This is an assessment of all of the risks and hazards that could happen on a construction site. This could be the spillage of chemicals, power outages, floods, fires, and earthquakes. The site losing its health and safety certificate should be considered a site risk.

> **Exam Tip**
>
> When purchasing a new system, the MTBF measures the reliability of the system. You might also seek a system with a low MTTR, so that it is reliable and can be repaired quickly.

In the next section, we will look at threat actors, vectors, and intelligence concepts.

Threat Actors, Vectors, and Intelligence Concepts

Let's look at threat actors, vectors, and intelligence concepts, starting with threat assessments.

Threat Actors

A threat assessment helps a company classify its assets and then looks at the vulnerabilities of that asset. It will look at all of the threats the company may face, the probability of the threat happening, and the potential loss should the threat be successful.

A threat actor is another name for a hacker or attacker who is likely to attack your company; they all have different attributes. They will investigate your company from the outside, looking for details on social media and search engines. Security companies provide an open source intelligence test and inform you of your vulnerabilities in terms of threat actors. Let's now look at threat actor types:

- **Hackers**: There are three different types of hackers. Let's look at each of them:

    a. **Black Hat**: The black hat hacker has no information because they are not authorized by the company.

    b. **Gray Hat**: The gray hat hacker is provided with limited information from the company as they might be participating in a bug bounty program.

    c. **White Hat**: The white hat hacker is a former black hat hacker who is employed by a company to test applications for flaws and vulnerabilities before their release. They have all of the information that they need, including the source code.

> **Exam Tip**
>
> A gray hat hacker may not be employed by you but depends on a bug bounty program to get paid.

- **Hacktivist**: A hacktivist is an external threat that defaces your website or breaks into your computer or network. They are politically motivated and seek social change. They want to bring awareness to their cause by gaining press coverage.

- **Competitor**: A competitor is another company in the same industry as your company that tries to steal your trade secrets and cause damage to your production system to prevent you from getting products to market. They hope to get these products to market before you to capture a higher market share.

- **Script Kiddie**: A script kiddie is a person who does not have high technical knowledge and uses scripts and code that they find to attack your company. They want to be seen as a famous hacker and gain notoriety. They have no preference regarding who they attack; they just want to be noticed. They will purchase tools from the dark web.

- **State Actors**: A state actor is another country that poses a threat to your country; their motivation is that they want to undermine your nation. They are well organized and well funded. An example of this is someone interfering with your country's election process.

- **Advanced Persistent Threat** (**APT**): An APT is an external threat that tries to steal data from your network, but they are there for an extremely long period of time. They are very sophisticated and could be funded by a foreign government.

- **Shadow IT**: This is where people plug their own computers and devices into your network without consent. These devices may not be patched over a period of time and may become vulnerable. This may result in a threat actor gaining an access to your network via this system and could lead to pivoting.

- **Criminal Syndicates**: Criminal syndicates target companies mainly to steal money. They either want to blackmail you into paying a ransom for the return of your data or they threaten to make that information public by publishing it on the internet or sell it to one of your competitors. They have people working for them that have a high level of sophistication and their motivation is financial wealth.

- **Insider Threat**: An insider threat is a disgruntled employee who might have been overlooked for promotion and so their relationship with their company has gone sour. They are also known as *malicious insider* threats and are the most difficult to protect yourself from as they are already inside your network.

> **Exam Tip**
>
> Shadow IT is where someone plugs an unauthorized device into your network, leaving it vulnerable to attack. Criminal syndicates will threaten you and their motivation is financial gain.

Attack Vectors

There are a few different types of attack vectors. Let's look at each of them in turn, starting with direct access:

- **Direct Access**: This is where an attacker physically gains access to your network so that they can install keyloggers, malware, and listening devices, or carry out pivoting.

- **Wireless**: Wireless networks are a good attack vector. They can be exploited by carrying out **Initialization Vector** (**IV**) attacks or placing an evil twin or rogue access point.

- **Email**: Email is a major attack vector with, attacks ranging from phishing, spear phishing, or simply attaching a payload to an email that looks like it was sent by a reputable source.

- **Cloud**: Attackers may target your cloud provider to gain access to your network. Most cloud services are accessed by the internet, and you need to ensure that your company's connections to the cloud are secure, especially those for roaming users such as salespeople. All the attackers need to do is to exploit one person and they can attack your network.

- **Supply Chain**: If your supply chain outsources parts of a contract to other contractors, this could lead to a third-party attack. The attacker may be able to get a job with a supplier who provides computers to you, say, and they could place a Trojan horse on that computer. They could also tamper with your critical HVAC systems, which is what happened to Target in 2013, where Target was attacked by the company that repaired the HVAC systems: `https://www.cybereason.com/blog/what-are-supply-chain-attacks`. Threat Post says that half of all attacks focus on the supply chain; you can read the article at `https://threatpost.com/half-all-attacks-supply-chain/143391/`.

- **Removable Media**: If you do not obtain your software from a reliable supplier, you may inadvertently purchase software that has hidden malware. Another example of removable media is that, you may find a USB left in a location at the entrance or reception area of your company. When you use it and click on the link it contains to find its owner, a script might run that gives an attacker total control of your system.

- **Social Media**: Posting information about your company on social media could lead to an attacker gaining information that would be helpful for them to launch an attack on your network. Attackers may befriend you and launch a watering hole attack or embed trojans in social media posts so that when you read the post, you download the trojan, resulting in a remote access trojan attack.

Exam Tip

The supply chain attack has become a major threat to companies. External agencies performing maintenance on the supply chain may even place an exploit when carrying out said maintenance.

Threat Intelligence Sources

Over the past 5 years, there has been an increase in cybercrime, and because of that, several threat intelligence sources have emerged so that companies can protect themselves against attacks. Let's look at some of these resources; we will start with **Open Source Intelligence (OSINT)**:

- **OSINT**: This is intelligence collected legally from the public domain and the internet. OSINT has consultants who are willing to provide their services to companies at a cost. The Malware Information Sharing Platform threat sharing website is an OSINT provider that can be found at `https://www.circl.lu/doc/misp/`. OSINT can be used in law enforcement and business intelligence to help identify the source of an attack.

- **Closed/Proprietary**: This is information collected by a commercial company, and the data is accurate due to the money that they spend gathering information. You will need to pay a fee to access this data.

- **Vulnerability Databases**: The **National Institute of Standards and Technology (NIST)** is a US Government body that provides a National Vulnerability Database, which comprises **Common Vulnerabilities and Exposures (CVE)** and uses the **Common Vulnerability Scoring System (CVSS)** to show the level of severity of each of the vulnerabilities. The MITRE ATT&CK framework is a database of threat actors, their techniques, and the vulnerabilities that they exploit. This helps security teams protect themselves against such attacks.

- **Public/Private Information Sharing Centers**: This is where commercial and government bodies work together to provide threat assessments for different types of industries; see *Figure 10.4*:

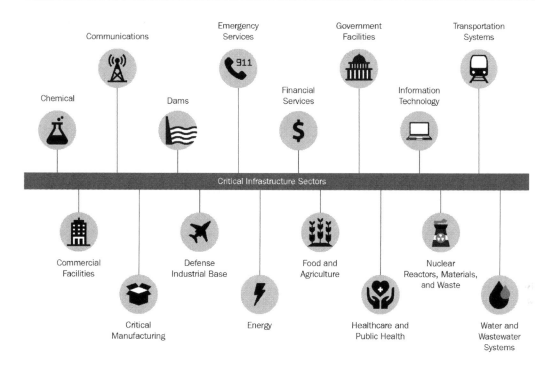

Figure 10.4 – Critical Infrastructure Sectors

The United States Department of Homeland Security wrote a critical infrastructure guide in October 2016. This was a threat assessment framework to help protect critical industry sectors.

- **Dark Web**: Governmental bodies trawl the dark web for any threats and then publish information on the threats that they find. Access to the dark web is by bulletin boards and not search engine, but the authorities access these sites by bribing those using the dark web. The attackers using the dark web hide their identity by using **TOR** software. TOR stands for **The Onion Router**. It is free software. TOR routing is like an onion as there are thousands of layers that are all encrypted to hide the true identity of the attacker. These layers relay traffic across thousands of networks to avoid detection.

- **Indicators of Compromise (IOCs)**: These provide information related to attacks within the IT security community and include IP addresses, file hashes, and URLs that are associated with malicious software. IOCs give a good understanding of the current threat landscape as the data is taken from malware that has been captured.

Exam Tip

The dark web depends on TOR software to avoid detection.

- **Structured Threat Information Exchange (STIX)/Trusted Automated Exchange of Indicator Information (TAXII)**: These are standards to prevent cyber-attacks. STIX was developed by MITRE and is a format to help distribute cyber threat intelligence. It defines the methods of attack and is divided into 18 domain objects, such as attack patterns, campaigns, indicators, and courses of action. TAXII works with STIX as it is an application that can distribute **Cyber Threat Intelligence (CTI)** over HTTP.

- **Automated Indicator Sharing (AIS)**: This provides the exchange of data about cyber-attacks. This is shared by the US federal government from the state level down to the local level, and private companies can participate in this program as well. STIX/TAXII is used for notifications.

  For example, say one of the participants in the AIS shares information on the malicious IP addresses and email addresses of an attacker; this will help prevent a second attack by this attacker as the awareness of the other participants about the attacker and their methods has been increased.

- **Predictive Analysis**: This filters big data (huge volumes of data) by using machine learning to identify patterns of cyber threats so that future attacks can be predicted.

- **Threat Maps**: These are real-time cyber-attack maps that show real-time attacks. There are a lot of these maps from *Bitdefender, Check Point, Norse map, Kaspersky*, and many more. A *Bitdefender* attack map is shown in *Figure 10.5*:

Figure 10.5 – Bitdefender Threat Map

- **File/Code Repositories**: GitHub was launched in 2008 so that application developers could share information about source code. A maintainer, who is typically the project leader, evaluates different versions of code that are held in separate repositories. Developers can share their personal files about vulnerabilities and the solutions for dealing with the vulnerabilities. Another source is `virustotal.com`, which holds information on malware signatures and code.

> **Exam Tip**
> STIX and TAXII distribute CTI updates over HTTP.

Research Sources

There are various other threat intelligence sources; let's look at some of them, starting first with vendor websites:

- **Vendor Websites**: Microsoft has produced its *Cyber Trust blog*, and Cisco has produced its *Security Blog* and *RSS feed*. Sophos has produced its *SophosLabs Threat Intelligence*, which can be found at `https://www.sophos.com/en-us/medialibrary/PDFs/factsheets/OEM-solutions/sophos-threat-intelligence-dsna.pdf`.

- **Vulnerability Feeds**: There are three main categories of vulnerability feeds. They are vendors, governments, and private sources. The best feeds are the *Department of Homeland Security AIS feed*, *FBI InfoGuard Portal*, *SABS Internal Storm Center*, and *Cisco Talos Intelligence Group*; the latter can be found at `https://blog.talosintelligence.com/`.

- **Conferences**: These are a great way for people in the cybersecurity world to keep pace with development and network with those involved in protection against cybercrime. These events are well attended and sponsored by various institutions. In January 2016, *SANS Threat Hunting and IR Summit and Training* was held in London, and it featured topics such as hacker tools, techniques and exploits, and incident handling. The second lecture was on advanced incident response, threat hunting, and digital forensics. These events are huge, worldwide, and can help increase awareness among industry professionals.

- **Academic Journals**: There are many academic journals publishing papers on cybersecurity. These include the **Journal of Cryptography** (**JOC**) and IEEE Security and Privacy. You have to purchase most of these journals.

- **Request for Comments (RFC)**: RFCs are created by the **Internet Engineering Task Force (IETF)**, whose aim is the development of standards for the internet. Some of these standards are advisory and some other standards are mandatory; as technology develops, so do the RFCs. A good example of this is *RFC1244*, the *Site Security Handbook*; this is the first attempt at providing guidance on how to deal with security issues on the internet. RFCs are written by experts in their fields.

- **Local Industry Groups**: In England, there is a group called the *Local Government Association*, whose aim is to provide good practice guidelines for local authorities for the prevention of cybercrime. There are local groups that help people report cybercrime. Victims may inform agencies such as the Cybercrime Support Network, which has produced a fraud log to help report cybercrime so that we can catch criminals.

- **Social Media**: Social media is a good source for researching cybercrime as many people publish articles on blogs so issues can be discussed. They also make people aware of cyber-attacks so that they don't become victims.

- **Threat Feeds**: These threat feeds are provided by security vendors to give people up-to-date information on bad actors, such as their IP addresses and malicious domains, so that the public is saved from becoming victims.

- **Adversary Tactics, Techniques, and Procedures (TTP)**: This is information on adversaries and the attack methods, tools, and techniques that they use. A good source of information for this is the MITRE ATT&CK framework, where you have a spreadsheet of adversaries and can drill down into relevant details.

In the next section, we will look at the importance of policies for organizational security.

The Importance of Policies for Organizational Security

Security policies are a good way to protect your environment against cybercriminals. Not having policies in place would mean that we would leave ourselves at the mercy of cybercriminals. Let's look at the policies that help keep our environments safe, starting with personnel policies, as personnel may be subjected to many types of social engineering attacks.

Personnel

Most cybercrime vulnerabilities relate to social engineering attacks carried out on employees. Therefore, we will put many policies in place to reduce the attack surface. Let's look at some of these policies, starting with on-boarding:

- **On-Boarding Policy**: Companies can allow a **Bring Your Own Device (BYOD)** policy for employees, and part of that process is carrying out on-boarding and off-boarding. An on-boarding policy states that any device must be checked for viruses, and any application that could cause damage to the company's network should be removed before the device is given access to the network. If someone fails to carry out onboarding properly, then the company could be infected by a virus.

- **Off-Boarding Policy**: When someone leaves your company, then the business data used on BYOD devices needs to be removed before departure. If off-boarding is not carried out properly, an ex-employee could leave with company business data on their device.

- **Separation of Duties**: Separation of duties is having more than one person participate in completing a task; this is an internal control to prevent fraud or error. Say a person worked in the finance department, collecting all money being paid in and authorizing all the payments being paid out. This would be better if there were two distinct finance jobs, where one person received money and another authorized payments, otherwise embezzlement can occur. A charity in the United Kingdom was defrauded out of £1.3 million over a period of 6 years this way. The aim of separation of duties is to have no one person doing the entirety of a task.

  For example, members of an IT team can make any changes they like to a network firewall; this represents a huge risk to the network. An auditor could recommend that each time a firewall rule is changed, it needs to be authorized by the *Change Advisory Board*, and that two people should be responsible for checking the changes to the firewall. With two people being responsible for making the changes, any errors should be eliminated. This is an example of the separation of duties.

  As another example, when I first got married, my wife and I opened a joint bank account that only my wages were paid into. My wife spent money from this account even though she had her own account. I paid in; my wife withdrew – a true separation of duties. Nowadays, I have my own account!

> **Exam Tip**
> Separation of duties can prevent financial fraud as whoever collects money cannot pay it out. This prevents someone from completing a whole transaction.

- **Acceptable User Policy (AUP)**: The purpose of the AUP is to let employees or contractors know what they can or cannot do with company computers and BYOD devices. It lays out the practices relating to how you can access the company network and the internet. It also outlines practices that are forbidden, such as using blogs and social media sites such as Facebook or Twitter while at work or installing pirated software.

- **Non-Disclosure Agreement (NDA)**: An NDA is a legally binding contract made between with an employee or a business partner, where they promise not to disclose trade secrets to others without proper authorization. The reason for this is to stop trade secrets or proprietary information from being sold on to competitors.

- **Background Checks**: Completing background checks on new employees may involve looking into criminal records and employment and education history, as well as driving license and credit checks. This is to ensure that what the person has stated on their CV (or resume) is correct. More stringent background checks are needed for those working with children or handling finances.

- **Exit Interview**: The purpose of an exit interview is to find out the reason why an employee has decided to leave an organization; this can be used to improve employee retention.

- **Job Rotation**: Job rotation is used for two main reasons – the first is so that all staff can be trained in all aspects of the jobs in the company. Employees may change departments every 6 months; this way, they get a better training experience. The second reason is that by rotating jobs, any theft or fraudulent activities can be discovered by the new person coming in.

- **Mandatory Vacations**: Mandatory vacations help detect whether an employee has been involved in fraudulent activities by forcing them to take holidays of a week or more. When people are involved in fraudulent activities, they tend not to take many holidays so that the fraud cannot be discovered. This is especially rife in jobs in which people have fiscal trust, such as someone working in finance or someone who can authorize credit card payments.

- **Least Privilege Policy**: This policy states that access to data should be restricted and that employees should be given the minimum access required for them to perform their job. In the military, it is known as the *need-to-know* principle, where if you don't need access, then you have no access.

- **Clean-Desk Policy**: A clean-desk policy (sometimes known as a *clear-desk policy*) is a company policy that specifies that employees should clear their desks of all papers at the end of each day. This prevents the cleaning staff or anyone else from reading those papers.

- **Rules of Behavior**: Rules of behavior lay down the rules for how employees should conduct themselves when at work. There should be no bullying, discrimination, or sexual harassment. Employees should work together for the benefit of the company, even if they are not from the same background. People should respect and tolerate other employees' religious beliefs even if they are not the same as their own beliefs and they disagree with them.

- **Adverse Action**: An adverse action is an action that is unlawful. The *Fair Work Act* defines a number of actions as adverse actions. Examples include threatening an employee, injuring them during their employment, or discriminating against them.

- **Policy Violations**: When employees or contractors do not follow the policies or procedures that they have agreed to, it may result in either disciplinary procedures or, if serious, instant dismissal. This is normally to do with behavior.

- **Social Media Analysis**: We need a good company policy on what we post on social media as we need to prevent useful information from being accessed by attackers.

- **User Training**: User training is vital to reducing the risk of being exploited by cybercriminals. (In the next section, we are going to look at different types of user training, starting by looking at the diversity of training techniques.)

Exam Tip

If you install pirated software onto a company computer, then you are in violation of the AUP.

Diversity of Training Techniques

Due to the increase in the number and sophistication of different types of attacks, companies must provide a diverse range of user security training and regular seminars. User training is vital to reducing the risk of being exploited by cybercriminals, and we are going to look at different types of user training here. Let's start by looking at Capture the Flag:

- **Capture the Flag**: These events are where red team members (posing as attackers) will have an exploitation-based exercise or blue team members (defenders) will have a threat that they need to deal with. Each member tackles their particular exercises, achieving one objective at a time until they meet their overall aim (which is known as capturing the flag). At this point, they can move on to another level of the exercise. Once they have completed a sufficient number of levels, they are fit to join their relevant teams. See *Chapter 5, Monitoring, Scanning, and Penetration Testing*, for information on red and blue teams.

- **Phishing Campaigns/Simulations**: Here the company sends phishing emails to their employees to see how they react. Personnel who fall victim to them are then given remedial training on phishing attacks.

- **Computer-Based Training (CBT)/Gamification**: This is where employees watch a video and are given questions after each section of the video to ensure that they understand the training. This is a form of *gamification*.

- **Role-Based Training**: Here the company carries out security awareness training and ensures that all employees are sufficiently trained for their job roles.

> **Exam Tip**
> Capture the Flag exercises help to train both red and blue team members, as each time they capture the flag, they move up one level in their training.

Third-Party Risk Management

Companies use a vast amount of third parties either for software or to provide a service, and since we do not control those third parties, we need to carry out risk assessments that look at the way we interact with those companies. Let's look at each of the interactions in turn, starting with supply chain management:

- **Supply Chain**: Your supply chain comprises the companies that you totally rely on to provide the materials you need to carry out business functions or make a product for sale. Let's say that you are a laptop manufacturer, and *Company A* provides the batteries and *Company B* provides the power supplies. If either of these companies runs short of batteries or power supplies, it stops you from manufacturing and selling your laptops. See *Supply Chain* under the *Attack Vectors* section earlier in this chapter.

- **Vendors**: When you purchase software, you must ensure that it is from a reputable vendor, because if the vendor cannot be trusted, they could be installing malware such as remote access trojans or spyware with the software. They could also have a backdoor built in. The more you integrate the products from a single vendor, the more you are reliant on them. If they go bankrupt, it could leave you vulnerable.

- **Business Partners**: A **Business Partnership Agreement** (**BPA**) is used between two companies who want to participate in a business venture to make a profit. It sets out how much each partner should contribute, their rights and responsibilities, the rules for the day-to-day running of the business, who makes the decisions, and how the profits are shared. It also has rules for the partnership ending either at a given point or if one of the partners dies.

- **Memorandum of Understanding** (**MOU**): An MOU is a formal agreement between two or more parties. MOUs are stronger than a gentlemen's agreement and both parties must be willing to make a serious commitment to each other, but they are not legally binding.

- **Memorandum of Agreement** (**MOA**): An MOA is similar to an MOU but serves as a legal document and describes the terms and details of the agreement.

- **Non-Disclosure Agreement** (**NDA**): An NDA is a legally binding contract made between an employee or a business partner where they promise not to disclose trade secrets to others without proper authorization. The reason for this is to stop trade secrets or proprietary information from being sold on to competitors.

- **Service Level Agreement (SLA)**: An SLA is a contract between a service provider and a company receiving the service. The agreement can be for either a fix or a response over a certain period of time and is measured by metrics.

- **End of Life (EOL)**: This is where a vendor stops selling a product and the availability of replacement parts and technical support is limited.

- **End of Service (EOS)**: This is where the vendor believes that the product has reached the end of its usefulness, maybe due to a new version of the product being released. They will not commit any more time or resources to maintain the product. Users can still use the product but must take into consideration that there will be no more security updates or technical support available from the vendor. This will mean that over time, such products will become vulnerable and pose a huge security risk to any company still using them.

> **Exam Tip**
> An SLA lays down how quickly a supplier should respond to an incident such as a failed printer. It is measured using metrics.

Data

Data is one of the most important assets that a company has, and it is important to ensure that policies are in place to ensure that it is classified, handled, stored, and disposed of in accordance with regulations such as GDPR or HIPAA. Let's look at the data aspects we need to consider, starting with classification:

- **Classification**: This is the process of labeling data with relevant classifications, so that we know if it is top secret, secret, confidential, or sensitive data. The classification determines how the data is handled.

- **Governance**: Data governance is the oversight and management that describes the security controls that are applied at each stage of the data-handling process, from creation to destruction. These procedures detail the processes used to manage, store, and dispose of data to ensure that you are compliant.

- **Retention**: Companies do not want to hold data any longer than they need to, as it reduces their liability; however, they may have to keep data in an archive after its usefulness to remain compliant. An example of this is medical data in the UK, which needs to be retained for 25 years.

Credential Policies

It is vital that credentials are kept safe to prevent unauthorized access to systems; therefore, it is vital that policies are in place to prevent vulnerabilities and unauthorized access. Let's look at the policies we need to put in place, starting with personnel-related policies:

- **Personnel**: Personnel accounts could use a shared account, where all members of the customer service team use the same account to email customers. The downside of this is that you cannot audit or monitor individual users. The other type of personnel account is the user account, which should be subjected to the principle of least privilege.

- **Third-Party**: A third-party credential could be a SAML token given by a cloud provider or **Security as a Service** (**SECaaS**) vendor, where the cloud provider manages your identity management. If we are doing remote administration, we could use SSH keys for Secure Shell, where the public key is installed on the target server.

- **Devices**: Devices have generic accounts with default password settings. As soon as you purchase a device, you need to change the default settings, as these are published on websites. Please go to `https://cirt.net/passwords` to see these passwords.

- **Service Accounts**: Service accounts are used to run applications such as anti-virus. They can run as local service accounts with the same rights as a user. A system account gives you a higher level of privilege, giving you full control.

- **Administrator/Root Accounts**: Administrative and root accounts in Linux need to be protected as they allow you to install software, make configuration changes, and access any file. These accounts should be restricted to a few IT personnel. When we install new systems, we need to ensure that we change the default account settings. The root account in Linux is called *superuser* and is not restricted; this account should not be used unless it is absolutely necessary. The administrator should have two accounts: a normal user account for day-to-day use and an admin account for administrative duties.

Organizational Policies

Organizational policies need to be in place to deal with changes in technology, risk, or security to maintain a secure working environment. Let's look at some of these policies, starting with change management:

- **Change Management**: When an audit is carried out and reports show that the controls in place are not secure enough, we either implement change management or write a new policy. A new policy changes an entire process, and change management amends existing processes.

- **Change Control**: Change control is where someone makes a request to those managing the implementation of a change to an existing control. Say that management would like to know about the financial benefits of a change, the saving it would make either in labor time or monetary value. Such changes need to be sent to the **Change Advisory Board** (**CAB**) to ensure that it is beneficial to the company.

- **Asset Management**: This is a process where each asset that belongs to the company has been tagged and is recorded in an asset register. Annual audits need to be carried out to ensure that all assets are accounted for.

Regulations, Standards, and Legislation

Regulations, standards, and legislation are put in place to ensure that compliance has been achieved, and most are legally enforceable. From these regulations and standards, we derive our policies to ensure compliance and prevent crime; if companies do not abide by these regulations, they will be fined. There are other industry frameworks that are only best practice and are not legally enforceable, but vendors will not support any product that has not been set up according to such best practices. In this section, we are going to look at regulations, standards, and legislation followed by a look at key frameworks, benchmarks, and secure configuration guides. Let's start with **General Data Protection Regulation** (**GDPR**):

- **General Data Protection Regulation** (**GDPR**): The **European Union's** (**EU's**) GDPR came into force on 25th May 2018, as a framework for data protection law. It is enforced by the EU **Information Commissioner's Office** (**ICO**) and protects the individual's right to the privacy of their data, such as name, date of birth, photographs, video footage, email addresses, and telephone numbers. GDPR aims at protecting the collection, use, and storage of this information. GDPR states that anyone selling products on their website to EU citizens must adhere to GDPR and that data can only be stored for its intended use. For example, after a purchase has been made, credit card details should no longer be stored without the consent of the user.

- **National, Territory, or State Laws**: In the US, there are national data laws – for example, the **Health Insurance Portability and Accountability Act (HIPAA)** for medical data and the **Gramm-Leach-Bliley Act (GBLA)** for financial services. States tend to have their own laws on personal data, but most are based on **Federal Information Security Management Act (FISMA)**, which protects government information and operations.

- **Payment Card Industry Data Security Standard (PCI DSS)**: PCI DSS deals with the handling and storage of data used for card payments. For more information, please go to `https://www.pcisecuritystandards.org/about_us/`.

> **Exam Tip**
> GDPR deals with the handing of data while maintaining the privacy and rights of an individual.

Key Frameworks

Several key frameworks have been designed, mostly by not-for-profit organizations, to help reduce the risk created by ever-increasing cybercrime levels and the adoption of the cloud by companies. Let's start with **Center for Internet Security (CIS)**:

- **CIS**: This is a not-for-profit organization that publishes information on cybersecurity best practices and threats and has tools to help harden your environment and provide risk management. CIS provides benchmarks for different operating systems and provides controls to help secure your organization. For more details, go to `https://www.cisecurity.org/cybersecurity-tools/`.

- NIST **Cyber Security Framework (CSF)**: NIST RMF/CSF is designed to focus on the individual and the risk they pose to cybersecurity. This replaces NIST's **Risk Management Framework (RMF)** and was designed to look at the risk that individuals pose to governmental agencies. Information on the CSF can be found at `https://www.nist.gov/cyberframework` and information on the RMF can be found at `https://csrc.nist.gov/projects/risk-management/rmf-overview`.

- **International Organization for Standardization** (**ISO**): ISO publishes standards that are internally agreed upon by experts. Listed here are the standards for information systems; let's first look at 27001:

  a. **27001** – Security techniques for *Information Security Management Systems*: `https://www.iso.org/standard/54534.html`.

  b. **27002** – *Code of Practice for Information Security Controls*. The aim of this standard is to improve the management of information: `https://www.iso.org/standard/54533.html`.

  c. **27701** – An extension to 27001/27002 for *Privacy Information Management – Requirements and Guidelines*: `https://www.iso.org/standard/71670.html`.

  d. **31000** – About managing risk for company organizations and management in general; information can be found on its website: `https://www.iso.org/standard/65694.html`.

- **Statements on Standards Attestation Engagements** (**SSAE**): SSAE 18 is an audit standard to enhance the quality and usefulness of **Service Organization Control** (**SOC**) reports. This is designed for larger organizations such as cloud providers, as the cost of a low-end report is in the region of $15,000.

- **SOC Type 2/3**: SOC reports are used to help a **Code Public Accountant** (**CPA**) carry out an audit to gain confidence in the services that you provide. This gives confidence to stakeholders and potential customers. Let's look at some SOC reports:

  a. **SOC Type 2 Reports**: These are reports on the internal controls of the security, processing, and handling of users' data to ensure that it is kept confidential and that privacy is maintained. There are two types: type 1 is to do with the suitability of the design of controls, and type 2 is to do with the effectiveness of the controls.

  The distribution of these reports is restricted as they provide lots of details on the company that has been audited.

  b. **SOC Type 3 Reports**: These are general-use reports, and they are less detailed and so can be freely distributed. More information on SOC reports can be found at `https://www.aicpa.org/interestareas/frc/assuranceadvisoryservices/serviceorganization-smanagement.html`.

> **Exam Tip**
> SSAE is an audit standard for SOC reports. SOC type 1 reports measure your security, and SOC type 2 reports are about data management. These have restricted access and are mandatory for every cloud provider.

- **Cloud Security Alliance**: The **Cloud Security Alliance (CSA)** is a not-for-profit organization that produces various resources to help **Cloud Service Providers (CSPs)**, such as online training, webinars, community discussion groups, and virtual summits. Please go to the following site for more information: `https://cloudsecurityalliance.org/online-resources/`. Let's look at the **Cloud Control Matrix (CCM)** and the CSA Reference Architecture:

  a. **CSA CCM**: This is designed to provide a guide on security principles for cloud vendors and potential cloud customers to assess the overall risk of a cloud provider: `https://cloudsecurityalliance.org/research/working-groups/cloud-controls-matrix/`.

  b. **CSA Reference Architecture**: The Reference Architecture contains best security practices for CSPs. Its website states its mission as being "*to promote research, development, and education of best practice and methodologies around a reference architecture for a secure and trusted cloud.*" It looks at different topics, such as security and risk, presentation services, application services, information services, **IT Operation and Support (ITOS)**, and **Business Operation and Support Services (BOSS)**.

> **Exam Tip**
> CSA CCM helps potential customers measure the overall risk of a CSP.

Benchmarks/Secure Configuration Guides

Every company faces the challenge of protecting its servers and computers from an ever-increasing amount of cybersecurity threats. There are many different types of servers, such as web servers, email servers, and database servers, and each of them has different configurations and services, so the baselines are different for each type of server. Vendors and manufacturers will provide platform/vendor guides so that their products can be configured as per their own best practices, ensuring that they perform as best they can. Let's look at various types, starting with platform-specific guides:

- **Platform-/Vendor-Specific Guides**: These guides roll out with new products so that they can be set up as securely as possible, making them less vulnerable to attack.

- **Web Servers**: There are two main web servers used by commercial companies. Microsoft has a web server called the *Internet Information Server*, and its rival is *Apache*. Web servers provide web pages for the public to view, and because they are in the public domain, they are prime targets for hackers. To help reduce the risk, both Microsoft and Apache provide security guides to help security teams reduce their footprint, making them more secure. Microsoft has created a user guide called *Best Practice to Protect Internet Facing Web Servers*, which can be found at `https://social.technet.microsoft.com/wiki/contents/articles/13974.microsoft-security-best-practices-to-protect-internet-facing-web-servers.aspx`. Web server security guides rely on the latest updates being in place, services that are not required being turned off, and the operating system being hardened to make it as secure as possible and reduce the risk of attack.

- **Operating Systems**: Most vendors, such as Microsoft, have guides that detail the best practices for installing their operating systems. This is to ensure that they are as secure and as reliable as possible.

- **Application Server**: Vendors produce guides on how to set up their application servers, such as email servers or database servers, to make them less vulnerable to attack.

- **Network Infrastructure Devices**: Cisco produces the best high-end network devices, and because the networking world is ever-evolving, Cisco has produced an infrastructure upgrade guide so that companies can use it for best practices when upgrading their network devices: `https://www.cisco.com/c/en/us/support/ios-nx-os-software/ios-15-4m-t/products-installation-and-configuration-guides-list.html`.

In the next section, we will look at the different privacy and sensitive data concepts.

Privacy and Sensitive Data Concepts

It is vital that private and sensitive data is labeled and handled correctly, as doing otherwise would adversely affect a company's reputation and could lead to a regulatory fine. Let's look at concepts relating to data, starting with the consequences of a data breach.

Organizational Consequences of Privacy Breaches

If a company suffers a data breach, there can be several repercussions. Let's look at some of them, starting with reputation damage:

- **Reputation Damage**: When a company suffers a data breach and it is known to the public, it can cause their brand to become tainted as they lose the respect of the public. This could reduce sales.

- **Identity Theft**: If any data held on a customer is stolen and then used for identity theft, the company will be sued for damages.

- **Fines**: Data breaches could result in regulatory fines. An example would be the EU GDPR, where the maximum fine is 20 million euros or 4% of the company's annual global turnover, whichever is greater.

- **IP Theft**: IP theft could result in copyrighted material, trade secrets, and patents being stolen by competitors, resulting in a loss of revenue. This data could be used in countries where a legal route to recover your data would be impossible.

> Exam Tip
>
> If a company suffers a data breach and that data is used for identity theft, the company could be sued by the individual affected.

Notifications of Breaches

There are national laws and regulations that are laid down on how data breaches should be reported and who they should be reported to. A data breach is normally where data has been stolen or there has been an accidental breach; this means that the policies currently in place are not effective. If someone accesses a file or database server, we need to find the account used so that we can remove it to prevent further breaches. Let's now look at the action we need to take once a breach has been discovered, starting with escalation:

- **Escalation**: Any data breach, no matter how small, should be reported immediately to the CEO as the company may face legal action later on. A company may face a fine if they have not been compliant with regulations.

- **Public Notifications and Disclosures**: We may have to contact the police, the regulator, customers, and any individuals affected by the breach. EU GDPR law allows a company 72 hours to notify those concerned. If you are in the UK, you must comply with the Data Protection Act 1988, which is statute law, and in the USA, if it is medical data, you must comply with HIPAA.

Data Types

There are various types of data and we need to have an appreciation of each type and its characteristics; let's start with different data classifications.

Classification

The first stage of risk management is the classification of the asset, which determines how we handle, access, store, and destroy data. We are now going to look at the different classifications of data so that we know how to handle the data. Let's start by looking at public data:

- **Public Data**: This is data that is available to anyone, such as yesterday's news, leaflets, or brochures that have been distributed everywhere. Anyone has access to this data.

- **Private Data**: Private data is data that an individual does not want to disclose; it could also be classified as sensitive data.

- **Sensitive Data**: This is data that is personal to an individual, such as sexual orientation-, politics-, religion-, race-, or health-related data: `https://ec.europa.eu/info/law/law-topic/data-protection/reform/rules-business-and-organisations/legal-grounds-processing-data/sensitive-data/what-personal-data-considered-sensitive_en`.

- **Confidential Data**: **Research and Development (R&D)** and legal data will be classified as confidential data; disclosure would cause damage to the company. This could also be called classified data.

- **Critical Data**: This is data that a company does not want to disclose; it could also be classified and encrypted to prevent someone from reading it.

- **Proprietary Data**: This is data generated by a company, such as its trade secrets, or work done by the R&D department.

- **Personally Identifiable Information (PII)**: This is information that can identify a person, such as their date of birth, biometric information, or their social security number.

- **Protected Health Information (PHI)**: This is information stored in a person's medical records.

- **Financial Information**: This is data about a company's bank account, share capital, and any investments that it has made. It could also be credit card information and payroll data.

- **Government Data**: This is data collected by governmental agencies, and there are strict rules on how it can be shared, normally only internally. Contractors working with the government will have strict rules that they need to follow when the contract has finished and the data used in the contract is to be disposed of.

- **Customer Data**: This is data that is held about each customer of an organization and should never be divulged; data on the account manager dealing with a customer is also classified as customer data.

> **Exam Tip**
>
> When a government contract ends, the contractor needs to dispose of government data in accordance with the original contract. They cannot just destroy the data.

Privacy-Enhancing Technologies

We are going to look at techniques that enhance the storage of PII information, making it impossible to be stolen. Let's look at these techniques, starting with data minimization:

- **Data Minimization**: Data minimization means that only necessary data should be collected. This data should only be held in accordance with regulations and this should be reflected in the data retention policy.

- **Data Masking**: This is where only partial data is left in a data field so that the original data cannot be stolen; for example, a field holding a credit card number may only show the last four digits, as follows:

```
**** **** **** 3545
```

- **Tokenization**: Tokenization is where meaningful data is replaced with a token that is generated randomly, and the original data is held in a vault. This is much stronger than encryption and it is stateless, and the keys are not stored locally.

- **Anonymization**: Recital 26 of the GDPR defines anonymized data as "*data rendered anonymous in such a way that the data subject is not or no longer identifiable.*" Identifiers such as the name of an individual should be removed, substituted, or distorted. We could use this to protect PII. For instance, we could view a social security number, but we can no longer identify the individual that it belongs to as their name has been removed.

- **Pseudo-Anonymization**: This is where data is modified or replaced by other information so that if you want to reverse the process, it would rely on another data source that is separate from the original. Article 4(5) of the EU GDPR states that the process of pseudo-anonymization is "*the processing of personal data in such a manner that the personal data can no longer be attributed to a specific data subject without the use of additional information provided that such additional information is kept separately and is subject to technical and organizational measures to ensure that the personal data are not attributed to an identified or identifiable natural person.*"

> **Exam Tip**
>
> Data masking is when only partial data is left in a data field. For example, a credit card could be shown as **** **** **** 1234. Tokenization is better than encryption as it replaces data with a token that is connected to a remote location where the original data is held.

Data Roles and Responsibilities

There are different roles and responsibilities for dealing with data, ranging from the owners who create the data to those that store and control it. Let's look at each of these roles and what areas they are responsible for. We will start with data owners:

- **Data Owners**: The data owners are responsible for classifying data and deciding who can access the data.

- **Data Controller**: The data controller is responsible for ensuring that all data that is collected and its storage is legal and follows compliance regulations. The data controller is responsible for investigations into data breaches.

- **Data Processor**: The data processor operates on behalf of the data controller, ensuring that the collection, storage, and analysis of data is done in accordance with regulations (GDPR Article 30).

- **Data Custodian/Steward**: The steward is responsible for labeling data, and the custodian stores and manages data, ensuring that is encrypted and that regular backup tapes are kept.

- **Data Privacy Officer** (**DPO**): Privacy law or data protection laws prohibit the disclosure or misuse of information about private individuals. It is the role of the DPO to ensure that the handling, use, retention, and disposal of PII data is in accordance with national law and regulatory frameworks.

> **Exam Tip**
>
> The DPO ensures that data is handled, stored, used, and disposed of according to national law and regulatory frameworks.

Information Life Cycle

The information life cycle comprises the life cycle of data, from data creation to data destruction; see *Figure 6*:

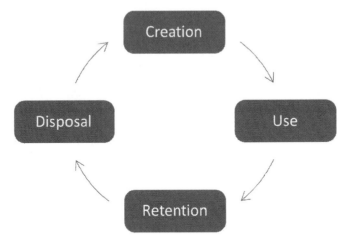

Figure 10.6 – Information life cycle

Let's look at each of these stages:

1. **Creation**: Data could be generated by someone filling in a form. It could also be collected via a mailshot.

2. **Use**: The data is accessed using the principle of least privilege and is only used for its intended purpose.

3. **Retention**: We adhere to the data retention policy so that we are compliant with regulatory frameworks. We may need to archive data for years.

4. **Disposal**: After the event that the data was collected for has passed, we must use the best and most effective data sanitizing method to ensure that there are no remnants of data left.

> **Exam Tip**
> The data owner classifies data, the steward labels it, the custodian stores and backs it up, and the administrator gives access to it.

Impact Assessment

This is where you evaluate the risk of collecting large amounts of data and look at tools that would reduce that risk.

For example, say you are working in a hospital, where consent needs to be provided by patients to allow doctors to operate on them. You might collect 1,000 of these forms a week and might decide to use a SharePoint server to store them so that they are centrally located and not lost through clerical errors.

Terms of Agreement

This is an agreement between the collector of data and the individual whose data is being collected; it outlines the purpose that the data is collected for.

Privacy Notice

Obtaining consent means that if I allow you to collect my personal data, you can only use it for the purpose that it was intended.

For example, say I have given you my email and my personal cell phone number to set up my account so that I can purchase goods. It is then illegal to send those details to your marketing department so that they can target me.

Review Questions

Now it's time to check your knowledge. Answer the questions, then check your answers, found in the *Assessment* section at the end of the book:

1. What is a vulnerability in relation to risk management?

2. What is the purpose of BPA?

3. What is multiparty risk?

4. What is IP theft?

5. What is the difference between an MOU and an MOA?

6. What is tokenization and why is it stronger than encryption?

7. One of the junior members of the IT team installs more copies of a piece of software than are allowed by the licenses that the company has purchased. What have they just carried out?

8. What is the purpose of an ISA?

9. How does the shadow IT threat actor operate and what type of attack could benefit from their actions?

10. What is an inherent risk?

11. What are the four stages of the information life cycle?

12. Why would you use STIX\TAXII?

13. What is the benefit of introducing a separation of duties in the finance department?

14. What is the purpose of a risk register?

15. What is an impact assessment?

16. A company has a leak in the roof, and before it can be repaired, there's heavy rain, resulting in 6 laptops being water-damaged. What type of disaster is this?

17. What is the purpose of job rotation?

18. What is the purpose of a privacy notice?

19. What is data masking?

20. If a company suffered a data breach, what would be the impact if one of their customers suffered identity fraud?

21. What is a SOC type 2 report and what is its distribution?

22. What is the purpose of mandatory vacations?

23. Why would an auditor look for single items that could cause the failure of whole computer systems?

24. What is the first stage in risk assessment?

25. What type of threat intelligence does the Malware Information Sharing Project provide?

26. Your company has carried out a tabletop exercise followed by a walk-through. What type of plan has just been carried out?

27. Why would a company introduce a clean-desk policy?

28. Why would someone use the website www.virustotal.com?

29. If someone brought their own laptop to be used at work, apart from an on-boarding policy, what other policy should be introduced?

30. What is the purpose of an exit interview?

31. What is the MITRE ATT&CK framework used for?

32. What is the purpose of GDPR?

33. What type of hacker might participate in a bug bounty program?

34. What do hackers that use tools from the dark web use to remain anonymous?

35. What is the purpose of Capture the Flag exercises?

36. What is the purpose of risk avoidance?

37. What is the purpose of risk transference?

38. Who uses AIS and what is its distribution?

39. What is the purpose of the ISO standard 27701?

40. What are rules of behavior?

41. What is the purpose of IOCs?

42. What is the motivation of a script kiddie?

43. Why would a company run an annual security awareness training program?

44. What would happen if I tried to sell my car and sent an email about it to everyone who worked in my company using my Gmail account?

45. Why would I make a risk assessment for one of my main suppliers?

46. What is the driving force of a BIA?

47. What is the relationship between the RPO and the RTO?

48. What information can be established from an MTTR?

49. What type of threat actor could damage a company's production system?

50. What type of threat actor would demand payment from you or threaten to publish customer information that you hold on social media?

51. What is the purpose of MTBF?

52. What is the purpose of SSAE?

53. What is the purpose of SLE and how is it calculated?

54. How can we calculate the ALE?

11
Managing Application Security

One of the main tasks that the cybersecurity team deals with is the management of applications used within the company, to ensure that they have no vulnerabilities and have been hardened. In this chapter, you will learn to deploy and manage applications effectively and select the appropriate development life cycle. You will learn about secure coding techniques, quality control, and testing. Let's begin by looking at implementing hosts and ensuring that they are secure before rolling them out.

In this chapter, we will cover the following topics:

- Implementing Host or Application Security
- Understanding the Security Implications of Embedded and Specialist Systems
- Understanding Secure Application Development, Deployment, and Automation

Implementing Host or Application Security

Within an organization, we use laptops, desktops, servers, and mobile devices such as tablets that can be used externally in unsecured environments such as hotels and airports. We therefore need to harden endpoints and their **Operating System (OS)** to ensure that they are as secure as we can possibly make them. There are various aspects that we need to look at, depending on the functionality of the device and where it is used. Let's look at all of the aspects that we need to take into consideration, starting with a system booting up.

Boot Integrity

When hosts are booting up, we need to ensure that they are protected as much as possible. We rely on them for being able to boot up securely before they are fully operational, and all of their protections are in place. We will now look at the UEFI and boot attestation:

- **Unified Extensible Firmware Interface (UEFI)**: The UEFI is a modern version of the **Basic Input/Output System (BIOS)** that is more secure and is needed for a secure boot of the OS. The older BIOS cannot provide a secure boot.

- **Early Launch Anti-Malware**: In a Windows computer, early launch anti-malware tests all drivers that are being loaded and prevents rogue drivers from loading.

- **Measured Boot**: This was first adopted with Microsoft Windows 8, where all components from the firmware up to the applications and software are measured and stores this information in a log file. This log file is then stored in the **Trusted Platform Module (TPM)** chip on the motherboard. Anti-malware can use this information to ensure that when the system boots up, the software is trustworthy. This log can be sent to a remote server that can assess the health status of the host.

- **Secure Boot and Attestation**: OSes such as Windows 10 can perform a secure boot at startup where the OS checks that all of the drivers have been signed. If they have not, the boot sequence fails as the integrity of the system has been compromised. This can be coupled with *attestation*, where the integrity of the software has been confirmed. An example of this would be using FDE, such as **BitLocker**, to ensure that the software has not been tampered with. The BitLocker keys are stored on a TMP chip on the motherboard.

  Example: Your company is a multinational company that requires an OS that can be used by both desktops and laptops and can provide both secure booting and attestation. You would most likely use Microsoft Windows 10, which can provide secure booting and BitLocker to carry out system attestation.

Endpoint Protection

It is important that the endpoints are protected from an attack. Let's look at each of the endpoint protections in turn, starting with anti-virus:

- **Anti-Virus**: Anti-Virus monitors websites that are being visited and the files that are being downloaded to ensure that they are not affected by viruses or trojans. Most modern anti-virus solutions have the ability to carry out the role of anti-malware.

- **Anti-Malware**: Anti-malware scans your computer for *adware* and *spyware*, and prevents malicious software from running. These cannot be detected by anti-virus programs.

- **Endpoint Protection and Response** (**EDR**): An EDR is an advanced solution that is better than anti-virus or anti-malware. It is a centralized console that continuously monitors the computer, and makes automatic alerts when a threat has been detected. It uses machine learning to detect threats and has the ability to detect file-less viruses.

- **Data Loss Prevention** (**DLP**): An endpoint DLP solution can be set up so that it can protect data on your computer from being stolen by using email or a USB drive. DLP can also protect any data that has a pattern match, such as PII information or sensitive data.

  Example: I have a file called *new business contacts* and I want to ensure that it cannot be stolen. It does not have a pattern match. However, I can use the DLP solution, select the file, and a pattern match will be assigned to the file. When someone tries to email the file, it will be blocked by the DLP system.

- **Next-Generation Firewall** (**NGFW**): An NGFW is more than a traditional firewall. It has the ability to act as a stateful firewall by carrying out deep packet filtering. It can also inspect application traffic to ensure that it is legitimate and use whitelisting to ensure that only approved applications are allowed to run. It can also act as an intrusion prevention device protecting against an attack, and it can inspect encrypted SSL and HTTPS packets.

- **Host Intrusion Prevention System (HIPS):** An HIPS is a software program that can be installed on a host to protect it against attack. It analyzes the behavior of a computer and looks for any suspicious behavior in log files and memory and takes the appropriate action to prevent attacks such as malware.

- **Host Intrusion Detection System (HIDS):** An HIDS, by its very nature, is a passive device that monitors patterns in the behaviour of a computer system. The HIDS uses a database that contains the settings for the computer, including the registry, critical system files, applications, and components. Its function is to alert the user to any discrepancies or attacks.

- **Host-Based Firewall:** A host-based firewall can be used to prevent unauthorized access to the desktop and can set up permitted rules for approved applications. The firewall in the following screenshot allows anti-virus updates, checkpoints, VPN, DNS name resolution, Firefox, and Java:

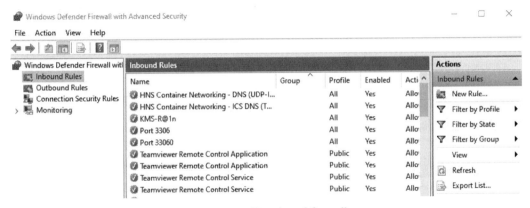

Figure 11.1 – Host-based firewall

The firewall acts as an additional layer of protection to the computer by controlling the traffic coming into it.

Databases

It is very important that we keep databases safe as they may contain PII information about individuals or credit card information. Let's look at what we can do to keep our database as secure as possible, starting with stored procedures:

- **Stored Procedures:** A SQL injection attack manipulates a SQL statement and then ends it by inserting 1=1. Instead of writing Transact-SQL statements, we can have the SQL script prewritten and saved in a stored procedure, for example, ABC. This prevents manipulation of the statement. We then insert ABC into the Transact-SQL, thereby preventing alteration. This is similar to what happens with a batch file.

- **Tokenization**: Tokenization is deemed more secure than encryption. When we encrypt data, we use a public key and then we can reverse the encryption by decrypting the data with the private key or by cracking the encryption. This means that an attacker could decipher the data. Tokenization takes sensitive data such as a credit card number and replaces it with random data. Therefore, it cannot be reversed. Refer to *Figure 11.2* to understand the process of tokenization:

Figure 11.2 – Tokenization

If you need to employ the service of a payment gateway, these are the e-commerce application service providers that can process direct debit or credit card payments. Two examples are Visa and Barclaycard, and information pertaining to these can be found here. There are many more providers besides:

- **Visa**: Information can be found at `https://www.visa.co.uk/dam/VCOM/regional/na/us/partner-with-us/documents/token-service%20-provider-product-factsheet-from-visa.pdf`.

- **Barclaycard**: Information can be found at `https://www.barclaycard.co.uk/business/news-and-insights/tokenisation`.

These payment gateway providers store the credit card details securely and generate a random token. Tokenization can help companies be **Payment Card Industry Data Security Standard** (**PCI DSS**)-compliant. They have the ability to replace protected health information, e-PHI, **Non-Public Personal Information** (**NPPI**), and ensure that health organizations are in compliance with **Health Insurance Portability and Accountability Act** (**HIPAA**) regulations.

- **Hashing**: A database contains a huge amount of data and we use hashing to index and fetch items from a database. This makes the search faster as the hash key is shorter than the data. The hash function maps out all of the data to where the actual records are held. Refer to the following diagram:

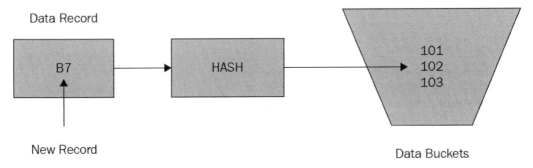

Figure 11.3 – Hash index

In the preceding diagram, you can see that the hash value is stored in a data bucket, which is a memory location where records are stored. A data bucket is known as a unit of storage.

- **Salting**: Salting passwords in a database means that we take the password stored in the database and add randomized numbers to increase the compute time for a brute-force attack.

Application Security

In today's world, we are all interconnected and use an ever-increasing amount of applications that can be targeted by attackers. Therefore, as a cybersecurity professional, we need to ensure that we harden these applications to prevent attacks. Let's look at the types of protection that we can put in place, starting with input validation:

- **Input Validation**: Controlling inputs to an application is vital to ensure that *buffer overflow*, *integer overflow*, and *SQL injection* attacks cannot be launched against applications and databases. Input validation is where data is entered either using a web page or wizard. Both are set up to only accept data in the correct format within a range of minimum and maximum values.

    Example: Have you ever completed a web form quickly and maybe put your zip code into another field? This results in an error in the form and it fails to process the submit button. The web form then has a list at the top, in red, of the incorrect parameters, with a red star next to each of them. Once you have corrected the entries, the form will accept them and submit.

- **Secure Cookies**: Cookies are used by web browsers and contain information about your session, and they can be stolen by attackers to carry out a session hijacking attack. We can set the secure flag on the website to ensure that cookies are only downloaded when there is a secure HTTPS session. You can do this in Java EE 6 by applying the following information to the web.xml file. An example is shown in the following code snippet:

```
<session-config>
<cookie-config>
<secure> 'true' </secure>
</cookie-config>
</secure-config>
```

- **Hypertext Transfer Protocol (HTTP) Headers**: HTTP headers are designed to transfer information between the host and the web server. An attacker can carry out *cross-site scripting* as it is mainly delivered through injecting HTTP response headers. This can be prevented by entering the **HTTP Strict Transport Security (HSTS)** header:

```
function requestHandler(req, res) {
    res.setHeader('Strict-Transport-Security', 'max-
age=31536000; includeSubDomains; preload');
        }
```

This means that HSTS ensures that the browser will ignore all HTTP connections.

- **Code Signing**: A code-signing certificate is procured that allows you to digitally sign scripts and executables to verify their authenticity and to confirm that they are genuine.

- **Allow List**: An allow list only allows explicitly allowed applications to run. This can be done by setting up an application whitelist. Firewalls such as pf-sense can have an allow list.

- **Block List/Deny List**: A block/deny list prevents explicitly blocked applications from being set up by using a blacklist to prevent banned applications from running. Firewalls such as pf-sense can have a block list.

- **Secure Coding Practices**: This is where the developer that creates software ensures that there are no bugs or flaws, so that they can prevent attacks such as *buffer overflow* or *integer injection*.

- **Static Code Analyzers**: When developers use static code analyzers, the code is not executed locally. Instead, they launch the static code analyzer tool. Then the source code is run inside the tool that reports any flaws or weaknesses.

- **Dynamic Code Analysis**: When developers use dynamic analysis, the code is run locally and then they use a technique called *fuzzing*, where a random input is inserted into the application to see what the output will be. White box pen testers use fuzzing to see the flaws and weaknesses in an application before it is rolled out to the production environment.

- **Manual Code Review**: This is where a developer reads code line by line to ensure that the code is written properly and that there are no errors. This is very tedious and time consuming.

- **Fuzzing**: This is where we will put random information into an application to see whether the application crashes or causes memory leaks or error information to be returned. The white box pen tester uses this to remedy any potential problems before a new application is released. The black box will use fuzzing to find any vulnerabilities with the application. This is also known as improper input validation.

Hardening

We need to ensure that we harden both the devices running the applications and the applications themselves against an ever-increasing cybercrime threat. In this section, we are going to look at different types of hardening techniques, which, when they are implemented, will keep our devices and applications safe. We are going to start by looking at open ports and services:

- **Open Ports and Services**: Ports used by applications are endpoints for connections. Each application or protocol will use different port numbers; it is like having TV channels. If you don't go to the sports channel, then you can't watch sport. Similarly, if you don't use the correct port, you cannot connect to your application. When you install an OS, some of these ports are open, so you need to close unused ports on your host-based firewall. This can be done on a Windows computer by using the netstat command to find the open ports. Referring to *Figure 11.4*, the port number is after the colon in the Local Address column. You can use the netstat -ano command to close the port that you are not using:

```
C:\WINDOWS\system32>NETSTAT

Active Connections

  Proto  Local Address           Foreign Address         State
  TCP    127.0.0.1:5939          DESKTOP-QR6R2DA:49758    ESTABLISHED
  TCP    127.0.0.1:7778          DESKTOP-QR6R2DA:49793    ESTABLISHED
  TCP    127.0.0.1:49669         DESKTOP-QR6R2DA:49670    ESTABLISHED
  TCP    127.0.0.1:49670         DESKTOP-QR6R2DA:49669    ESTABLISHED
  TCP    127.0.0.1:49758         DESKTOP-QR6R2DA:5939     ESTABLISHED
  TCP    127.0.0.1:49793         DESKTOP-QR6R2DA:7778     ESTABLISHED
  TCP    127.0.0.1:49794         DESKTOP-QR6R2DA:49795    ESTABLISHED
  TCP    127.0.0.1:49795         DESKTOP-QR6R2DA:49794    ESTABLISHED
  TCP    192.168.0.118:49672     r-54-45-234-77:https     CLOSE_WAIT
  TCP    192.168.0.118:49677     DE-HAM-PLS-R012:5938     ESTABLISHED
  TCP    192.168.0.118:49748     ams10-004:http           ESTABLISHED
  TCP    192.168.0.118:49753     40.67.255.199:https      ESTABLISHED
```

Figure 11.4 – Netstat

Applications use a service to run and when you first install an OS, there are a lot of services running by default, some of which you may never use. For example, the telnet service will allow remote access to your computer in clear text, so we would need to disable those services. In a Windows computer, if you type `services.msc` in the `run` command, you can see which services are running and then just disable those that you are not using.

- **Registry**: The registry is a database of all the settings on your computer, and gaining access to the registry can allow someone to cause damage to the computer. If you make a change in control, that change is reflected in your registry. There are a group of settings called *hives* and there are five main hive keys. These start with HKEY_. You can see these five keys in *Figure 11.5*, starting with HKEY_CLASSES_ROOT. You can access the registry by using the `regedit` command:

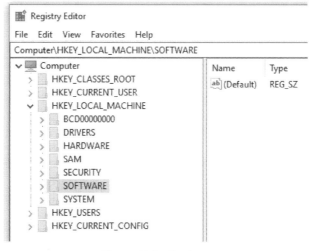

Figure 11.5 – Registry

The Docker tool allows you to isolate applications into a separate space called *containers*. The registry can now be isolated into a separate container, making it more secure.

- **Operating System**: In order to harden an OS, it is important that the OS has the latest patches and updates. Subscribing to security bulletins from the vendor helps to get updates when new patches are released.

- **Patch Management**: Patch management is where the cybersecurity team obtains updates from the vendors. They test the updates on a computer in a sandbox to ensure that it will not cause any damage to either the OS or the installed applications. Patch management such as the Microsoft WSUS server has the ability to roll out vendor updates and third-party updates. Once the updates have been tested, they can be set up to automatically update your OS.

Full Disk Encryption (FDE)

FDE is used on computer systems to encrypt the whole hard drive as it holds data at rest. FDE uses X509 certificates to encrypt the full disk, but needs a TPM chip on the motherboard to store the keys. Microsoft's BitLocker is an example of this, and if it thinks the drive has been tampered with it, locks the drive and a 48-character key is then required to unlock it. Let's look at aspects of FDE, starting with the TPM chip:

- **Trusted Platform Module (TPM)**: The TPM chip is stored on the motherboard and is used to store the encryption keys so that when the system boots up, it can compare the keys and ensure that the system has not been tampered with.

- **Hardware Root of Trust**: When we use certificates for FDE, they use a hardware root of trust that verifies that the keys match before the secure boot process takes place.

Self-Encrypting Drives (SEDs)

The OPAL storage specification is the industry standard for self-encrypting drives. This is a hardware solution. Therefore, they outperform other encryptions as they are software solutions. They don't have the same vulnerabilities as software and therefore are more secure. The SEDs are **Solid State Drives** (**SSDs**) and are purchased already set to encrypt data at rest. The encryption keys are stored on the hard drive controller. Therefore, they are immune to a cold boot attack and are compatible with all OSes. The drives have a security mechanism allowing the drive to be locked in order to prevent unauthorized users from accessing the data. Only the computer user and the vendor can decrypt the drives.

Hardware Security Module (HSM)

An HSM is similar to TPM chips, except that it is removable. The *Key Escrow* uses an HSM to store and manage private keys, but smaller ones can be used for computers.

Sandboxing

Sandboxing is where we can install an application in a virtual machine environment isolated from our network so that we can patch, test, and ensure that it is secure before putting it into a production environment. In a Linux environment, this is known as *Chroot Jail*.

Now that we have an idea of host and application security, let's understand the security implications of embedded and specialist systems.

Understanding the Security Implications of Embedded and Specialist Systems

An embedded system has its own software built into the device hardware. Some are programmable and some are not. Embedded systems are found in consumer products used for health monitoring, automotive, medical, and household products. Some examples follow in the next section.

Internet of Things (IoT)

IoT comprises small devices, such as ATMs, small robots, and wearable technologies, that can use an IP address and connect to internet-capable devices. We must ensure that we change the default usernames and passwords for these devices to prevent someone from hacking them. From a security point of view, supporting IoT items is a nightmare because of the diversity of the devices. Most users of IoT devices are not aware that they have default username and passwords, and so they are vulnerable to attack. You should change the default settings immediately after purchase. Let's look at some of these devices in the following diagram:

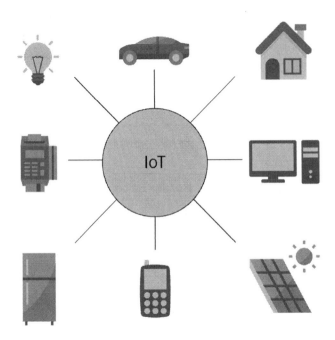

Figure 11.6 – IoT devices

The devices shown in the preceding diagram have been explained in detail in the following points:

- **Smart Devices**: Smart devices, such as a smart TV or refrigerators, can connect to a home network and gain access to the internet. If we do not change the default username and passwords, they are vulnerable to attacks. Default passwords for these devices can be found at www.cirt.net. Most home users are unaware that they have a password, and so are vulnerable to attack. If we look at a smart refrigerator, the owner can connect to it from the supermarket, using an app on their cell phone, to see what is in the fridge as it has a direct connection to the internet.

- **Home Automation**: A home automation system will control alarms systems, lighting, climate, entertainment, alarm systems, and kitchen appliances. Since most home automation devices have a direct internet connection, this makes them vulnerable to attack.

  Example: An Alexa stores all conversations that take place in its vicinity. Therefore, if you don't delete the voice history on a regular basis, an attacker can gain access to those conversations. To prevent this, you should say *Alexa, delete what I say today*. You need to watch where you place the device as it has a camera. You can turn the camera off by simply saying, *Alexa, turn off the camera*. You change the wake-up word in case you have a friend called *Alexis* and this also prevents other people giving commands to your device.

- **Wearable Technology**: The use of wearable technology has increased in recent years, from monitoring health and performance to sending texts and receiving calls on your watch. Some devices such as *Fitbit* are encrypted, but others are vulnerable as they use Bluetooth.

- **Sensors**: These could be used to detect motion, alert you when systems fail, or allow you to measure occupancy as they can detect motion and the use of electricity.

- **Facilities Automation**: Companies can use IoT devices to help them manage and secure their environments. Some companies have a smart building system that can provide the following:

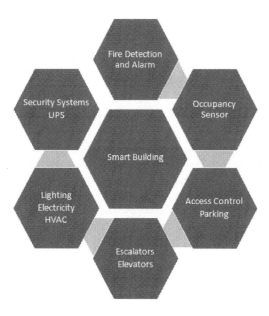

Figure 11.7 – A smart building system

As these devices are connected to the main control unit and all have an internet capability, they could be attacked from the internet. The attacker could tamper with the systems so that it provides false positive information, or they could launch a denial-of-service attack. They could use selective forwarding that would filter out messages or they could eavesdrop and carry out man-in-the-middle attacks.

Real-Time Operating System (RTOS)

RTOS are more reliable than desktops or servers as they are normally used for real-time applications since they process data immediately, thereby preventing buffering and buffer overflows. If a task or process does not complete within a certain time, the process will fail. RTOS could be used for military systems or where robots are being used in production to ensure that processes are completed quickly.

Multifunctional Printers (MFPs)

MFPs are an all-in-one device consisting of at least two of the following – printer, scanner, fax, or photocopier. The weakness of each of these is that they all have a network interface and could be attacked through that interface. Any default setting or passwords must be changed.

Surveillance Systems

Surveillance systems can check cameras, speak to those on the camera, automate lights, and set alarms, and this can all be done from a smart phone. Surveillance systems now tend to be networked and are used for security of a business or your home and the footage can be used in evidence for legal purposes. They could be attacked from the internet and the attacker could steal the information that they contain. Therefore, the default username and passwords must be changed immediately.

Example 1: You are at work when the surveillance systems alerts you that someone has rung your door bell. You can now see the person who has picked up a parcel from your porch, you can shout at them to drop the parcel, and can send the footage to the police.

Example 2: The police are dealing with a riot. The police are dressed in riot gear and there are police vehicles equipped with camera systems. These will be used to record the event in real time. The footage can be sent back to an incident control room, in real time, where the police can see whether any of the rioters are on their internal police systems.

System on a Chip (SoC)

An (SoC) is an integrated circuit on a microchip that connects the functionality of a computer on a small microchip. Life support devices use SoC.

Heating, Ventilation, and Air Conditioning (HVAC)

HVAC is very important for server rooms and for server farms that are located in data centers as they regulate the temperature by using hot and cold aisles, as shown in *Figure 11.8*:

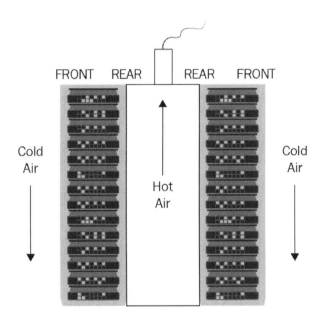

Figure 11.8 – HVAC

The cold aisle is where the cold air comes in and that faces the front of the servers. The rear of the servers face one another. They push hot air out into the hot aisles, and this is allowed to escape through a chimney. This way, the temperature can be regulated, and this ensures the availability of the IT systems. Critical systems could fail if the temperature gets too hot, and the security teams will know whether offices are occupied according to the HVAC system usage register.

Specialized Devices

Specialized devices are more expensive bespoke devices that provide a unique purpose. For example, there are *man overboard* devices that detect someone falling into the water. We are going to look at these in the following points, starting with medical devices:

- **Medical Devices**: These can include infusion devices that measure fluids that are given to patients in hospitals. Ambulances will carry life-support systems, such as *defibrillators*, that are used to save a person's life if they have just suffered from cardiac arrest. The defibrillators will have an SoC installed as it gives out instructions on how to use it, but if it detects a pulse, it will not send a charge, as shown in *Figure 11.9*:

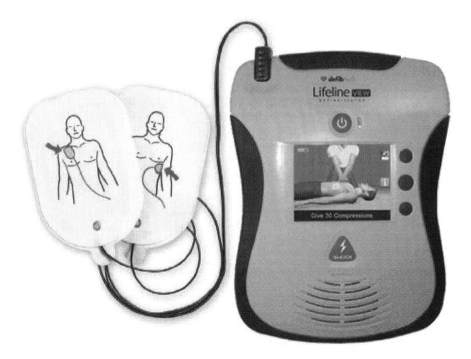

Figure 11.9 – Defibrillator

- **Luxury Vehicles**: Some luxury vehicles have embedded systems that produce a wireless hotspot in the car so that, when you are driving along, your passengers can connect to the internet. Others have the ability to carry out automatic self-parking. There have been many trials recently of self-driving cars; vendors, such as Google, are still trying to perfect their systems.

- **Drones**: For many years, people have been flying model aircraft that also have embedded systems, but in the past 2-3 years, unmanned aerial vehicles called drones (**Unmanned Aerial Vehicles (UAV)**) have been making the headlines. The military can use these drones to carry out surveillance of areas where it is too dangerous to send manned aircraft, and they could also be armed to carry out attacks.

- **Smart Meters**: These can be used to show you the amount of electricity or gas that you are using. This helps to reduce your energy bills.

Embedded Systems

An embedded system is both hardware and software combined in a single device. Some such devices will have updates, but some have no update mechanism, making them vulnerable to attack. Examples of embedded systems include the following:

- **Raspberry Pi**: This is a credit card size computer that allows you to run program languages such as Python or Scratch. The Raspberry Pi can be plugged into a monitor or computer.

- **Field-Programmable Gate Array** (**FPGA**): This is as close to creating your own chip as you can possibly get. The FPGA takes code and stores it in multiple hardware blocks. The hardware block contains register and logic units. These are not like microchips that have a function. The FPGA has absolutely no function at all. It has no processor, and this makes it very flexible. Each block can be programmed to perform a single function. FPGAs are super-fast as they have Gbps capability with built-in transceiver and serial decoding. You could use a FPGA to build your own supercomputer.

  Example: If you have built your own microcontroller and you want to change it, but it does not have enough processing power to change it, then you are stuck. However, if you had built your processor inside an FPGA and you had sufficient resources, you could increase your processor power and that would allow you to perhaps put in a **finite impulse response** (**FIR**) filter between two pins and achieve your aim.

- **Arduino**: This is an open source programmable microprocessor/microcontroller. These boards are programmable through a USB. They are able to read inputs whether it be a light on a sensor, or an activity such as turning on a LED, publishing something online, or activating a motor. They can be run from a 9-volt battery and can be used to control electronic components. The Arduino has shields, and these allow you to add wireless or Bluetooth to it so that it could be used to build a robot.

Supervisory Control and Data Acquisition (SCADA)

SCADA systems are automated control systems that can be used for water, oil, or gas refineries, or industrial and manufacturing facilities, where there are multiple phases of production. The architecture of a SCADA system can be seen in the following diagram:

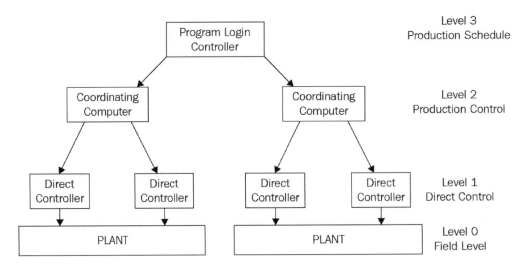

Figure 11.10 – SCADA system

The security of the SCADA system is paramount. A network firewall prevents unauthorized access to the network, and then an NIPS is used as an additional layer. If further segmentation is required, VLANs could be used internally. This is no different to protecting a corporate network.

Example: Iran had a uranium enrichment facility that was a SCADA system, but it suffered an attack from the Stuxnet virus that attacked the centrifuges. The Stuxnet virus was discovered in 2007, but many believe it could have been there in 2005. Uranium enrichment is an example of using the SCADA methodology in a production environment.

Industrial Control System

Several types of control systems and instrumentation used for industrial process control are generally encompassed as the **Industrial Control System** (**ICS**). They are used for water, telecommunications, health, chemicals and pharmaceuticals, water supply, and treatment.

Communication Considerations

In today's world, there are various different connection methods for mobile devices, and we need to be able to identify the best selection for a given scenario. Let's look at these by first looking at cellular:

- **Cellular**: This is where tablets and phones are using 3G, 4G, or 5G to connect to their provider without needing any other devices. Cellular connections are encrypted to prevent anyone seeing who is logging on or stealing your data. The problem that cellular faces is that, if there are no masts nearby and the device has a setting of no service, they will not work.

- **Narrow-Band**: These are short-range, wireless applications that are used, for example, with security **radio-frequency identification** (**RFID**) or keyless vehicle entry products.

- **Baseband Radio**: This is used for audio signals over a radio frequency, for example, when truck drivers go onto a specific channel to talk to another truck driver.

- **Subscriber Identity Module** (**SIM**) **cards**: These are small computer chips that contain your information that allows you to connect to your telecoms provider to make calls, send text messages, or use the internet.

- **Zigbee**: These chips are integrated with microcontrollers and radios. They are powered by a battery as they are low cost and low power. Examples of use include Abode smart security system, Bosch security systems, and Honeywell thermostats.

Constraints

There are many constraints associated with embedded devices, due to their size. Most devices, such as Zigbee and Arduino, are battery-operated and even cell phones such as the iPhone have a battery that lasts about 7 hours. Most embedded systems have a smaller processor. They may be 8- or 16-bit, compared to a laptop, which has a 64-bit processor. They are therefore restricted in terms of their compute time. Other limitations are as follows:

- **Network**: Embedded systems are not scalable, and some can only communicate through Wi-Fi or Bluetooth and are short ranged. It is difficult to transfer data from one system to another.

- **Crypto**: PKI needs at least a 32-bit processor, and embedded devices are limited to 8 or 16, so you will need significant overhead when trying to authenticate, and this may well be very slow.

- **Hardware Upgrade/Patching**: Most embedded devices cannot have their hardware upgraded, and some do not have the ability to patch. In fact, some vendors do not produce patches.

- **Range**: Many embedded systems may have a very short range, and so are not scalable.

- **Cost**: Embedded systems are mainly customized, and when the new product is released, the cost of purchase is outside the range of normal users.

- **Implied Trust**: When you purchase an embedded system, you need to hope that there is implied trust, where the system operates as described in the sales brochures. You may not be able to troubleshoot these devices.

Now that we have understood the security implications, we will look at secure application development, deployment, and automation in the next section.

Understanding Secure Application Development, Deployment, and Automation

There are two main models of the **Software Development Life Cycle (SDLC)**, the first being an older version that is called Waterfall, where each stage is completed before the next stage commences. This is known as a cascade model. The newer, faster, and more flexible model is called Agile, which is similar to Scrum, where several stages of development can occur simultaneously. Agile is customer focused, where each part of the project is called a sprint, so if I have three stages, then there are three sprints and the project concludes when all the sprints are complete.

Before applications can be used in a production environment, we must ensure that they are as secure as possible so that we mitigate the risk of being attacked by an outside agency. We are going to look at these in turn, starting with the software diversity.

Software Diversity

A compiler takes code and converts it into binary machine language. Software diversity is where a developer can take code and obfuscate it with a compiler so that an attacker cannot reverse engineer the code, allowing them to find vulnerabilities in the code. An **Application Programming Interface (API)** is created to allow systems to be programmed to talk to one another. Using a complier to obfuscate API methods will make it harder for attackers to reverse engineer the code.

Elasticity

Elasticity is the process of increasing resources when they are needed. The cloud is a pay-as-you-go model where your resources can be increased at the drop of a hat.

Scalability

This is where an application can take more users than originally planned with little or no increase in cost.

Environment

When we are designing an application, we need a secure environment for development, testing, and staging before moving the application into production. This environment is shown in *Figure 11.11*:

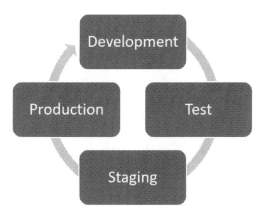

Figure 11.11 – Environment

Let's look at each of these in turn:

- **Development**: The first stage of developing an application is to use the most secure programming language for the task at hand. There may be more than one application developer involved in the development. The application will go through different versions before it is complete, and these can be tracked by using version numbers.

- **Testing**: Developers integrate all of their work into a single application, software testers ensure that the functionality of the program fulfills the specifications. They may also employ a secure coding freelancer to carry out regression testing to ensure that the application is fit for production. At this stage, we are not looking at how it affects the production environment, as this is completed at staging.

- **Staging**: This is where we ensure quality assurance before we roll it out to production. We test the new application with real data in a sandbox environment so that the end users who will be using the applications ensure it is fit for purpose and that all the reports that they need are available. At this stage, the application is signed off as being fit for purpose. The quality assurance of the product is fulfilled.

- **Production**: The production environment is where the application goes live, and end users have the support of the IT team. The end users will be asked to give as much feedback as they can if the application has any problems that were not picked up beforehand.

Automation/Scripting

Automation is where processes are set up to carry out tasks automatically with the need for human intervention, using either scripts or a graphical user interface. Scripts are precompiled instructions that are automatically launched when the script is activated. This leads to fewer errors than carrying out tasks manually, where humans make mistakes. Let's now look at other aspects of the SDLC:

- **Continuous Integration**: This is the process where multiple software developers consolidate and test the code that they write to ensure that the different input codes do not conflict. This happens in the developing and testing environments.

- **Continuous Validation**: This is where the application is tested to make sure that it is fit for purpose and fulfills the original specification.

- **Continuous Delivery**: This is the process of fixing bugs before the application moves into production. This happens in the staging environment.

- **Continuous Deployment**: This is the process of pushing out new updates into production software, for example, patching.

- **Continuous Monitoring**: This is to log any failures by the application so that steps can be taken to remedy them.

- **Automated Courses of Action**: We can automate courses of action, for example, an **Network Intrusion Detection System** (**NIDS**) will detect threats, and the NIPS will prevent the threat from happening.

Provisioning and Deprovisioning

The concept of application provisioning is the life cycle of designing, preparing, creating, and managing the applications, and ensuring that there are no flaws in the security before release. Deprovisioning is when the application meets its end of life and we remove the application and either migrate the data to the new system or dispose of it, ensuring that we do so in accordance with local regulations, such as HIPAA, GDPR, or the Data Protection Act 1998.

Integrity Measurement

We measure application integrity to ensure that the application performs as it should do and conforms to data industry standards and regulations. Before the application is written, a third-party coding expert should carry out regression testing to ensure that there are no flaws in the code. The application itself is measured to ensure that it does what it is meant to do. We test that the security features are safe and that no vulnerabilities exist. Anything found out of the ordinary should be addressed quickly.

Secure Coding Techniques

Although most people who work in networking or security are not application developers, CompTIA has introduced secure coding into the syllabus. This section needs to be understood, so it is written in the simplest format we could think of:

- **A Race Condition**: This is where two instructions from different threads try to access the same data at the same time. When the developer wrote the application, the threads should have been programmed to access the data sequentially.

   Example: Two guys buy tickets for the Super Bowl final, and when they arrive at the stadium, they find that they have been allocated the same seat. That's a great profit for those selling the ticket, but a bad deal for those purchasing the ticket.

- **Proper Error Handling**: When we develop IT systems, we want the errors that are sent back to users to be very short and generic so that an attacker has very little information to use and launch the further attacks. However, we want the information logged in relation to errors to be as detailed as possible so that the security administrators know why the error occurred.

- **Proper Input Validation**: Input validation is controlled by using either wizards or web pages where the following is laid out:

  a. Is it alphabetical?

  b. Is it numerical?

  c. Is it a certain format, such as a zip code or telephone number?

  d. What are the minimum and maximum numbers of characters?

  If the data is not input in the correct format, it will not be accepted. Input validation on web pages lists errors in red at the top of the page with the incorrect entries. This prevents SQL injection, integer overflow, and buffer overflow attacks.

- **Stored Procedure**: A stored procedure is a pre-written SQL script that might ask you for a list of all the customers who have purchased items costing over $1,000 in the last 7 days. When this is written, it is saved as a stored procedure called *ABC*. When I run the ABC stored procedure, it will give me all of the information I require, and an attacker won't be able to modify the script inside.

- **Obfuscation/Camouflage**: *Obfuscation* is the process where you take source code and make it look obscure, so that if it was stolen, it would not be understood. Obfuscation masks the source code so that it cannot be understood by competitors.

  Example 1: **Exclusive OR (XOR)** is a binary operand from Boolean algebra. This operand will compare two bits and will produce one bit in return, two bits that are equal to 0, and two bits that are equal to 1. This is the opposite to binary. For example, we are going to use the word *tread* in ASCII format and then we are going to insert a key using the word *hello* so that we can complete an XOR operation. Refer to the following diagram:

	T	R	E	A	D
XOR (Original Input)	01010100	01110010	01100101	01100001	01100100
Key	01101000	01100101	01101100	01101100	01101111
Output	00111100	00010111	00001001	00001101	00001011

Figure 11.12 – XOR

From the preceding XOR, you can see that the data has been obscured.

Example 2: *ROT 13* is a variation of the *Caesar* cipher. As there are 26 letters in the alphabet, we are rotating the letters 13 times. The key to ROT 13 would be as follows:

Letter	A	B	C	D	E	F	G	H	I	J	K	L	M
ROT 13	N	O	P	Q	R	S	T	U	V	W	X	Y	Z
Letter	N	O	P	Q	R	S	T	U	V	W	X	Y	Z
ROT 13	A	B	C	D	E	F	G	H	I	J	K	L	M

Figure 11.13 – ROT 13

When receiving the message *GVZR SBE GRN*, we would apply ROT 13, but instead of going forward 13 places to decipher, we would simply go back 13 places, and the message would be *TIME FOR TEA*.

- **Code Reuse/Dead Code**: Developers like to keep code libraries where they store their source code. If they need to develop an application, they may start with old code and then modify it for the new application. Dead code is code that is never executed. It also consumes resources and should be removed as it serves no purpose.

- **Memory Management**: It is important that, when a developer writes an application, they control how much memory it can consume as this can create performance issues. Memory leaks are where written applications consume more memory than they need and, over a period of time, starve other applications of the memory that they need.

- **Use of Third-Party Libraries**: The use of apps on mobile devices is a fierce marketplace where, as soon as you purchase a domain name, someone has emailed you offering you a good deal on mobile apps for your business. There are many third-party libraries that have many pieces of code, and although they may not be perfect, this is a fast way to get your application to market. There are many third-party libraries for Android and JavaScript that have grown in popularity.

- **Software-Developer Kits (SDKs)**: An SDK is a set of software development tools that a vendor creates to make application development easier.

  Example: Microsoft has the Windows 10 SDK, which provides the latest headers, libraries, metadata, and tools for building Windows 10 apps. Further information can be found at `https://developer.microsoft.com/en-us/windows/downloads/windows-10-sdk/`.

- **Data Exposure**: Sensitive data is normally encrypted to prevent it from being stolen by attackers; this would include passwords and credit card details. We should limit the amount of data allocated to a user who is using an application, and we should also use input validation and DLP to protect our data.

- **Normalization**: Each database has a list of tables that are broken down into rows and columns. In a large relational database, data may be retained in multiple places. The goal of normalization is to reduce and eliminate the redundancy to make fewer indexes per table and make searching much faster.

- **Server-Side versus Client-Side Execution and Validation**: Website code will either run as server-side code or client-side code. Let's look at each of these in turn, starting with server-side code:

  a. **Server-Side – Known As the Backend**: Server-side validation is where the user's input is sent to the server, where it is validated and then the response is sent back to the client. Programming languages such as C# and .NET are server-side.

  b. **Client-Side – Known As the Frontend**: Client-side validation is done locally on the client so there is no network traffic. Script languages such as JavaScript, VBScript, or HTML5 attributes are used for this type of validation on the browser side.

  Client-side validation is much quicker, but an attacker can exploit the JavaScript and bypass the client side. Server-side validation takes much longer and can use input validation to check that the input is valid and to stop the attacker in their tracks.

Open Web Application Security Project (OWASP)

The **Open Web Application Security Project (OWASP)** is an international not-for-profit organization that provides an up-to-date list of the most recent web application security concerns. They rely on donations to exist. Their mission statement is *to improve software security through open source initiatives and community education*. They provide the following resources:

- Tools and resources

- Community and networking

- Education and training

They run seminars all over the world for the security of web, cloud, mobile devices, applications, and software development and maintenance.

Review Questions

Now it's time to check your knowledge. Answer the questions, and then check your answers, which can be found in the *Assessments* section at the end of the book:

1. Name three types of mobile device connection methods

2. What is an embedded electronic system? Give two examples.

3. What is the purpose of a SCADA system?

4. What category of device are my smart TV and wearable technology?

5. What is home automation?

6. What is the purpose of SoC?

7. If a process does not suffer buffer overflow, but fails within a specified period of time and this causes the process to fail, what method am I using?

8. What is the most likely way an attacker would gain control of an MFP?

9. What is the purpose of the security team controlling the HVAC in a data center?

10. Someone at work has suffered a cardiac arrest and the first aid delegate takes out a defibrillator that gives instructions of the steps to take. What had been built into the device to give these instructions?

11. Give an example of embedded systems that can be used with vehicles.

12. What is a UAV? Give two examples.

13. What is the main problem with a race condition when using an application?

14. What is the perfect way to set up error handling in an IT system?

15. Explain input validation and name three types of attacks that this could prevent.

16. How can I prevent a SQL injection attack other than with input validation?

17. What is the purpose of code signing?

18. What is the purpose of obfuscation?

19. What is dead code and how should it be treated?

20. If I am an Android developer, what can I obtain from the internet to help me get an application to market quickly?

21. What is the purpose of a measured boot?

22. What is needed for a secure boot – UEFI or BIOS?

23. If BitLocker is checking upon boot up that the software has not been tampered with, what is this known as?

24. What is the purpose of an endpoint protection and response solution?

25. Why do we use fingerprinting?

26. What type of firewall can act as an intrusion prevention device, a stateful firewall, and can inspect encrypted SSL and HTTPS packets?

27. Why is tokenization deemed more secure than encryption?

28. What is the purpose of secure cookies?

29. What is the purpose of using HSTS?

30. When a developer wants to analyze code when it is running, what type of code analyzer will they use?

31. What is the benefit of using the Docker tool to protect your registry?

32. Why would a cybersecurity team change the SSD hard drives in the company's laptop to an Opal drive?

33. As part of application development, when would you apply quality assurance?

12
Dealing with Incident Response Procedures

To protect businesses against disasters, it is vital that we have solid incident response plans and procedures. There are many different types of incidents a company will face, for example, dealing with a flood is totally different to dealing with the failure of a server's hardware. They will have many plans in place, one for each incident, and it is vital that employees know their role in the plan in order for it to be effective. The plan must be exercised at least on an annual basis to be effective. Let's look at each of these in turn, beginning with the incident response procedures.

This chapter will deal with incident response and will be divided into the following elements:

- Incident Response Procedures
- Utilizing Data Sources to Support Investigations
- Knowing how to Apply Mitigation Techniques or Controls to Secure an Environment
- Implementing Cybersecurity Resilience

Incident Response Procedures

Before we start making incident response plans, we need to have a process in place, and the process we are going to use is as shown in *Figure 12.1*:

Figure 12.1 – Incident response process

The incident response process must be carried out in order, starting with stage 1, which is the preparation phase. Let's look at these stages in order:

- **Preparation**: The preparation phase is where the different incident response plans are written and kept up to date. System configurations are documented as well.

- **Identification**: Once an incident has occurred, it is important that the appropriate incident response plan is invoked, and that stakeholders and the incident response team for that particular incident are notified.

- **Containment**: At this stage, we will isolate or quarantine computers, to prevent the attack from spreading any further and collect the volatile evidence.

- **Eradication**: In the eradication phase, we want to destroy the source of the incident. For example, if it is a virus, we want it totally removed. We will remove the virus or delete infected files, patch the system, and turn off any services that we don't need, so that it is hardened.

- **Recovery**: In the recovery phase, we are getting the company back to an operational state, hopefully within the **Recovery Point Objective (RPO)**. For example, imaging machines, restoring data, or putting domain controllers or infected machines back online after cleansing.

- **Lessons Learned**: Lessons learned is a detective phase where we pull together all of the facts and plan to prevent a re-occurrence in the future. Failure to carry this out will lead to a re-occurrence.

Example: A domain controller is infected with a virus. The first stage is containment, where we take it off the network. The next stage is eradication, where we remove the virus and patch the server. The last stage is recovery, where the clean server is put back online. After the incident has been dealt with and we are back up and running, we carry out lessons learned, where we look at how the domain controller got the virus in the first place and prevent it from happening again.

Disaster Recovery Exercises

There are three types of exercises that you can carry out to ensure that your company is ready for any disaster. These are structured walk-throughs, tabletop exercises, and simulations. Let's look at all three of them:

- **Tabletop Exercise**: A tabletop exercise is a paper-based, hypothetical exercise where all parties meet around a table and discuss how they would deal with a disaster scenario.

- **Structured Walk-Through**: A structured walk-through is where a mock disaster is enacted physically with all parties involved. An example of this would be carrying out a fire drill where we mobilize the fire crew.

- **Simulations**: The white team organizes and measures the responses to this event. The simulation is based on a given scenario and they mobilize the disaster recovery plans. The red and blue teams are briefed about the scenario and their roles, with the red team attacking and the blue team defending.

Attack Frameworks

There have been different attack frameworks developed to help cybersecurity teams to better prepare themselves for cyber attacks. We are going to look at three different models, so let's start with the MITRE ATT&CK Framework.

MITRE ATT&CK Framework

Mitre is a US Government-sponsored company whose aim is to help prevent cyber attacks. They developed an online framework that can be used by the general public and they have many matrices. They give information about adversaries and their attack methods. They use the acronym *ATT&CK* to help you understand better the attack vectors used by the attackers. If you go on to the *Mitre* website (`https://attack.mitre.org`), you will find a huge spreadsheet that you can use to find information on adversaries, their attack methods, and how to mitigate these attacks. This aids everyone from cybersecurity teams to threat hunters, so let's look at each of these in turn. Let's look at the breakdown of the acronym:

- **Adversarial**: This looks at the behavior of potential attackers who are put into different groups. An example would be *APT28*, a Russian group who allegedly interfered with the US election in 2016.

- **Tactics**: This is the medium by which the attack will be carried out. We could look at a phishing attack from which we can drill down, and it will explain how phishing attacks are launched.

- **Techniques**: These are a breakdown of the processes of how an attack will be launched.

  More information on drive-by compromise can be found at the following link: `https://attack.mitre.org/techniques/T1189/`.

- **Common Knowledge**: This is the documentation relating to the adversaries' tactics and techniques.

Cyber Kill Chain

Lockhead Martin originally developed the *kill chain*, a military model to identify the steps an enemy would take to attack you. It was then adapted to become the *cyber kill chain*, a framework to aid cybersecurity teams in terms of becoming more aware of potential cyber attacks (`https://www.lockheedmartin.com/en-us/capabilities/cyber/cyber-kill-chain.html`). Refer to *Figure 12.2*:

Stages of the Cyber Kill Chain	
Reconnaissance	Calling employees, sending emails, social engineering, dumpster diving
Weaponization	Create malware payload
Delivery	Delivery medium such as USB, email, web page
Exploitation	Executing code via a vulnerability
Installation	Installing malware on the asset
Command and Control	Infected system sends back information to the attacker
Action on Objectives	'Hands-on keyboard' – attack complete

Figure 12.2 – Cyber Kill Chain

The idea behind that was to give cybersecurity teams an awareness so that they could identify and prevent attacks at an early stage. For example, we could create a security awareness program, warning employees against phishing, and also to report unusual calls from outside agencies. The attacker might then be stopped at the reconnaissance phase.

The Diamond Model of Intrusion Analysis

This model is a framework for gathering intelligence on network intrusion attacks. This comprises four key elements: adversary, capabilities, infrastructure, and victims, and these are interconnected:

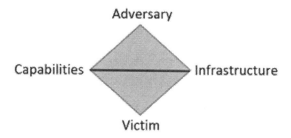

Figure 12.3 – Diamond Model of Intrusion Analysis

This model was used by the intelligence community until it was declassified in 2013. More information can be found at `https://apps.dtic.mil/sti/pdfs/ADA586960.pdf`. A breakdown of the preceding model follows:

- **Adversary**: This is the threat actor group, and we can use the MITRE ATT&CK model to identify who they are and what attacks they use.

- **Capabilities**: This is where the adversary develops an exploit that they use to carry out the attack. These are also laid out in the MITRE ATT&CK model.

- **Infrastructure**: This is how the attacker can get to the victim. This could be via email, IP address, or remote access.
- **Victim**: This is the person targeted by the adversary.

Example: If we look at the *Stuxnet* virus, we know the capabilities were four zero-day viruses targeting the Siemens **Industrial Control System (ICS)**. Secondly, we know that the infrastructure used was USB sticks, and that the victim was the *Iran Nuclear Enrichment Facility*. All of this information has been discovered a piece at a time and then when we have this information, we now search for an adversary. The attack is very sophisticated. Therefore, we can narrow down the search for an adversary to someone who is well funded and capable of this sophisticated attack. You can see from this example how we can narrow down who the adversary is. Siemens, China, India, the US, and Israel were all considered. The hardest part of the diamond is to find the adversary.

We can combine the Diamond model for every step of the kill chain to detect adversaries. We can also use the MITRE ATT&CK model to find other information in the Diamond model.

Let's look at other aspects that are important in terms of a successful incident response.

Stakeholder Management

When we have an incident, there are five groups of stakeholders that we need to inform and manage. These are creditors, directors, employees, governmental bodies, and the shareholders who are the owners of the business. We notify the stakeholders and we remind them that their responsibility is to ensure that the press do not have knowledge of the incident as this could severely affect your company's reputation. Knowledge of the incident may be common knowledge maybe a month after it has been dealt with.

Communication Plan

This is the medium for informing all stakeholders of the incident where we would use encryption such as PGP or S/MIME to ensure that the event does not become public knowledge. A list of contacts should be maintained that includes the government, police, customers, suppliers, and internal staff.

Disaster Recovery Plan

Disasters range from natural disasters, such as hurricanes and floods, to hardware failure, malicious insider attacks, and the accidental deletion of data. The main aim of a disaster recovery plan is getting the company back up and running so that it can generate income. We need to identify the most critical assets and ensure that they are up and running first. We will run disaster recovery exercises periodically to gain experience of executing the plan. As technology frequently changes, we need to update the disaster recovery plan to facilitate the changes.

Business Continuity Plan (BCP)

This does what it says on the tin. Keep the business up and running no matter what disasters are on the horizon. We need to complete a business impact analysis to identify a single point of failure so that we can build in some redundancy. We should have vendor diversity built into our BCP. We need to focus on the **Recovery Point Objective** (**RPO**), so that we can identify how long we can operate without our data and the time in which we have to complete disaster recovery and return to an operational state. Let's look at the four phases of the BCP plan:

- **Initial Response**: This determines how a company should conduct itself in the early stages of the disaster. We would activate the plan by calling the IRP team members.

- **Relocation**: At this stage, we should move to a backup hot site or work from home so that the business can operate.

- **Recovery**: At this stage, once we have relocated, we will make an assessment of the damage and what action we need to take; for example, the restoration of data, the reimaging of desktops, and the restoration of critical servers.

- **Restoration**: Restore the original site back to its former glory or find an alternate permanent business premises.

Continuity of Operations Planning (COOP)

COOP was developed by the United States federal government. This was their version of a **Business Continuity Plan** (**BCP**). It looks at each type of disaster and puts processes in place for the government so that they can work with limited resources, providing critical services until the incident has been mitigated.

Incident Response Team

When an incident occurs, it is important to get an incident response team together to deal with the incident, which is made up of members in the following roles:

- **Incident Response Manager**: A top-level manager who takes charge.

- **Security Analyst**: Technical support to the incident.

- **IT Auditor**: Checks that the company is compliant.

- **Risk Analyst**: Evaluates all aspects of risk.

- **HR**: Sometimes employees are involved in the incident.

- **Legal**: Gives advice and makes decisions on legal issues.

- **Public Relations**: Deals with the press to reduce the impact.

- **Cyber Incident Response Team**: The cyber incident response team must move rapidly and have up-to-date training for the variety of incidents that they may encounter. They may have to use third-party specialists in some aspects of cybercrime.

Roles and Responsibilities

Each member of the incident response team needs to understand their roles and responsibilities within the team to make the team effective.

Retention Policies

We need to first of all classify the data that we may require following a disaster. We need to create a data retention policy for all PII and sensitive information as well as unclassified data. For legal and compliance reasons, you may need to keep certain data for different periods of time; for example, some financial data needs to be retained for 6 years, whereas medical data may need to be kept for 20-30 years, depending on the type. A data retention policy ensures that legal and compliance issues are addressed.

In the next section, we will learn how to utilize data sources to support investigations.

Utilizing Data Sources to Support Investigations

There are many different types of data sources that cybersecurity teams can utilize to gain more knowledge and a clear understanding of how much damage has been done and the extent of the incident. Let's look at the different types of data sources that we can search to support investigations, starting with a vulnerability scan output.

Vulnerability Scan Output

The vulnerability scanner can identify various vulnerabilities, such as missing patches, open ports, services that should not be running, and weak passwords. This will help you avoid attacks such as SQL injection, buffer overflows, denial of service, and other type of malicious attacks.

SIEM Dashboards

Security Information Event Management (**SIEM**) dashboards are very useful to the security operations centers as they provide information in real time. Let's look at the types of data that could be found on a SIEM dashboard, staring with sensors:

- **Sensor**: Sensors are deployed across your network to monitor and collect changes collected by the log files to give visibility as events occur.

- **Sensitivity**: The SIEM system can monitor PII and sensitive information to ensure that we are compliant. An example would be to ensure that all **Health Insurance Portability and Accountability Act** (**HIPAA**) regulations are observed so that organizations are compliant. The SIEM system has the ability to maintain a Personal Data Breach Register to ensure that we have, for example, GDPR compliance.

- **Trends**: A SIEM system can identify trends in hardware breakdown and performance issues, so that they predict when we may need to carry out maintenance in the future, thereby preventing breakdowns. We will have separate categories of events, such as application, system, and security events.

- **Alerts**: Log files provide information about events on hosts and network devices but are not automated. A SIEM system can set up alerts so that when certain information appears in the log files, the security team is notified immediately. Another way would be to install agents on devices so that when an event is triggered, the SIEM system correlates the events and notifies the security team in real time.

- **Correlation**: The SIEM correlates and aggregates the log files from multiple sources and from that it can generate a single report that provides a picture of events.

Log Files

Log files play a massive part in providing evidence for investigations. There are many different types of log files. Let's look at each of these in turn and identify the type of information from each of these log files. We will start with network log files:

- **Network**: This log file can identify the IP address and the MAC address of devices that are attached to your network. The log files from the NIDS and NIPS can be very important and we can track users by using the log files from a proxy server. We can identify DDoS traffic as it arrives due to the duplicate entries and be able to stop it.

- **System**: System log files have information about hardware changes, updates to devices, and time synchronization, and they log group policy events and whether they have been successful.

- **Application**: Application log files contain information about a software application, when it was launched, whether it was successful, or whether it carries warnings about potential problems or errors.

- **Security**: Security log files contain information about a successful login or an unauthorized attempt to access the system. This can identify attackers trying to log in to your computer systems.

- **Web**: Web servers log many types of information about the web requests and can be very useful in identifying events. Let's look at the type of information collected about each web session: IP address request, Date and time, HTTP method, such as GET/POST, Browser used, and HTTP Status code. These can be broken down into the following:

  a. 100 series, request received; an example would be 102 processing request.

  b. 200 series, successful login attempt.

  c. 300 series, more action needed to complete the request.

  d. 400 series, client-side error; an example would be 403, where you are forbidden access, or 404 file not found.

  e. 500 series, server-side error, failure to carry out a request; examples would be 500 internal server error, 502 bad gateway, where an upstream proxy returns an invalid response, or 503 service is unavailable.

- **DNS**: This log contains all DNS information, such as zone transfer, name resolution queries, DNS server errors, DNS caching, and DNSSEC.

- **Authentication**: This log gives information about login events, and whether they are successful or not. One of the best resources for authenticating log files in a domain environment would be a RADIUS server, which maintains a log of when people log in and out. Therefore, it is able to not only authenticate users, but to track them as well. Authentication log files are also kept on a domain controller or remote users coming in via a VPN server.

- **Dump Files**: Dump files is when a computer crashes (commonly known as the *blue screen of death*), and all of the contents in the memory are saved in a dump file (.dmp). These dump files can be analyzed by using a tool such as the *Blue Screen Review*.

- **VoIP and Call Managers**: These systems provide information on the calls being made and the devices that they originate from. They also measure the quality of the call by logging the **Mean Optical Score** (**MOS**), jitter, and loss of signal. Each call is logged where you can see inbound and outbound calls, the person making the call, and the person receiving the call.

- **Session Initiation Protocol (SIP) Traffic**: SIP is used for internet-based calls and the log files show the 100 events, known as the *INVITE*, the imitation of a connection, that relates to ringing and then 200 OK is followed by an acknowledgement. If users cannot connect to their SIP calls, this log file can be used to troubleshoot them.

Log Managers

The following log managers perform the same basic functions. Let's look at each of them in turn:

- **Syslog**: The system logging protocol (syslog) collects event logs from various devices and then sends them to a central syslog server. In the Linux version, these logs are called syslogd and syslog daemon, which stores the log files in the var/log/syslog directory.

- **Rsyslog**: This is an advanced syslog server. It is called rocket-fast as it has a high performance. It obtains the data and then transforms it to send the outputs to the destinations such as a SIEM server.

- **Syslog-ng**: This was developed by *Balabit IT Security Ltd* as a free open source protocol for Unix and Linux systems.

Journalctl

Journald collects and stores log data in binary format, and *journalctl* is able to query and display these logs in a readable format. It is used in a Linux environment.

Nxlog

This is an open source log management tool that helps identify security risks in a Linux/Unix environment.

Bandwidth Monitors

These can be used to understand your network traffic flow. They can monitor changes in traffic patterns and identify devices on your network that are causing bottlenecks and could detect broadcast storms and potential denial-of-service attacks.

Metadata

This is data that provides information about other data. Let's look at the different types of metadata, starting with email:

- **Email**: Email headers contain detailed information about an email. It shows the source, destination, and the route through the email providers to the recipient. This can be used when phishing emails are received so that you can identify the perpetrator.

- **Mobile**: Telcom providers retain information about phone calls, including calls made, calls received, text messages, internet usage, and location information. These can be used during an investigation to provide evidence that could lead to a conviction.

   Example: A German politician filed a lawsuit against *T-Mobile* for the release of his cell phone metadata that they had gathered from his phone. He received 35,830 records – 6 months' usage. He gave this data to *ZEIT Online* and they could identify his daily movements, phone calls, text messages, and internet usage.

- **Web**: Website metadata provides information about every page created on a website, including who was the author, date created, images, videos, and spreadsheets.

- **File**: When investigations are being carried out, the file metadata can be used to track information, such as the author, date created, date modified, and file size.

Network Monitoring

The following products can be used for network monitoring. Let's look at this in turn, starting with NetFlow:

- **Netflow**: This is a CISCO product that monitors network traffic, so that they can identify the load on the network. This helps you utilize your network traffic efficiently. During an investigation, it can help identify patterns in network traffic.

- **Sflow**: This is a multi-vendor product that gives you clear visibility of network traffic patterns. This can help identify malicious traffic so that we can keep the network secure and safe.

- **IP Flow Information Export (IPFIX)**: This product can be used to capture traffic from the node itself. This data can then be exported to a collector within the node.

  Example: IPFIX can be used to identify data traveling through a switch and this can be used for billing purposes. It can take IP Flow information and both format the data and forward it to a collector.

Protocol Analyzer Output

A protocol analyzer such as *Wireshark* can capture data traveling across the network. Law enforcement has been used to replay commands to network devices and allowed to capture and replay video traffic.

In the next section, we will learn to apply mitigation techniques or controls to secure an environment.

Knowing How to Apply Mitigation Techniques or Controls to Secure an Environment

Should we find that we have a vulnerability, we need to take action to mitigate the risk, so let's look at some of the techniques or controls that we can use. We might have to reconfigure the endpoint security solutions. We are going to look at applications.

Application Approved List

We can use application whitelisting where the approved applications are listed. This means that if an application is not listed, it cannot be launched. Some devices such as pf-sense have Allowed Lists.

Application Block List/Deny List

We can blacklist applications that are deemed dangerous, such as Kali Linux. If it is on the blacklist, it is totally banned and cannot be placed on the whitelist. Some devices such as pf-sense firewall have Block Lists.

Quarantine

If we find a device has been infected with a virus, we can remove it from the network by quarantining it. We can also use **Network Access Control** (**NAC**) so that devices that are not patched or are vulnerable are placed in a quarantine network where a remediation server applies patches to the system before it is allowed back on to the network.

Configuration Changes

As new attacks emerge and new technologies are implemented, we may have to make some configuration changes to secure our environment. Let's look at devices, starting with a firewall:

- **Firewall Rules**: Firewalls can be used to block traffic and we can use either an MDM solution or group policy to change the configuration on endpoint devices.

- **Mobile Device Management (MDM)**: An MDM solution can be used to push configuration changes to mobile devices. The password policy may change, or we might remove the ability to use the camera on mobile phones. The MDM solution will push out the new configuration changes.

- **Data Loss Prevention (DLP)**: There may be a security risk of credit card information leaving the company or data that has a pattern match has been exfiltrated. We may use a regular expression to ensure that this data does not leave via email. Good examples of data that DLP prevents leaving our environment are PII and sensitive information.

- **Content Filter/URL Filter**: We might update the content filters on either a proxy server or a **Unified Threat Management** (**UTM**) firewall due to security events. The content filter blocks the target website; for example, a gambling website and the URL filter prevents the endpoints from visiting a website that has been subject to an attack.

- **Update or Revoke Certificates**: If the endpoints have reported *trust errors*, this means that we may have to update the certificate because it has expired or revoke the certificate because it has been compromised.

Isolation

We may have to air gap research and development endpoints to isolate them from the network to protect them against a network-based attack.

Containment

If the security team finds that an endpoint has been compromised and may be infected by a virus, they will contain it so as to stop the malware spreading.

Segmentation

We might have to use storage segmentation or containerization to keep personal and business data separate on a mobile device. We may have to segment devices that have become vulnerable, such as an unpatched printer where there are no updates.

Security Orchestration, Automation, and Response (SOAR)

Orchestrations are the process of running multiple automations to perform complex tasks. Automations are the process of scripting a single activity. These systems are used to collect threat-related data from multiple sources and use playbooks and runbooks. Let's look at each of these in turn:

- **Playbooks**: Playbooks contain a set of rules and actions to enable the SOAR to identify incidents and take preventative action.

- **Runbooks**: These are automated routines to automate many phases of the playbook and so can respond to different types of events.

In the next section, we will learn to implement cybersecurity resilience.

Implementing Cybersecurity Resilience

It is important that companies have redundancy or fault tolerance built in so that they are protected from cyber attacks.

Redundancy

Redundancy is the process of when one part of a system fails but we have the ability to keep the system running. It could also be referred to as fault tolerance. Let's begin by looking at the different types of redundancy that companies could deploy. We will start with disks and then move on to geographical dispersal.

Disk

There is a need for the disk setup on servers to provide redundancy, sometimes known as *fault tolerance*. In simple terms, this means that if one or more disks fail, the data is still available. There are different **Redundant Array of Independent Disks (RAID)** levels, so let's look at each of these in turn, starting with RAID 0:

- **RAID 0**: RAID 0 uses a minimum of two disks with a maximum of 32 disks; see *Figure 12.4*:

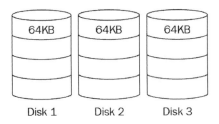

Figure 12.4 – RAID 0

This is known as a *stripe set*, as the data is written across *Disks 1-3* in 64 KB stripes. Should one disk fail, then all of the data will be lost, so RAID 0 does not provide fault tolerance or redundancy. The benefit of RAID 0 is its faster read access, so it may be used for the proxy server's cache.

- **RAID 1**: RAID 1 is two disks, known as a *mirror set* where you have an original disk that is live with a copy on the second disk. See *Figure 12.5*:

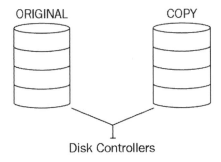

Figure 12.5 – RAID 1

RAID 1 is fault tolerant, and so should *Disk 1* fail, you would *break the mirror* and then activate *Disk 2*. At a later stage, we will add another disk and then re-establish the mirror set.

- **RAID 5**: RAID 5 has a minimum of three disks and is known as a *stripe set with parity*. It is written across the disks in 64 KB stripes just like RAID 0 but, when each stripe is written, one of the disks has a single parity block for each line of data. The parity is shown as shaded in *Figure 12.6*:

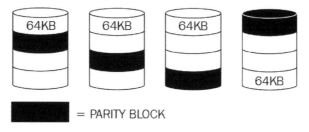

Figure 12.6 – RAID 5

Example: The following diagram (*Figure 12.7*) represents a RAID 5 set where we are using a mathematical equation to represent the disk set so that you can see the impact of losing one disk and then losing two disks:

Figure 12.7 – RAID 5 as a mathematical equation

Each of the disks has a numerical value. For example, if *Disk 3* fails, the equation would be (*7 +? = 10*) and the answer would be *3*. If we lose a second disk, *Disk 1*, the equation would then be (*? + ? = 10*) and you could not work it out. The same happens if you lose two disks; parity cannot recreate the missing data.

- **RAID 6**: RAID 6 has a minimum of four disks and the same configuration as RAID 5, but it has an additional disk that holds another copy of the parity:

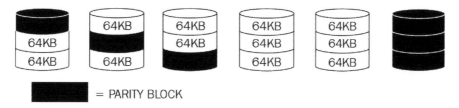

Figure 12.8 – RAID 6

A RAID 5 disk set can afford to lose one disk and the data will still be available as it has single parity. The good thing about a RAID 6 set is that it can lose two disks and still be redundant as it has double parity.

- **RAID 10**: RAID 10 is also known as *RAID 1+0*. This is a RAID configuration that combines both mirroring and striping to protect data. It has a mirrored set that is then striped. As long as one disk in each mirrored pair is functional, data can be retrieved:

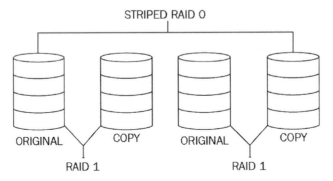

Figure 12.9 – RAID 10

From this diagram, you can see a *RAID 1* on the left and then it is striped, meaning you could lose an entire dataset.

- **Multipath**: This is normally used by a SAN storage solution where there is more than one network path between the SAN storage and the target server. This prevents a single point of failure and provides redundancy as well as a load-balancing capability.

Geographic Dispersal

This practice has been adopted by the business community for years, but governmental bodies have been slower to adopt this practice. We use hot and warm sites that are in different regions and also use different power suppliers. Data is replicated between different regions within the same country to ensure that even if there is a natural disaster or power outage within one of the regions, they can still keep operating. As soon as records are created, they are replicated to the other hot sites chosen. This ensures that there is a redundant set of data and resiliency against disasters. Warm sites have their data delivered by courier. Cold sites cannot be used as they contain no data.

Network

There is a need to make our network more resilient and, from the preceding disk multipath, you can see that when using a SAN, we use multiple paths between the host and the SAN storage. Let's now look at other types of network storage, starting with network card teaming:

- **Network Interface Card (NIC) Teaming**: In a server environment, there are dual network cards, and these are paired together to give maximum throughput. Also, should one adapter fail, the other adapter can be used for load balancing, performance, and increased throughput. Windows 10 has *teaming* capability.

- **Load Balancers**: Enterprise load balancers such as *Kemp* and *F5* can balance many types of network traffic, including a high volume of web and email traffic. The load balancer understands the status of each server and if the server is down even for maintenance, it balances the traffic between the other nodes.

Power

Power is the most critical resource for any computer system and it is important that we have redundancy. Let's look at the different types, starting with the **Uninterruptible Power Supply (UPS)**.

- **Uninterruptible Power Supply (UPS)**: The UPS is basically a battery that is a standby device so that when the computer power fails, it kicks in. It is designed to keep the system going for a few minutes, to allow the server team to close the servers down gracefully. It can also be used to clean up the power coming from the national grid, such as spikes, surges, and voltage fluctuations. This protects the servers from being damaged.

- **Generator**: A generator is a standby device that is powered by diesel, gasoline, propane, or natural gas. When the power from the national grid fails, a generator can be started to give electricity to a company. Hospitals will have a number of generators available to protect those people in intensive care or those in operating theatres when the power outage occurs.

- **Dual Supply**: Most servers will have a dual power supply so that if the power unit fails, then the other power supply keeps the server running.

- **Managed Power Distribution Units (PDUs)**: A managed PDU allows you to remotely connect and monitor the power. The PDU distributes clean power to multiple, critical network resources, such as servers, routers, switches, and data centers.

Replication

Replication is a method for the immediate transfer of data and virtual machines within a network. Let's first of all look at a **Storage Area Network (SAN)** and then virtual machines:

- **Storage Area Network**: A SAN is a hardware device that contains a large number of fast disks, such as **Solid-State Drives (SSDs)**, and is isolated from the LAN as it has its own network:

    a. **Host Bus Adapters (HBAs)**: The cheapest form of redundancy for a SAN is to use two HBAs with each node. This will give you two separate paths to them.

    b. **SAN Fabric**: A SAN fabric is a collection of servers, storage, switches, and other devices. We could use two SAN fabrics, *Fabric 1* and *Fabric 2*. These two fabrics are separate. We could have the SAN nodes connecting one HBA to *Fabric 1* and the other HBA to *Fabric 2* to provide redundancy.

- **Virtual Machine Replication**: Virtual machine replication is where a backup copy of a virtual machine is kept on another host so that if a disaster happens, you still have redundancy.

On-Premises versus the Cloud

In this chapter, we have looked at on-premises redundancy using RAID and we could also consider hosting a backup of our environment in the cloud. We could replicate data in the cloud so that if we have a disaster, we could switch quickly to the cloud. All we would need is internet connectivity.

Backup Types

Backing up our data has always been a good method of data redundancy, so let's look at each of these in turn, starting with the full backup:

- **Full Backup**: A full backup is a backup of all of your data. However, some companies might only be able to back up all of their data over the weekend, so they will use either an incremental or differential backup in the middle of the week. This can be seen in the exam as the *fastest physical backup*.

- **Incremental**: An incremental backup backs up the data since the last full backup or the last incremental backup. An incremental backup will need the full backup, from the start, and then all of the incremental backups.

- **Differential**: A differential backup will back up the data since the last full backup. The problem with this is that if we have a full backup at the start of the week and then a differential backup every day, they will grow progressively larger each day. A differential backup will always be two tapes: the full backup from the start and the latest differential.

  Example: We will compare the different types of backup. We will start the backup every day, but will suffer data loss on the Friday, and we will see for how many tapes we need to recover our data. Our full backup will be 50 GB of data, and every day, we will produce 5 GB of data. You can see this from the following table. How many tapes are needed for each type of backup to recover your data?

- **Daily Copy**: This could be the copy of the data on any day, but this is in addition to a planned tape cycle.

- **Full**: The latest full backup is 65 GB. Every day, we back up more and more.

- **Incremental**: Starts off with the full backup but needs all of the incremental backups.

- **Differential**: Starts off with the full backup but needs the latest differential backup:

Backup	Mon	Tues	Wed	Thurs	Fri	Tapes to recover
Full (F)	F 50 GB	F 55 GB	F 60 GB	F 65 GB	X	F 65 GB Thurs
Incremental (I)	F 50 GB	I 5 GB	I 5 GB	I 5 GB	X	F 50 GB Mon 3 X I—Tues, Wed, Thurs
Differential (D)	F 50 GB	D 5 GB	D 10 GB	D 15 GB	X	F 50 GB Mon D 15 GB Thurs

Figure 12.10 – Backup examples

- **Network Location**: A backup can be performed to a file shared on a server in the network. The server would have some sort of RAID redundancy or the storage would be part of a SAN.

- **Backing Up – To Tape**: A backup can be backed up to magnetic tape, and this would be the slowest form of restore. Additionally, a copy of the backup tape can be stored offsite in case the company has a fire and burns down.

- **Disk**: This could be a complete backup to a USB or removable hard drive. It could also be a copy of a disk on another server.

- **Copy**: This could also be done using the *xcopy* facility to copy to another server on the network. A better way of making a copy across the network is to use *robocopy* because, if there is a network failure, robocopy knows when the copy left off and ensures complete data transfer.

- **Network Attached Storage (NAS)**: You will use an NAS box when you want to store over 5 TB of data and your data is accessed by using a **Universal Naming Convention (UNC)** path rather than a **Logical Unit Number (LUN)**, which a SAN uses. This is a good option when you are starting to run out of storage.

- **SAN Storage**: When you have a vast amount of storage, a SAN is your best solution. It is good for databases such as SQL or email. You will have a fast connection to it. Cloud providers store all of your cloud data on a SAN.

- **Cloud Storage**: It is quite common to use cloud storage to hold your data from the iCloud, provided by Apple, Google Drive, provided by Google, OneDrive, provided by Microsoft, or Dropbox, provided by Dropbox, Inc. The consumer versions of cloud storage allow you to have limited storage space but offer to sell you a business version or additional storage by charging a monthly subscription fee.

- **Image**: Rather than rebuilding a desktop from scratch and taking hours, you can capture an image using products such as *ghost*. This means you can reimage a desktop in about 40 minutes.

- **Online versus Offline**: When we look at online versus offline backups, we need to first of all look at the amount of data we need to back up. When it is offline storage, we need to ensure that all forms of backup media are labeled; for example, if we are using tape, we need to ensure that its shelf life has not expired or when we go to get our backup, the tape might be corrupt. An online backup is much faster to recover, and is available any time of the day or night. We just need a connection method to gain access.

- **Offsite Storage**: If we are backing up to media, we should keep a copy offsite in case of a natural disaster such as fire or floods. We need to ensure that the travel distance from and to the offsite storage is not too great as this will slow down the recovery process.

Data Sanitization

It is very important that we dispose of data in the most secure manner to ensure that it cannot be stolen. We are going to look at sanitizing data on paper followed by data on media.

Paper Data

When we are disposing of data, the best way of doing this, in order, is as follows:

- **Burn**: When we burn paper, it will never come back and we might get a third party to do this and provide us with a destruction certificate.

- **Pulping**: If burning is not available, pulping, which turns the data into paper mache, is the best option.

- **Shredding**: This is the third best way of disposing of data; a cross-cut shredder is best.

Media Data

When disposing of data that is stored on media such as a hard drive or DVD/CD ROM, the best ways to dispose of the data are as follows:

- **Shredding**: You can shred a metal hard drive into powder, and this is the best method.

- **Pulverizing**: This is where you take a sledge hammer and smash it into small pieces.

- **Degaussing**: This is where an electrical charge is sent across the disk.

All of the above will render the media unusable. If you want to reuse the media, you need to choose wiping or formatting as the method of sanitization.

> **Exam tip**
> If you want to reuse a hard drive, then you need to sanitize it by either wiping or formatting it.

Non-Persistence

Non-persistence is when the computer system becomes corrupt, and you can roll it back to a former state. Let's look at each of these in turn, starting with *revert to known state*:

- **Revert to Known State**: In a Windows environment, you can save the system state, and the system's settings, to removable media. If the computer is corrupt, then you can repair the computer and then insert the media and revert to the system state data.

- **Last Known Good Configuration**: This is where the system has recorded the configuration state as you log in. This can be reverted to at a later stage.

Example: In a Windows environment, when you successfully log in, all of the computer's settings are saved in a clone set (duplicate). Should the operating system not boot up, we restart the computer and invoke the last known configuration.

- **Live Boot Media**: A copy of the operating system is saved to a USB flash drive or DVD. Then you will be able to boot from the removable media.

High Availability

High availability could involve using clustering between servers or perhaps having a backup data center, as shown here in *Figure 12.11*:

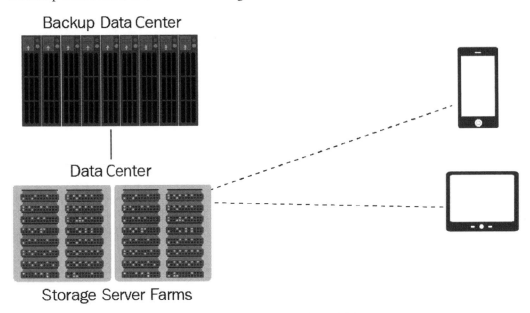

Figure 12.11 – Data center high availability

In *Figure 12.11*, you can see a backup database for the storage farm. Scalability is where you can add additional nodes to the solution.

Restoration Order

Once a disaster has happened, it is important that we look at the services necessary for getting a company back up and running. We would rank them as *critical*, *essential*, or *non-essential*, and we would work on getting the most crucial service up and running first. We would start with power, then our network infrastructure and critical servers, and then restore data before going back online.

Diversity

Companies need to use diversity within their organization so that they can be prepared for any disasters. Let's look at diversity in vendors.

Vendors

We need to purchase the same technologies from different vendors just in case one of the businesses either goes out of business or faces failure. An example of this would be purchasing broadband from two different companies. This is because it is a critical area of a business and should one provider suffer a disaster, then the other would provide the service.

Review Questions

Now it's time to check your knowledge. Answer the questions, and then check your answers, which can be found in the *Assessments* section at the end of the book:

1. What RAID model has a minimum of three disks? How many disks can it afford to lose?

2. What RAID models has a minimum of four disks?

3. What is the difference between RAID 5 and RAID 6?

4. Where will a diskless virtual host access its storage?

5. What types of disks does a SAN use?

6. What is an example of cloud storage available to a personal user?

7. At what stage of incident response procedures would you reduce the services running on a computer on a domain controller that is infected with malware?

8. During a disaster recovery exercise, the IRP team is given a scenario to respond to. What type of exercise are they likely to carry out?

9. Why would a cybersecurity team use the MITRE ATT&CK Framework?

10. What are the four key elements of the Diamond Model of Intrusion Analysis framework?

11. Why are the roles and responsibilities of the IRP team important?

12. What type of file is created when your computer suffers a blue screen of death?

13. What is the purpose of SFlow?

14. What type of HTTP status code lets you know you have made a successful connection to a web server?

15. What is the purpose of a SOAR system playbook?

16. What is the benefit of network card teaming?

17. What is the purpose of a UPS?

18. What can be installed on a node of a SAN to provide redundancy?

19. Why would a company use two different vendors for their broadband?

20. What is the purpose of an incident response plan?

21. Name three different categories of incident.

22. Name three different roles required to deal with an incident.

23. What should the help desk do when an incident has just been reported?

24. What is the purpose of an incident response exercise?

25. What is the first phase of the incident response process and what happens there?

26. What is the last phase of the incident response process?

27. What would happen if the last process of the incident response process was not carried out?

28. What happens during the containment phase of the disaster recovery process?

29. What happens during the eradication phase of the disaster recovery process?

30. What happens during the recovery phase of the disaster recovery process?

Section 4:
Mock Tests

This section has two mock exams with full explanations that will help you understand whether ready you are to take the test. The sample exam questions and answers will give you all the confidence you need to prepare for the exam.

This section comprises the following chapters:

- *Chapter 13, Mock Exam 1*
- *Chapter 14, Mock Exam 2*

13
Mock Exam 1

1. You are an administrator for a college that has 10 intranet web servers, and you need to install an X509 certificate so that they can support HTTPS. You need to use the solution that is the most cost-effective. Which of the following will you use for the certificates?

   a. Wildcard

   b. Domain

   c. Self-signed

   d. SAN

2. Which of the following threat intelligence sources is likely to provide much more accurate data?

   a. OSINT

   b. Public/private information sharing centers

   c. Closed/proprietary

   d. Threat maps

3. A cybersecurity administrator wants to add comments to a log file that they are monitoring. Which tool is best for this?

   a. Nmap

   b. Head

   c. Logger

   d. Tail

4. A cybersecurity team has been attacked by a group of hackers from the internet. The cybersecurity team wishes to find all of the email addresses of this group. Which tool would be the best for this?

   a. Dimitri

   b. The harvester

   c. Curl

   d. Logger

5. Which of the following tools can be used for banner grabbing?

   a. Curl

   b. Telnet

   c. Nmap

   d. netcat (nc)

6. A cybersecurity analyst has just finished reading the monthly release from a security advisory. They have now started searching the log files on all of the database servers. What task are they completing?

   a. Log analysis

   b. Risk mitigation

   c. Security administration

   d. Threat hunting

7. A vendor has stopped selling a product, but they still sell a limited number of replacement parts. Which of the following describes the product?

   a. Legacy

   b. End of life

   c. End of service

   d. Retired

8. A security administrator needs to implement secure authentication between two car manufacturers who are going to work on a joint venture. Which of the following should they adopt?

   a. Kerberos

   b. OAuth

   c. Single sign-on

   d. SAML

9. Which of the following regulations deals with credit card purchases and financial transactions?

   a. GDPR

   b. HIPAA

   c. PCI DSS

   d. All of the above

10. Which of the following can be used to protect data stored on mobile telephones? Select two.

    a. TLS

    b. SSL

    c. FDE

    d. Remote wipe

    e. Screen locks

    f. Cable locks

11. You are the security administrator for the British secret service. What type of access method will you use for secret and top-secret data?

   a. You will use DAC, with the owner of the data giving access.

   b. You will use MAC, with the custodian of the data giving access.

   c. You will use DAC, with the security administrator giving access.

   d. You will use MAC, with the security administrator giving access.

12. John goes to a sports website and gets the following error: **THIS WEBSITE CANNOT BE TRUSTED**. What two actions does the website administrator need to take to resolve this error?

   a. Ask the key escrow to store his private key.

   b. Ensure that the website uses a valid SAN certificate.

   c. Update the root certificate into the client computer's trusted root certificate authority's store.

   d. Verify whether the certificate on the server has expired.

13. You are the security administrator for a large multinational company and you have read a security bulletin that mentioned that the CRL for certificate validation has many security flaws. Which of the following will you implement?

   a. Certificate stapling

   b. Certificate pinning

   c. OCSP

   d. Key escrow

14. A security administrator discovers that an attacker used a compromised host as a platform for launching attacks deep in a company's network. What terminology best describes the use of the compromised host?

   a. Brute force

   b. Active reconnaissance

   c. Pivoting

   d. Passing point

15. A security administrator has noticed the following output collected by the SIEM system: Pinging Server 1 with 45,000 bytes of data:

```
Reply from 192.0.0.1: bytes=45000 time<1ms TTL=128
Reply from 192.0.0.1: bytes=45000 time<1ms TTL=128
Reply from 192.0.0.1: bytes=45000 time<1ms TTL=128
Reply from 192.0.0.1: bytes=45000 time<1ms TTL=128
```

What type of attack has been detected?

a. Integer overflow

b. Buffer overflow

c. XSS

d. SQL injection

16. During automation, which of the following is used to identify failures and helps detect security incidents. Select the best option.

a. Continuous validation

b. Continuous monitoring

c. Continuous integration

d. Continuous development

e. Automated courses of action

f. Continuous development

17. A large company is looking to purchase a cybersecurity company and would like a very detailed report about the security controls, in particular, the handling of data, ensuring it is confidential. What reports would the large company want to read so that it can make a good decision on whether to buy or not?

a. SOC 4 reports

b. SOC 1 reports

c. SOC 2 reports

d. SOC 3 reports

18. You are a security administrator for a large multinational company, and you have recently removed data from a data field, and it is now being held by a payment provider. What have you just implemented?

    a. Tokenization

    b. Obfuscation

    c. Data masking

    d. Encryption

19. The network administrator is going to set up a VPN that ensures that both the header and payload are encrypted. What did the security analyst recommend?

    a. IPSec in tunnel mode

    b. IPSec in split-tunnel mode

    c. IPSec in transport mode

    d. IPSec in full-tunnel mode

20. You are the CEO of a large multinational company and you are looking to move to the cloud. Which of the following will help you assess the overall risk of a cloud provider?

    a. CSA reference architecture

    b. CSA CCM

    c. NIST

    d. CASB

21. The security administrator is going to open a risk register for the company. What will be recorded in the risk register?

    a. Risk mitigation techniques

    b. Risk descriptions, the owner, and the mitigation strategies

    c. The annual risk audit report

    d. All of the above

22. An auditor made a recommendation in an annual audit last year that an embedded device be patched immediately. A year later, a second audit made the same recommendation and noted the fact that the outcomes from the last audit had not been adhered to. What is the reason that the patching has not been carried out? Select the most likely reason.

    a. The audit recommendation has been ignored.

    b. The company disagreed with the audit recommendation.

    c. The vendor is not producing any more patches as it is end of life.

    d. There is no interface for patching.

23. The IT manager is designing a BIA plan and is calculating the amount of time in a disaster recovery system that the company can operate without its data. What are they measuring?

    a. RTO

    b. A single point of failure

    c. SLA

    d. RPO

    e. MTTR

24. A security administrator wants to know which services are running on their mail server. What two tools are they most likely to use?

    a. NIDS

    b. Nmap

    c. ipconfig

    d. netstat

    e. Nbtstat

    f. Autopsy

25. Company A is due to upgrade all of its IT systems and has been investigating moving to the cloud as there is no capital expenditure since the CSP provides the hardware. Company A would still like to control the IT systems in the cloud. Which cloud model would best serve Company A's needs?

    a. Software as a Service (SaaS)

    b. Infrastructure as a Service (IaaS)

    c. Monitoring as a Service (MaaS)

    d. Platform as a Service (PaaS)

26. Which of the following RAID systems uses four disks that give you the best resiliency?

    a. RAID 0

    b. RAID 1

    c. RAID 2

    d. RAID 5

    e. RAID 6

27. A data owner is responsible for the classification of data and deciding who can access the data. Who is responsible for ensuring that the collection of data is legal, that the storage is legal, and that compliance has been carried out at all times? Select the best choice.

    a. Data custodian

    b. Privacy officer

    c. Data controller

    d. Data steward

28. You are a security administrator, and the IT director has tasked you with collecting the volatile memory on server 1 as it is currently experiencing a cyber-attack. Which of the following are the two best forms of volatile memory to collect?

    a. Secure boot

    b. Swap/page file

    c. USB flash drive

    d. ROM

    e. RAM

29. At what stage of the SDLC are computer systems no longer supported by the original vendor?

    a. Sandboxing

    b. End-of-life systems

    c. Resource exhaustion

    d. System sprawl

30. Company A has just developed a bespoke system for booking airline tickets. What is it called if a freelance coding specialist tests it for security flaws?

    a. Code review

    b. Static code review

    c. Regression testing

    d. Dynamic code review

31. You are the security administrator for a company that has just replaced two file servers. Which of the following is the best solution for disposing of hard drives that used to store top-secret data?

    a. Hashing

    b. Degaussing

    c. Low-level formatting

    d. Shredding

32. You are the security administrator for an airline company whose systems suffered a loss of availability last month. Which of the following attacks would most likely affect the availability of your IT systems?

    a. Spear phishing

    b. Replay

    c. MITM

    d. DoS

33. Company A has suffered a DDoS attack, and the company has decided that its RPO should be set at 4 hours. The directors are holding a board meeting to discuss the progress that is being made. During this meeting, the IT manager has mentioned the RTO, and the CEO looks confused. How can you explain the meaning of RTO to the CEO?

    a. Acceptable downtime

    b. Return to operational state

    c. Measure of reliability

    d. Average time to repair

34. Which of the following will prevent an SSL man-in-the-middle attack?

    a. Certificate pinning

    b. Input validation

    c. Certificate stapling

    d. Kerberos

35. The security team has identified an unknown vulnerability and isolated it. What technique is best for investigating and testing it?

    a. Steganography

    b. Fuzzing

    c. Sandboxing

    d. Containerization

36. You are the security administrator for your company, and the IT manager has asked you to brief them on XML authentication methods. Which of the following should you tell them uses XML-based authentication? Select all that apply.

    a. TOTP

    b. Federation Services

    c. Smart card

    d. SSO

    e. SOAP

    f. SAML

37. An attacker tries to target a high-level executive but has to leave a voicemail as they did not answer the telephone. What was the intended attack, and what attack was eventually used? Select all that apply.

    a. Whaling

    b. Vishing

    c. Phishing

    d. Spear phishing

38. The auditor has been investigating money being stolen from a charity, and they have discovered that the finance assistant has been embezzling money, as they were the only person who dealt with finance, receiving donations and paying all of the bills. Which of the following is the best option that the auditor could recommend to reduce the risk of this happening again?

    a. Hashing

    b. Job rotation

    c. Separation of duties

    d. Mandatory vacations

    e. Encryption

39. James has raised a ticket with the IT help desk. He had been tampering with the settings on his computer and he can no longer access the internet. The help desk technicians have checked the configuration on his desktop and the settings are the same as everyone else's. Suddenly, three other people have also reported that they also cannot connect to the internet. Which network device should be checked first?

    a. Switch

    b. Router

    c. Hub

    d. Repeater

40. Your company is opening up a new data center in Galway, Ireland. A server farm has been installed there and now a construction company has come in to put a 6-foot mantrap at the entrance. What are the two main reasons why this mantrap will be installed?

    a. To prevent theft

    b. To prevent tailgating

    c. To prevent unauthorized personnel from gaining access to the data center

    d. To allow faster access to the facility

41. What type of trust model do cloud providers use?

    a. Full trust

    b. Bridge trust

    c. Web of trust

    d. Zero trust

42. What two factors does a forensic examiner need when they are going to investigate a cloud-based attack. Choose two.

    a. Right-to-audit clause

    b. Access token

    c. Volatile evidence

    d. Search warrant

43. An auditor has just finished a risk assessment of the company, and they have recommended that we need to mitigate some of our risks. Which of the following are examples of risk mitigation?

    a. Turning off host-based firewalls on laptops

    b. Installing antivirus software on a new laptop

    c. Insuring your car against fire and theft

    d. Outsourcing your IT to another company

    e. Deciding not to jump into the Grand Canyon

44. You work for a very large company that has undergone an audit and the auditor has been looking at the amount of data that you hold. The auditor made recommendations about reducing data retention times for PII and sensitive data. Which of the following concepts is the auditor looking at?

    a. Tokenization

    b. Data retention policy

    c. Data masking

    d. Data minimization

    e. Anonymization

45. Which of the following obtains the consent of a user for the collection of only a minimal amount of personal data for an intended purpose?

    a. GDPR

    b. Terms of agreement

    c. Privacy notice

    d. Impact assessment

46. The cybersecurity team has set up a honeypot to track the attack vector of a newly released malware. As they review the virus, they notice that the hash value of the malware changes from host to host. Which of the following types of malware have been detected?

    a. Virus

    b. RAT

    c. Worm

    d. Logic bomb

    e. Polymorphic virus

47. The cybersecurity team has looked at the latest trends and identified that there has been an increase in brute-force attacks. Which of the following is a random value that can be appended to the stored password to make it more difficult for a brute-force password attack to be carried out?

    a. Obfuscation

    b. Nonce

    c. Data masking

    d. Salting

48. You are the security administrator for a software manufacturer and recently you stopped two new products from being sold as you found security flaws. Which of the following was not completed properly when the software was being developed? At what stage should more action have been taken?

    a. Software auditing

    b. Quality assurance

    c. Code signing

    d. Staging

    e. Development

    f. Testing

49. An auditor is carrying out an annual inspection of a SCADA network and finds that the programmable logic controllers (PLCs) have not been updated since last year. Upon further investigation, it is discovered that the company manufacturing these PLCs has gone into liquidation, making these controls end-of-life systems. The manufacturer is currently looking for another company to make an upgraded PLC. Which of the following recommendations should the auditor make to the management team to mitigate the risk in the short term?

    a. Remove the PLCs from the manufacturing infrastructure.

    b. Produce their own updated PLCs for the firmware.

    c. Set up a SIEM system for real-time monitoring of the SCADA system.

    d. Place the PLCs in a VLAN.

50. The auditor has carried out an inspection of the finance department and has made recommendations that the file server holding the financial data and the desktops of the financial department should use IPsec to secure the sessions between them. The network administrator is going to ensure that only the payload is encrypted. What did the security analyst recommend?

a. IPsec in tunnel mode

b. IPsec in split-tunnel mode

c. IPsec in transport mode

d. IPsec in full-tunnel mode

Mock Exam 1 Assessment

1. Answer: c

    Concept: A self-signed certificate is the cheapest certificate for internally facing servers.

2. Answer: c

    Concept: Closed/proprietary threat intelligence is funded by the company producing the report. More money would have been spent on creating the report and it will provide more accurate information as this information will be sold on to other companies.

3. Answer: c

    Concept: The logger command allows you to insert comments into a log file.

4. Answer: b

    Concept: The harvester is written in Python and allows you to search and collate the email addresses of a company on search engines such as Google.

5. Answers: a, b, c, d

    Concept: Telnet, curl, Dimitri, nmap, and nc can all be used for banner grabbing.

6. Answer: d

    Concept: When a new security update has been released, threat hunting is the process of searching current and historical logs for the symptoms of an attack.

7. Answer: b

    Concept: If it is end-of-life, the vendor will not produce any updates, but will sell the limited spare parts that they still have. With end-of-service, the vendor stops everything – no spare parts, nothing.

8. Answer: d

   Concept: Third-party authentication is federation services that use SAML.

9. Answer: c

   Concept: **Payment Card Industry Data Security Standard (PCI DSS)** deals with card payments.

10. Answer: c, e

    Concept: Data at rest is protected by FDE and access to the mobile telephone can be protected by screen locks and strong passwords.

11. Answer: d

    Concept: MAC is used as the access method for classified data and the security administrator is responsible for giving users access to the data once the person has been vetted and access is justified.

12. Answer: c and d

    Concept: A certificate needs to be valid and trusted by the computer.

13. Answer: c

    Concept: Only CRL and OCSP can provide certificate validation. Normally, if the CRL is going slow, you would implement an OCSP. In this case, if you remove the CRL, you need to implement an OCSP.

14. Answer: c

    Concept: Pivoting involves using a weak host to launch an attack further in the network. In virtualization, it is called VM Escape.

15. Answer: b

    Concept: This shows 45,000 bytes of data. It should have been 32 bytes. It is too much data, therefore a buffer overflow.

16. Answer: b

    Concept: Continuous monitoring detects system failure and any security breaches.

17. Answer: c

    Concept: SOC 2 reports produce a very detailed report on the internal controls of a company relating to security, data processing, and the handling of user's data to ensure it is confidential and privacy is maintained.

18. Answer: a

    Concept: Tokenization replaces data with a token that links to a payment provider who holds the data. This is better than encryption as it is stateless, whereas with encryption the keys are held locally.

19. Answer: a

    Concept: IPSec in tunnel mode is used externally on a VPN where both the header and the payload are encrypted.

20. Answer: b

    Concept: **Cloud Security Alliance Cloud Controls Matrix (CCM)**: This is designed to provide a security principles guide for cloud vendors and potential cloud customers to assess the overall risk of a cloud provider.

21. Answer: b

    Concept: The risk register lists the risks, each risk has an owner, and the owner will decide to accept, mitigate, transfer, or avoid the risk.

22. Answer: c

    Concept: An end-of-life system is no longer supported by the vendor and no patches will be made.

23. Answer: d

    Concept: When a disaster hits, the amount of time a company can operate without access to its data is called the **Recovery Point Objective (RPO)**.

24. Answer: b, d

    Concept: Nmap is used to create an inventory and can tell what operating system a host has and what services it is running. Netstat can tell which services are running through its port number.

25. Answer: b

    Concept: IaaS provides bare-metal hardware. Then, you need to install the software, configure it, and patch it.

26. Answer: e

    Concept: RAID 6 uses a minimum of four disks, uses double parity, and can lose two disks.

27. Answer: c

    Concept: The data controller is responsible for ensuring that all data that is collected, and its storage, is legal and follows the compliance regulations. The data controller is responsible for investigations into data breaches.

28. Answers: b and e

    Concept: Always collect the volatile evidence before stopping a cyber-attack in order to detect the source. Volatile memory evaporates if the power is switched off. RAM is volatile and the swap/page file is where applications run when RAM is full.

29. Answer: b

    Concept: End-of-life systems are no longer operational or supported by the vendor.

30. Answer: c

    Concept: Regression testing is part of program development, and in larger companies is done by code-testing specialists.

31. Answer: d

    Concept: You can shred a whole hard drive down until it looks like powder—let someone try to put that back together again.

32. Answer: d

    Concept: DDoS and DoS attack the availability of IT systems, as they both aim to take them down.

33. Answer: b

    Concept: The RTO means that the system is now back up and running. This can also be known as the return to operational state.

34. Answer: a

    Concept: Certificate pinning prevents SSL M-I-M attacks.

35. Answer: c

    Concept: Sandboxing is where we put an application in an isolated virtual machine to test patches, or maybe just because the application is too dangerous to run on our network.

36. Answer: a, b, and f

    Concept: SAML is an XML-based type of authentication used in federation services; TOTP is also XML-based.

37. Answer: b

Concept: The intended attack was vishing, and because he left a voicemail the actual attack was vishing, as leaving a voicemail is a vishing attack.

38. Answer: c

Concept: Separation of duties prevents one person from authorizing the whole transaction, and also prevents fraud. The CA signs the X509 certificates.

39. Answer: b

Concept: A router gives you access to the internet; on a computer, it is known as the default gateway.

40. Answer: b, c

Concept: A mantrap provides a safe and controlled environment in the data center as it allows you to control access.

41. Answer: d

Concept: Cloud providers use a zero-trust model where everybody needs to prove their identity.

42. Answer: a, c

Concept: To obtain the volatile evidence from a cloud provider, you will need a right to audit clause.

43. Answer: b

Concept: Risk mitigation involves reducing the risk of an attack or event. These are basically technical controls.

44. Answer: d

Concept: Data minimization is the process of collecting only the necessary data for a purpose and then retaining it only for a period required by compliance.

45. Answer: c

Concept: A privacy notice obtains consent to collect my personal data and only use it for the purpose that it was intended.

46. Answer: e

Concept: A polymorphic virus mutates, therefore the hash value will change.

47. Answer: d

    Concept: Salting appends a random value to a password before it is hashed

48. Answer: b, d

    Concept: Staging is where the software is tested with real data and the quality assurance of the product should have been tested and assured prior to moving the software from staging into production.

49. Answer: d

    Concept: You can place the vulnerable PLCs into a VLAN to segment them from the network.

50. Answer: c

    Concept: IPSec in transport mode is used server to server internally where only the payload is encrypted.

14
Mock Exam 2

1. You are a security administrator and you wish to implement an encrypted method of authentication for your wireless network. Which of the following protocols is the most secure for your wireless network?

   a. WPA2-PSK

   b. EAP-TLS

   c. PEAP

   d. PAP

2. You work on the cybersecurity team of a large multinational corporation, and you have been alerted to an attack on the web server inside your screened subnet that is used for selling your products on the internet. You can see by running netstat that you have an unknown active connection. What should be the first step you take when investigating this incident?

   a. Isolate the web server by disconnecting it from the network to prevent further damage.

   b. Disconnect all external active connections to ensure that any attack is stopped.

   c. Run a packet sniffer to capture the network traffic to identify the attacker.

   d. Take a screenshot of the damage done to the website and report the incident to the police.

3. I need to purchase a certificate that I can install on five internet-facing mail servers. Which of the following is the most cost-effective solution?

   a. PEM certificate

   b. Wildcard certificate

   c. Subject Alternative Name (SAN) certificate

   d. Root certificate

4. You are the operational manager for a financial company that has just suffered a disaster. Which of the following sites will you choose to be fully operational in the smallest amount of time?

   a. Cold site

   b. Warm site

   c. Hot site

   d. Off site

5. The serious crimes agency has just taken control of a laptop belonging to a well-known criminal that they have been trying to track down for the last 20 years. They want to ensure that everything is done by the book and that no errors are made. What is the first step in their forensic investigation, prior to starting the chain of custody?

   a. Make a system image of the laptop.

   b. Place it in a polythene bag and seal it.

   c. Hash the data so that data integrity is assured.

   d. Ask for proof of ownership of the laptop.

6. If an attacker is looking for information about the software versions that you use on your network, which of the following tools could they use? Select all that apply:

   a. Netstat

   b. Port scanning

   c. Nmap

   d. The harvester

7. Footage of people relaxing in their homes started appearing on the internet without the knowledge of the people being filmed. The people being filmed were warned by relatives and co-workers, resulting in an enquiry being launched by the police. Initial evidence reported a similarity in that they had all recently purchased IoT devices, such as health monitors, baby monitors, smart TVs, and refrigerators. Which of the following best describes why the attacks were successful?

   a. The devices' default configurations had not been changed.

   b. Their houses had been broken into and hidden cameras were installed.

   c. The victims' wireless networks were broadcasting beyond the boundaries of their homes.

   d. The manufacturers of the devices installed hidden devices, allowing them to film.

8. You are the network administrator for an IT training company that has over 20 training rooms that are all networked together in their Miami office. Last week they suffered an attack from the internet. What solution should be deployed to prevent this in the future?

   a. Create a VLAN on the switch and put the corporate admin team in the VLAN.

   b. Install a router in the LAN and place the corporate admin team in the new subnet.

   c. Create a NAT from the firewall and put the corporate machines in that network.

   d. Install a proxy server.

9. A security administrator looked at the top five entries from a report received from a SIEM server that showed the following output:

Name	Invalid Login Attempts
John Templeton	220
George Scott	219
Mary Shaw	219
Ian Neil	219
Joe Shipley	219

What type of attack did the SIEM system discover:

a. Password history

b. Password spraying

c. RAT

d. Dictionary attack

10. Your organization has many different ways of connecting to your network, ranging from VPN and RAS to 802.1x authentication switches. You need to implement a centrally managed authentication system that will record periods of access. Select the two most suitable methods of authentication:

    a. PAP

    b. TACACS+

    c. NTLM

    d. RADIUS

11. From a security perspective, what is the major benefit of using imaging technology, such as Microsoft WDS server or Symantec Ghost, on image desktop computers and laptops that are being rolled out?

    a. It provides a consistent baseline for all new machines.

    b. It ensures that all machines are patched.

    c. It reduces the number of vulnerabilities.

    d. It allows a non-technical person to roll out the images.

12. A company that is allowing people to access their internet application wants the people who log in to the application to use an account managed by someone else. An example of this is using their Facebook account with a technology called OpenID Connect. Which of the following protocols is this based on? Select the best choice:

    a. Kerberos

    b. SAML

    c. OAuth 2.0

    d. Federation Services

13. A security administrator has discovered that members of the sales team are connecting their own laptops to the company network without permission. What type of threat to the network have they discovered?

    a. Malicious insider

    b. BYOD

    c. Shadow IT

    d. Competitor

14. You are the security administrator for a medium-sized company that needs to enforce a much stricter password policy via group policy. The aims of this policy are to do the following:

- Prevent using the same password within 12 password changes.

- Ensure that users cannot change the password more than once a day.

- Prevent weak passwords or simple passwords, such as 123456 or password, from being used.

Select the options that you will need to fulfill all of these goals:

a. Enforce password history

b. Minimum password length

c. Passwords must meet complexity requirements

d. Minimum password age

e. Maximum password length

15. You provide a service for people who have recently fulfilled their contract with their mobile phone provider to unlock their phone and then install third-party applications on it. They will then no longer be tied to using the mobile phone vendor's app store. Which of the following techniques will you use to achieve this? Select all that apply:

a. Tethering

b. Sideloading

c. Slipstreaming

d. Jailbreaking or rooting

e. Degaussing

16. Which of the following is a standard for data privacy and handling?

a. SSAE

b. NIST

c. PCI DSS

d. GDPR

e. ISO 31000

17. You are the security administrator of a multinational company that has recently prevented brute-force attacks by using account lockout settings with a low value using group policy. The CEO of the company has now dictated that the company will no longer use account lockout settings as he read an article about it and got the wrong impression. Facing this dilemma, how can you ensure that you can make it more difficult for brute force to be successful?

    a. Obfuscation

    b. Salting

    c. XOR

    d. ROT 13

18. You want to protect the admin password for a wireless router. Which of the following wireless features would be most appropriate to achieve this objective?

    a. WPA2-Enterprise

    b. TKIP

    c. WPS

    d. PSK

    e. CCMP

19. Why would a network administrator install a Network Intrusion Detection System (NIDS)? Select the two best options.

    a. It identifies vulnerabilities.

    b. It identifies new network hosts.

    c. It identifies viruses.

    d. It identifies new traffic patterns.

    e. It identifies new web servers.

20. A web server was the victim of an integer overflow attack. How could this be prevented in the future?

    a. Install a proxy server.

    b. Install a SQL injection.

    c. Input validation on forms.

    d. Install a web application firewall.

21. An attacker managed to access a guest machine and then attacked the database server and managed to exfiltrate the credit card details of 20,000 users. What type of attack did they carry out?

    a. VM escape

    b. VM sprawl

    c. System sprawl

    d. VM containerization

22. Which of the following attacks cannot be detected by any monitoring systems?

    a. Pass-the-hash

    b. Man-in-the-middle

    c. Zero-day virus

    d. Smurf attacks

23. You are the system administrator for a multinational company that wants to implement two-factor authentication. At present, you are using facial recognition as the method of access. Which of the following would allow you to obtain two-factor authentication? Select all that apply:

    a. Palm reader

    b. Signature verification

    c. Thumb scanner

    d. Gait

    e. Iris scanner

24. The security auditor has just visited your company and is recommending change management to reduce the risks from the unknown vulnerabilities of any new software introduced into the company. What will the auditor recommend for reducing the risk when you first evaluate the software? Select the best two practices to adopt from the following list:

    a. Jailbreaking

    b. Sandboxing

    c. Bluesnarfing

    d. Chroot jail

    e. Fuzzing

25. You are the owner of a small business that has just installed a terminal for allowing payment by credit/debit card. Which of the following regulations must you adhere to?

    a. SSAE

    b. NIST

    c. PCI DSS

    d. GDPR

    e. ISO 31000

26. You are the security administrator for a multinational corporation and you recently carried out a security audit. Following the audit, you told the server administrators to disable NTLM and enable Kerberos on all servers. Which of the following types of attack best describes why you took this action?

    a. It will improve the server's performance.

    b. To prevent a man-in-the-middle attack.

    c. To prevent a pass-the-hash attack.

    d. To prevent a poodle attack.

27. The political adviser to the Prime Minister of the United Kingdom has returned from the two months of summer break that all staff are entitled to. He has applied for an immediate transfer to another department, stating that his health is bad, and the job was far too intense. When his replacement arrives, he finds that, during the summer recess, the political adviser has shredded all documents relating to a political inquiry that has involved his cousin. The police are immediately called in and say that they cannot prosecute the political adviser due to a lack of evidence. What precautions could the Houses of Parliament security team take to prevent further events such as this from happening in the future?

    a. Create a change management document to ensure that the receptionists are more vigilant to people coming in out of hours.

    b. Enforce time-based access restrictions so that nobody can access the IT systems during summer breaks.

    c. Enforce separation of duties to ensure that any document that is destroyed has been witnessed by a second person.

    d. Enforce mandatory vacations to prevent him coming in during the recess.

28. You are the administrator for a large multinational organization. You wish to purchase a new biometric system. Which of the following is a critical factor when making the purchase?

a. High FAR

b. Low FRR

c. Low FAR

d. Low CER

e. High CER

f. High FRR

29. You work in the forensics team of a very large multinational corporation, where an attack has happened across three different sites in two different countries. You are now going to install a SIEM server to collect the following log files from all of the locations.

- Security logs

- DNS logs

- Firewall logs

- NIPS logs

- NIDS logs

What is the first action that you need to take before collating these logs?

a. Apply time normalization to these logs.

b. Copy them into a worm drive so that they cannot be tampered with.

c. Sort out the sequence of events by site.

d. Install a Network Time Protocol (NTP) server.

30. You are working for the serious crimes unit of the United Nations and have been given a laptop to investigate. You need to ensure that the evidence you are investigating has not been tampered with during your investigation. How are you going to prove this to the court when it is time to present your findings? Which of the following techniques will you adopt to best prove this? Select all that apply:

    a. MD5

    b. 3DES

    c. SHA1

    d. Blowfish

31. Fifteen developers are working on producing a new piece of software. After 4 weeks, they all submit the code that they have produced, and it has just been moved into the development phase of the software development. All of this code will be automated. What has just been carried out?

    a. Continuous validation

    b. Continuous monitoring

    c. Continuous integration

    d. Continuous development

    e. Automated courses of action

32. You are the security administrator for a multinational corporation that has an Active Directory domain. What type of attack uses HTML tags with JavaScript inserted between the `<script>` and `</script>` tags?

    a. Cross-site scripting

    b. Man-in-the-middle

    c. Cross-site forgery attack

    d. SQL injection

33. You are the system administrator for an Active Directory domain and deal with authentication on a daily basis. Which of the following would you use as multifactor authentication?

    a. Smart card

    b. Kerberos

    c. WPS

    d. TOTP

34. A company has just installed a new wireless network and has found that some devices are interfering with other wireless devices. Which of the following have the administrators failed to carry out? Choose the best two.

    a. Heat map

    b. Checking wireless channels

    c. Site survey

    d. Low-power directional antennas

35. You are the security administrator for a multinational company, and you know that one of your X509 certificates, used in at least 300 desktop machines, has been compromised. What action are you going to take to protect the company, using the least amount of administrative effort?

    a. Email the people involved and ask them to delete the X509 from their desktop immediately.

    b. Carry out certificate pinning to prevent the CA from being compromised.

    c. Revoke the root CA X509 so it is added to the CRL.

    d. Revoke the X509 so it is added to the CRL.

36. A biometric system has been letting in unauthorized users ever since it had a patch upgrade. Which of the following is being measured?

    a. CER

    b. FAR

    c. FRR

    d. CVE

37. Which of the following is footprinting?

    a. Creating a list of approved applications

    b. Listing network connections

    c. Creating a diagram about network connections and hosts

    d. A list of approved applications

38. You need to install a new wireless access point that should be as secure as possible, while also being backward compatible with legacy wireless systems. Which of the following do you choose to implement?

    a. WPA2 PSK

    b. WPA

    c. WPA2 CCMP

    d. WPA2 TKIP

39. You are the security administrator for a multinational corporation based in Miami, and your company has recently suffered a replay attack. Following lessons learned, you have decided to use a protocol that uses timestamps and USN to prevent replay attacks. Which of the following protocols is being implemented here? Select the best answer:

    a. Federation Services

    b. EAP-TLS

    c. Kerberos

    d. RADIUS Federation

40. A company recently suffered a break-in, where the company's research and development data was stolen, and the assembly line was damaged. Which of the following threat actors is most likely to have carried this out?

    a. A criminal syndicate

    b. A competitor

    c. A script kiddie

    d. A nation state

41. You are the new IT director of a small, family-owned business that is rapidly expanding. You have submitted your annual budget for the IT team and the owners of the company want to know why you have asked for funds for vendor diversity. They have asked you to provide two good reasons as to why they should grant you the funds. Which of the following are the most suitable reasons why you wish to implement vendor diversity?

    a. Reliability.

    b. Regulatory compliance.

    c. It is a best practice in your industry.

    d. Resilience.

42. You are the network administrator for a large multinational corporation, and you have captured packets that show that the administrators' credentials between their desktop and the network devices are in clear text. Which of the following protocols could be used to secure the authentication? Select the best choice.

    a. SNMP V 3

    b. Secure Shell

    c. SCP

    d. SFTP

43. You are the auditor of a large multinational corporation and the SIEM server has been finding vulnerabilities on a server. Manual inspection proves that it has been fully hardened and has no vulnerabilities. What are the two main reasons why the SIEM server is producing this output?

    a. There was a zero-day virus.

    b. False negatives.

    c. False positives.

    d. The wrong filter was used to audit.

44. You are the purchasing manager for a very large multinational company, and you are looking at the company's policy of dealing with the insurance of laptops. Last year, the company lost a record number of laptops. Your company is losing 10 laptops per month and the monthly insurance cost is $10,000. Which of the following laptop purchases would prevent you from purchasing insurance?

    a. A budget laptop at $1,300 each

    b. A budget laptop at $1,200 each

    c. A budget laptop at $1,000 each

    d. A budget laptop at $1,001 each

45. Which of the following is a measure of reliability?

    a. MTTR

    b. MTBF

    c. MTTF

    d. RPO

46. A research and development computer that holds trade secrets needs to be isolated from other machines on the network. Which of the following is the best solution?

    a. VLAN

    b. PVC

    c. Air gap

    d. Containment

47. Which of the following constitutes risk transference? Choose two:

    a. Outsourcing your IT support

    b. Purchasing anti-virus software

    c. Identifying and classifying the asset

    d. Purchasing cybersecurity insurance

48. Which of the following are the characteristics of a third-party to third-party authentication protocol that uses XML-based authentication?

    a. Single sign-on (SSO)

    b. Kerberos

    c. SAML

    d. Secure Shell

49. A cybersecurity administrator is looking at a customer database and has noticed the following against the credit card of a customer:

    ★★★★ ★★★★ ★★★★ 3456

    What has the administrator come across?

    a. Tokenization

    b. Obfuscation

    c. Data masking

    d. XOR

50. A security administrator found that a domain controller was infected by a virus. They isolated it from the network and then removed the virus and turned off the telnet service? Which of the following has the administrator just carried out?

a. Containment

b. Eradication

c. Recovery

d. Lessons learned

Mock Exam 2 Assessment

1. Answer: b

   Concept: EAP-TLS is a secure wireless authentication protocol, as it uses certificates. An X509 certificate is installed on the endpoint. This is the most secure EAP standard.

2. Answer: c

   Concept: The first stage in any attack is to capture the volatile evidence. In this incident, you would capture the network traffic to identify the source of the attack.

3. Answer: b

   Concept: A wildcard certificate can be used on multiple servers, normally those that are internet facing.

4. Answer: c

   Concept: The hot site should be up and running with data that has been replicated.

5. Answer: a

   Concept: The first step is to create a system image or, if it is a hard drive, create a forensic copy.

6. Answer: c

   Concept: A **Network mapper (Nmap)** can identify new hosts on the network, identify what services are running, and identify what operating systems are installed. It can also be used for banner grabbing.

7. Answer: a

   Concept: IoT home-based automated devices should have the default configurations of the username and password changed. Most users do not realize that these passwords exist.

8. Answer: c

Concept: A NAT hides the internal network from external users.

9. Answer: b

Concept: Password spraying is where an attacker obtains a list of employees and then tries common passwords against each account.

10. Answer: b and d

Concept: AAA servers are used for centralized authentication as they provide authentication, authorization, and accounting. They can record all log-ins and log-outs in a database.

11. Answer: a

Concept: When you build an image, all of the applications will have the same settings and updates and therefore will be consistent. A baseline consists of the applications that are installed at the current time.

12. Answer: c

Concept: OAuth 2.0 is the industry-standard protocol for authorization. It is used by OpenID Connect, where people can be authenticated using their Facebook or Google account.

13. Answer: c

Concept: A shadow IT threat is where someone connects their device to a private network without permission.

14. Answers: a, c, d

Concept: The password history is the number of passwords that you need to remember before you can reuse them. Password complexity requires users to use three of the four following characters in the password: lowercase, uppercase, numbers, and special characters not used in programming. A minimum password age set to 1 means that you can change the password only once a day, preventing password rotation until you get back to the original password.

15. Answers: b and d

Concept: Sideloading involves loading third-party applications onto an unlocked mobile Phone. Jailbreaking (iOS), or rooting (Android), is where the phone has been unlocked, removing the vendor's restrictions on the mobile phone.

16. Answer: d

    Concept: GDPR is a framework for data protection law ensuring the privacy rights of individuals. It deals with data privacy and data sharing.

17. Answer: b

    Concept: Salting appends random characters to a password before it is hashed. As the passwords are then longer, brute-force attacks need more processing and computation resources to crack them.

18. Answer: e

    Concept: CCMP uses AES for encryption and is the strongest wireless security.

19. Answer: b, d

    Concept: A NIDS uses sensors and collectors to identify changes to the network.

20. Answer: c

    Concept: Input validation prevents buffer-overflow attacks, integer-overflow attacks, and SQL injection by restricting the input to a certain format.

21. Answer: a

    Concept: VM escape can be used for a lateral attack on the virtual host or the other virtual machines.

22. Answer: c

    Concept: A zero-day virus is a newly released virus, and no monitoring system can detect it until it receives an update in about 7 days' time. There are no patches for it either.

23. Answer: b and d

    Concept: Facial recognition is something you use for authentication. b and d are both something you do – you have a unique signature, and your gait is how you walk.

24. Answer: b and d

    Concept: Sandboxing and chroot jail (Linux version) allow you to isolate an application inside a virtual guest machine.

25. Answer: c

    Concept: **Payment Card Industry Data Security Standard (PCI DSS)** lays out the regulations for the handling and storage of financial information.

26. Answer: c

    Concept: Disabling NTLM or enabling Kerberos will prevent pass-the-hash attacks. Kerberos is the best of the two as passwords are held in an encrypted database.

27. Answer: b

    Concept: Time-based access restrictions would have prevented someone from accessing the system during the holidays.

28. Answer: d

    Concept: When the FAR and FRR are equal, this is known as the CER. A system with a low CER is the best choice as it has very few errors.

29. Answer: d

    Concept: We need to install an NTP server to synchronize the time of all of the servers so that the events can be put into a sequence of events.

30. Answer: a and c

    Concept: Hashing proves data integrity. SHA1 and MD5 are both hashing algorithms.

31. Answer: c

    Concept: Continuous Integration is where code from multiple sources is integrated together.

32. Answer: a

    Concept: **Cross-Site Scripting (XSS)** uses HTML tags or JavaScript.

33. Answer: a

    Concept: A smart card is "something you have," inserting the card into the reader is "something you do," and then when you insert the PIN, it is "something that you know."

34. Answers: a, c

    Concept: A site survey should be carried out prior to installing a wireless network as it maps out all of the items that would interfere with a wireless connection. A heat map shows the coverage with blue/green areas showing poor connectivity and red showing great connectivity.

35. Answer: d

Concept: Once a certificate has been compromised, it should immediately be revoked so it is added to the CRL.

36. Answer: b

Concept: Unauthorized users are allowed. Look at the middle initial in FAR – it is A for allow.

37. Answer: c

Concept: Footprinting maps out network topology including active hosts.

38. Answer: d

Concept: WPA2 is the most secure and TKIP is backward compatible. WPA also works with legacy but is not the best choice.

39. Answer: c

Concept: Kerberos issues tickets for authentication, and each change has a different **Updated Sequence Number (USN)** and timestamps. It prevents both replay and pass-the-hash attacks.

40. Answer: b

Concept: The R&D department creates a lot of the company's trade secrets; therefore, a competitor would steal them to beat you to the marketplace. If they damaged your production line, it would prevent you from getting a product to market.

41. Answer: a and d

Concept: Vendor diversity involves getting a service from two different providers at the same time. Vendor diversity provides reliability and resilience. For example, if broadband from one provider fails, then the second provider's broadband should still be up and running.

42. Answer: b

Concept: **Secure Shell (SSH)** is used for secure remote access and credentials are protected.

43. Answer: c and d

Concept: If we are using the wrong configuration for the SIEM server, we will get poor monitoring, resulting in false positives. This would also happen if you scanned the wrong type of host.

44. Answer: c

Concept:

```
SLE = ALE/ARO
ALE = 12 x 10,000 = $120,000
ARO = 12 X 10 = 120 laptops a year
Single loss expectancy = $120,000/120 = $1000
```

Explanation: The cost of losing the laptops is $120,000, the same as purchasing the insurance. You should not take out the insurance in the hope that next year you may lose fewer laptops, as a record number of laptops has already been lost.

45. Answer: b

Concept: **Mean Time Between Failures (MTBF)** is the measure of the number of failures. If I purchased a car and it broke down every day for the next week, I would take it back, as it would be unreliable.

46. Answer: c

Concept: An airgap isolates a computer from the network as it has no physical or wireless connections. The only way to extract data is by removable media.

47. Answers: a, d

Concept: Risk transference is where you transfer the responsibility of the risk to a third party, purchasing insurance of any kind and outsourcing your IT are examples.

48. Answer: c

Concept: Federation services is a third-party-to-third-party authentication method that uses SAML, an XML-based method for authentication. SAML passes credentials to the **Identity Provider (IdP)**.

49. Answer: c

Concept: Data masking masks all or some of the data held in a field.

50. Answer: b

Concept: Removing viruses and turning off services are carried out at the eradication phase.

Assessment

Chapter 1 – Understanding Security Fundamentals

1. The three components of the CIA triad are confidentiality, where the data is encrypted, integrity, where the data uses hashing, and availability, where the data is available, for example, by restoring data from a backup.

2. A CCTV camera without any film inside is used as a deterrent, as criminals would not know that there is no film inside.

3. Confidentiality means preventing other people from viewing the data; the best way to keep data confidential is to encrypt it.

4. The best way to control entry into a data center is to install a mantrap.

5. An air gap is where a computer or device has no physical connections, such as Wi-Fi, or an Ethernet cable isolating it from your network.

6. The three control categories are managerial, operational, and physical.

7. Choose three of the following physical controls: Lighting, cameras, robot sentries, fences, gate signage, industrial camouflage, security guards, badges, key management, proximity card, tokens, biometric locks, electronic locks, burglar alarms, smoke detectors, internal protection, conduits, HVAC, cable locks, airgap, laptop safe, USB data blocker, vault, and Faraday cage.

8. Researching an incident requires detective controls where all of the evidence is gathered.

9. Hashing provides data integrity where the hash value is measured before and after accessing data. If the values match, it has integrity.

10. Corrective controls are the actions you take to recover from an incident. You may have to restore data from a backup.

11. Firewall rules are designed to mitigate risk and they are technical controls.

12. A smart card, a CAC card, or a PIV card are all used in conjunction with a PIN.

13. In a MAC model, the custodian stores and manages the data. The administrator grants access to the data.

14. In a DAC environment, the data owner decides who has access to the data.

15. Least privilege is the process of giving an employee the minimal permissions to perform their job.

16. The Linux permission of 764 gives the owner read, write, and execute access, the group read and write access, and other (users) read access.

17. This is called rule-based access control where the access is applied to the whole department.

18. The two people from finance are using role-based access control where a subset of a department is carrying out a subset of duties.

19. The defense in depth model has multiple layers to protect data and resources. If the outer layer fails, then the next layer should perform the protection. Many layers need to be broken through before gaining access to the data or resource.

20. When someone leaves the company, we should disable the account and reset the password so that it cannot be used.

21. The EU GDPR regulations state that if a website that is hosted by someone in the US is accessed by someone from within the EU, that website needs to be GDPR-compliant.

22. If a company puts a right to audit clause into a contract, it gives them the right to audit the supplier at any time. This way, the company can look at the company records and check the quality of the products and materials being used.

23. Chain of custody is a record of who has collected the evidence and provides a log of who has handled the data. The original data must be intact and there must not be any break in the chain.

24. The US released The CLOUD Act so that they could obtain evidence from other countries for the purposes of an FBI investigation. The UK government released the COPOA act to seek data stored overseas and give their law enforcement faster access to evidence held by providers.

25. Stage C of Cloud Forensic Process 26 is to ascertain the type of technology behind the cloud.

Chapter 2 – Implementing Public Key Infrastructure

1. A CA has a root certificate, which it uses to sign keys.

2. You would use a private CA for internal use only; these certificates will not be accepted outside of your organization.

3. You would use a public CA for B2B activities.

4. If you were a military, security, or banking organization, you would keep the CA offline when it is not being used to prevent it from being compromised.

5. An architect would build the CA or intermediary authorities.

6. The CA would sign the X509 certificates.

7. Certificate pinning can be used to prevent a CA from being compromised and fraudulent certificates being issued.

8. If two separate PKI entities want to set up cross-certification, the root CAs would set up a trust model between themselves, known as a bridge trust model.

9. PGP uses a trust model known as a web of trust.

10. A **Certificate Revocation List (CRL)** is used to determine whether a certificate is valid.

11. If the CRL is going slow, an OCSP is used as it provides faster validation.

12. Certificate stapling/OCSP stapling is where a web server uses an OCSP for faster certificate authentication, bypassing the CRL.

13. A **Certificate Signing Request (CSR)** is a new certificate request.

14. The key escrow stores and manages private keys for third parties.

15. A hardware security module is used by the key escrow as it securely stores and manages certificates.

16. When a user's private key becomes corrupt, the DRA recovers the data by obtaining a copy of the private key from the key escrow.

17. Each certificate can be identified by its OID, which is similar to a serial number.

18. A private certificate is in P12 format with a `.pfx` extension.

19. A public certificate is in P7B format with a `.cer` extension.

20. A PEM certificate is in Base64 format.

21. A wildcard certificate can be used on multiple servers in the same domain.

22. A **Subject Alternative Name (SAN)** certificate can be used on multiple domains.

23. Code-signing software is similar to hashing the software and ensuring the integrity of the software.

24. Extended validation is normally used by financial institutions as it provides a higher level of trust for the X509; when it is used, the URL background turns green.

25. The Caesar cipher is a substitution cipher; an example would be ROT 4, where each letter would be substituted by a letter four characters along in the alphabet.

26. Encryption is when plain text is taken and turned into ciphertext.

27. Symmetric encryption is used to encrypt large amounts of data as it uses one key.

28. DH is an asymmetric technique that creates a secure tunnel; during a VPN connection, it is used during the IKE phase and uses UDP port 500 to create the VPN tunnel.

29. The first stage in encryption is key exchange. During asymmetric encryption, each entity will give the other entity its public key. The private key is secure and never given away.

30. Carol uses Bob's public key to encrypt the data, and then Bob will use his private key to decrypt the data. Encryption and decryption are always done by the same key pair.

31. George must obtain the old private key to decrypt the data as the encryption was done with a different key pair.

32. Janet will digitally sign the email with her private key and John will check its validity with Janet's public key, which he would have received in advance.

33. A digital signature provides both integrity and non-repudiation.

34. ECC will be used to encrypt data on a smartphone as it is small and fast and uses the DH handshake.

35. AES-256 will be used to encrypt a military mobile telephone.

36. Two key-stretching algorithms are bcrypt and PBKDF2.

37. Key stretching salts the password being stored so that duplicate passwords are never stored, and it also increases the length of the keys to make things harder for a brute-force attack.

38. Streams encrypt one bit at a time and block ciphers take blocks of data, such as 128-bit modes. A block cipher will be used for large amounts of data.

39. CBC needs all of the blocks of data to decrypt the data; otherwise, it will not work.

40. Hashing ensures the integrity of data; two examples include SHA-1 (160 bit) and MD5 (128 bit).

41. Encryption is used to protect data so that it cannot be reviewed or accessed.

42. A hash is one-way and cannot be reversed.

43. POODLE is a man-in-the-middle attack on a downgraded SSL 3.0 (CBC).

44. DHE and ECDHE are both ephemeral keys that are short-lived, one-time keys.

45. The strongest encryption for an L2TP/IPSec VPN tunnel is AES and the weakest is DES.

46. A session key ensures the security of communications between a computer and a server or a computer and another computer.

47. Data-at-rest on a laptop is protected by FDE.

48. Data-at-rest on a tablet or smartphone is protected by FDE.

49. Data-at-rest on a backend server is stored on a database, so it needs database encryption.

50. Data-at-rest on a USB flash drive or external hard drive is done via full disk encryption.

51. Data-in-transit could be secured by using TLS, HTTPS, or an L2TP/IPsec tunnel.

52. Data-in-use could be protected by full memory encryption.

53. Obfuscation is used to make the source code look obscure so that if it is stolen, it cannot be understood. It masks the data and could use either XOR or ROT13 to obscure the data.

54. Perfect forward secrecy ensures that there is no link between the server's private key and the session key. If the VPN server's key was compromised, it could not decrypt the session.

55. A collision attack tries to match two hash values to obtain a password.

56. Rainbow tables are a list of precomputed words showing their hash value. You will get rainbow tables for MD5 and different rainbow tables for SHA-1.

57. Steganography is used to conceal data; you can hide a file, image, video, or audio inside another image, video, or audio file.

58. DLP prevents sensitive or PII information from being emailed out of a company or being stolen from a file server using a USB device.

59. Salting a password ensures that duplicate passwords are never stored and makes things more difficult for brute-force attacks by increasing the key size (key stretching).It appends the salt to the password making it longer than before hashing.

Chapter 3 – Investigating Identity and Access Management

1. A password is most likely to be entered incorrectly; the user may forget the password or may have the Caps Lock key set up incorrectly.

2. When purchasing any device, you should change the default username and password as many of these are available on the internet and could be used to access your device.

3. Password history is the number of passwords you can use before you can reuse your current password. Some third-party applications or systems may call this a password reuse list.

4. Password history could be set up and combined with a minimum password age. If you set the minimum password age to 1 day, a user could only change their password a maximum of once per day. This would prevent them from rotating their passwords to come back to the old password.

5. A complex password uses three of the following: uppercase and lowercase letters, numbers, and special characters not used in programming.

6. If you set up an account lockout with a low value, such as 3, the hacker needs to guess your password within three attempts or the password is locked out, and this disables the user account.

7. A smart card is multi-factor or dual-factor as the card is something you have, and inserting it into a card reader is something you do, and the PIN is something you know.

8. A password, PIN, and date of birth are all factors that you know; therefore, it is single-factor.

9. Biometric authentication is where you use a part of your body or voice for authentication, for example, your iris, retina, palm, or fingerprint.

10. Federated services are an authentication method that can be used by two third parties; this uses SAML and extended attributes, such as an employee's ID or email address.

11. **Security Assertion Mark-up Language (SAML)** is an XML-based authentication protocol used with federated services.

12. Shibboleth is a small, open source Federation Services protocol.

13. **Lightweight Directory Authentication Protocol (LDAP)** is used to store objects in X500 format and search Active Directory objects such as users, printers, groups, or computers.

14. A distinguisher name in the ITU X500 object format is cn=Fred, ou=IT, dc=Company, dc=Com.

15. Microsoft's Kerberos authentication protocol is the only one that uses tickets. It also uses timestamps and updated sequence numbers to prevent replay attacks. It also prevents pass-the-hash attacks as it does not use NTLM.

16. A **Ticket-Granting Ticket (TGT)** process is where a user logs in to an Active Directory domain using Kerberos authentication and receives a service ticket.

17. Single sign-on is where a user inserts their credentials only once and accesses different resources, such as email and files, without needing to re-enter the credentials. Examples of this are Kerberos, Federation Services, or a smart card.

18. Pass-the-hash attacks exploit older systems such as Microsoft NT4.0, which uses NT LAN Manager. You can prevent this by enabling Kerberos or disabling NTLM.

19. OpenID Connect is where you access a device or portal using your Facebook, Twitter, Google, or Hotmail credentials. The portal itself does not manage the account.

20. The first AAA server is Microsoft RADIUS, using UDP port 1812 – it is seen as non-proprietary. The second is Cisco TACACS+ and uses TCP port 49. Diameter is a more modern secure form of RADIUS that is TCP-based and uses EAP.

21. Accounting is an AAA server where they log the details of when someone logs in and logs out; this can be used for billing purposes. Accounting is normally logged into a database such as SQL. RADIUS Accounting uses UDP port 1813.

22. A VPN solution creates a secure connection from a remote location to your corporate network or vice versa. The most secure tunneling protocol is L2TP/IPSec.

23. PAP authentication uses a password in clear text; this could be captured easily by a packet sniffer.

24. An iris scanner is a physical device used for biometric authentication.

25. Facial recognition could be affected by light or turning your head slightly to one side; some older facial recognition systems accept photographs. Microsoft Windows Hello is much better as it uses infrared and is not fooled by a photograph or affected by light.

26. Type II in biometric authentication is Failure Acceptance Rate, where people that are not permitted to access your network are given access.

27. **Time-Based One-Time Password** (**TOTP**) has a short time limit of 30–60 seconds.

28. HOTP is a one-time password that does not expire until it is used.

29. A CAC is similar to a smart card as it uses certificates, but the CAC is used by the military and has a picture and the details of the user on the front, as well as their blood group and Geneva convention category on the reverse side.

30. IEE802.1x is port-based authentication that authenticates both users and devices.

31. A service account is a type of administrative account that allows an application to have a higher level of privileges to run on a desktop or server. An example of this is using a service account to run an anti-virus application.

32. A system administrator should have two accounts: a user account for day-to-day tasks, and an administrative account for administrative tasks.

33. When you purchase a baby monitor, you should rename the default administrative account and change the default password to prevent someone from using it to hack into your home. This is known as an **Internet of Things** (**IoT**) item.

34. A privileged account is an account with administrative rights.

35. When monitoring and auditing are carried out, the employees responsible cannot be traced from more-than-one-person shared accounts. Shared accounts should be eliminated for monitoring and auditing purposes

36. Default accounts and passwords for devices and software can be found on the internet and used to hack your network or home devices. Ovens, TVs, baby monitors, and refrigerators are examples, and therefore pose a security risk.

37. The system administrator is using a standard naming convention.

38. When John Smith leaves the company, you need to disable his account and reset the password. Deleting the account will prevent access to the data he used.

39. Account recertification is an audit of user accounts and permissions that is usually carried out by an auditor. This is also referred to as a user account review.

40. A user account review ensures that old accounts have been deleted and that all current users have the appropriate access to resources and not a higher level of privilege.

41. A SIEM system can carry out active monitoring and notify the administrators of any changes to user accounts or logs.

42. Following an audit, either change management or a new policy will be put in place to rectify any area not conforming to company policy.

43. The contractor's account should have an expiry date equal to the last day of the contract.

44. Rule-based access should be adopted so that the contractors can access the company network between 9 a.m. and 5 p.m. daily.

45. Time and day restrictions should be set up against each individual's user account matching their shift pattern.

46. Account Lockout with a low value will prevent brute-force attacks.

47. Create a group called IT apprentices, and then add the apprentices, accounts to the group. Give the group read access to the IT data.

48. The credential manager can be used to store generic and Windows 10 accounts. The user therefore does not have to remember the account details.

49. The company should have disabled the account and reset the password. A user account review needs to be carried out to find accounts in a similar situation.

50. To copy and install the public key on the SSH server and add to the list of authorized keys.

51. This is where a user logs in to a device from one location, and then they log in from another location shortly afterward, where it would be impossible to travel that distance in the time between logins.

52. This is known as a risky login as I have used a secondary device to log in to Dropbox.

53. A password vault is an application that stores passwords using AES-256 encryption and it is only as secure as the master key.

54. They would use a dynamic KBA that would ask you details about your account that are not previously stored questions.

55. FAR allows unauthorized user access, and FRR rejects authorized user access.

56. Privileged Access Management is a solution the stores the privileged account in a bastion domain to help protect them from attack.

57. Some people don't realize that there are generic accounts controlling the devices that make them vulnerable to attack.

58. Some devices being used do not belong to a domain, for example, an iPad, so every connection should be considered unsafe.

59. Biometric authentication allows unauthorized users access to the system.

Chapter 4 – Exploring Virtualization and Cloud Concepts

1. Elasticity allows you to increase and decrease cloud resources as you need them.

2. **Infrastructure as a Service (IaaS)** requires you to install the operating systems and patch the machines. The CSP provides bare-metal computers.

3. SaaS is a custom application written by a vendor and you cannot migrate to it.

4. The major benefit of a public cloud is that there is no capital expenditure.

5. A private cloud is a single-tenant setup where you own the hardware.

6. A public cloud is multi-tenant.

7. A community cloud is where people from the same industry, such as a group of lawyers, design and share the cost of a bespoke application and its hosting, making it cost-effective.

8. The CSP is responsible for the hardware fails.

9. The CASB ensures that the policies between on-premises and the cloud are enforced.

10. On-premises is where you own the building and work solely from there.

11. A hybrid cloud is where a company is using a mixture of on-premises and the cloud.

12. Distributive allocation is where the load is spread evenly across a number of resources, ensuring no one resource is over-utilized. An example of this is using a load balancer.

13. **Security as a Service (SECaaS)** provides secure identity management.

14. A diskless virtual host will get its disk space from an SAN.

15. A VLAN on an SAN will use an iSCSI connector.

16. An SAN will use fast disks, such as SSDs.

17. A host holds a number of virtual machines – it needs fast disks, memory, and CPU cores.

18. A guest is a virtual machine, for example, a Windows 10 virtual machine. A snapshot can be used to roll back to a previous configuration.

19. Sandboxing is where you isolate an application for patching or testing or because it is dangerous. A chroot jail is for sandboxing in a Linux environment.

20. A snapshot is faster at recovering than any other backup solution.

21. A Type 1 hypervisor is a bare-metal hypervisor. Some examples are Hyper-V, ESX, and Xen.

22. A Type 2 hypervisor is a hypervisor that sits on top of an operating system, for example, VirtualBox, which could be installed on a Windows 10 desktop.

23. HVAC keeps the servers cool by importing cold air and exporting hot air. If a server's CPU overheats, it will cause the server to crash.

24. A community cloud is where people from the same industry share resources.

25. Cloud storage for personal users could be iCloud, Google Drive, Microsoft OneDrive, or Dropbox.

26. Fog computing is an intermediary between the device and the cloud. It allows the data to be processed closer to the device. It reduces latency and cost.

27. It allows data storage to be closer to the sensors rather than miles away in a data center.

28. A container allows the isolation of the applications and its files and libraries so that the application is independent.

29. Infrastructure as code allows you to automate your infrastructure, for example, using PowerShell DSC.

30. This is the combination of business and IT functions into a single business solution.

31. These are policies that state the actions and access levels someone has in relation to a particular resource.

32. This is where a virtual machine or host has run out of resources. The best way to avoid this is to use thin provisioning.

33. VM escape is where an attacker will use a vulnerable virtual machine to attack the host of another virtual machine. The best protection against this attack is to ensure that the hypervisor and all virtual machines are fully patched.

34. A cloud region consists of multiple physical locations called zones; data can be spread across multiple zones for redundancy.

35. Secrets management uses a vault to store keys, passwords, tokens, and SSH keys used for privilege accounts. It uses RSA 2048-bit keys to protect the secret management access key.

36. LRS replicates three copies of your data to a single physical location. This is the cheapest option. ZRS is where three copies of the data are replicated to three separate zones within your region.

37. They would be used as a form of network segmentation.

38. Resources that need access to the internet, for example, company web servers. A NAT gateway and an internet gateway would also be on these subnets.

39. Resources that should not have direct internet access, such as database servers, domain controllers, and email servers.

40. A VPN connection using L2TP/IPSec should be used to connect to a VPC.

41. The default route of 0.0.0.0 should be pointing to either the NAT gateway or the internet gateway. When network traffic does not know where to go, it will be sent to the default route as a last resort.

42. The third-party tools will offer more flexibility.

Chapter 5 – Monitoring, Scanning, and Penetration Testing

1. The white box tester can access the source code.

2. It would prevent you from monitoring or auditing an individual.

3. The gray box pen tester would be given at least one piece of information; normally they get limited data.

4. Rules of engagement must be established.

5. He would have regular meetings with the client, who would tell him if he has been discovered.

6. The scope determines whether the pen test is black, gray, or white.

7. The pen tester would give the internal IT team their IP address so that they can establish whether or not it is the pen tester or an attacker.

8. The credentialed vulnerability scan has more permissions than a non-credentialed one and has the ability to audit, scan documents, check account information, check certificates, and provide more accurate information

9. The cleanup phase is where the systems are returned back to the original state.

10. Open source intelligence; this is legal intelligence that is obtained from the public domain.

11. They fulfill the role of the attacker.

12. They fulfill the role of the defender.

13. They organize and judge the cybersecurity events, ensuring reports are accurate and the correct countermeasures are recommended.

14. They carry out the rules of both the red and blue teams; these are external consultants or auditors.

15. You must deal with the most critical vulnerabilities first.

16. When a monitoring system and manual inspection differ. For example, a SIEM system says there is an attack, and a manual inspection confirms that there is no attack.

17. When a monitoring system and manual inspection agree on events.

18. An intrusive scan will cause damage whereas a non-intrusive scan is passive and won't cause damage.

19. Regression testing is where a coding expert checks the code written for an application to ensure that there are no flaws.

20. Dynamic analysis is evaluating a program where it is running in real time.

21. The syslog server collects data from various sources in an event logging database. It filters out legitimate events and forwards the rest of the data to the SIEM server for further analysis.

22. A SIEM server puts events into chronological order. If the clocks are not synchronized, then events cannot be put into sequential order.

23. The IT team carry out threat hunting in their own systems to try and discover whether they have been subjected to a cyber attack.

Chapter 6 – Understanding Secure and Insecure Protocols

1. When using Kerberos authentication, a TGT session is established, where the user obtains an encrypted service ticket. Kerberos uses USN and timestamps to prevent replay attacks.

2. IPSec in tunnel mode is used with an L2TP/IPSec VPN session where both the AH and ESP are encrypted.

3. IPSec in transport mode is server to server on a LAN where only the ESP is encrypted.

4. SSH is a secure protocol that replaces Telnet.

5. A router connects external networks and routes IP packets.

6. A switch is an internal device connecting computers being used in the same location.

7. Spotify is a subscription service where the user pays a monthly fee. It is a pay-per-use model.

8. Port security is where a port on a switch is disabled to prevent someone from using a particular wall jack.

9. 802.1x authenticates users and devices connecting to a switch. Normally, the user or device has a certificate to authenticate them without the need to disable ports on the switch. An unauthorized user is prevented from using the port as they have no certificate.

10. The three portions of a distinguished name from left to right are CN, OU, and then DC.

11. DNSSEC, which produces RRSIG records that prevent DNS poisoning.

12. A computer might not receive an IP address from a DHCP server due to resource exhaustion or network connectivity.

13. Both a SIEM server and a Microsoft domain controller using Kerberos authentication are dependent on an NTP server to keep the clock times on the hosts up to date. Otherwise, the SIEM server cannot put events into chronological order and Kerberos clients cannot log in.

14. The building administrator would normally have companies located in the same physical location connected to the same switches. They could provide departmental isolation by using VLANs.

15. The spanning tree protocol prevents switches from looping, which slows the switch down.

16. A network administrator could use SMTP v3 to securely collect the status and reports from network devices.

17. A network administrator could use AES as the strongest protocol for an L2TP/IPSec VPN as it can use 256 bit.

18. A pass-the-hash attack is a hash collision attack against NTLM authentication. Kerberos prevents this attack and Kerberos uses Active Directory, which stores the passwords in an encrypted database.

19. **Transport Layer Security (TLS)** protects data in transit.

20. S/MIME can be used to digitally sign emails between two people.

21. SRTP is used to secure videoconferencing traffic.

22. SIP is used to manage internet-based calls and can be used with Skype to put calls on hold and transfer them.

23. LDAP uses TCP port 389 and is used to manage directory services. It can be replaced by LDAPS TCP port 636, which is more secure.

24. The format is NETBIOS, where the name is up to 15-characters long with a service identifier. In this example, the host is called Ian; <00> indicates the workstation service and <20> indicates the server service.

25. FTPS is used to transfer large files as it uses two ports: 989/990.

Chapter 7 – Delving into Network and Security Concepts

1. The web application firewall is normally installed on a web server as its job is to protect web applications from attack.

2. Implicit Deny is used by both the firewall and the router. If there is no allow rule they get the last rule which is deny all. This is known as Implicit Deny.

3. **Unified Threat Management (UTM)** is a firewall that provides value for money as it can provide URL filtering, content filtering, and malware inspection, as well as firewall functionality.

4. A router connects different networks together and works at Layer 3 of the OSI reference model.

5. A switch connects users on an internal network, normally in a star topology.

6. A **Network Address Translator** (**NAT**) hides the internal network from those on the external network.

7. An inline NIPS is where the incoming traffic passes through and is screened by the NIPS.

8. A **Host-Based IPS** (**HIPS**) is installed inside the guest virtual machine to protect it from attacks.

9. A **Network-Based IPS** (**NIPS**) is placed behind the firewall as an additional layer of security. The firewall prevents unauthorized access to the network.

10. A NIPS can passively monitor the network as it can fulfill the functionality of a NIDS if there is no NIDS on your network.

11. A signature-based NIDS works off a known database of variants, whereas an anomaly-based one starts with the database and can learn about new patterns or threats.

12. A passive device that sits inside your network is a NIDS.

13. If one of the monitoring systems reports a virus and you manually check and find no virus, this is known as a false positive.

14. You should enable port security, where you turn the port off on the switch. This will prevent further use of the wall jack.

15. To prevent a rogue access point from attaching to your network, you would enable 802.1x on the switch itself. 802.1x ensures that the device is authenticated before being able to use the post.

16. A managed switch uses 802.1x, which authenticates the device but does not disable the port when port security merely disables the port. 802.1x, therefore, provides more functionality.

17. Web caching on a web server keeps copies of the web pages locally, ensuring faster access to the web pages and preventing the need to open a session to the internet.

18. The purpose of a VPN is to create a tunnel across unsafe networks from home or a hotel to the workplace.

19. In the IKE phase of an IPSec session, Diffie Hellman using UDP port 500 sets up a secure session before the data is transferred.

20. The purpose of a VPN concentrator is to set up a secure session for a VPN.

21. The most secure VPN tunnel is L2TP/IPSec, which uses AES encryption for the ESP.

22. IPSec in tunnel mode is used across the internet or external networks, and IPSec in transport mode is used between hosts internally.

23. When setting the site-to-site VPN, it should be used in always-on mode as opposed to dial-on-demand.

24. A load balancer should be used to manage a high volume of web traffic as it sends the requests to the least-utilized node that is healthy.

25. SDN is used in a virtual environment when the routing requests are forwarded to a controller.

26. The screened subnet is a boundary layer that hosts an extranet server; it is sometimes known as the extranet zone. It used to be called the DMZ.

27. If you set up a honeypot, which is a website with lower security, you will be able to monitor the attack methods being used and then be able to harden your actual web server against potential attacks.

28. Network access control ensures that devices connecting to your network are fully patched. There are two agents: one that is permanent and another that is dissolvable that is for single use.

29. A SIEM server can correlate log files from many devices and notify you of potential attacks.

30. If data is backed up to a **Write-Once Read-Many** (**WORM**) drive, the data cannot be deleted or altered.

31. A port mirror can make a copy of the data going to a port and divert it to another device for analysis. A tap is another device that can be used for the same purpose. However, a tap is more expensive.

32. DNSSEC creates RRSIG records for each DNS host and a DNSKEY record used to sign the KSK or ZSK.

33. An IPSec packet has the authenticated header that uses either SHA-1 or MD5 and an **Encapsulated Payload** (**ESP**) that uses DES, 3DES, or AES.

34. If you cannot get an IP address from a DHCP server, you would receive a `169.254.x.x` IP address. This is known as APIPA. This could be caused by network connectivity or resource exhaustion.

35. It is an IP version 6 address and you can simplify it by changing the leading zeros to `2001:123A::ABC0:AB:DCS:23`.

36. An HTML5 VPN has no infrastructure to be set up as it uses certificates for encryption.

37. This would be IPSec in tunnel mode and would be used externally.

38. The purpose of a jump server is to allow a remote SSH session to a device or a virtual machine in a screened subnet or the cloud.

39. This is where the host is sent to the same server for the session.

40. Both of the load balancers are working close to capacity and if one of these load balancers fails, then the users would find that the traffic is slower.

41. A VLAN can be used for departmental isolation on the same switch.

42. East-West traffic moves laterally between servers within a data center.

43. A zero-trust network is where nothing is trusted, and every user or device must prove their identity before accessing the network. This would be used in the cloud.

44. Angry IP is an IP scanner that would scan an IP range to determine hosts that are active or inactive.

45. `curl` and `nmap` could be used for banner grabbing.

46. The harvester tool is used to collect the email addresses of a particular domain from search engines such as Google.

47. They can use the `dnsenum` tool.

48. It allows anonymous port scanning so that it cannot be traced back to you

49. You could use the tool called `cuckoo` to carry out this activity.

50. This is to prevent rogue DHCP servers from operating openly on your network.

51. It could be resource exhaustion, where the DHCP server has run out of IP addresses or it could be network connectivity between the client and the DHCP server.

Chapter 8 – Securing Wireless and Mobile Solutions

1. Visitors and employees on their lunchtime break might access a guest wireless network.

2. The FAT wireless controller is standalone; it has its own setting and DHCP addresses configured locally. A thin wireless controller pushes out the setting to multiple WAPs.

3. The WAP master password is the admin password, and it should be encrypted to protect it.

4. Wi-Fi Analyzer can troubleshoot wireless connectivity and discover the SSID inside a packet going to the WAP.

5. MAC filtering controls who can access a WAP. If your MAC address is not added to the WAP, then you are denied access.

6. To prevent interference by overlapping the wireless channels.

7. He would ensure that the WAPs are placed where there is no interference.

8. No, because it is not secure.

9. WEP is the weakest as it only has 40-bit encryption.

10. You are giving them the **Pre-Shared Key** (**PSK**).

11. It is WPA2-CCMP as it uses AES encryption that is 128 bits

12. **Simultaneous Authentication of Equals** (**SAE**) replaces the PSK; it is more secure as the password is never transmitted, and it is immune to offline attacks

13. Wi-Fi Enhanced Open is the WPA3 equivalent of Open System Authentication; it does not use a password and prevents eavesdropping.

14. This is WAP3 as it has AES encryption up to 256 bit, whereas WPA2 only uses 128-bit encryption.

15. With WPS, you push the button to connect to the wireless network. It is susceptible to a brute-force attack as it has a password stored on the device.

16. A captive portal can ask you to agree to an AUP and provide additional validation, such as your email address or Facebook or Google account details.

17. Wi-Fi Easy Connect makes it very easy to connect IoT devices such as a smartphone by simply using a QR code.

18. A certificate on the endpoint as TLS needs an x509 certificate.

19. They have violated the **Acceptable Use Policy** (**AUP**).

20. If they adopt BYOD, they might have to support hundreds of different devices, whereas if they adopt CYOD, there would be a limited number of devices to make support easier.

21. You could use your cellular phone as a hotspot.

22. If your cell phone is lost or stolen, then you should remote wipe it.

23. You should use screen locks and strong passwords, and use FDE to protect the data at rest.

24. You could tag the laptops and set up geofencing to prevent thefts. RFID is another option.

25. You could segment the data using storage segmentation or containerization.

26. To segment business data and prevent applications outside of the Knox container from accessing resources inside the container.

27. **Near-Field Communication (NFC)**

Chapter 9 – Identifying Threats, Attacks, and Vulnerabilities

1. Because you have parted with money, this is a subtle form of ransomware.

2. A fileless virus piggybacks itself onto a legitimate application, and they both launch together. Using Malwarebytes would alert you of both launching at the same time.

3. Credential harvesting is done by a phishing attack where you are warned that an account has been hacked, and it gives you a link to a website to resolve it. That way, when you try to log in, they collect your details.

4. Pretexting is where an attacker manufactures a scenario such as saying that there is suspicious activity on your account, and they ask you to confirm your account details. This way, they can steal them.

5. An attacker obtains the details of a legitimate invoice and sends the company reminders that it needs to be paid, but they substitute the bank details with their own.

6. An attacker works out what standard naming convention a company is using, and they then obtain the names of employees from the internet. They then try common passwords against those accounts.

7. An attacker leaves a malicious USB drive inside a company where it can be found. There is only one shortcut, so when the finder puts it in their computer to try and find the owner, they click on the only visible file and get infected. The attacker can now control their computer.

8. Artificial intelligence uses machine learning to teach the machine to think like a human and detect attacks. So, if it is tainted, it will ignore attacks by the attackers.

9. When you go to a restaurant, please ensure that the server does not disappear with your card; make sure it is always visible to you.

10. An on-path attack is an interception attack, for example, a replay or man-in-the-middle attack.

11. Operational technology is where we have removed CCTV standalone systems that were air-gapped and we now use a fully integrated solution that is fully connected, leaving them vulnerable to attacks.

12. An example of crypto-malware is ransomware where the victim's hard drive is encrypted and held to ransom. It could also have popups.

13. A worm replicates itself and can use either port 4444 or 5000.

14. A Trojan inserts a .dll into either the SysWOW64 or System 32 folder.

15. A Remote Access Trojan (RAT) is a Trojan that sends the user's username and password to an external source so that a remote session can be created.

16. A rootkit virus attacks the root in the Windows/System 32 folder, or in a Bash shell in Linux. For Windows, you may reinstall the OS, but the virus will still be there.

17. A logic bomb virus is triggered by an event; for example, a Fourth of July logic bomb would activate when the date on the computer was July 4. It is triggered by time, scripty, .bat/.cmd files, or a task scheduler.

18. A keylogger is a piece of software that could run from a USB flash drive plugged into the back of a computer, which then records all the keystrokes being used. It can capture sensitive data that is typed in, such as bank account details and passwords.

19. A botnet is a group of computers that have been infected so that they can be used to carry out malicious acts without the real attacker being identified. They could be used for a DDoS attack.

20. A phishing attack is when a user receives an email asking them to fill in a form requesting their bank details.

21. Spear phishing is a phishing attack that has been sent to a group of users.

22. A whaling attack targets a CEO or a high-level executive in a company.

23. A vishing attack can use a telephone or leave a voicemail.

24. Social engineering tailgating is where someone has used a smart card or entered a pin to access a door, and then someone behind them passes through the door before it closes, entering no credentials.

25. Social engineering exploits an individual's character in a situation that they are not used to. This is hacking the human, putting them under pressure to make a snap decision.

26. Dressing as a police officer could be part of an impersonation attack.

27. If you let a fireperson into the server room to put out a fire, that is a social engineering urgency attack.

28. If I am using an ATM and someone films the transaction, this is a subtle shoulder surfing attack.

29. Fake software that will not install is a hoax. An email alert telling you to delete a system file as it is a virus is also a hoax.

30. A watering hole attack infects a trusted website that a certain group of people visits regularly.

31. An email that looks like it has come from your company's CEO telling you to carry out an action is a social engineering authority attack.

32. This is a social engineering consensus attack, where the person being attacked wants to be accepted by their peers.

33. An attack with multiple SYN flood attacks is a DDoS attack.

34. A Man-in-the-Middle (MITM) attack is an on-path attack where a connection between hosts is intercepted and the conversation is changed and then replayed, but the people involved still believe that they are talking directly to each other.

35. A reply attack is similar to an MITM attack, except the intercepted packet is replayed at a later date.

36. A POODLE attack is an MITM attack using an SSL3.0 browser that uses Cipher Block Chaining (CBC).

37. A man-in-the-browser attack is a Trojan that intercepts your session between your browser and the internet; it aims to obtain financial transactions.

38. Kerberos authentication uses USN and timestamps and can prevent a replay attack, as the USN packets and the timestamps need to be sequential.

39. Enabling Kerberos or disabling NTLM would prevent a pass-the-hash attack.

40. XSS uses HTML tags with JavaScript.

41. A zero-day virus has no patches and cannot be detected by NIDS or NIPS, as it may take the anti-virus vendor up to 5 days to release a patch.

42. Domain hijacking is where someone tries to register your domain, access your hosted control panel, and set up a website that is similar to yours.

43. Bluejacking is hijacking someone's Bluetooth phone so that you can take control of it and send text messages.

44. Bluesnarfing is when you steal someone's contacts from their Bluetooth phone.

45. An ARP attack is a local attack that can be prevented by using IPSec.

46. `strcpy` can be used for a buffer overflow attack.

47. An integer overflow inserts a number larger than what is allowed.

48. An attack that uses the phrase `1=1` is a SQL injection attack.

49. Input validation and stored procedures can prevent a SQL injection attack. Stored procedures are the best.

50. Session hijacking is where your cookies are stolen so that someone can pretend to be you.

51. Typosquatting is where an attacker launches a website with a similar name to a legitimate website in the hope that victims misspell the URL.

52. Shimming and refactoring are used for driver manipulation attacks.

53. Digital signatures are susceptible to a birthday attack.

54. Rainbow tables are pre-computed lists of passwords with the relevant hash in either MD5 or SHA-1.

55. Salting passwords inserts a random value and prevents dictionary attacks, as a dictionary does not contain random characters.

56. Two tools that can be used for key stretching are bcrypt and PBKDF2.

57. A brute-force attack is the fastest password attack that will crack any password, as it uses all combinations of characters, letters, and symbols.

58. An account locked with a low value is the only way to prevent a brute-force attack.

59. If account lockout is not available, the best way to slow down a brute-force attack is to make the password length longer or to salt passwords.

60. Using passwords for authentication is more prone to errors as certificates and smart cards don't tend to have many errors.

61. An evil twin is a WAP that is made to look like a legitimate WAP.

62. Using an 802.1x authentication switch can prevent an attack by a rogue WAP, as the device needs to authenticate itself to attach to the switch.

63. A wireless disassociation attack is where the attacker prevents the victim from connecting to the WAP.

64. An attacker needs to be within 4 cm of a card to launch an NFC attack.

65. A pivot is where you gain access to a network so that you can launch an attack on a secondary system.

Chapter 10 – Governance, Risk, and Compliance

1. A vulnerability is a weakness that an attacker could exploit.

2. A BPA is used by companies in a joint venture and it lays out each party's contribution, their rights and responsibilities, how decisions are made, and who makes them.

3. A multi-party risk is where someone wins a contract and sub-contracts to a third party who could sabotage your systems.

4. This is where your intellectual property has been stolen, for example, trade secrets, copyright, and patents.

5. A memorandum of understanding is a formal agreement between two parties, but it is not legally binding, whereas a memorandum of agreement is similar, but is legally binding.

6. Tokenization is where data is replaced by a stateless token and the actual data is held in a vault by a payment provider.

7. He has carried out a software licensing compliance violation.

8. An **Interconnection Security Agreement** (**ISA**) states how connections should be made between two business partners. They decide on the type of connection and how to secure it; for example, they may use a VPN to communicate.

9. Shadow IT would connect their own computers to your network without your consent and could lead to pivoting.

10. An inherent risk is a raw risk before it has been mitigated.

11. The four stages of the information life cycle are creation, use, retention, and disposal.

12. They work together so that **Cyber Threat Intelligence** (**CTI**) can be distributed over HTTP.

13. If we adopted separation of duties in the finance department, we would ensure that nobody in the department carried out both parts of a transaction. For example, we would have one person collecting revenue and another person authorizing payments.

14. A risk register lays out all of the risks that a company faces; each risk will have a risk owner who specializes in that area and decides on the risk treatment.

15. Impact assessment is where you evaluate the risk of collecting big data and what tools can be used to mitigate the risk of holding so much data.

16. This is an example of an environmental threat.

17. Job rotation ensures that employees work in all departments so that if someone leaves at short notice or is ill, cover can be provided. It also ensures that any fraud or theft can be detected.

18. A privacy notice gives consent for data only to be collected and used for one specific purpose.

19. This is where data is stored, showing only portions of the data; for example, you might see only the last four digits of a credit card, as follows: **** **** **** 1234.

20. They are most likely going to be sued by the customer.

21. It deals with the effectiveness of controls and has limited access as it provides a detailed report about a company.

22. Mandatory vacations ensure that an employee takes at least 5 days of holiday and someone provides cover for them; this also ensures that fraud or theft can be detected.

23. He is measuring BIA as the most important factor to avoid is a single point of failure.

24. The first stage in risk assessment is identifying and classifying an asset. How the asset is treated, accessed, or scored is based on the classification.

25. The Malware Information Sharing Platform provides **Open Source Intelligence (OSINT)**.

26. This is an example of a functional recovery plan.

27. A clean desk policy is to ensure that no documents containing company data are left unattended overnight.

28. This is a code repository that holds information about malware signatures and code.

29. Someone bringing their own laptop is called BYOD and this is governed by two policies: the onboarding policy and the **Acceptable Use Policy (AUP)**. The AUP lays out how the laptop can be used, for example, accessing social media sites such as Facebook or Twitter is forbidden while using the device at work.

30. An exit interview is to find out the reason why the employee has decided to leave; it may be the management style or other factors in the company. The information from an exit interview may help the employer improve their working conditions and therefore have a higher retention rate.

31. MITRE ATT&CK is a spreadsheet that shows groups of adversaries, which can be drilled down to see the attack methods and tools used by them.

32. GDPR was developed by the EU to protect an individual's right of privacy.

33. That would be a gray hat hacker as he is provided with limited information.

34. They would use Tor software, The Onion Router, which has thousands of relays to prevent detection.

35. This is training for both red and blue teams where they capture a flag when they achieve each level of training. When they have completed all levels, they are fit to become full-blown red or blue team members.

36. When a risk is deemed too dangerous or high risk and could end in loss of life or financial loss, we would treat the risk with risk avoidance and avoid the activity.

37. Risk transference is where the risk is medium to high and you wish to offload the risk to a third party, for example, insuring your car.

38. Automated Indicator Sharing was invented by the US federal government to exchange data about cyber attacks from the state down to the local level.

39. 27701 was developed as a standard as an extension of 27001/27002 to be used for privacy information management.

40. Rules of behavior are how people should conduct themselves at work to prevent discrimination or bullying.

41. IOC informs members of their IT security community of IP addresses, hashes, or URLs where they have discovered newly released malware.

42. A script kiddie wants to be on the national news and TV as they seek fame.

43. Annual security awareness training advises employees of the risk of using email, the internet, and posting information on social media websites. It also informs employees of any new risks posed since the last training.

44. Sending an email to everyone who works in your company using your Gmail account is a violation of the AUP and could lead to disciplinary action.

45. A manufacturing company would carry out a supply chain risk assessment because they need a reputable supplier of raw materials so that they can manufacture goods.

46. Business impact analysis is just money; it looks at the financial impact following an event. The loss of earnings, the cost of purchasing new equipment, and regulatory fines are calculated.

47. The **Recovery Point Object** (**RPO**) is the acceptable downtime that a company can suffer without causing damage to the company, whereas the **Recovery Time Object** (**RTO**) is the time it takes for the company to return to an operational state – this should be within the RPO.

48. **Mean Time to Repair** (**MTTR**) is the average time it takes to repair a system, but in the exam, it could be seen as the time to repair a system and not the average time.

49. A competitor would seek to damage your production systems and steal your trade secrets.

50. Criminal syndicates would threaten you and demand payment as they are financially driven.

51. **Mean Time Between Failure** (**MTBF**) is the measurement of the reliability of a system.

52. SSAE assists CPA in carrying out the auditing of SOC reports.

53. **Single Loss Expectancy** (**SLE**) is the cost of the loss of one item; if I lose a tablet worth $1,000, then the SLE is $1,000.

54. The **Annual Loss Expectancy** (**ALE**) is calculated by multiplying the SLE by the ARO (the number of losses per year). If I lose six laptops a year worth $1,000 each, the ALE would be $6,000.

Chapter 11 – Managing Application Security

1. Mobile devices can connect through cellular, wireless, and Bluetooth connections.

2. Embedded electronic systems have software embedded into the hardware; some use SoC. Examples are microwave ovens, gaming consoles, security cameras, wearable technology, smart TVs, medical devices, such as defibrillators, or self-driving cars.

3. SCADA systems are industrial control systems used in the refining of uranium, oil, or gas, or the purification of water.

4. Smart TVs and wearable technology are classified as IoT devices.

5. Home automation is where you can control the temperature, lighting, entertainment systems, alarm systems, and many appliances.

6. An SoC is a low-power integrated chip that integrates all of the components of a computer or electronic system. An example would be the controller for a defibrillator. Think of it as an operating system stored on a small chip.

7. The **Real-Time Operating System** (**RTOS**) processes data as it comes in without any buffer delays. The process will fail if it is not carried out within a certain period of time.

8. An attacker would most likely gain control of an MFP through its network interface.

9. When a security team controls the HVAC in a data center, they can ensure that the temperature is regulated and the servers remain available. They also know which rooms are occupied based on the use of air conditioning and electricity.

10. An SoC gives instructions on the steps to take when using a defibrillator; however, if it detects a pulse, it will not send a charge.

11. An example of embedded systems is vehicles that are either self-parking or self-driving.

12. Unmanned aerial vehicles are drones or small, model aircraft that can be sent to areas where manned aircraft cannot go. They can be fitted with a camera to record events or take aerial photographs; an example of these would be to determine the spread of a forest fire.

13. A race condition is when two threads of an application access the same data.

14. The perfect way to set up error handling is for the user to get generic information but for the log files to include a full description of the error.

15. Input validation is where data that is in the correct format is validated prior to being inserted into the system. SQL injection, buffer overflow, and integer overflow are prevented by using input validation.

16. The best way to prevent a SQL injection attack is by using stored procedures.

17. Code signing confirms that the code has not been tampered with.

18. Obfuscation is taking code and masking the data, making it obscure so that if it is stolen, it will not be understood. XOE and ROT13 could be used for obfuscation.

19. Dead code is code that is never used but could introduce errors into the program life cycle; it should be removed.

20. Using a third-party library will help a developer obtain code from the internet to help make an application and get it to market quickly. There are many for Android and JavaScript.

21. The measured boot logs information about the firmware and application and stores this log in the TPM chips. This can be used to check the health status of the host and anti-malware can check during the boot process that the software is trustworthy.

22. UEFI is a modern version of the BIOS and is needed for secure boot.

23. Checking the integrity of the software as it is being loaded is known as attestation.

24. It is a centralized console that continuously monitors the computer and makes automatic alerts when a threat has been detected. It uses machine learning.

25. Fingerprinting is the deep analysis of a host.

26. An NGFW has the ability to act as a stateful firewall by carrying out deep packet filtering.

27. Tokenization takes sensitive data, such as a credit card number, and replaces it with random data, so it cannot be reversed. Encryption can be reversed.

28. We can set the secure flag on the website to ensure that cookies are only downloaded when there is a secure HTTPS session.

29. HSTS ensures that the web browser only accepts secure connections and prevents XSS.

30. They will use dynamic code analysis so that they can use fuzzing to test the code.

31. The Docker tool allows you to isolate applications into a separate space called containers. The registry can now be isolated in a separate container, making it more secure.

32. Opal is a self-encrypting drive where the encryption keys are stored on the hard drive controller and are therefore immune to a cold boot attack and are compatible with all operating systems. They do not have the vulnerabilities of software-based encryption. As a hardware solution, they outperform software solutions.

33. Quality assurance is completed during the staging environment where users test the new application with real data.

Chapter 12 – Dealing with Incident Response Procedures

1. RAID 5 has a minimum of three disks and you can afford to lose one disk without losing data.

2. RAID 6 has a minimum of four disks.

3. RAID 5 has single parity and can lose one disk, whereas RAID 6 has double parity and can lose two disks.

4. A diskless virtual host will get its disk space from an SAN.

5. An SAN will use fast disks, such as SSDs.

6. Cloud storage for personal users could be iCloud, Google Drive, Microsoft OneDrive, or Dropbox.

7. Eradication is where we remove viruses and reduce the services being used. It should be isolated, and this is the containment phase. The virus would be removed in the eradication phase, and then be placed back online. This is the recovery phase.

8. A simulation is where the IRP team is given a specific scenario to deal with.

9. This is an aid to help prepare your business against different adversaries. You can drill down from an adversary into the tactics and techniques that they use. You can then take mitigation steps to avoid being attacked.

10. The four key elements are adversary, capabilities, infrastructure, and victims.

11. If they understand their roles and responsibilities, it can make them more effective when a disaster happens.

12. The contents of memory are saved in a dump file and this can be used to investigate the event.

13. It gives you clear visibility of network traffic patterns and can identify malicious traffic.

14. An HTTP status code of 200 OK lets you know that a successful connection has been made.

15. Playbooks contain a set of rules to enable the SOAR to take preventative action as an event occurs.

16. It can help load balance the network traffic and provide redundancy if one card fails.

17. The UPS is basically a battery that is a standby device so that when the computer power fails, it kicks in. It is designed to keep the system going for a few minutes to allow the server team to close the servers down gracefully. It can also be used to clean up the power coming from the National Grid, such as spikes, surges, and voltage fluctuations.

18. Two **Host Bus Adapters** (**HBAs**) on each node will give two separate paths to them.

19. This would be diversity, so that if one vendor had a disaster, the other would keep providing the broadband.

20. An incident response plan is written for a particular incident and lays out how it should be tackled and the key personnel required.

21. The different categories of incidents are as follows:

    a. Unauthorized access

    b. Loss of computers or data

    c. Loss of availability

    d. Malware attack

    e. DDoS attack

    f. Power failure

    g. Natural disasters, such as floods, tornadoes, hurricanes, and fires

    h. Cybersecurity incidents

22. The different roles required to deal with an incident are as follows:

    a. **Incident response manager**: A top-level manager takes charge.

    b. **Security analyst**: Provides technical support for the incident.

    c. **IT auditor**: Checks that the company is compliant.

    d. **Risk analyst**: Evaluates all aspects of risk.

    e. **HR**: Sometimes, employees are involved in the incident.

    f. **Legal**: Gives advice and makes decisions on legal issues.

    g. **Public relations**: Deals with the press to reduce the impact on the company's reputation.

23. The help desk identifies the incident response plan required and the key personnel that need to be notified.

24. An incident response exercise is for carrying out the incident response plan and planning for any shortfalls.

25. The first phase of the incident response process is the preparation phase, where the plan is already written in advance of any attack.

26. The last phase of the incident response process is lessons learned, where we review why the incident was successful.

27. If we do not carry out lessons learned, the incident may re-occur. Lessons learned is a detective control where we try to identify and address any weaknesses.

28. This is where we isolate or quarantine an infected machine.

29. This is where we remove malware and turn off services that we do not need.

30. This is where we put infected machines back online, restore data or reimage desktops.

Other Books You May Enjoy

If you enjoyed this book, you may be interested in these other books by Packt:

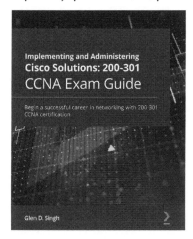

Implementing and Administering Cisco Solutions: 200-301 CCNA Exam Guide

Glen D. Singh

ISBN: 978-1-80020-809-4

- Understand the benefits of creating an optimal network
- Create and implement IP schemes in an enterprise network
- Design and implement virtual local area networks (VLANs)
- Administer dynamic routing protocols, network security, and automation
- Get to grips with various IP services that are essential to every network
- Discover how to troubleshoot networking devices

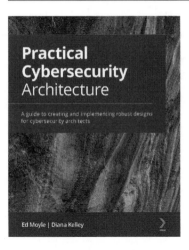

Practical Cybersecurity Architecture

Ed Moyle, Diana Kelley

ISBN: 978-1-83898-992-7

- Explore ways to create your own architectures and analyze those from others
- Understand strategies for creating architectures for environments and applications
- Discover approaches to documentation using repeatable approaches and tools
- Delve into communication techniques for designs, goals, and requirements
- Focus on implementation strategies for designs that help reduce risk
- Become well-versed with methods to apply architectural discipline to your organization

Leave a review - let other readers know what you think

Please share your thoughts on this book with others by leaving a review on the site that you bought it from. If you purchased the book from Amazon, please leave us an honest review on this book's Amazon page. This is vital so that other potential readers can see and use your unbiased opinion to make purchasing decisions, we can understand what our customers think about our products, and our authors can see your feedback on the title that they have worked with Packt to create. It will only take a few minutes of your time, but is valuable to other potential customers, our authors, and Packt. Thank you!

Index